'DAILY SPIRITUAL DIET'

3rd Quarter
September-December

ELIZABETH DAS

English

Copyright © 2023 *ELIZABETH DAS*.

All rights reserved for audio, eBook (digital), and paper book. No part of this book may be used or reproduced by any means, graphic, electronic, or mechanical, including photocopying, recording, taping or by any information storage retrieval system without the written permission of the author except in the case of brief quotations embodied in critical articles and reviews. Because of the dynamic nature of the internet, any web address links contained in this book may have changed since publication and may no longer be valid. Any people depicted in stock imagery provided by Thinkstock are models, and such images are beings used for illustrative purposes only. Certain Stock imagery © Thinkstock. Excerpt From: *Elizabeth Das*: "DAILY SPIRITUAL DIET"

DAILY SPIRITUAL DIET ISBN

ISBN: 978-1-961625-06-8 Paperback
ISBN: 978-1-961625-01-3 Ebook EPUB

Library of Congress Control Number: 202344250

CONTACT: nimmidas@gmail.com nimmidas1952@gmail.com

YOUTUBE CHANNEL "DAILY SPIRITUAL DIET' BY ELIZABETH DAS

PREFACE

On Jan 1, 2018. I was at home alone, resting on the sofa. I heard my Lord's voice commanding me to write. In my spirit, He meant for me to do it every day. I clarified my process and topics and verbalized my intention to write daily. Divine communication gave me the inspiration for writing. As per the divine plan, I harked to the message for the day shared by the LORD. I wrote the content. I recorded it and uploaded it on YouTube. For 365 days, I took notes from the Lord. I have a message for all who will accept it. Under the instructions of the Holy Spirit, I learned Satan organizes religion, organizations, denominations, and non-denominations. These systems do not have the power to help you follow Jesus; instead, they will lead you to another building with a brand name, where you will learn about Jesus, but not about His power and His might. I once read an article by a satanic prophetess who claimed that to establish Satan's kingdom, we must convert people to the majority religion, which is Christianity. How can the Kingdom of Jesus be destroyed? Use the same proven tactics. Focus on what is prohibited. If Jesus overturned a table, constructed a den, and confined thieves there. The chief advantage of calling a structure a church is that people will not understand that their physical body embodies the church of Jehovah God. In addition, individuals who are impoverished, malnourished, addicted, alcoholic, spiritually controlled, or oppressed will not attain salvation.

Rather than relying on individuals trained and taught by the Holy Spirit, establish a theological school that covers all of our divided and contradictory teachings and trains men for teaching and preaching.

This is an excellent plan! This plan not only sounds good but can also be successful. Continue focusing on women since they can serve as our spokespeople. She still enjoys window shopping, finding good deals, and living a glamorous lifestyle.

They display godliness but reject true power. These types of doctrines may gratify the desires of the greedy, the lustful, and those driven by pride. I have realized that living within the confines of formal religious communities can hinder individuals from seeking and finding God through personal inquiry and prayer. The religious leadership may be a promoter of certain literature that may be the work of false teachers or prophets. It may also impede the home meetings from reaching out to our family, neighbors, and friends. This is defining total control. In addition, religious organizations are preachers of the WORD, but they are not always practitioners of the WORD. Their instructions distract believers from doing what Jesus commanded, directing them to obey group leaders. The teachings are effective only if you follow them without deviation. We are following everything but the teachings of Jesus. I recommended you study the teachings of Jesus, as he instructed his followers to do so. Jesus declared he is the path, the truth, and the Life. Following Jesus is the way to attain eternal life. I needed many years of searching to break free from Satan's deceptive hold and discover the Truth. The Lord has provided us with clear guidance on how to recognize His loyal disciples and how not to be led astray by Satan's deceptive schemes.

The text says that the apostle will work wonders, healings, and miracles in the city. Instead of religious restrictions, shouldn't we focus on these fruits out there? The New Testament says that the Lord will come and live in us when we repent and are immersed in Jesus' name to wash away our sins. Therefore, we become Holy Spirit residents, or as some may say, the house of the Lord Jesus. It is now that our body serves as the church. While it is necessary to establish fellowship with our brothers and sisters in Christ from home to home and city to city, building establishments are unnecessary. One is called to work.

We must preach the good news of the gospel, which includes performing supernatural acts such as healing the sick, restoring the brokenhearted, casting out demons, and restoring sight to the blind. Supernatural power comes from the Holy Spirit. The Spirit does all healing, miracles, and deliverance living within us. We need to go out and work as Jesus did. Learning the Lord's ways requires surrendering and yielding to His Spirit. If we do not do this, we will not acknowledge creating God who suffers from various ailments, such as oppression, possession, sickness, brokenness, physical disabilities, and depression. The Lord will take care of everything, and you will go back home feeling joyous. This is a testament to the brilliance of the plan of God! There are many rewards for being a disciple of God. Access to provisions, protection, peace, and working privileges are bonuses. As a follower, you will inherit a beautiful mansion in the eternal paradise of heaven. Life's journey will soon end. This book may help you understand God's plan with clarity. I have been studying the Bible through practice, and you, too, can be a student by abiding by its teachings. May the Lord send you faithful prophetic, evangelistic, pastoral, teaching, and apostolic ministers to equip you for service in the armies of God. Follow Jesus.

Amen.

Elizabeth Das

Contents

SEPTEMBER

SEPTEMBER 1 2
A DOOR WILL BE OPEN FOR THE RIGHTEOUS! 2
SEPTEMBER 2 5
LOOK FOR THE ROOTS! 5
SEPTEMBER 3 8
LEARN BY OBEYING! 8
SEPTEMBER 4 11
LIVING IN THE PRESENT, CREATING DESTINY! 11
SEPTEMBER 5 14
ARE YOU DOING FATHER'S BUSINESS? 14
SEPTEMBER 6 17
LAZY AND SLUMBER 17
SEPTEMBER 7 20
LEAN NOT ON YOUR UNDERSTANDING! 20
SEPTEMBER 8 23
WHAT GOD IS LOOKING FOR? 23
SEPTEMBER 9 26
ONLY YOU CAN UNLOCK YOURSELF! 26
SEPTEMBER 10 29
HOW DO YOU INTRODUCE JESUS? 29
SEPTEMBER 11 32
SERVE GOD WITH HIS CONDITION ANDSTANDARD! 32
SEPTEMBER 12 35
PEOPLE WHO ARE CALLED BY GOD! 35
SEPTEMBER 13 38
TALK REASONABLY! 38
SEPTEMBER 14 41
HOLD ON TO THE HAND OF GOD! 41
SEPTEMBER 15 44
THE TARGET IS ON YOUR FAITH! 44
SEPTEMBER 16 47
GET FREEDOM BY FORGIVING! 47

SEPTEMBER 17	50
WHAT IS RELIGION?	50
SEPTEMBER 18	53
WHERE DO YOU HAVE THE BATTLE?	53
SEPTEMBER 19	56
DIFFERENT MEASURE OF FAITH!	56
SEPTEMBER 20	59
DO NOT LET THE LORD DEPART FROM YOU!	59
SEPTEMBER 21	62
PROMOTION AND DEMOTION!	62
SEPTEMBER 22	65
THE HIGHEST NAME OF JEHOVAH IS JESUS!	65
SEPTEMBER 23	68
LORD, OPEN SPIRITUAL EYES!	68
SEPTEMBER 24	71
BRING THE DEVIL TO CAPTIVITY!	71
SEPTEMBER 25	74
YOUR CHOICES DEFINE YOUR TITLE!	74
SEPTEMBER 26	77
HOW TO SUSTAIN IN DISASTER!	77
SEPTEMBER 27	80
ARE YOU OPPRESSED IN YOUR NATION?	80
SEPTEMBER 28	83
WITCH, WIZARD, ENCHANTER, MAGICIAN!	83
SEPTEMBER 29	86
DO NOT DESTROY THE TEMPLE OF GOD!	86
SEPTEMBER 30	89
I COME TO SEE THE LORD!	89
OCTOBER	
OCTOBER 1	93
GOD BEAUTIFIES MEEK WITH SALVATION!	93
OCTOBER 2	96
FINISHED WELL!	96
OCTOBER 3	99
TESTIMONY!	99

OCTOBER 4	102
UNKNOWN WAY, HOLD HIS HAND!	102
OCTOBER 5	104
GOD IS UNDER HOUSE ARREST!	104
OCTOBER 6	107
REDEEM BY FULFILLING CONDITIONS!	107
OCTOBER 7	110
TREASURE HIDES IN THE BIBLE!	110
OCTOBER 8	113
THE BATTLE BELONGS TO THE LORD!	113
OCTOBER 9	116
CELEBRATE JESUS!	116
OCTOBER 10	119
REASON TO CHOOSE RELIGIONS!	119
OCTOBER 11	122
RAISE GOD'S GIVEN CHILDREN FOR GOD!	122
OCTOBER 12	125
REPETITION MAKES US PERFECT!	125
OCTOBER 13	128
HAVE YOU PREPARED YOURSELF?	128
OCTOBER 14	131
HAVE YE RECEIVED THE HOLY GHOST?	131
OCTOBER 15	134
THE ACCUSATION AND ALLEGATION ARE THE OLD TACTICS OF THE DEVIL!	134
OCTOBER 16	137
MYSTERY OF CHRIST!	137
OCTOBER 17	140
GOD IS CONCERNED ABOUT WHAT CONCERNS YOU!	140
OCTOBER 18	143
THE MIND IS A DEVIL'S WORKSHOP. GOD WORKS WITH HEART!	143
OCTOBER 19	146
YOUR WORD IS THAT POWERFUL!	146
OCTOBER 20	149
LET PEOPLE HEAR HEAVENLY TALK!	149

OCTOBER 21	152
RECEIVER OR REJECTOR!	152
OCTOBER 22	155
THE BELIEVER RECEIVES WHAT THEY CLAIM!	155
OCTOBER 23	158
TALK TO GOD IN HIS LANGUAGE!	158
OCTOBER 24	161
PRIVILEGES OF CALLED AND CHOSEN!	161
OCTOBER 25	164
WHO IS JESUS?	164
OCTOBER 26	167
NOT HOW YOU BEGIN, BUT HOW YOU FINISH!	167
OCTOBER 27	170
PLANT THE WORD AS A SEED!	170
OCTOBER 28	173
THY KINGDOM COME ON EARTH!	173
OCTOBER 29	176
ARE YOU BLOOD BOUGHT?	176
OCTOBER 30	179
GET TRANSPARENT!	179
OCTOBER 31	182
CHECK SHORT CIRCUITS IN YOUR SPIRIT!	182
NOVEMBER	
NOVEMBER 1	186
WHAT KIND OF CHURCH DOES GOD WANT?	186
NOVEMBER 2	189
THE ONLY AUTHORITY YOU PLEASE IS GOD!	189
NOVEMBER 3	192
ONE GOD IN THREE ROLES OR THREE GODS?	192
NOVEMBER 4	195
ALL PROMISES COME WITH THE TRIAL!	195
NOVEMBER 5	198
WAKE UP MY PEOPLE!	198
NOVEMBER 6	201
KNOWLEDGE NEEDS AN APPLICATION!	201

NOVEMBER 7	204
NO ONE BUT THE LORD JESUS CAN FIX IT!	204
NOVEMBER 8	207
THE PLANTATION BRINGS PLENTY!	207
NOVEMBER 9	210
PICK THE SPIRITUAL WIFE!	210
NOVEMBER 10	213
DO NOT LET YOUR DREAM DIE!	213
NOVEMBER 11	216
DAMAGE OF THE PRAYERLESSNESS!	216
NOVEMBER 12	219
FOLLOW THE EASY INSTRUCTION OF GOD!	219
NOVEMBER 13	222
PERMANENT LOSS OVER MOMENTARY GAIN!	222
NOVEMBER 14	225
WLORD, ENLARGE MY TERRITORY!	225
NOVEMBER 15	228
WHAT MATTERS THE MOST?	228
NOVEMBER 16	231
WHO HAS OCCUPIED THE HOUSE?	231
NOVEMBER 17	234
ACTION ALERT!	234
NOVEMBER 18	237
SEE-THROUGH THE EYES OF THE PROPHET!	237
NOVEMBER 19	240
BE SENSITIVE TO YOUR SURROUNDINGS!	240
NOVEMBER 20	243
NOT CONVERTING, BUT PROCLAIMING THE TRUTH!	243
NOVEMBER 21	246
PREPARE YOUR HEART!	246
NOVEMBER 22	249
THANKSGIVING!	249
NOVEMBER 23	252
MAY THE PROPHECY COME TRUE!	252

NOVEMBER 24	255
SPIRITUAL ILLITERACY!	255
NOVEMBER 25	258
GOD GIVES INABUNDANCE NO NEED TO TOIL!	258
NOVEMBER 26	261
CARELESS LEADERS CAUSE CHAOS IN THE NATION!	261
NOVEMBER 27	264
YOUR CHOICES REFLECT YOUR HEART!	264
NOVEMBER 28	267
SPIRITUAL EXERCISE!	267
NOVEMBER 29	270
HAPPY ARE YE!	270
NOVEMBER 30	273
GOD'S MANAGEMENT IS THE BEST!	273
DECEMBER	
DECEMBER 1	277
FORBIDDEN BY GOD!	277
DECEMBER 2	279
PRAYER GIVES BIRTH!	279
DECEMBER 3	282
DON'T COME SHORT!	282
DECEMBER 4	285
PRAYER REDESIGNS!	285
DECEMBER 5	288
IF YOU ENFORCE GOD'S LAW!	288
DECEMBER 6	291
BREACH OF CONTRACT!	291
DECEMBER 7	294
I KNOW MY GOD!	294
DECEMBER 8	297
WHAT DOES CHRISTIAN THINK?	297
DECEMBER 9	300
RELIGIOUS PEOPLE ARE PRESUMPTUOUS.	300
DECEMBER 10	303
CHRIST GAVE!	303

DECEMBER 11	306
YIELD TO THE SPIRIT OF GOD!	306
DECEMBER 12	309
GOD GOT ALL!	309
DECEMBER 13	312
WHO ALLOWED TARE?	312
DECEMBER 14	315
DON'T LET ANYONE CONTROL YOU!	315
DECEMBER 15	318
POSITION YOURSELF TO SAVE!	318
DECEMBER 16	321
PRESS THROUGH!	321
DECEMBER 17	324
USE YOUR TALENT!	324
DECEMBER 18	327
BE A MEDIATOR!	327
DECEMBER 19	330
IMPORTANCE OF THE ROOT!	330
DECEMBER 20	333
TIME INVESTMENT.	333
DECEMBER 21	336
OBEDIENCE IS THE FOUNDATION!	336
DECEMBER 22	339
CRITICISM!	339
DECEMBER 23	342
DO YOU SEE THE STING OF DEATH IN SIN?	342
DECEMBER 24	345
DO YOU HAVE ROOM FOR ME?	345
DECEMBER 25	348
JESUS MADE ME ROYAL!	348
DECEMBER 26	351
IT WOULDN'T WORK!	351
DECEMBER 27	354
THE MIND IS THE GREATEST ASSET!	354

DECEMBER 28	357
IMPORTUNITY!	357
DECEMBER 29	360
I AM OPEN TO THAT!	360
DECEMBER 30	363
GOD HAS NOT CALLED LAZY OR COWARDLY!	363
DECEMBER 31	366
HEAR, OBEY AND SUBMIT!	366

SEPTEMBER

SEPTEMBER 1

A DOOR WILL BE OPEN FOR THE RIGHTEOUS!

But God will shut the door for the unrighteous. Now, what is righteous? Righteous Meant:

law-abiding, pure, blameless. Definition according to the Strong concordance: the approval of God or divine approval. Your action or reaction has God's approval. Another way to walk in the light of God's laws, precepts, and commandments. These people get the favor when they stand before the King.

Esther 5:2 And it was so, when the king saw Esther the queen standing in the court, that she obtained favour in his sight: and the king held out to Esther the golden sceptre that was in his hand. So Esther drew near, and touched the top of the sceptre. 3 Then said the king unto her, What wilt thou, queen Esther? and what is thy request? it shall be even given thee to the half of the kingdom.

Wherever righteous go, the door will be open. The Lord touches the Heart of others to favour only if you are in the will of God. Keep God's law by fearing Him. Please keep the God-given commandments, and statutes in any and every situation. No compromising, adding, and subtracting! Then the Lord will open the door of the prison.

Acts 12:5 Peter therefore was kept in prison: but prayer was made without ceasing of the church unto God for him. 7 And, behold, the angel of the Lord came upon him, and a light shined in the prison: and he smote Peter on the side, and raised him up, saying, Arise up quickly. And his chains fell off from his hands. 8 And the angel said unto him, Gird thyself, and bind on thy sandals. And so he did. And he saith unto him, Cast thy garment about thee and follow me.

It is God's word to pray without ceasing. If you pray, then supernatural help will come from heaven. It is His will that you continue knocking, asking, and seeking. Do not give up, do not give in, but pray till you see the help from heaven. Prayer is the righteousness of God. Righteousness meant the right action in the sight of God.

Isaiah 60:11 Therefore thy gates shall be open continually; they shall not be shut day nor night; that men may bring unto thee the forces of the Gentiles, and that their kings may be brought.

God will feed you in the famine if you believe. When God speaks to the land to produce 100-fold, the land has to obey the Lord. If you are righteous, hear what God tells you. The Lord is! The Lord wants us to walk on earth as His children, kings, kids, and highly favored. But learn to wait on Him, and continue in His will

SEPTEMBER 1

and direction. May the Lord help us understand how much we lose our blessings by not listening to God. Our righteousness is called a filthy rag.

Isaiah 64:6 But we are all as an unclean thing, and all our righteousnesses are as filthy rags; and we all do fade as a leaf; and our iniquities, like the wind, have taken us away.

Our ways are unprofitable and hopeless. How many have noticed that we have chosen different ways than God's and nothing works? But do we justify, argue, and be careless about the outcome of our actions? The Lord said, wait on me and let me do it. The human replies, no, I will bless you if I make money. God, please bless my messy ways. The way of man is called ways of unrighteousness. Our God is good.

We have confidence if we live by the laws of God.

Psalm 112:4 Unto the upright there ariseth light in the darkness: he is gracious, and full of compassion, and righteous.

When I was going through a physical trial, God made a way of tutoring where there was no way. I had no way to survive through a brief check of 1,100.00. My house payment was almost $1,300.00. There were many dues. Since my injury, I have to pay for everything, plus all the utility bills. But during that time, God anointed me to teach math. I had some students who helped me out financially. I never found students before, but when I had temporary memory loss, I found math students. Now think how good God is. My God taught this student. They were happy when F and C students achieved A and A+. It was God who opened the doors. All that I learned during my disability stage was to trust. He said, Trust me, I will take care of you. He spoke the same word twice at different times.

No matter what situation you are going through, please do it right. Many find a way of lying or getting through the wrong sources. I know the Lord is our shepherd, Jehovah Jireh, and caretaker. The beauty is discovering how He opens the door. We never think it will work, but it does. Just wait on the Lord.

John 10:9 I am the door: by me if any man enter in, he shall be saved, and shall go in and out, and find pasture.

Jesus is the door for all. Do not be in a hurry. Our God opens the door when the other door closes. God said I would open new doors when the door closes on us. Do you think it will happen? He said, do not worry. I can help you and provide for you. Give your troubles and worries to the Lord. Our God said I was at the door.

People who walk with God know how God opens the door. He said it and meant it. It would be best if you walked upright. Do not deviate from the path of righteousness. He is a good God.

Many times it seems no doors are opening, then you pray and fast and God will open the door. The devil can stop and block, but trust and continuing to do right will change the scenario. The power of God makes the impossible possible.

Righteous men and women have never to worry. They know God is faithful. But the unrighteous will suffer loss.

Luke 13:24 Strive to enter in at the strait gate: for many, I say unto you, will seek to enter in, and shall not be able. 25 When once the master of the house is risen up, and hath shut to the door, and ye begin to stand without, and to knock at the door, saying, Lord, Lord, open unto us; and he shall answer and say unto you, I know you not whence ye are: 26 Then shall ye begin to say, We have eaten and drunk in thy presence, and thou hast taught in our streets. 27 But he shall say, I tell you, I know you not whence ye are; depart from me, all ye workers of iniquity. 28 There shall be weeping and gnashing of teeth, when ye shall see Abraham, and Isaac, and Jacob, and all the prophets, in the kingdom of God, and you yourselves thrust out.

Remember Moses, Joseph, Daniel, and others being righteous slaves but God opens the door to be top, above, head, and promoted. Be bold and courageous to stand alone. The door will be open for the righteous, but the door will be closed for the unrighteous.

LET US PRAY

Heavenly righteous father, your laws and precepts are right. Teach us the righteousness of God to find favor in any nation or place. Many doors can open for the righteous, but the unrighteous door will be closed. Give us courage and boldness to do right. Our God can save and keep us against every odds we face. You have power over the king, places, and situations. God can solve our situation if we stand on His word. Lord, your word will take us to the path of righteousness, so help us. Help us teach our children righteousness, so they also are blessed. Many parents are very busy and forget to teach their children. Many suffer from trouble because of that. Our righteousness keeps the door open. We thank you for the Word of God. The Holy Spirit teaches us the Word. In Jesus' Name Amen,! God bless you!

SEPTEMBER 2

LOOK FOR THE ROOTS!

Are you lost in the wrangling of maybe, maybe not? Or you do not know what the solution is. Are you responding, oh well, or I think or I wonder and try to find what and how to solve the problem? Your problem could be physical, spiritual, emotional, mental, or financial. There is a source behind it.

John 9:2 And his disciples asked him, saying, Master, who did sin, this man, or his parents, that he was born blind? 3 Jesus answered, neither hath this man sinned, nor his parents: but that the works of God should be made manifest in him.

God knows the reason or cause of the roots of the problems. Omniscient that is all-knowing, God can help if you ask, seek, and knock. Inquire of God, what is the reason for my sickness? If you are poor, then check where you are robbing the Lord. Check where you are investing your money. Do you give to one who comes to pray, preach, and teach you the truth? Do not let the true laborer, prophet, or teacher go out of your door without you blessing them. Nowadays, we have many denominations, churches, and organizations robbing people of misleading and deluding. They always come up with projects to steal money. They don't have a project to turn the world upside down, cast out demons, heal the sick, or do miracles in Jesus's name. I have many who came asking for money, and I do not mind giving if it is necessary. But if they have not learned how to fish, then I must teach them to catch fish. If I give them two fish, they will come back the next day asking for more, but if I teach them to fish, they will have fish for the rest of their life. So, teach them through the Word of God how money flows for our dispensation.

Luke 6:38 Give, and it shall be given unto you; good measure, pressed down, and shaken together, and running over, shall men give into your bosom. For with the same measure that ye mete withal it shall be measured to you again.

If people are paying tithes and offerings to the church and give nothing to the laborers, then they lose big blessings. Remember, they are laborers. If you want to be blessed, bless laborers.

Mark 9:41 For whosoever shall give you a cup of water to drink in my name, because ye belong to Christ, verily I say unto you, he shall not lose his reward.

If you take care of the needs of laborers, then God will give you provision and protection. There will be no alcohol, sicknesses, or divorces attached to your family. No woman will come and take away your wealth by giving divorces by suing. The God almighty will rebuke all kinds of sickness, disease, breaking, and falling apart. Word of God should not be the business or the Lord will label you as a thief. Malachi 3:10,11.

Let us see some roots of curses on you, your family, and your land.

Deuteronomy 28:15 But it shall come to pass, if thou wilt not hearken unto the voice of the Lord thy God, to observe to do all his commandments and his statutes which I command thee this day; that all these curses shall come upon thee, and overtake thee:

Sometimes people ask me to invite them to the US because it offers a good life. I said, if you bring Jesus to your country, then your family, land, animal, business, health, children, and everything will be blessed. Bring Jesus, the only wealthy God in your country, who blesses us. Open the Bible and find the reason, the roots, the cause of poverty, sickness, curse, and calamity. God said to seek the roots of your calamities, diseases, and pain. God will heal and bless you if you repent. That is turned away from sin. An impotent man was sick for 38 years. Jesus revealed to him the roots or cause of the sickness.

John 5:14 Afterward Jesus findeth him in the temple, and said unto him, Behold, thou art made whole: sin no more, lest a worse thing come unto thee.

The man was sick of Palsy; Jesus knows the roots of it.

Matthew 9:2 And, behold, they brought to him a man sick of the palsy, lying on a bed: and Jesus seeing their faith said unto the sick of the palsy; Son, be of good cheer; thy sins be forgiven thee.

He arose and walked. When sins are forgiven, the sickness demons have to get out of your body. Pharisees, priests, and blind leaders got upset. The same situation is today: blind and greedy leaders will argue instead of rejoicing. Find the roots of problems, believe in God and not false prophets, teachers, and blind religious authority. As you know, the roots of sickness are sin or generational curses, or someone has done something to you. Like witchcraft, spell, or spoken evil prayer to you. As you baptize in the name of Jesus, (remember not father, son, and the Holy Ghost), then the blood of the lamb will come to wipe away your sins. And you will be healed, delivered, and set free. Do not argue for baptism in Jesus's name; it is the commandment for the forgiveness of sins and not a suggestion.

Psalm 103:3 Who forgiveth all thine iniquities; who healeth all thy diseases;

Why do people have problems with the name 'Jesus'? Peter, Paul, or any Apostles and prophets of Jesus did not argue against the NAME, Jesus.

Acts 22:16 And now why tarriest thou? arise, and be baptized, and wash away thy sins, calling on the name of the Lord.

Your sicknesses, diseases, and curses will be washed away in the blood which is hidden under the NAME, Jesus. The name above every name! In the name of Jesus, every knee shall bow, and tongue confesses He is the Lord of Lords and King of Kings. Amen! Find the roots of your problems, sicknesses, and diseases and solve them by the instruction given in the word of God. Amen!

LET US PRAY

Heavenly Father, our loving God, father of all creation, we come to you. We asked you to forgive all our sins. Help us not to argue or follow the lost religious leaders but obey your word, which is in the black-and-white book Bible. You are going to judge us by the Word written in the Bible. Help us, Lord, to believe and obey. Your Word is not suggestions but commandments. Our problem can be solved if we believe and obey the word and not the false teachers and prophets. Sin is the root of sicknesses and curses. Rebellion runs in us. Lord, give us courage and boldness to obey your Word. Help us not to follow false teachings and doctrine. We want our family healthy, wealthy, and blessed in Jesus's name. Amen! God bless you!

SEPTEMBER 3

LEARN BY OBEYING!

God manifested in flesh called Jesus. He learned everything by obedience.

Hebrews 5:7 Who in the days of his flesh, when he had offered up prayers and supplications with strong crying and tears unto him that was able to save him from death, and was heard in that he feared 8 Though he were a Son, yet learned he obedience by the things which he suffered; 9 And being made perfect, he became the author of eternal salvation unto all them that obey him;

Obedience is better than sacrifice. King Saul was a good example of disobedience. He had many excuses. If you are disobedient like King Saul or Eve and Adam, or other examples from the Bible, then you will not learn. Have you seen people go from denomination to non-denomination, search scriptures on the computer, constantly study, and never come to the knowledge of the truth? A simple answer: God needs someone who listens and obeys. Not too smart, listen to everyone but God. There is disobedience and rebellion in us. How sad? Even God in the flesh learns by keeping all commandments. In the flesh, He prayed. Why? All flesh has to pray.

Palmas 65:2 O thou that hearest prayer, unto thee shall all flesh come.

All flesh must connect with God through prayer. Spirit God came in flesh and needed to connect with Spirit God. Direct channel to God in prayer. If we pray, then there is God to answer. Stay connected with God by believing and obeying. Use the channel step by step. The result will be awesome. The life of those who walked with God followed the instruction book Bible. They were head first, blessed, above, and favored. But like King Saul was afraid of people and took over the priest's job, was not just removed but removed with curses. Not obeying God brings curses to your offspring and throughout your bloodline. In the Bible, God instructed humanity on how to bless. It went in the hand of Satan, who is a twister, liar, and wicked. The enemy of your soul will always try to pull and push you out of the last step of reaching promises. You are safe and settled in God. Paul encountered God on Damascus Road so the Galatians, Corinthians, and Ephesians found the Lord. Jesus said, follow as written and established by the apostles and prophets. Lord Jesus never built the church. Remember, you are the church, not the building.

Ephesians 2:20 And are built upon the foundation of the apostles and prophets, Jesus Christ himself being the chief corner stone;

The original truth of apostles and prophets' teaching continued in the first century.

Acts 2:42 And they continued stedfastly in the apostles' doctrine and fellowship, and in breaking of bread, and in prayers.

What happens if you build on the foundation of truth, having a revelation of Jesus? Flesh and blood can give you confusion and are a product of religions to misguide. Listening to religious leaders will take you to the Broadway of destruction! How can we lose sight, way, and blessings? Just listen and obey the false teachers and prophets. They Feel accepted, loved, and fit in the standard of Satan. There is no casting demon out, no blind eyes open, and no one rises from the dead. Do not see Spirit's operation to amaze the people. Isn't your life monotonous? My life may seem lonely but exciting since I see new people almost every day. I see the miracle, healing, and God doing signs and wonders through me. Have you ever wondered why Christianity is dying and boring? They are holding people by giving them a position in churches. I knew the Bible but never stopped searching for it. Was searching for the sign following true prophets and teachers. I do not want to be an antichrist. The theologian never had the revelation of Jesus but is full of arguments. Excuse me, go get the revelation from God before speaking of Jesus. He will tell you who Jesus is. Just like He did to Peter, Paul, and many. Jesus said you would do greater if I live within you.

John 14:12a Verily, verily, I say unto you, He that believeth on me, the works that I do shall he do also; and greater works than these shall he do.

The Lord said I should do more than that. I am in search of that and not stuck in one building where lost seats, blind lead blind, deaf do not want to hear, and sick stay sick. Yesterday, I greeted a few people. He said I am cancer-free. I remembered praying for Him at Children's Hospital in Dallas. Another person, I prayed, and God said, he was watching pornography. So I confronted him, He said, yes. He said please pray for my deliverance. Jesus wanted Him to read more Bible. The Word is light, food, sword, and lamp. Jesus asked me to circle him and pray. So we all held hands around him and prayed for deliverance. Well, none of this I knew. Lord knows since I am the servant of God. I am working for Him to let others know what they must do. God knows no matter where and what you do. If you are losing the job, you can keep the job. Meaning we do not align you with God. You must align with the Lord. His word by obeying and doing what the Lord says. Your journey at the end will be beautiful. Learn to listen to God. Run from the false religious leaders, so-called pastors, and false prophets and teachers. May the Lord give you love for Jesus. He loves you to give you the New Testament with the Help of the Holy Spirit. Receive the Holy Spirit by evidence of speaking in a tongue, but allow the Holy Spirit to do its work through you.

Acts 19:2 He said unto them, Have ye received the Holy Ghost since ye believed?Meet true Apostles and prophets like Paul and Peter, so you also can receive the Holy Spirit.

Acts 19:6 And when Paul had laid his hands upon them, the Holy Ghost came on them; and they spake with tongues, and prophesied.Paul knew it since Jesus said, speaking in tongues is one sign that should follow.

Mark 16:17 And these signs shall follow them that believe; In my name shall they cast out devils; they shall speak with new tongues;

Find yourself a true disciple who can baptize you in Jesus's name. By laying a hand you will receive the spirit of God. I received the Holy Spirit by evidence of speaking in tongue. I ran away from the antichrist theologians. They always watch me since our spirits clash. Who does not want the name of Jesus when they go under the water for remission or forgiveness of sins? Antichrist will never baptize you with that name above every name. That name washes away my sins, and I put on Jesus.

Galatians 3:27 For as many of you as have been baptized into Christ have put on Christ.

Obey His Word. Word is the highest authority. Why don't you tell the antichrist religious leader that it is written; it is written as Jesus said to the devil? Love your soul and obey to continue the book of Acts, so you can also write many books.

John 21:25 And there are also many other things which Jesus did, the witch, if they should be written every one, I suppose that even the world itself could not contain the books that should be written. Amen.

LET US PRAY

Our heavenly father, we all have a blinder on the eyes and mind. Remove to know you as it says in your Word. We must obey the truth and fear you. God said it and meant it. It is fearful to fall into the hands of God. We saw what happened to Eve and Adam, King Saul, Priest Eli, and many who did not obey you. But seeing all who obeyed was and will be blessed and used by God. We learn your doctrine if we are like a babe, obedient and submissive. We want all that you have stored for us, so Help me Lord to believe, submit, and obey you in Jesus's name. Amen! God bless you!

SEPTEMBER 4

LIVING IN THE PRESENT, CREATING DESTINY!

Do you consider your actions today to impact the future? Many people are so obscure. When they see the circumstances, situations, and surroundings, their vision gets blurry. But if you see through the eyes of the Lord, you will see the mountain move, a pool of water in the desert, and a crooked path straighten up.

May the Lord help us to see through the eyes of God as future kings, queens, counselors, teachers, prophets, and powerful instruments in God's kingdom.

A beautiful future begins today if you act rightly. The one who decides the future is you and no one. See all around, cannot see the highway to promise land through the ocean. Do you think like God, He said nothing is impossible. I do not mind letting God think of me. God thinks beautifully, He wants me to construct today and not in the future. I am ready to let God think for me. I do not want to see just the slavery of Egypt, but I let God think that this slavery turns into freedom as soon as I go yonder the ocean.

May the Lord, let you be free, worry less, hopeful, whole and not broken, living in abundance and not in scarcity.

Psalms 139:13 For thou hast possessed my reins: thou hast covered me in my mother's womb. 14 I will praise thee; for I am fearfully and wonderfully made: marvellous are thy works; and that my soul knoweth right well. 15 My substance was not hid from thee, when I was made in secret, and curiously wrought in the lowest parts of the earth. 16 Thine eyes did see my substance, yet being unperfect; and in thy book all my members were written, which in continuance were fashioned, when as yet there was none of them. 17 How precious also are thy thoughts unto me, O God! How great is the sum of them!

Our creator was thinking about my future. The beginning may be tiny, but the future could be the star of the sky. The Lord does for us as we allow Him.

God manifested in flesh not just to kill time, walk here and there, and go back to heaven. He was busy in presence preparing for the future. His future was bright since He was doing what He came on earth for. To pay His life through the blood, life is in blood. He was taking back what the devil made a mockery of. Devil thought, oh well, I have done to finish His creation. Jesus came and rescued me, said no devil no, leave my creation. Lord said, I will not allow this; I will come as a humble man and not as the king of kings. I will come as a humble servant and not as Lord of Lords. He redirected the future of His creation by establishing what He came for.

God said, why are you seeing yourself bound, blind, slave, druggy, brokenhearted, lame, deaf, confined to the bed, living a hopeless life? I want you to think of something impossible, beyond your imagination, to construct your future today.

Jeremiah 33:2 Thus saith the Lord the maker thereof, the Lord that formed it, to establish it; the Lord is his name; 3 Call unto me, and I will answer thee, and show thee great and mighty things, which thou knowest not.

A Lady in the prison had never heard about the Lord Jesus. The preacher of faith came there and introduced them to the mighty Jesus. The preacher said you can do all things. You can ask without doubting you will receive it. This lady in prison was good, but somehow she ended up in jail. Not doing the crime, but breaking some kind of law was spending time in jail. She never read the Bible, so she requested one. As she opened the Bible to read, she could not put it down. She said this is marvelous. I never knew this kind of Jesus.

She used her time reading the Word, praying, and believing in God. She dares to say, Lord; I want a paid-off house on the beach. One day, she heard a voice telling her she would be out on a certain date. She believed that voice. Even though that day court was closed, the Judge was on vacation. Well, guess what? She saw the jailer standing at her cell, opening the door to give her news; you are free. It was the same day that God spoke to her. Then as she came out, being a writer, her books were getting published, and she already started earning. Her dream of the paid-off house on the beach also came true.

I love the work of the supernatural. Who holds your success? The key is in your hand. Open the Bible, obey by believing the Word, and see what happens to your future. Your future does not need lottery tickets or someone's will. Your future builds by hearing, fearing, believing, and obeying the true God.

No matter what you say or believe, you build your future by doing and living in the present, hoping for the best for the future.

Joshua 1:8 This book of the law shall not depart out of thy mouth; but thou shalt meditate therein day and night, that thou mayest observe to do according to all that is written therein: for then thou shalt make thy way prosperous, and then thou shalt have good success. 9 Have not I commanded thee? Be strong and of good courage; be not afraid, neither be thou dismayed: for the Lord thy God is with thee whithersoever thou goest.

All that you think today will happen tomorrow? Do better planning for a better future.

The day I received the Holy Spirit and was baptized, in Jesus's name, was indescribable. I cannot explain since it was the supernatural. I wanted to tell the entire world what happened to me when I was baptized in Jesus's name. The Lord said that you shall know the truth and the truth will set you free.

I started coming against the devil and its false teaching. I never heard Jesus's name baptism. The devil buried the truth under the false teaching and doctrine. I started teaching and preaching to all whom I met. If there is only one saved still it is worth it.

I know Noah constructed the ark to rescue the world from a future flood. How many listened? How many listened when Lot and His family were rescued from the fire and brimstone? The wife looked back instead of looking forward to the future, and she was destroyed.

Friends, look ahead to your future and do not let this world hold you. It is burning everywhere. Look at lava burning in many big, rich countries and states. It is time to wake up and prepare for your future. You may say what can rescue us from the coming calamities?

1 Peter 3:20 Which sometime were disobedient, when once the longsuffering of God waited in the days of Noah, while the ark was a preparing, wherein few, that is, eight souls were saved by water. 21 The like figure whereunto even baptism doth also now save us (not the putting away of the filth of the flesh, but the answer of a good conscience toward God,) by the resurrection of Jesus Christ:

Maybe you are laughing at this moment since the future is not predictable today, but it will happen. The sinner needs to rescue themselves from future calamities by baptizing in the Name of Jesus to wash away their sins. Baptism is your arc, so prepare now in Jesus's name. Amen!

LET US PRAY

our heavenly father, as we know the history, repeats but let it positively be a reminder to us. We need your blessings and wisdom to prepare as five wise. Also to help and teach the truth and not the religion for their better future. Our God said and will do it. We know many have gone astray, busy in this world, compromised by pleasing others and not God. Lord, as Noah preached, we must also preach the gospel by death, burial, and resurrection to rescue the soul. Lord have mercy, give your people wisdom to depend on you. We know many are called, but few are chosen. I want to be in a few chosen ones. We stand for the truth, for the bright future of ours, and for others who are willing in Jesus's name. Amen! God bless you!

SEPTEMBER 5

ARE YOU DOING FATHER'S BUSINESS?

Well, someone makes the Bible as their pocket income, personal profit, religion, and Satan's business like a priest, high priest, and Pharisee.

Jesus said.

Luke 2:49 And he said unto them, How is it that ye sought me? wist ye not that I must be about my Father's business?

When parents couldn't find their Son, Jesus, they returned to Jerusalem looking for him. On asking, Jesus replied, I am in my father's business. We must work on our assignment. Our job is to follow in the footsteps of our father. We have a job and we must do as demanded.

Jesus said I am working as my father does, this answer upset Pharisees.

What was Jesus doing? Lord Jesus was fixing the legs, body, and eyes, setting people free and all that only the creator can do. Creation works can be done by the creator alone. I can do the same and greater work if I have a Creator living in me. I have the authority and power given by the Lord.

The creator is not limited, but creation is. Thank you, Jesus. When the Lord came, He was busy going around doing God's business. Many impotent men were by the pool, but the Lord healed one who was sick for 38 years and no wise did anything.

It was the Sabbath day. Religious people found fault against the Lord Jesus.

John 5:16 And therefore did the Jews persecute Jesus, and sought to slay him, because he had done these things on the sabbath day. 17 But Jesus answered them, My Father worketh hitherto, and I work. 18 Therefore the Jews sought the more to kill him, because he not only had broken the sabbath, but said also that God was his Father, making himself equal with God.

Son of God meant God in the flesh. Having one God and knowing His coming in the flesh upset the religious leaders. Jesus was the God manifested in the flesh. One God believer knows that is blasphemy; it is the matter of slaying. Jesus is claiming in this scripture that He is walking God. That is what it means when you say Son of God. Jesus came to work but the one who should cooperate called priests, or high priests, now called pastors or bishops, wanted to kill Him. Be careful to investigate yourself! Are you working for or against the kingdom of God? It is dangerous to fall into the hands of God.

Check your assignment, call, and get diligent in work. Remember, we all have a calling.

Matthew 16:15 And he said unto them, Go ye into all the world, and preach the gospel to every creature. 16 He that believeth and is baptized shall be saved; but he that believeth not shall be damned. 17 And these signs shall follow them that believe; In my name shall they cast out devils; they shall speak with new tongues; 18 They shall take up serpents; and if they drink any deadly thing, it shall not hurt them; they shall lay hands on the sick, and they shall recover. 19a So then after the Lord had spoken unto them, he was received up into heaven

So it is my job to preach the gospel with signs and wonders, healing the sick, casting out demons, and baptizing people in Jesus's name. Remember, it is the business of God, our Father, and you have a job offer. You can apply, with many benefits if you accept.

Matthew 22:14 For many are called, but few are chosen. God gave us His Spirit with His authority to work.

Matthew 9:37 Then saith he unto his disciples, The harvest truly is plenteous, but the labourers are few; 38 Pray ye therefore the Lord of the harvest, that he will send forth labourers into his harvest.

The time has come when we see many churches, but they are raising for their type to fill up the pew and support the pocket. May the Lord make His disciples regain the quality to work for God as Peter and Paul did. We must do the work of our Father, cast out the demons, heal the sick, and preach the Gospel with signs following as Jesus did.

In the past, after receiving my healing, I worked with Br. James in a healing and deliverance meeting. We went home to home, town to city to state as they invited us. Yes, we had many meetings; people were healed, delivered, and saved. We worked for years until I left California for Texas. I saw the work of God, short lag, and hand growth. Intellectually challenged receive deliverance, demon talk, and give information on how they are working in the body. I was not aware of the demon world, where demons manifest, talk, and give information. In Jesus' name, they have to speak the truth and I saw the information was mind-boggling.

I do not limit myself. I know I have the truth and the truth can set people free. Satan tries to block my work, but the devil is a liar. I am so glad that God has my back. I am crazy about Jesus and His truth. He is true and good. I need no one but Jesus alone. It is the Lord who works through me and does all. It is most important that people get saved. Salvation is more important than healing and deliverance. I built over the foundation laid by the Apostle and prophets of old. I just have to continue the plan of salvation of repentance, Baptisms in Jesus's name, and receiving the Holy Spirit by evidence of speaking in tongues. It is the most amazing work since we are building our churches on the right foundation. Do not try laying another foundation.

Ephesians 2:20. And are built upon the foundation of the apostles and prophets, Jesus Christ himself being the chief corner stone;

I have seen the work built on sand destroyed. Jesus is nowhere in their foundation. We see this at the end time, which is now. Christians are powerless. People go to witch doctors, help cometh from the hospital. Many have compromised since there is no spiritual growth around them.

I used to work in the post office. After working for 20 years, I had an injury. Having great faith, I never thought I would have to take retirement for this situation. I was not healed, but the Lord said, I take away your job and you work for me. So I did. The work of God will manifest if you are in the will and way of God. I never worry about the paycheck since God has my back. Later, finding the disciple of Jesus Br. James prayed, and I was healed and walked. True disciples are not sitting in a pew because religious authorities will reject them.

Acts 17:6a These that have turned the world upside down are come hither also;

Work according to the will and ways of God, you can also turn the world upside down. The truth will attract the new convert.

Acts 2:47b And the Lord added to the church daily such as should be saved.

Acts 2:41 Then they that gladly received his word were baptized: and the same day there were added unto them about three thousand souls.

Acts 4:4 Howbeit many of them which heard the word believed; and the number of the men was about five thousand.

How important it is to work for the Lord. The calling is for all and not some. Our job description is in the Book of Acts. Many attend church, but no one knows they are Christian because they are not. They accept the brand names of organizations, denominations, or non-denominations. I know when you are working for God, have no time for yourself. Many times it is so funny that they act like they love God and truth, but you find out they are working for their religious organization and against Jesus. Work for the Lord, He will bless you. God took away my job; I am now working for God and spreading His truth. Have never had a problem with food or clothes. I live in the US with a little retirement check, but God has provided. God has stretched my little income, multiplied, and added. He has done great that I do not have to depend on anyone since Lord Himself said, "I will take care of you". I do not have to work under organizations of denominations or non-denominations. My father runs a business. I want His name blessed and glorified in Jesus's name. Amen!

LET US PRAY

Heavenly Father, your narrow way and the strait that is (restricted) gate will take us to heaven. Thank you for opening our eyes as you did to many who love you with all heart, mind, soul, and strength. There is a power in your truth. Lord, you have given us a job. We want to hear from you the words, Well done thou good and faithful servant: thou hast been faithful over a few things, I will make thee ruler over many things: enter thou into the joy of thy lord. I want our God to be glorified and not any religion, denomination, or leader. We know the mission of Jesus was to work and our mission must continue in His work to give Him glory, honor, and praise which belongs to the owner and creator of the earth, heaven of heavens in Jesus's name Amen! God bless you!

SEPTEMBER 6

LAZY AND SLUMBER

We need the worker to further the kingdom of God. A worker who can work in season out the season instant. Jesus was doing work until His strength was gone. Jesus healed the ear of the servant in the garden of Gethsemane, even though He was worn out and going through agony. Our problem is we are not paying attention as the word of God speaks to us. The time has come when the people have fallen asleep. The spirit of slumbers has taken over. People have stopped praying and fasting. Many do not go out to minister. If you have stopped reading the Bible and witnessing, then you are in slumber mode. Wake up. Darkness, poverty, and trouble will take over you when the world says peace, peace.

1 Thessalonians 5:3 For when they shall say, Peace and safety; then sudden destruction cometh upon them, as travail upon a woman with child; and they shall not escape.

When sudden destruction takes over life? When people are falling spiritually asleep. Remember, this is a spiritual battle called war against the devil, who is an enemy of humanity. Living on Earth is a war zone. Wake up and pray! Laziness is part of humans. We must remember that we are called laborers, workers in the vineyard. In times like these, we should pray and fast instead of eating and drinking.

A few days ago I was in the restaurant; my eyes were toward the door. Each person entered with a big belly. I mean scary big. I thought this individual could die anytime. Not one, but many men had a big belly. What happened? Do they know fasting and prayer, go out to witness? Food becomes toxic when the fullness of bread like Sodom and Gomorrah comes. People eat so much that they feel like they are drunk and sleepy. No one preaches to the Ants, but they remember their work. It is funny that we need much help and still we are lazy for the work of God. We do not practice what we have heard and learned. Your body is the temple of Jehovah God. Make sure you put the good food in your mouth.

Lord said; Proverb 6:6 Go to the ant, thou sluggard; consider her ways, and be wise: 7 Which having no guide, overseer, or ruler, 8 Provideth her meat in the summer, and gathereth her food in the harvest.

Here God is using an insignificant insect called Ants, very busy, teaching us a lesson. They are always carrying something to survive. They know that there will be a time when they need a supply. We need supply for a bad time. Our God has made those little unique ants. Ant uses the time to work. We have physical and spiritual laziness.

The planner is always ahead of the problem. Joseph was like an ant.

Ephesians 5:16 Redeeming the time, because the days are evil.

Indeed, you can also store your prayers, and supplications, and work for the bad days. You know that when you take more calcium; it stores in your body. We use it when it's needed. In many places, I see people storing dry food and spending money on dehydrated food for a bad time. God stored your prayer up for your children and their children for the future trouble they might go through. It works for many generations. Our God keeps our work established by a prayer for a future time. Even Jesus prayed for us. How nice! Daniel prayed three times a day. It helped him when he was in the lion's den. When I was going through the trial, some Christian coworker said, God will answer your prayer. God stored it for you. Yes, He does. Would you do your children and many generations after yours a favor? Pray for them. God will store it and will remember it for them.

Once I met a farmer, who said, the farm just sold across his and made millions of dollars. He said I knew the current owner's grandfather and also knew the day he bought the farm for 100 dollars an acre. He said I was just a school kid the day the man purchased the farm. Now it is sold for millions of dollars. A grandkid is older and so happy since that money made him a millionaire. Your prayer does the same. I am grateful that my mom and father prayed for us and grand and great-grandchildren. We are receiving the blessings of their righteous prayer. You may say they do not deserve to be millionaires. Does not matter what you think. Someone stored wealth for them. God has provided the provision to us through prayer. I value prayer. At 3:50 am, my alarm rings. I wake up and pray. No matter if I am tired, sleepy, or sick. I wake up and pray. I cannot afford to stay in bed. Last few years I haven't slept all night. The devil releases his army from hell. Demons go around stealing, killing, and destroying. It is no time for me to allow the devil to do any harm. I damage the devil since I have authority with power. Who has power and authority? Why do people tarry in the upper room to receive the Holy Spirit? I tried for the Holy Spirit after I had received water baptism in Jesus's name. It took a while, but I got the Holy Spirit by evidence of speaking in another tongue. Now I empty hell and fill up heaven with soul. I do not mind working since I have the truth and only truth sets us free. Great is our Lord to appoint us to work on His vineyards with higher wages.

1 Tim 5:18b The labourer is worthy of his reward.

Our God said, if you are lazy, slumber then time will come on you unaware. God warns us.

Proverb 6:10 Yet a little sleep, a little slumber, a little folding of the hands to sleep: 11 So shall thy poverty come as one that travelleth, and thy want as an armed man.

Shake yourself and put your body to work. Work is the Lord's idea. When God created man, he first found the work; he made the first vineyard and asked men to dress it. All have to work no matter what. One brother said, my wife and her family do not approve. Since I work without a paycheck. All do not bring a paycheck; some bring pure blessings, security, and God. I do a lot of work from morning to evening but not making any money. Yes, God summoned me, work for me and I will take care of you. I never lose my time or am lazy around. I have invested in every field and done so much work. Someone is thinking of a salary in terms of dollars. I am thinking of salary in terms of blessings. Money does little, but blessings much more and stretches to eternity. So get rid of lazing and slumber. Look at Jesus and what He did. Did not have a 9 to 5 Job but a job that stores blessings for eternity. Amen!

LET US PRAY

Heavenly Father, the greedy, money-hungry people do not value or admire our work. You admire our work, and we work for God Almighty. Our wages are secured and saved not just for us, but after many generations. We thank you for giving us a distant vision, a vision of eternity, and a wise heart. The lazy and slumbered physically and spiritually do not receive food and blessings since they do not have the wisdom and desire to work for you. Your work is great since a natural man cannot figure it out, but we do. Your example of not slumbering the crucifixion night shows we have to be ready all the time. Even if our body is not cooperative, or tired, but must push and press through in Jesus's name. Amen! God bless you!

SEPTEMBER 7

LEAN NOT ON YOUR UNDERSTANDING!

The Bible is God's book written by the Spirit God. The man used his pen to take dictation from God. Individual stenographers for the Holy Spirit!

When you are reading, working, or anything for the Spirit of God, you need divine understanding. First time I heard from a Bible teacher that you need the Holy Spirit to understand the Bible. I just scratch my head. Never knew that people wait on God for everything. He read the following scripture, and I realized, yes, I do.

1 Corinthians 2:10 But God hath revealed them unto us by his Spirit: for the Spirit searcheth all things, yea, the deep things of God.11 For what man knoweth the things of a man, save the spirit of man which is in him? even so, the things of God knoweth no man, but the Spirit of God.13 Which things also we speak, not in the words which man's wisdom teacheth, but which the Holy Ghost teacheth; comparing spiritual things with spiritual.14 But the natural man receiveth not the things of the Spirit of God: for they are foolishness unto him: neither can he know them, because they are spiritually discerned.15 But he that is spiritual judgeth all things, yet he is judged of no man.16 For who hath known the mind of the Lord, that he may instruct him? but we have the mind of Christ.

We lean on the teaching of our family, preacher, and teachers but never get hold of God. Get Hold of God and seek Him. Seek Him for everything. It is a must. You may think you are a hundred percent right, being a hundred percent wrong. The Holy Spirit will teach you and guide you. Well, the religious organization does not believe in receiving the Holy Spirit. They justify what you receive when you accept Jesus Christ as your personal Savior. Lie after lie. Satan leads organizations, denominations, or non-denominations, and not by the Holy Spirit. It is obvious how many people are stumbling, falling, and doing the opposite of what God said since they are leaning on false teachings. I was one of them.

Religion had rooted the Trinity doctrine in me. During that time, I did not have the revelation of Jesus Christ. I was struggling to understand the Bible. In one meeting someone said, Lord, will reveal you by one scripture. All of the Bible is a revelation and not a personal interpretation by denomination, organization, or non-denominational. Wait on God and not on your understanding.

I minister all over the world to different nationalities and religious people. The hardest to minister is religious Christians and once I was there too. I received the truth of one God because of God's mercy. I was visiting different churches to seek God. By the grace of God, I found people who had the truth. They differed from

SEPTEMBER 7

religious people. Religion is without foundation but spiritual sounded confident, experienced, and not stubborn but firm.

Get revelation from God. It makes a big difference. Who else but God? He knows it all.

A few years ago, I was visiting a back home in California. I was shopping for a new phone, and it was too expensive. I heard God speaking to me to go to a particular store. So I asked a friend to drive me there. She said, I know, they did not have it since I inquired. I said, but the Lord asked me to go there. She knew my walk with God, so she drove me to that store. The store salesman didn't want to show the product on sale. While talking to the manager, I said, God said, you have a special price for a certain product which I need. He realized I knew what he was hiding. He showed me the product was an online buy. I purchased it at a cheap price. No need to lean on anyone. See, we can't wait. I have learned to ask, knock, and seek. May the Lord make us like David and not Soul.

Today I had a phone call from a good Christian friend. I know her; she is sincere. But she started some kind of business. After starting it, she called me to pray for it. I knew in the Spirit that it was not God's will. God would help if you asked. He would not take over unless you say I surrender Lord, bring me out. She is in such a critical situation that I have to counsel her. She agreed she must surrender to God. Even if she is in the ditch, entangles herself, or dips into problems, God will bring her out. You do not know down the road what can happen. God wants to help us if we have His approval, green light, and blessings. Do not think someone can accomplish something means you can follow their steps. I think twice and pray many times before making small and big decisions. With God's approval, we will be successful. May the Lord teach us to lean on Him and not on our understanding.

Proverb 3:5 Trust in the Lord with all thine heart; and lean not unto thine own understanding. 6 In all thy ways acknowledge him, and he shall direct thy paths.

Every person can develop a relationship with God if they lean on God and not on their understanding. May the Lord help us! God is real. He will answer, lead, guide, and teach if you learn to lean on God. Many people have never learned to listen to God. Some individuals continue to fall and endure defeat, sickness, oppression, and failure. Lean on God; He has a plan for you and me and all. Only do not become like Eve and Adam, King Saul, King Jeroboam, and King Zedekiah. Those fearful of the situation see no future for themselves. Nonetheless, there is a luminous world that exists outside your awareness and acknowledgement.

Do not talk yourself out of the big beautiful plan of God. Fast and pray. Many wise heathen kings did not know the God Jehovah but took counsel from His people. Isn't that nice? Why Christians cannot depend on God? We follow what our parents or surroundings practice. Get a heavenly vision. Lean on God, He will give you the flight of an Eagle, eyesight of the farthest, and a better bird's view than you can imagine. Please do not lean on your understanding. Always remember when you are leaning on God; Satan will send someone, perhaps not in snake form but a beautiful woman or money, or any other type or shape, to tear your dawn. May the Lord give you the strength to lean on Him! Isn't it funny all those who wait on God have the plan of the devil to throw them out? When you are praying, asking, seeking, and knocking, someone will drop by to misguide you. Please counsel with the Lord, He will come on time. Do not rush or go astray since He knows the season of your blessings. Wait, Red light!

Our God is living and is well aware of our being. Many kings of the Nation did significant damage, not leaning on God. Their mistakes caused many calamities, brought slavery, and made nations of Israel idolatry. God wiped Israel out in the end. Learn to lean on God and not on your understanding. God Bless you!

LET US PRAY

Lord, sometimes we think you are too far away. Not knowing whether or not you listen. Lord, our reading knowledge clashes with people who themselves are not saved and brings confusion. Lord, teach us to lean on God and not anyone. The plan is yours. You are the creator; you know the best and no one else. We ask you to help us lean on you with all our hearts to find the right direction. You are the Pilot and never be the copilot. You take over the reign of our life and be the sailor of the boat. Thank you for your time and concern to bless us. Your purpose to create us is to bless, and you will if we listen and obey. Help us lean not to our understanding since it is limited and misleading. So we surrender to you, help us in Jesus's name. Amen! God bless you!

SEPTEMBER 8

WHAT GOD IS LOOKING FOR?

God is looking for the one who listens and obeys. Incline their ear with the heart to HIS voice. Do not show others how great they are, but how great God is. Lean and navigate life through the Holy Spirit. Is it true God is looking for us?

Yes, He is looking for one who is like;

2 Chronicles 16:9 For the eyes of the Lord run to and fro throughout the whole earth, to shew himself strong in the behalf of them whose heart is perfect toward him.

I always look for the one who loves the Lord with all his heart, mind, soul, and strength. Since I have no denomination but I am winning a soul for the kingdom of King Jesus. I always pray to the Lord, bring those whom you have picked so I do not waste my time. Time is very short, let us be honest. God says I wrote some names in the book from the foundation of the world.

Ephesians 1:4 According as he hath chosen us in him before the foundation of the world, that we should be holy and without blame before him in love: 5 Having predestinated us unto the adoption of children by Jesus Christ to himself, according to the good pleasure of his will,

Some people love God with everything in them and will accept the truth. They are different, and wouldn't be afraid of religious leaders. They can walk alone in any country like Daniel and many who separated themselves from God. God is looking for the one who is called but also chooses not to play the dirty game like Judas. If you are playing a dirty game with the truth, that means God has given you the spirit of delusion. What is a delusion? Delusion is a misbelief, misunderstanding, error, mistake. The so-called Christian religion is like this. Do not worry about them, since the Bible says.

2 Thessalonians 2:9 Even him, whose coming is after the working of Satan with all power and signs and lying wonders,10 And with all deceivableness of unrighteousness in them that perish; because they received not the love of the truth, that they might be saved.11 And for this cause God shall send them strong delusion, that they should believe a lie:12 That they all might be damned who believed not the truth, but had pleasure in unrighteousness.

Damn means permanent punishment in hell. What God is looking for after He shed His blood by putting on the flesh? In the New Testament Church, He is looking for His bride. His bride must accept Jesus as her God and Savior. A personal commitment! No hindrances to any type of religion. Allow the Word to be your highest and above all, to obey. God will prepare you as you repent and accept His invitation by baptizing only In Jesus's name. The name which is above all His Old Testament names. Then receive the Holy Spirit, which is Jesus, coming to you. By receiving the Holy Spirit, He will come within.

Ephesians 5:25 Husbands, love your wives, even as Christ also loved the church, and gave himself for it; 26 That he might sanctify and cleanse it with the washing of water by the word, 27 That he might present it to himself a glorious church, not having spot, or wrinkle, or any such thing; but that it should be holy and without blemish.

This Bride has to prepare for a wedding with the groom of Jesus. Jesus is not looking for one who is not listening and rebellion, people pleaser, power-hungry. The Bible says God is preparing His bride who suffered on earth by the so-called religious authority as He did. No problem, since this is eternal separation from those who have the form of godliness but reject the power.

Revelation 19:7 Let us be glad and rejoice, and give honour to him: for the marriage of the Lamb is come, and his wife hath made herself ready. 8 And to her was granted that she should be arrayed in fine linen, clean and white: for the fine linen is the righteousness of saints.

After washing our sins in the blood of Jesus by baptizing in the precious and matchless name of Jesus, we have now put one Jesus.

Galatians 3:27 For as many of you as have been baptized into Christ have put on Christ.

Now spend time with Him by learning the Word. If you want to know Him, then find true teachers and prophets who can help you understand His Word. Follow the Word of God and not religion. Nowadays, we have many denominations to bewitch people. Why? Since they do not have a love for Jesus. They do not care for His Word and truth. God knows them. Do not waste your time after them. Since Jesus says,

2 Corinthians 4:3 But if our gospel be hid, it is hid to them that are lost: 4 In whom the god of this world hath blinded the minds of them which believe not, lest the light of the glorious gospel of Christ, who is the image of God, should shine unto them.

God sends delusions and turns them over to the god of this world, which is Satan. Be careful! Love God, surrender, trust, obey, and submit to the Lord Jesus. I understood the one who is easy to win, never contaminated by false teaching. The power of the false doctrine of Satan can only work if you are not seeking, asking, and knocking for God. It is a heart condition. The heart is called the deceitful and wicked. Jesus came to earth at that time Priest and high priests had already contaminated God's people. Once you are contaminated by false teachers, then there is no hope for you. God came to set an example. He was walking among them, but still, they couldn't recognize Him.

John 14:8 Philip saith unto him, Lord, show us the Father, and it sufficeth us. 9 Jesus saith unto him, Have I been so long time with you, and yet hast thou not known me, Philip? he that hath seen me hath seen the Father; and how sayest thou then, Show us the Father?

See how Jesus answers them. How silly and blind? Many search all their life but never find the truth since they don't have the love for the truth. Love the truth and not the blind leaders and authority. Some will indeed say, Lord, haven't we cast out demons, heal the sick in your name? Jesus will say to go away, I never knew you. I am preparing myself and others for Jesus. I want to meet Him. All I long for is Jesus. I live in the US, have seen world-class things, and enjoyed it, but there is no comparison with my Jesus. No one can buy me. I am sold out to Jesus. Nothing can stop me since I have followed Jesus all the way. Jesus is looking for the one who is sold out. Submit and obey His voice and His alone. Amen!

LET US PRAY

Heavenly Father, we thank you. We have the Word of God. Open the eyes and ears, so we see and hear your voice alone. It is the God we have to hear and no one else. Thank you for manifesting in flesh to purchase us with your blood. You have given your blood, which is your life. I want to say thank you for being merciful for washing away my sins. It is God who did it himself for me by putting on flesh. I thank you for giving me your name, which is above all my name. In the name of Jesus, every knee shall bow, and the tongue confesses that Jesus is the living and only God. You were Father in creation, Son in redemption for your bride and Holy Spirit to comfort, empower, guide, and teach us. We welcome the Holy Spirit within us, in Jesus's name. Amen! God bless you!

SEPTEMBER 9

ONLY YOU CAN UNLOCK YOURSELF!

One who can hear, see, obey, believe, and submit to the Word is you. No one but you!

The Word of God says, *John 8:31 Then said Jesus to those Jews which believed on him, If ye continue in my word, then are ye my disciples indeed; 32 And ye shall know the truth, and the truth shall make you free. So the key is the truth. You must seek the truth and not religion.*

Joining a name-brand organization will ruin you. Allowing the Holy Spirit to teach you will do mighty works. A man was a murderer named Soul, fishermen Peter, John, James, and Andrew, tax collector Matthew, and many more who found the truth and unlocked the treasure. To set yourself free needs your cooperation with the creator.

The Bible says, *John 8:36 If the Son, therefore, shall make you free, ye shall be free indeed.*

God can free you if you follow the direction, instruction, and command given in the Word of God. You listen to God, or you are on your own.

Satan, the snake, interpreted the word of God, and Eve followed it. What happens then? Do not do any personal interpretation that satisfies your lust for eyes, flesh, and pride in life. It is God or your lust and pride. Satan is called the father of the lie, misguider

John 8:43 Why do ye not understand my speech? even because ye cannot hear my word. 44 Ye are of your father the devil, and the lusts of your father ye will do. He was a murderer from the beginning, and abode not in the truth, because there is no truth in him. When he speaketh a lie, he speaketh of his own: for he is a liar, and the father of it.

The word of God is God. Use the word of God all the time. If you hear the Word of God, then learn by keeping it. It will keep you from following the deceptive voice of Satan. Who hears a deceptive voice? Window shoppers for pride and lust? Do not go window shopping, don't have to keep up with Joneses. I want what my neighbor has to be a prideful character. Wait on the Lord! You are going to be blessed by the Lord with everything you need. It is the Lord's freedom, but your choices will lock you up in debt, jealousy, lying, stealing, and bad habits. Do not deceive committing lust by rejecting God's command. Do not blame anyone but yourself, since the devil has no business for the people who hear God and obey His voice.

You cannot tell God not to send me to hell since I am misguided by Satan. Satan never picked fruits or never looked. Satan never put the fruit in the mouth, but you did. Why? Because you wanted to be like God. It is you who sins. You check your heart. Deception is in your heart. It starts in your heart. David's sins inspired him to write the confession song,

Psalms 51:7 Purge me with hyssop, and I shall be clean: wash me, and I shall be whiter than snow.10 Create in me a clean heart, O God; and renew a right spirit within me.This is available in the New Testament. When you are baptized in the name of Jesus, God will wipe out your sins.

Act 22:16 And now why tarriest thou? arise, and be baptized, and wash away thy sins, calling on the name of the Lord. (Jesus)Sickness caused by sin will be wiped away in the water. God will deliver you from all curses.

This only can be done by you. You can unlock yourself from the illnesses connected with sin.I have seen uncountable cases where people come out of the water in Jesus's name, speaking in their tongue. It is the Gift when you go in the water to wash away your sins. Now, who can take you to water? No one but you! The Lord will never push you. The Lord gave you Word, and you do or deny it.How easy for the one who is like babes to find the truth.

Isaiah 28:9 Whom shall he teach knowledge? and whom shall he make to understand doctrine? them that are weaned from the milk, and drawn from the breasts.10 For precept must be upon precept, precept upon precept; line upon line, line upon line; here a little, and there a little:11 For with stammering lips and another tongue will he speak to this people.12 To whom he said, This is the rest wherewith ye may cause the weary to rest; this is the refreshing: yet they would not hear.Be like a babe.

The baby would not tell mom and dad what to do. The baby is the follower. That is why the baby is safe in the hands of the Lord. Let us be like a babe who depends on the Father, the Creator, to guide and to teach. Remember, you do as the Word said to unlock and lose yourself from the bondage. I can teach, but you are the one who follows.When I give Bible study, the one who listens and obeys is a joy to my heart. But some hear the Prophecy, the teaching of the word of God still does not obey.I see their life has no progress, very smart, smarter than God, and cannot obey the voice of God, which is the word of God. I spend much time in prayer, teaching, and guiding, but then if they reject me, I walk away from them. You show them over two scriptures for the doctrine, but still; they accept tradition, and false teaching and follow the crowd. The false teachers and prophets are the most difficult, despite that, it is not their fault as I think it depends on the individual.

Matthew 10:14 And whosoever shall not receive you, nor hear your words, when ye depart out of that house or city, shake off the dust of your feet.15 Verily I say unto you, It shall be more tolerable for the land of Sodom and Gomorrah in the day of judgment, than for that city.Follow Jesus's word for unlocking, to set yourself free.

Some denominations, false teachers, pastors, Satan, and his devilish doctrine have deceived many. God asked Adam to follow Him, and not to another voice. But the biggest enemy was within them. You alone can bring in a curse or blessings. You alone can bring freedom or bondage. It's possible to lock or unlock yourself. Follow Jesus and obey His Word. Truth is a powerful weapon to unlock you from the bondages, sicknesses, and calamities. You are responsible for the consequences. Amen!

LET US PRAY

Lord, God, you came to set the captive free. You gave us freedom even in the Garden of Eden. Our choices brought us bondages, curses, and trouble not paying attention. Not inclining our ears to you! Help us, Lord, since we are not better than Eve and our ancestors who failed you. We asked you to give us the desire to follow you and not organizations, denominations, and lost religious authorities. Help us open the Bible by opening our hearts and minds to receive the truth. Your Word is true and will bless and unlock us if we believe, obey, and submit. So, Lord, help, give us courage and boldness to follow you in Jesus's name. Amen! God bless you!

SEPTEMBER 10

HOW DO YOU INTRODUCE JESUS?

In Matthew 4, Satan questions Jesus, *"If thou art the Son of God..."* Satan knew Jesus was God, manifested in the flesh. He knows who Jesus is.

James 2:19 tells us, "Thou believest that there is one God; thou doest well: the devils also believe, and tremble."

Satan knows the Word of God. He knows,

Isaiah 9:6 "For unto us a child is born, unto us a son is given: and the government shall be upon his shoulder: and his name shall be called Wonderful, Counsellor, The mighty God, The everlasting Father, The Prince of Peace."

He knows, *John 1:1,14, "In the beginning was the Word, and the Word was with God, and the Word was God... And the Word was made flesh, and dwelt among us, (and we beheld his glory, the glory as of the only begotten of the Father,) full of grace and truth."*

Jehovah God put on flesh to shed precious, sinless blood. That is why He was the Son of God and not the son of Joseph. Here is the Son of God, the letter "S" is capitalized. Jesus did not come with a divine nature, but the divine God put on flesh. Remember, Satan knows Jesus is Jehovah's God since he was in heaven at one time before being expelled. But we, being created, need revelation from the Holy Spirit to introduce who Jesus is.

In Mark 5:6, the demons that possessed a man saw Jesus coming, and came and worshiped Him knowing that Jesus was that one true God in flesh. "6 But when he saw Jesus afar off, he ran and worshipped him, 7 And cried with a loud voice, and said, What have I to do with thee, Jesus, thou Son of the most high God? I adjure thee by God, that thou torment me not. 8 For he said unto him, Come out of the man, thou unclean spirit."

Who did the disciple think Jesus was?

Mark 8:27 reads, And Jesus went out, and his disciples, into the towns of Caesarea Philippi: and by the way he asked his disciples, saying unto them, Whom do men say that I am? 28 And they answered, John the Baptist; but some say, Elias; and others, one of the prophets."

Then Jesus asked them in verse *29*, *"And he saith unto them, But whom say ye that I am? And Peter answereth and saith unto him, Thou art the Christ."*

Peter was the only one who knew who Jesus was. You are blessed, if you know who Jesus is, because Jesus said in

Matthew 16:17, *"And Jesus answered and said unto him, Blessed art thou, Simon Barjona: for flesh and blood hath not revealed it unto thee, but my Father which is in heaven.*

No man, teacher, or Bible college, can teach you who Jesus is. We can only build the true Church of Jesus Christ on the revelation of who Jesus is; all else is just building on sinking sand. Jesus told Peter that his revelation of Jesus would stand against the gates of hell.

Jesus said to Peter in *Matthew 16:18 And I say also unto thee, That thou art Peter, and upon this rock I will build my church; and the gates of hell shall not prevail against it.19 And I will give unto thee the keys of the kingdom of heaven: and whatsoever thou shalt bind on earth shall be bound in heaven: and whatsoever thou shalt loose on earth shall be loosed in heaven.*

King Herod and Jews said about Jesus in *Mark 6:14 And king Herod heard of him; (for his name was spread abroad:) and he said, That John the Baptist was rose the dead, and therefore mighty works do shew forth themselves in him. 15 Others said, That it is Elias. And others said, That it is a prophet, or as one of the prophets.16 But when Herod heard thereof, he said, It is John, whom I beheaded: he has risen from the dead.*

During the time of Jesus people did not know who He was. To know the identity of Jesus needs revelation.

Saul of Tarsus (later called Paul) received a revelation of Jesus on his way to Damascus. Acts 9:15. We all need revelation and manifestation of Jesus.

Ephesians 4:13 tells us, "Till we all come in the unity of the faith, and of the knowledge of the Son of God, unto a perfect man, unto the measure of the stature of the fulness of Christ:"

Jesus is the expressed (or exact image) of Jehovah God. Just like your photo is the exact (or express image) of your person.

Hebrews 1:1 tells us, "God, who at sundry times and in divers manners spake in time past unto the fathers by the prophets, 2 Hath in these last days spoken unto us by his Son, whom he hath appointed heir of all things, by whom also he made the worlds; 3 Who being the brightness of his glory, and the express image of his person..."

Paul introduced Jesus as the visible image of God. He writes in

Colossians 1:15 "Who is the image of the invisible God, the firstborn of every creature:..."

Again, Paul writes, *in 2 Corinthians 4:4 "In whom the god of this world (Satan) hath blinded the minds of them which believe not, lest the light of the glorious gospel of Christ, who is the image of God, should shine unto them."*

No flesh and blood (natural man) can know who Jesus is except by the Spirit. No human, or theologian, or master of a Torah is needed. It is your search, love, and revelation. Therefore, many denominations are in error. Most of the time, theologians, priests, high priests, and religious leaders do not have a revelation of Jesus.

The demons, devils, and fallen angels knew who Jesus was since they were spirit beings. Spirit knows the spirit world. Satan (Lucifer) and all the fallen angels that came down from heaven knew Jesus since they were spirits and not flesh and blood. Of course, they are all antiChrist, so they will not let you know who Jesus is.

I have seen many confused organizations, and denominations hold to this antiChrist doctrine of not accepting Jesus as the One and only true God, manifested in the flesh. Paul, being Saul, was in this category, but His love for God found the mercy of Jesus. God intervened since Paul had a love for God and was not looking for a position of power. He was not jealous, greedy, a liar, money, or power-hungry like the priest high priests were. He was not categorized as the "generation of the vipers" but he loved God.

Today, we have many organizations and denominations since they do not have a revelation of who Jesus is. Isn't that strange since Jesus said if you obey me, if you love me, and if you keep my commandment, I will reveal to you who I am? I pray you know the Jehovah God of the Old Testament as Jesus (in the flesh) of the New Testament, by revelation from God!

LET US PRAY

Lord, many walks confused, not knowing who you are. Lord, we need not just a revelation of you but know you as coming God to conquer and rule, as King of King and the Lord of the Lord. The world will know you at that time and kneel and confess that you are the Jehovah God. But today we want all to know and revere you. Many claims to know Jesus since they attend a building called church and were born in a religious family. Lord, we want to know you in your might and power, so we can give you your rightful place. We have the God Jesus, the Highest name, the name above all names that you took in the past. We cast out demons, heal the sick, pray, and baptize in Jesus's precious name. Jesus's name is the authorized name above all names you had. It is the name we bow and confess that you alone are worthy of honor, wisdom, knowledge, riches, glory, power, and strength in Jesus's name. Amen! God bless you!

SEPTEMBER 11

SERVE GOD WITH HIS CONDITION AND STANDARD!

Why do we have so many religions, churches, and organizations? We are no better than Cain, Eve, Adam, and all who decided their destiny, knowing it would not work. Jesus did all that it takes to fulfill the law. Establish doctrine exactly as God instructs it in the Word, which is the only highest authority. That is why I teach by showing them two or more scriptures.

Matthew 5:17 Think not that I am come to destroy the law, or the prophets: I am not come to destroy, but to fulfil.

Two or more witnesses must establish every doctrine, belief, or policy. The Lord instructed us to find two witnesses, proofs, or evidence given in the Bible. God has always kept two or three proofs to establish His doctrine or teaching. God gave exact instructions for fasting. You can water it down by adding and subtracting the scriptures. Quickly, we should search for two or more scriptures on fasting, following the instructions exactly as given.

First evidence.

Esther 4:16 Go, gather together all the Jews that are present in Shushan, and fast ye for me, and neither eat nor drink three days, night or day: I also and my maidens will fast likewise; and so will I go in unto the king, which is not according to the law: and if I perish, I perish.

Second evidence, *Exodus 34:28a And he was there with the LORD forty days and forty nights; he did neither eat bread nor drink water.*

We saw two scriptures for fasting and let us see one more scripture to establish doctrine. Do not let your imagination ruin the power of fasting.

Jonah 3:5 So the people of Nineveh believed God, and proclaimed a fast, and put on sackcloth, from the greatest of them even to the least of them. 7 And he caused it to be proclaimed and published through Nineveh by the decree of the king and his nobles, saying, Let neither man nor beast, herd nor flock, taste anything: lets them not feed, nor drink water:

See, even idol worshipers of Nineveh knew how to fast since they were aware of godly fasting. And It worked since they fasted as given instruction in the word. What happens if we water down the instruction of God?

Simply, people are rebellious, stiff necks, and stubborn Hebrews and us too. Why don't we see God moving, and can't cast out the demon? Believe me, demonic hindrances wouldn't be removed if you add or subtract to the Word of God.

God said to worship Him in Spirit and truth. Lord Jesus said do not preach without having His knowledge. Start His work by knowing who Jesus is. God used Peter for Jews and Paul for Gentiles. Both had a revelation of Jesus. The first condition, flesh, and blood cannot reveal the identity of Jesus. It confirmed that the spirit was revealed to Peter and Paul. Paul's knowledge couldn't help. Do not go to the religious organization to find Jesus, go to God and His Word. Serve God with His condition and at His standard. Mary Joseph agreed to work at His condition. People fasted fulfilling His condition and saw the result. Word is the highest authority, so open the Bible and seek two or three Scriptures to establish any doctrines. God reveals the truth to the one who seeks God, so do not worry about those who reject you not having the same revelation. If you love God, then God will teach you. Others will wander in darkness and not find the truth. Religious leaders rejected Jesus since religion is a man's level and conditions, but the relationship is at God's level and conditions. Thousands of religions are there since it is a men's program using the Word and interpreting for personal productions of the Bible. Go check their churches; nothing is working, but it is full of people just like them having stubborn and strong delusions. Why? You are the church and you are not called to sit on a pew or chairs, go work, and learn the word. Return home rejoicing!

Let us see the doctrine of baptism. Find two or three scriptures. First,

Acts 2:38 Then Peter said unto them, Repent, and be baptized every one of you in the name of Jesus Christ for the remission of sins, and ye shall receive the gift of the Holy Ghost.

Let us see the second witness in the Bible

Acts 8:16 (For as yet he was fallen upon none of them: only they were baptized in the name of the Lord Jesus.)

Let us find the third witness of the Cornelius family.

Acts 10:48 And he commanded them to be baptized in the name of the Lord.

Just study the early church history for water baptism. Now the Bible is the word of God. We need no personal interpretation but the only witness of two or three scriptures to establish doctrine. God received the Holy Spirit by evidence of speaking in the tongue by two or more scriptures in the Bible. Are you ready to obey God's condition to stand, and then reject false teachers, prophets, and religions? A disciple, Paul, and others followed Jesus by carrying the Cross. Moses did exactly what it took, so He meet the God of Abraham and David as well. God kicked out King Saul and other kings, who added their two senses. It is His condition to come on earth, leaving heaven to become poor for us.

In Jesus' condition, all the disciples cast out demons, healed the sick, opened the blind eyes of the lame, and raised the dead. You can do it if you are walking in His doctrine established by the two or more witnesses in the Word. Word is the highest authority, not this church, organization, and the false prophet and teacher deviated from the truth established by one scripture. Blind leaders can only lead the blind. It is His condition to go into the world and preach the truth. His disciple will speak in tongues if you do not, which means you do not have Holy Spirit Baptism. Heavenly language is a prayer language. If you are not following the condition of Jesus, then you will see the sick, oppressed, possessed churches preparing people for Satan to take over.

Lord said, quench not the Spirit. To repent, and then wash all sins in the Blood hidden under the name of Jesus will bring you to God's condition to serve Him at His level. Repent words came first from John Baptist, Jesus, disciples, and others. In the past, the Lord wanted a kingdom ruled by Him, but they asked the king. It was His desire and condition to stay alert so the devil does not steal the truth. The Lord gave commandments, precepts, laws, and statutes, so we walk with His conditions to reach the level that He prefers for His people to serve Him. How nice that we have written records, but if that written instruction of the Bible goes to the hand of the greedy, liar, false teacher, pastors, and prophets, then you will work on their level and with their conditions for their religion. Satan has changed the Bible, so you never reach God's level. It is the God whom you serve who has fixed the standard. So open the Bible and study, ask, knock, seek, and obey the truth. Jesus is the way, truth, and life to reach Him. Only truth counts and not the teaching of the religions. My Lord, open your eyes to see and ear to hear. It is the Lord who does all the work, so get humble, get instructions, and follow the Word and doctrine of the Lord.

LET US PRAY

Lord, we thank you for the Word doctrine and template to follow. It is the mercy of God who gave the example with His Spirit. Amazingly, we have evidence of receiving the Holy Spirit by speaking in tongues. How beautiful to have the truth? The obedient babes you will teach the doctrine. It is at the mercy of God that we can worship and serve God at your level. You are Holy and will teach righteous and obedient doctrine. We seek till we find and never compromise in Jesus's name! Amen! God bless you!

SEPTEMBER 12

PEOPLE WHO ARE CALLED BY GOD!

The Bible says no one comes to me except I draw them nigh to him. So coming to God is personal and unique for you, born in a Christian family. I hear great testimonies about a new convert, born in a nominal Christian family, or Hindu or Muslim family, which are incredible. I hear many testimonies, and it is clear how God alone can draw them. It is the Lord who calls us.

John 6:44 No man can come to me, except the Father which hath sent me draw him: and I will raise him at the last day. 65 And he said, therefore said I unto you, that no man can come unto me, except it was given unto him of my Father.

From the above scriptures, we know only God can draw us to Him. The creator has a rope to pull us. Only God calls us. God has not made our robot, so respond when He calls.

Matthew 22:14 For many are called, but few are chosen.

We have to prove and pass all tests to fulfill our calling. Being born into a Christian family does not qualify us for the Kingdom. But as He said, you can not enter the Kingdom of God unless you are.

John 3:5 Jesus answered, Verily, verily, I say unto thee, Except a man be born of water and of the Spirit, he cannot enter into the kingdom of God.

Lord Jesus, the God manifested in Flesh has to go through the trial on the mountain. He prayed and fasted. Spirit God in flesh, leaving us an example, did all that it took for His creation to be saved. God came in flesh known as lamb just to shed the blood. To shed the blood was not the only purpose. His other purpose was to leave an example for us.

1 Peter 2:21 For even hereunto were ye called: because Christ also suffered for us, leaving us an example, that ye should follow his steps:

The human in the flesh needs a template to follow. Jesus, being God, did all, so what is our problem? Why do we argue? Follow false doctrine and not search to find the way of Jesus. He is the only truth of eternal life. I have learned from Seventh-day Adventists, Mormons, and Jehovah's Witnesses plus attended the

Methodist. In the US, I attended a Pentecostal church. I did not stop searching. God called me so I know the mercy and grace of God leads me to the truth. It did not happen naturally. I prayed and fasted to find the truth. I would follow none of these religious organizations. Later I went to many churches in Los Angeles, in West Covina. Someone came and told me the truth. Oh my God, I had never heard of that before. The state of Gujarat where I lived did not know what I found. I did not know that the truth has the power to bury an old person and raise them in Newness. I am called doesn't mean I got a ticket to heaven. No, there is work to do. Jesus is the example; we must follow to turn a life around.

Matthew 16:24 Then said Jesus unto his disciples, If any man will come after me, let him deny himself, and take up his cross, and follow me.

When you are called to follow Jesus, you are called to join an army. I meet many people coming out of their religious denominations, Muslim and Hinduism, not knowing they are in the war zone with Satan. Make sure you understand it is difficult, but you are victorious since you have the power of the Holy Spirit. If you are attending the religious church where they teach, once saved, always saved, isn't that a joke? Go in and take ashes, that is another lie. You don't have a demon. That is another lie. When you accept Jesus, you receive the Holy Spirit right away; it is a lie, no hope for you. That is why it says many are called, but few are chosen. While narrow faces restrictions, Broadway remains unrestricted and attracts many who seek to destroy.

The Strait is the gate meaning restricted gate. When people are called by God and picked after passing, their test is different. When I teach, I show them the written Word; they grasp and go live with it. I am especially dealing with one Hindu guy. Today, he said when I did not know the Bible, I still knew that Jesus was the only God. He is the One and only God. Well, I studied the false and confusing doctrine of the Bible; I had many false teachings hindering me. But I depended on God. I stood on the Word of God and believed that it would happen as it says. The latter revelation came in some meetings. People who don't have a lot of confusion about false prophets and teachers are the ones I learn from. I am still like a babe and want to know more and more.

Isaiah 28:9 Whom shall he teach knowledge? and whom shall he make to understand doctrine? them that are weaned from the milk, and drawn from the breasts.

Be like a child.

Matthew 18:3 And said, Verily I say unto you, Except ye be converted, and become as little children, ye shall not enter into the kingdom of heaven.

Matthew 19:14 But Jesus said, Suffer little children, and forbid them not, to come unto me: for of such is the kingdom of heaven.

Mark 10:15 Verily I say unto you, Whosoever shall not receive the kingdom of God as a little child, he shall not enter therein.

Do not become a theologian, baptist, JW, Methodist, alliance, CNI, Pentecostal, or whatever. Accept the truth like a child. If you give a dollar to a child, he will accept it; the child will jump up and down. One time after Church I told my niece, I will buy you lunch, she jumped up and down. She believed it. Remember, we have to accept what thus saith the Lord. Teenagers and denominational people are difficult to talk to. When Angel asked Philip to go south of Jerusalem to Gaza, Philip did. He met Eunice; the Spirit asked Philip to go near, and he did and asked him do you understand?

He said no. *Acts 8:35 Then Philip opened his mouth, and began at the same scripture, and preached unto him Jesus. 36 And as they went on their way, they came unto a certain water: and the eunuch said, See, here is water; what doth hinder me to be baptized? 37 And Philip said, If thou believest with all thine heart, thou mayest. And he answered and said, I believe that Jesus Christ is the Son of God. 38 And he commanded the chariot to stand still: and they went down both into the water, both Philip and the eunuch and he baptized him.*

These kinds of people are called, and the Lord will send them a true teacher. Sometimes I meet these kinds of people. They are a joy. They will never say, Oh I am this and that, but accept and turn to God. There is a difference.

Revelation 17:14 These shall make war with the Lamb, and the Lamb shall overcome them: for he is Lord of lords, and King of kings: and they that are with him are called, and chosen, and faithful.

Praise God! He chooses after calling. Only the faithful will make it to heaven. Amen!

LET US PRAY

Lord, we thank you for calling us. Prepare us in your boot camp to fight with the unseen enemy. Rulers of the darkness are the opponent; we do not see, but God you have shown us how to fight. We love you, God, that you have many troubles and trials to go through, but your promises are with us. You will never leave us or forsake us. Thank you, Lord! This is what we want and keep in our hearts that your promises are yes, but we have to believe and claim it. The first is last and the last will be first. Help us run this race in your condition and not ours. We want to stay humble, not just us, but our land healed from poverty, sicknesses, disease, and demonic operations, in Jesus's name. Amen! God bless you!

SEPTEMBER 13

TALK REASONABLY!

You must talk with knowledge of someone or something. I find people have no knowledge and talk like they know everything. I lived in California for 25 years, which doesn't mean I know all about California. We must know subjects before debating or discussing them. Especially for God! How can I talk about God without knowing or experiencing a true God? You ask God, search, and seek for Him. Half-knowledge is worse than ignorance.

Proverb 1:5 A wise man will hear, and will increase learning; and a man of understanding shall attain unto wise counsels: 7 The fear of the Lord is the beginning of knowledge: but fools despise wisdom and instruction.

Talking on any subject without knowing, but you glance or overheard someone does not make you an expert. It shows how foolish you are. You expose your foolishness. May the Lord give you wisdom. Nowadays, everyone wants to talk about God; I mean the True God Jesus. But never heard, searched, read, and studied Him. Riots going on in the World for the true God, and it sounds so foolish, unlearned, and ignorant. One knows all about God. Something made by hand cannot walk, talk, speak, or think is not gods. Do not discuss the almighty God when you are worshiping hand products. Not knowing and speaking about the everlasting, omniscient, omnipotent, creator, and wonder-working God will bring trouble. It is inappropriate to even take the name of Jesus from the unholy and unrighteous mouth.

Hebrews 10:31 It is a fearful thing to fall into the hands of the living God.

Make sure you understand God is not science, space, or any other subject. It is the creator who created you. Be careful!

Psalm 90:11 Who knoweth the power of thine anger? even according to thy fear, so is thy wrath.

So any time I talk about God; I make sure God reveals it or I know what I am talking about. Otherwise, one voice will be louder than the other trying to prove I am right without knowledge. You can be wrong in thinking right.

Proverb 4:7 Wisdom is the principal thing; therefore get wisdom: and with all thy getting get understanding.

All prophecies coming true show that the time is closer to the coming of Jesus. The Bible says, for my namesake, they will hate you. There will be famine, earthquakes, and no more islands, and mountains. Get ready to see the outcome of the prophecy at hand. Read Mark 13, Luke 17:2037; 21:836; Matthew 24.

2Timothy 3:15 Timothy 4:17. These days, media and government control prove the fulfillment of Bible prophecy. It also proves ignorance. Some wicked forces lead or drive people to want to take over. So why is this? It shows the creation loves darkness rather than light. Creation loves evil rather than good. Good is evil and evil is good. May the Lord make us sensible. How can you speak about things you do not know? Is Christianity being converted or a reversal of a misleading path? People walking in darkness, lost after the dumb and deaf man-made idols, now found the true God. An idol can have any shape or name, but none of them have a mind, brain, or living organism. May the Lord open our spiritual eyes to see and seek Him. If you want to know God, you must ask Him. I would do so since the Bible is the Word of God.1 Corinthians 8:5 For though there be that are called gods, whether in heaven or in earth, (as there be gods many, and lords many,) It is common sense that you and someone else claim to be you, then they have to prove their identity.

We have identity cards, birth certificates, passports, and other identity proofs to prove that I am the real or original one. May I say that if we are careful about our identity, then why are we so confused or lazy not to find this one true God? If you do, then the end of the battle is poverty, sorrow, destruction, sickness, diseases, oppression, possession, and darkness. May the Lord help you find the truth of the Bible which has the power to set you free from the ignorant. Sensible talk is transparent. There is a piece of evidence behind it. There is a power behind it to support what it claims to be. If you just are talking or arguing, that means you have religion and not relations. You will be one of those religious authorities trying to promote and pressure you to accept what they believe.

God revealed in His word about the end time,

2 Thessalonians 2:3 Let no man deceive you by any means: for that day shall not come, except there come a falling away first, and that man of sin be revealed, the son of perdition; 4 Who opposeth and exalteth himself above all that is called God, or that is worshipped; so that he, as God sitteth in the temple of God, shewing himself that he is God. 5, Remember ye not, that, when I was yet with you, I told you these things?

Now, ignorant, untaught, or inexperienced shouldn't talk about the subject of God unwisely. In the past, my first experience of Christianity was when I went into the water in Jesus's name. My purpose to go under the water was to receive the forgiveness of my sins as explained in the Word of God. Let me tell you if you do, then all your arguments will be dissolved. You will experience forgiveness and will be grateful. You tell me, who would not be happy when they find something so precious? Now Jesus said I came for my creation, to heal, deliver, and set free. If we follow Jesus, we must do the same and not argue. The natural man wouldn't know about supernatural things. What will you do when a person is a lunatic, the demon possesses? You need the power and finger of God. The instruction is in the Bible by the true God. Now, if you and I, as a Christian, follow the exact instructions of the Bible, then it will work.Who can stop us from following our Father if we find Him? Who gave you the right to stop one who experienced the truth and then believed? If you are blind, ask for help, but do not stop the progress of others. It does not need anyone's permission unless you are biased or a hater of Christians. Christianity is not a religion; it is the mighty experience of deliverance from the darkness, poverty, sickness, and demons. I advise you to open the Bible and follow. If you find anything wrong, then go talk to the creator, since it is the creator's book. It is to guide you to all blessings, truth, and prosperity. Talk sensibly or you are unwise and ignorant. God bless you.

Proverb 24:4 And by knowledge shall the chambers be filled with all precious and pleasant riches. 5 A wise man is strong; yea, a man of knowledge increaseth strength. 6 For by wise counsel thou shalt make thy war: and in a multitude of counselors, there is safety.

LET US PRAY

Heavenly Father, we thank you for the time at hand. All prophecy will come to pass, then look up, and lift your heads; for your redemption draweth nigh. We see riots, killing, and destruction everywhere. This is the time of darkness. May the Lord help us reach many and bring them out of the fiery burning hell. Hell was no exit door. Give your people a desire to witness those who are ignorant. Our God is merciful, He alone can heal the brokenhearted, provide, heal the sick, and deliver. It is our job being children of the living God to help those who are without and helpless. We thank you since the doctor's charges are extreme, but our God does it for free. Help us Lord in Jesus's name. Amen! God bless you!

SEPTEMBER 14

HOLD ON TO THE HAND OF GOD!

We see children holding their parent's hands. They will not hold a stranger's hands. Husband and wife holding each other's hand. They hold until they are married, once they are divorced, the hand changes. Children grow up, and they do not need their hands anymore. People get older when they need a hand again. I was in India; I saw the elderly always hold others' hands. We need to hold hands, but we can change hands as well. But the hand of God will never change. That is the hand you need to hold tight. It is the unchangeable hand.

May the Lord always help us remember that the hand of the Lord will reach you to save you from the miry clay, and deep trouble, and will protect you. Years ago I heard the story of this So. Indian prophet. After His conversion, He came to the Northwest. Our parents always welcomed people who came in the name of Jesus. That brought many blessings to our home. This man's name was Mr. Pardeshi. He had a sccular job in South India. The Angel came to His office asking him to follow. He said no; I have a job wife and child to take care of. The angel came the following day and asked to do the same; he replied the same. On the third, as Angel asked him to follow, Mr. Pardashi dropped and followed him. South India has many mountains and valleys. So Angel took him to the pick of the mountain and dropped him and disappeared. For days and weeks, he waited for the angel to escort him. Being weak, he thought, I cannot go down. His beard got long, thirsty, and hungry. He prayed, Lord, please kill me here. I am not capable of going down. That time, he saw one hand come from heaven and touched his tongue and he gained complete strength. The light came to his eyes, and his body received the strength and he started climbing down. The man sought God in his desperation when he was on the mountain. God anointed the man with great anointing. If he walked on the street, possessed people to fall backward. The demon came out of the people in his presence. This man came to Gujarat state and baptized my mom in Jesus's name. My mom said I was sick and was healed.

The hand of God touched Br. Pardeshi and it revived him. You need the hand of God to touch you. Things happen with the Lord's right hand. It is the hand of power. God is a spirit, so the right hand is an allegory.

1 Peter 5:6 Humble yourselves therefore under the mighty hand of God, that he may exalt you in due time:

Isaiah 48:13 Mine hand also hath laid the foundation of the earth, and my right hand hath spanned the heavens: [when] I call unto them, they stand up together.

Our God uses the hand as an allegory, which is a metaphor or analogy.

The Bible says God is Spirit. John 4:24 God is a Spirit:

We use our hands to touch, work, or pray over people.

I use my hand to pray over people. People tell me of feeling hot when I lay my hands on them. They also confirm that they feel something came out of their hand and feel free and light or tired. Our hand is what God is talking about. Heavenly matters can only be understood if they are explained in earthly ways. God uses the parable so you and I can understand. I cannot talk about the US to people who have never visited the US.

Isaiah 41:9 Thou whom I have taken from the ends of the earth, and called thee from the chief men thereof, and said unto thee, Thou art my servant; I have chosen thee, and not cast thee away.10 Fear thou not; for I am with thee: be not dismayed; for I am thy God: I will strengthen thee; yea, I will help thee; yea, I will uphold thee with the right hand of my righteousness.

The Lord explains things, bringing us to our level so we can understand. God being Spirit fills heaven and earth. We understand with an earthly mind that His hands are mighty to save us. God uses the parable to explain the heavenly matter with earthly elements. God made our hands help. We use our hands to cook, clean, feed, comb, work, write, and do the work. We do not use legs for a hand. So our hand in the hand of God becomes a powerful hand. Our hands can raise the dead, heal the sick, and cast out demons. It can only happen if we allow our hand to be in the hand of God. Our hands only train to work but never for God's work, even though it is given by God.

God said in the Word of God. *Mark 16:18 They shall take up serpents; and if they drink any deadly thing, it shall not hurt them; they shall lay hands on the sick, and they shall recover.*

How can you do all the above work and take up the serpent? We work with our hands and also lay hands on the sick. May the Lord help us understand God is using our hands to do His work. We put our hand in the will of God. The Will of God needs your hand. If God does not use His hand, you will be drawn. You wouldn't be rescued. So remember that we need to be His unchangeable hand. It is the Lord who said you use your hand. As God anoints our hand to pray over others, it becomes the hand of Jesus.

Mark 8:25 After that he put his hands again upon his eyes, and made him look up: and he was restored, and saw every man clearly.

Luke 13:13 And he laid his hands on her: and immediately she was made straight, and glorified God.

Luke 4:40 Now when the sun was setting, all they that had any sick with divers diseases brought them unto him; and he laid his hands on every one of them, and healed them.

Acts 9:17 And Ananias went his way, and entered into the house; and putting his hands on him said, Brother Saul, the Lord, even Jesus, that appeared unto thee in the way as thou camest, hath sent me, that thou mightest receive thy sight, and be filled with the Holy Ghost.

To see the Power of Hand as it becomes the hand of the Lord. It is the unchangeable hand of God to do great work. Use your hand, thinking it will do great if it works for the Lord. He gave us an example. How you lay your hands on sick people. Put your hand on the oppressed, possessed people to see the work of God. The supernatural work will manifest only if your hand moves, works, and operates for Jesus's work. Amen!

LET US PRAY

Heavenly Father, we come before your altar. We know how important our hands are if we use them for you. It is the unchangeable hand of God to rescue, heal, deliver, and set the captive free if we do it your way. Lord, you are Spirit, but you use our hand. Our hand metaphor is understandable since we use the hand to work. May the Lord help us use our hands to do the mighty kingdom work. We let the doctors, nurses, or others use theirs, but one who must use them is us. We are Holy Spirit-filled people who must use our hand for our creation. To further your kingdom depends on the unchangeable hand of God, which is mine. It cannot be otherwise. Thank you for giving us two hands, not one. May the Lord anoint today for the many tasks of God. We dedicate our hand to be an unchangeable hand for the kingdom's work, in Jesus's name. Amen. God bless you.

SEPTEMBER 15

THE TARGET IS ON YOUR FAITH!

Faith moves the mountain. Mountain of debt, worry, trouble, sicknesses, diseases, and name it. If you have faith, you can do what you desire to be. Nothing is stronger than your faith. But the devil also knows, so he tries to do his best to create a situation that seems greater, bigger, impossible, and unusual just to shake your faith. Faith is a powerful positive weapon, and the devil knows it can quench the fiery dart of Satan.

Ephesians 6:16 Above all, taking the shield of faith, wherewith ye shall be able to quench all the fiery darts of the wicked.

1 Thessalonians 5:8 But let us, who are of the day, be sober, putting on the breastplate of faith and love; and for an helmet, the hope of salvation.

Faith is the shield of your hope. Through faith, you will overcome. It will save your children, and it will restore your marriage. Faith can deliver people and set them free.

Your faith in the Lord can protect hope. If you believe and pray for every or any situation, then faith will bring the expected result. The outcome of prayer is not what you prayed for, but the faith is. Have faith in God, believe, and He will do it. Always shield your faith with the blood of Jesus and the Holy Spirit. God anointed King David when he was just a kid. Satan monitored him to destroy the plan of God. Have you received many promises from God? Are you waiting for it? Are you praying for different things to happen in your life? The Devil is targeting your faith. Shield your faith. Read the scripture of testimony. If my faith is targeted, worried, fear, and doubt building up against me, then I read Hebrew 11 to destroy the fiery dart of the enemy. Your faith varies from day to day and from situation to situation. The teacher's son was suffering from a serious condition. I said Jesus can heal the kidney. I thought the man believed in healing since he was a teacher in the religious church. Instead, he answered, oh it is the kidney, so we need the doctor. I could not believe the Sunday school teachers' unbelief. I thought all things are possible; nothing is impossible for God. I know the Lord created our body, so who can be more knowledgeable than God? He alone can do the best job. I understood that not the position you hold, but your relationship with the Lord. More than anything, you need a relationship. Your knowledge of Him is most important. I spend more time reading the Bible. I do not hear many messages, but the Word which is God. When the Word = God, robbed in flesh, was a different story. The creator is the Word. God framed heaven and earth by speaking the Word. The Word you speak shows where you stand with God. When you speak the Word with faith, then you are creating what you said.

Genesis 1:1 In the beginning God created the heaven and the earth.3 and God said, Let there be light: and there was light.

SEPTEMBER 15

Hebrews 11:3 Through faith we understand that the worlds were framed by the word of God, so that things which are seen were not made of things which do appear. Do you understand that your vocabulary must be what you desire to see? Go wild in your imagination and expect an incredible result. Speak Your imagination, it will create the supernatural. Words are the most important factor since life and death are on your tongue.

Proverb 18:21 Death and life are in the power of the tongue: and they that love it shall eat the fruit thereof.

People do not know that unseen hope takes physically if you speak and pronounce it with your tongue. The Lady called me and said that they found a lump, and it was breast cancer. I said, no it is not. She went to the doctor and found out it was not and was excited. She said I remembered you told me it is not cancer. See, I said and believed. I believe it since I read the Bible and my faith is in the Word of God. Teach your children to speak the truth and be positive. The word brings forth life or death. Many children die because their parents whisper evil in their ears. They spread poison through their mouth; it is no surprise why their children are wicked. Who is the wicked trainer? Parents, not neighbors. We always speak blessings over our enemy, since it has the power to change them.

Jesus said.

Mark 5:34 And he said unto her, Daughter, thy faith hath made thee whole; go in peace, and be whole of thy plague. The man asked Jesus to send the word.

Luke 7:9 When Jesus heard these things, he marvelled at him, and turned him about, and said unto the people that followed him, I say unto you, I have not found so great faith, no, not in Israel.

It is the power of God that runs through the faith by declaring it. Lord is good! He is happy when someone trusts Him! Know and believe Him for all the impossible. When I go anywhere, I go by faith. My faith in God is high. I have no faith in anyone, anybody, or anything. I have faith in God for everything. The Lord can and will if you believe and proclaim. God has given over five thousand promises. Think about what can happen if you believe. No doubt we all have to act and believe. Nothing comes without action.

The action is the push to your faith.

James 2:17 Even so faith, if it hath not works, is dead, being alone. 20 But wilt thou know, O vain man, that faith without works is dead?

The obstacles of mountains, oceans, valleys, and hindrances can go away if you have faith in God for it. You speak, and He will make it happen. It is a Word game. I must level the game of Word with the word of God. Our God has done amazing things. The desert has become a pool of water by believing in it. He has burned the cities with brimstone and fire. He said and pronounced it. Let your action be pleasing to the Lord. Each of your actions attached to faith has great blessings. May the Lord teach us with His Spirit since the Holy Spirit teaches us. The devil has many arrows, but as you stand with determination, immovable, and steadfastness, no devil in hell can move you. None can steal your promises or destroy you, in Jesus's name. Amen!

LET US PRAY

Heavenly Father, the faith like a mustard seed, has the power to move a mountain. We all have faith to certain degrees, so help us, Lord. We know the power is in the tongue, so help us speak the positive word for petitions. Lord, we need positive faith, since we lack faith. We believe in many things, but for the Lord, we fail. Through your stripe, we are healed. Still, we go to the doctor. Lord, help us not to worry about all the situations we face. The Word and prayer are unimportant to us. So help us, Lord, we must be the wealthiest in the faith. We strive for the things which have no eternal value. Help us put faith in the work. Faith and the workforce have power. Lord, Daniel, Joseph, Esther, and many others saw the situation was beyond, but their faith went with their work and drew the attention of the World. We want the world to pay attention when we speak. The devil backs off by seeing our faith. None of its arrows can work. Bless us with faith by covering us with your blood in Jesus's name. Amen! God bless you!

SEPTEMBER 16

GET FREEDOM BY FORGIVING!

Many people are sick and the reason behind it is that there is no forgiveness in their system. I have met some people; I know very well, who have a mighty forgiving nature. If anyone does wrong to them, right away, give it to God. I am so glad for their great example. Since they live for God and carry no garbage, they walk clean. Some people like to carry what happened to them years ago. They carry garbage in their heart. It is a destructive memory whenever they think of it. If you want to be free, then forgive. When you go to the altar, just leave it there and do not pick it up. Many cry at the altar and leave their burdens there. Ask God to take revenge and say it is yours; I give it to you. Some people get up from an altar and pick up the burden instead of just leaving. They return home thinking the same way. They stay sick, vomit, and become sicker. Do not contaminate others by talking about your situation, also contaminate yourself. Leave it to God. To take revenge is God, so this is God's job and not yours. If you give it to God, you will experience His peace and blessings. Obey the commandments of God. I remember when I was going through a hard time at work. There was a supervisor who was harassing me. She was using her power to hurt me. I was upset and lost my sleep over it. I was thinking about how to get revenge. Thank God, one time in Bible study I heard this Scripture.

Mark 11:25 And when ye stand praying, forgive, if ye have ought against any: that your Father also which is in heaven may forgive you your trespasses.

It was a little hard to forgive, but since I couldn't afford to lose my sleep over this woman; I went into my room and forgave her. I was free from pain, hurt, and anger. From that day on, my sleep came back to me. Believe me, you will be free from all this hurt, anger, and pain if you forgive. May the Lord give you the strength to forgive those who did wrong to you. A person may not understand their wrongdoing. But you remember what happened years and years ago by harboring unforgiveness. Your body is now full of sickness, and disease. You poison your children and their children over silly matters. May the Lord give us an understanding that we all do many wrongs. Still, people forgive and go on. No one is perfect, and if you want someone's forgiveness, then you must forgive others. Your freedom is in one word, Lord, I forgive so and so who did wrong to me. Fear God, unforgiveness is a dangerous route. Many times you may wonder why I am so sick, unhappy, act, and react badly. It is because of evil in your heart, and unforgiveness in your heart. A heart is wicked, and deceitful, out of it comes our life, action, and reactions. You react to what you keep in your heart. At a particular workplace, my coworker did something wrong to me. One morning he came to me, folded his hands together, and said, please sister, forgive me. It shocked me. He was not even a Christian. The person realizes, recognizes, and has a clean conscience. How wonderful to hear the word, forgive me; I was wrong. God forgives them as well. Big people can forgive. At the same place, another guy was evil and nasty. He was doing wrong to me continuously. He also lied to me. Later, I heard he died young. He confessed to a coworker that what he did to me was wrong. I had already moved to the US at that time but friends gave me the news of his demise. I was sorry to hear, but he received the recompense. I serve the mighty God, and the best for me is to let it handle in God's court. Friends, do not walk with closed eyes. You will not have peace. Be humble and say, Lord, forgive me. The Lord forgave all who did wrong to Him. It gave them a chance to repent and receive salvation.

Luke 6:27 But I say unto you which hear, Love your enemies, do good to them which hate you, If you forgive them, you will continue with the plan of God. God knows how to save you from the enemies. Your enemies can fall into your hand but do not take revenge.

1 Samuel 24:4 And the men of David said unto him, Behold the day of which the Lord said unto thee, Behold, I will deliver thine, enemy, into thine hand, that thou mayest do to him as it shall seem good unto thee. Then David arose and cut off the skirt of Saul's robe privily. 6 And he said unto his men, The Lord forbid that I should do this thing unto my master, the Lord's anointed, to stretch forth my hand against him, seeing he is the anointed of the Lord.

Live within your limit. One day, the Lord wiped out Saul and his children. David kept his hand clean. The mighty man of war killed the bear and lions. This King Saul was a piece of cake for him, but he never did wrong.

1st Samuel 31:3 And the battle went sore against Saul, and the archers hit him; and he was sore wounded of the archers. 6 So Saul died, and his three sons, and his armourbearer, and all his men, that same day together.David became King.

2nd Samuel 2:4 And the men of Judah came, and there they anointed David king over the house of Judah. See, never take revenge;

God has an arrow to wipe out your enemy. By the same token, He can protect you from the arrows if you leave matters in God's hands. But if you do not forgive and do not let God be God, then He will let the enemy shoot you out of the way of His plan. God gives us many chances to change. Do not say, I am what I am because of what someone did to me. It is your choice to dwell in the past or forgive and keep going free. Unforgiveness is like drinking poison wishing your enemy to die. Forgive, get well, get free, get forgiveness for your sins. I saw God take revenge as I left the matter in His hands. I wished no harm, knowing it was God's job. Have you seen someone who is always sick? Talk to them for a few minutes and find out how bitter they are. One lady was working with me; I noticed she always had a nervous breakdown. After I had retired, she came to visit me. She started talking about her childhood. Her stepmom and father made her eat all of her plates, so she was still angry about it. She was already over 50. Then she said, my sister did this and my brother did that. So all the garbage made her sick. Sometimes she has to stay in the mental hospital because of past incidents. She always called me for prayer. Once she called me on Sunday, knowing I would go to church on Sunday. For not answering the phone, she left the message, "Never try to call me since you did not answer my phone." I tried to call her, but she never picked up my phone and later she changed her phone number. See how unforgiving? Now I am not saying to keep evil people closer who do wrong to you. Love them at a distance but do not harbor any unforgiveness, Amen! God bless you!

LET US PRAY

Lord, we thank you for giving us the privilege of forgiving those whose stress passes against us. It is great to receive forgiveness for our sins with great health and healing. Our Lord has given us an example by forgiving our sins. It is freedom for our souls. Forgiveness sets us free from someone's power over us. Lord, make us understand that we also are going to need forgiveness from someone. It is a benefit for Christians. Forgiveness has a positive influence on us. Our progress depends on our forgiveness. We only see the Lord work against our enemy if we forgive. The Lord is the righteous judge and knows how to take care of our enemy. Many are dead, dying, sick, or in prison, for not doing God's way. Please learn to forgive to be healed and also you will receive forgiveness in Jesus's name. Amen! God bless you!

SEPTEMBER 17

WHAT IS RELIGION?

This is what God showed me about religious people. Religion is like a headless, legless body. Religious communities have no choice in deciding. They follow the ruler of their religion. Religion makes people headless and legless. Please determine to find God. Let the Holy Spirit lead, guide, and teach you. If the Holy Spirit leads you, then you will have your head and leg, and you can move on. You can go wherever you want to go. Not only that, your mind will work. Besides, eyes and ears wouldn't shut down. Nobody will tell you what and how to see, hear, and think. Please allow the Holy Spirit to do the job. Allow the Holy Spirit to develop, advantage, and empower you. Remember, you allow religious leaders to cut off your head and leg. The same thing happened when the Israelites asked for the king. They didn't want Jehovah God as their captain. Keeping God's ways would have the head, so don't choose other than the Holy Spirit. Your ways are lower than God's Way.Moses started the work of having a relationship with the Lord. But the priest and high priest at the time Lord Jesus was walking on earth did not know God. The head knowledge of the Torah is what they had, but no relationship. They had only laws, commandments, and precepts but did not know how to live a holy life.

When you join any denomination or religion, then they will cut off your head and legs. Since they want to rule over you. They go by pulling and choosing scriptures to keep you away from God and keep you under them. Why are you choosing these denomination rulers, and religious leaders over you, since God has given you the Holy Spirit? False teachers, prophets, and pastors remove the truth by twisting the scriptures. Take a little safeguard and give God a chance. Let God take care of His business. Let the author of the Bible be the teacher. Do not sacrifice your head and leg and give yourself for bondage. May the Lord give you love for yourself and God. No need for extra help to misguide or mislead you. We have many lovers of powers, positions, and greed to manipulate if you allow them to do so.The priest and High Priest did the same in the end. People have to obey and serve on priest commands. They took control of their life. They brought customs and made the word of God non-effectual.

Mark 7:6 He answered and said unto them, Well hath Esaias prophesied of you hypocrites, as it is written, This people honoureth me with their lips, but their heart is far from me.7 Howbeit in vain do they worship me, teaching for doctrines the commandments of men. 8 For laying aside the commandment of God, ye hold the tradition of men, as the washing of pots and cups: and many other such like things ye do. 9 And he said unto them, Full well ye reject the commandment of God, that ye may keep your own tradition.13 Making the word of God of none effect through your tradition, which ye have delivered: and many such like things do ye.

SEPTEMBER 17

The religious leader cuts your relationship with the creator off. Religious people allow leaders to cut their heads and legs off. So they cannot go any further but backward. Religion brings darkness.Leaders do not know God and do not know the intention or plan of God. God's agenda was wiped out, and they placed their agenda and customs. So no matter what the Bible says, it will not penetrate them. The Word of God becomes vain. The truth is out, without truth, no one is set free. Only truth has power and not religion, custom, or false teaching. False teaching will keep you bound and you will only hear the priest and religious authority.Now you are headless and legless. You cannot think since you have no head to think, cannot see since you have no eyes and ears. So when the Lord Jesus came, they knew only what their religion had said and taught. Religious leaders only want you to see and hear what they want you to. Blind and deaf and brainless can't see, hear, or think.One time I gave a lady to use my Bible study book. She said I liked this Bible study, but I will tear off the scripture on One God. Can you believe this? I said, but God said in the very first commandment, I am one. Isaiah said there is none beside and none after me. So you simply need help from God to know Him, and He will if you love Him. Now she was approved by the religious leader of that city.The Bible says the Lord gave us authority, but acknowledges the Lord as He is doing all. King Saul got a position from God, Judas got the position from God. Do not hang God, do not betray God, do not sell God. God will kick you out if you do.

The Word of God is above and unchangeable; it stands forever. This lady said, no, I will not. So remember, God called many and some of them tried to take over. You are not smarter than God. If God is talking to you, then learn to keep your relationship smooth by keeping His commandments and not being too prideful. If you go over God, they will kick you out because of arrogance.We have all kinds of religions. Their roots are deep, and they are misguided by false teachers and prophets. God has called you, but joining religion and getting a position makes you conceited. Some get a big head, not knowing that the religious authority has cut their head off. You have no head.People become nearsighted and forget that God has promised us a land beyond the river. It is the road and the journey through the mountain, ocean, river, and desert. May the Lord deliver you from the religious demon or religious drug. It is oppression and possession.There are 4,200 religions In the world. These people walk confused and lost without heads and legs. They may go nowhere or wouldn't accept the truth since they all have no head or legs. May the Lord give your body back. How can you see without it? How can you go to the real God?

Isaiah 42:16 And I will bring the blind by a way that they knew not; I will lead them in paths that they have not known: I will make darkness light before them, and crooked things straight. These things will I do unto them, and not forsake them. 17 They shall be turned back, they shall be greatly ashamed, that trust in graven images, that say to the molten images, Ye are our gods. 18 Hear, ye deaf; and look, ye blind, that ye may see. 19 Who is blind, but my servant? or deaf, as my messenger that I sent? Who is blind as he that is perfect, and blind as the LORD'S servant?

May the Lord help you before it is too late. We are now entering the misguiding era of confusion. Truth is for the Babe, the humble and righteous. Lord, give us the love for the truth more than their religions. God Opens the door and promotes them next to the kings, making them a queen. God gives them wisdom, and there is always a light that shines for them. May the Lord Bless you in Jesus's name. Amen!

LET US PRAY

It is God's will and desire for us to have a relationship with Him. The Creator has a beautiful plan for us, but the devil has a plan to steal, kill, and destroy. Our God is ready to answer if you ask. The Lord desires His creation to come to Him and not via misguided and misleading religious authority. There are many false spirits out there. Lord, help us discern them. Help us not to believe all the spirits. Some will stop us from baptizing in the name of Jesus Christ and are called the Antichrist. They will not let you receive the spirit of God since they are the antichrist. But it is an open channel with God, an open invitation if we remove the stopper, blocker, and hindered harm. May Lord Jesus help us in Jesus's name. Amen! God bless you!

SEPTEMBER 18

WHERE DO YOU HAVE THE BATTLE?

All battles start in the spirit realm and can only win in the spirit realm. Any battle or problem can be solved if you know how to come against the spiritual darkness. The origin of battles is in the Spirit world. Cause of the battles are Satan and not humans. All wars are planted, plotted, and designed in the spiritual realm. Later manifest in the physical world. When you see the movement in the physical realm, do not be surprised. Do not look around. They planned it in the spiritual realm before it takes the physical form. Today we're going to learn step by step how to come up against a battle and win.

Let's get ready. The devil is an expert at ruining God's creation. He played the destruction through the flood. Each dispensation has a plan of punishment for those who disobeyed God. Do not be deceived by religious authorities whom you believe and trust as Godgiven authority. May I say, have a relation with God! Follow Jesus to win your battles. When people go to another nation as a slave, or for the job and if the Word of God is not in them, then they are done. What you need is the truth that is the Word of God and you can enjoy your freedom.

Matthew 9:14 Then came to him the disciples of John, saying, Why do we and the Pharisees fast oft, but thy disciples fast not? 15 And Jesus said unto them, Can the children of the bridechamber mourn, as long as the bridegroom is with them? but the days will come, when the bridegroom shall be taken from them, and then shall they fast.

What can happen if you don't fast? There was a case where they could not cast out the demon and the Lord showed the reason.

Matthew 17:19 Then came the disciples to Jesus apart, and said, Why could not we cast him out? 20 And Jesus said unto them, Because of your unbelief: for verily I say unto you, If ye have faith as a grain of mustard seed, ye shall say unto this mountain, Remove hence to yonder place; and it shall remove; and nothing shall be impossible unto you. 21 Howbeit this kind goeth not out but by prayer and fasting.

The Lord had given them authority over demons. Remember, it will only work if we align with the Word of God. Fasting with prayer helps.

Luke 10:17 And the seventy returned again with joy, saying, Lord, even the devils are subject unto us through thy name.

As they cast out demons having authority still God taught the lesson of the importance of fasting and prayer to cast out demons. The Lord said many things through one incident. First, you need faith and second; you must fast. Do not do Daniel's diet. Remember, you are not playing with an ordinary, but a mastermind, Satan. The devil is very strong. That is why we say stronghold. Legions had the power to destroy man. Satan comes to steal, kill, and destroy. So we are not dealing with ants or mosquitoes. Lord explicitly explains.

Mark 3:27 No man can enter into a strong man's house, and spoil his goods, except he will first bind the strong man; and then he will spoil his house.

Authority given to us with conditions prepares itself accordingly. God has always said to receive B to fulfill A. Knowledge is a must, otherwise the devil will fool you. After you bind the tiger, lions, and bears, you may be free to move around. As you bind the territorial demons, watchers, gatekeepers of the places, or from the body, then you can do well. The devil said, Do not torment me. Why? Jesus knows how to torment the devil.

Legions demon said, Mark 5:7 And cried with a loud voice, and said, What have I to do with thee, Jesus, thou Son of the most high God? I adjure thee by God, that thou torment me not.

In the name of Jesus, you can bind the devil and evil spirits, break their power, blind and then cast them out. Condition is that you must fast and pray. Fasting makes you physically weak, but spiritually strong. I stand toward east, west, north and south and bind all demons and tell them to get out. We do not see but have believed since the devil and his army rule in the air.

Ephesians 2:2 Wherein in time past ye walked according to the course of this world, according to the prince of the power of the air, the spirit that now worketh in the children of disobedience:

Humans have limits on hearing and seeing into the spiritual realm. When you have to see the spiritual realm, ask for spiritual eyesight.

2 Kings 6:16 And he answered, Fear not: for they that be with us are more than they that be with them. 17 And Elisha prayed, and said, Lord, I pray thee, open his eyes, that he may see. And the Lord opened the eyes of the young man; and he saw: and, behold, the mountain was full of horses and chariots of fire round about Elisha.

You should ask God to allow you to see the spirit world. The Spirit World decides and operates through humans. The Holy Spirit is teaching the truth, but the evil spirit misguides and twists the truths. What is the truth? God's Word is the truth. False teachers and prophets will say, just have a simple faith. Will this work when there is a battle against Satan and its army? Would you believe the one who is working for Satan? You need all the truth all the way. Satan's plan or trap looks amazing in the beginning, but in the end, you will see the destruction. I deal with the demonic world and it seems like it is never as difficult as it is now. You show people the truth, but the false teaching of the denominational churches will brainwash them. False teaching is so deep that it is difficult for them to see the truth. What happened? Organization, denominations and non-denominations do not have all truth. Thieves have overthrown the prayer and made it fit for their business. Just like the earlier priest and high priest crucified the Lord.

John 14:30 Hereafter I will not talk much with you: for the prince of this world cometh, and hath nothing in me.

See, God gave the power to the power of darkness, which is Satan.

Luke 22:53 When I was daily with you in the temple, ye stretched forth no hands against me: but this is your hour, and the power of darkness.

Friends, Jesus was not weak, but to fulfill the plan and purpose, He allowed the devil to take over. Many said I didn't want to speak about the devil, demon, and fallen angels. Why? I always talk about the operation of the spiritual darkness in the world. I want to learn how to bring the devil and His army down. Knowledge of truth gives us freedom. Learn the right way all the way and not halfway. You will win all battles. We fight in victory. We won the battle since Jesus won 2000 years ago. Claim it and run with it.

LET US PRAY

Heavenly Father, we thank you for winning the battle for us. Thank you for teaching me how to win the battle with your example. We know no one is above the battle. Many give in or give up when they are in battle, not knowing how to fight. God said loud and clear in His teaching what to do. The prince of Persia, Prince of Ephesus, Prince of India, or the US has many deceptive plans to trap. The devil wants us to fall and defeat us. It is the same tactic the devil used in the garden of Eden. It is the little leaven, but it leaveneth the whole lump. The same results, we die the day we break the commandment, not physically but eternally. Lord, we do not have any excuse since you recorded in the word of God. Sin is the leaven, and it is the food of Satan. Lord, help us pay attention. Be sincere to do right in Jesus's name. Amen! God bless you!

SEPTEMBER 19

DIFFERENT MEASURE OF FAITH!

Our God pleases with your faith. That means, if you believe God can do it, it makes Him Happy.

Let us see the level of faith according to God's language and standards.

Great Faith, *Luke 7:9 When Jesus heard these things, he marvelled at him, and turned him about, and said unto the people that followed him, I say unto you, I have not found so great faith, no, not in Israel.*

This shows that the World can see your faith. God even said that it is brilliant and surprising.

Little Faith; *Matthew 8:26 And he saith unto them, Why are ye fearful, O ye of little faith? Then he arose, and rebuked the winds and the sea; and there was a great calm.*

God gives the title to your faith. Faith is the substance of the things you hope for. So if you hope for something, then make sure you apply enough faith to receive it.

Matthew 16:8 Which when Jesus perceived, he said unto them, O ye of little faith,

Luke 8:25a And he said unto them, Where is your faith?

Enough Faith to receive more than you desire.

Luke 8:48 And he said unto her, Daughter, be of good comfort: thy faith hath made thee whole; go in peace.

The lady was sick and spent all her money. Ultimately, faith made her whole meaning complete. She spoke the word with faith. If you have no faith, having the Lord walking next to you will not work. A relationship can be established through your faith in God.

Mark 4:40 And he said unto them, Why are ye so fearful? how is it that ye have no faith?

Receive according to your faith! The Lord is teaching us that your miracle, healing, and provision will depend on the measure of your faith.

Matthew 9:29 Then touched he their eyes, saying, According to your faith be it unto you.

Saving Faith Luke 7:50 And he said to the woman, Thy faith hath saved thee; go in peace.

Full of Faith! Before passing, you must have faith!

Acts 6:8 And Stephen, full of faith and power, did great wonders and miracles among the people.

Faith is the most requisite factor on your part for God to move on to a situation. God does not answer your prayer, but your faith. So keep the faith. How to keep faith if you do not know the person? I have faith in no one but God. As you know, the Lord has taken away my job for almost twenty-plus years. God promised me I would take care of you, just work for me. Ever since I go out and work and never worry about the money or bills. All runs smoothly by faith. I believe all works fine since dollars do not design my life, but by faith in the Lord. I do not have the church (which is building) to pastor to have a stream of money flow. And I have no one who backs me up with the money. Not only that, I support many laborers working in the field. I go out to places to pray. I have done a lot of translation work by hiring translators and printing material. Besides, all the material I gave away was free. I have a wonderful investment in the kingdom of God. The soil blessed by God is abundant, yielding thirty, sixty, and one hundredfold.

Pray for the Country India. When I tried to invest money by publishing books, printing them, and giving them away for free, I found out the printer stole my money. The land has briers. Nothing grows but ruins. The thief who stole my money said, she, that means I am wrong. Can you believe this? These religions wouldn't stop the work of the mighty God. I complained to the father of the printer and he was even worse. Like father, like son. Later Lord showed me I was fighting the spirit of dogs and tigers. They both have the personality of tearing you down. The work of God is and will be torn down by the religious authorities as it did when Jesus was walking on earth.

Have faith in God. Some land produces Judas, tares, brier, and hypocrites. Most of whom I met there had destructive demons. It will work behind your back to harm. The Lord has mercy on their soul. Faith is such a wonderful virtue. It helped me to continue my work. God can protect us. Remember, the evil Spirit uses these people. God also has faith in us to send us out. God is full of faith, but He acts according to our faith. He said I wouldn't give you more than you take. That shows the measure of faith required exactly for the measure of a trial. If God gives more trials than our faith, it will harm us. God knew Job's faith, so He tried him accordingly.

When you pray, please pray with great faith, since it is according to your faith, you will receive the answer. I receive many calls, and I have to pray for them. Many times I see an enormous problem, and they completely depend on my intercession. I am glad that I have great faith in God when I pray. Another day, someone called early in the morning to pray. She has been calling me, and she said, in the past, you prayed, I saw the notable result. Praying both times, I saw the Lord did mighty things. So my prayer of faith helped her to come out of trouble. That shows that if you pray for someone with faith, it will help. Jesus prayed all the time. Many parents prayed for their children. That shows anyone can intercede if you allow them to.

James 5:14 Is any sick among you? let him call for the elders of the church; and let them pray over him, anointing him with oil in the name of the Lord:15 And the prayer of faith shall save the sick, and the Lord shall raise him up; and if he has committed sins, they shall be forgiven him.

When someone has no money, then they borrow money from those who have. Faith is like borrowing my faith for their problem. My mom was a woman of faith. Her life witnessed great faith and was not rich, but very rich in faith. She prayed for anything and received all that she desired. She can stop or start the clock by her faith. All is well if you have faith. God's work requires faith and not money. If it is, then all rich people will be happy. Rich people attract greedy people. The faith of the poor attracts God. They have no money to go to the doctor or for their needs. They go to God with faith, and they receive what they desire.

Since the Bible says: *James 2:5a Hearken, my beloved brethren, Hath not God chosen the poor of this world rich in faith,*

Can our faith level increase? Yes,

Romans 10:17 So then faith cometh by hearing, and hearing by the word of God.

I hear the Bible all day long and my faith is sky high. It was the Lord who spoke to me in my fiery trial of the year 2000 that you will come out as gold. Omniscient God knows the level of faith we carry. Faith can be tested. We must learn the Bible for our dealing, action, and behavior. live rich on earth, having faith above and beyond. Amen! God bless you,

LET US PRAY

Only Jesus, as your word says, let it be according to your faith, so help us prepare our faith before we come to the Altar. Our matter can be determined by our faith. Thank you for giving us a measure of faith. Our Lord is magnificent. He has done many wonderful things as we approach the throne room by faith. Faith is all that is required and has to be on the Word of God. Jesus is manifesting the written Word of God. We ask for faith in every situation. May the Lord today shield our faith with His blood. Our faith can move the mountains of worry, fear, sickness, and trouble. It is the Lord who said I am not a respecter of people but definitely of the faith. Little faith will establish little, negative faith will do nothing, but great faith will open the prison door, highway in the ocean, fire, and lions will have no power over us. So we thank you for the word which helps us to have faith in you in Jesus's name. Amen, God bless you.

SEPTEMBER 20

DO NOT LET THE LORD DEPART FROM YOU!

It is dangerous to be without God. You will be in darkness without light since the Lord is the Light. The Lord is your creator and Father; you will be an orphan without Him. You will be without direction if the Lord departs from you. The Lord is Love, and the devil is hate. You will produce the fruit to whom you follow. You wouldn't like anyone if you did not have love. As you receive the Holy Spirit, you will have a character of your own father.

John 14:18 I will not leave you comfortless: I will come to you. 23 Jesus answered and said unto him, If a man love me, he will keep my words: and my Father will love him, and we will come unto him, and make our abode with him.

In the New Testament, Jesus is the Jehovah in the flesh. And the Holy Spirit comes to us. We are living in a time when the Holy Spirit comes within and empowers us. How beautiful! The Lord comes to live in you if you obey Him. If you repent and baptize in the name above all names, which is Jesus, then your sins are forgiven, and now you are clean. Sins are gone, then the Lord fills us with His Spirit. Our God is good, He would not let us leave comfortless.

John 14:16 And I will pray the Father, and he shall give you another Comforter, that he may abide with you forever. 26 But the Comforter, which is the Holy Ghost, whom the Father will send in my name, he shall teach you all things, and bring all things to your remembrance, whatsoever I have said unto you.

Now the Lord gives His Spirit if you obey the Lord!

Acts 5:32 And we are his witnesses of these things; and so is also the Holy Ghost, whom God hath given to them that obey him.

If you are not obeying the Lord as the Word of God says, the Lord will not give you His Spirit. Do not say you have the Holy Spirit, since you do not. The disciples obeyed Jesus all the way and received the Holy Spirit on the day of Pentecost. God gave the Holy Spirit to you to work for the Lord and not against. Stop working against the Lord. Ask for the Holy Spirit. When the Lord anointed King Saul by the prophet, the Spirit was on him but not in. During the Old Testament, God gave the Spirit to do supernatural work. In the New Testament time, your body is a church and not a building. Dispensation of grace, the Holy Spirit came on the day of Pentecost. It birthed the church or bride for Jesus. They received the Holy Spirit by speaking in tongues, and we do the same today. I spoke in the tongue when I received the Holy Spirit. Do not believe otherwise. I never have seen, or the Bible does not agree with this false doctrine of having spirit when you accept Jesus. King Saul had the Spirit but departed later.

1 Samuel 10:1 Then Samuel took a vial of oil, and poured it upon his head, and kissed him, and said, Is it not because the Lord hath anointed thee to be captain over his inheritance?

As Prophet Samuel anointed the King Soul, the Spirit did not come upon him, but Samuel said,

1 Samuel 10:6 And the Spirit of the Lord will come upon thee, and thou shalt prophesy with them, and shalt be turned into another man.10 And when they came thither to the hill, behold, a company of prophets met him; and the Spirit of God came upon him, and he prophesied among them.

King Saul's heart overflowed with contentment and peace as long as he followed God's commands. But as soon as He stopped listening to God, the Spirit of God departed from King Saul. You cannot afford this.

1 Samuel 16:14 But the Spirit of the LORD departed from Saul, and an evil spirit from the LORD troubled him.

King Saul went crazy. He killed the priest of God. He shedded much innocent blood in Israel. See, the work of the Spirit is so distinct. When the Lord's Spirit comes, then you can do great and mighty. But as the evil spirit comes, then you become destructive. The Holy Spirit created heaven and earth since God is Spirit. It gives power to you. Not by might nor by power, but by thy Spirit. The work of the Spirit is supernatural. Evil Spirit being legions in the man's body could not be bound by the chain. The spirit possesses an immense strength. Flesh becomes powerless to fight spirits.

A person without the Holy Spirit becomes fearful.

John 20:19a Then the same day at evening, being the first day of the week when the doors were shut where the disciples were assembled for fear of the Jews,

No one can do mighty work except the mighty God. And if He comes to you, then you can do it through Him.

Peter's boldness radiated as he welcomed the Holy Spirit into his life.

Acts 4:13 Now when they saw the boldness of Peter and John, and perceived that they were unlearned and ignorant men, they marvelled; and they took knowledge of them, that they had been with Jesus.

Acts 4:31 And when they had prayed, the place was shaken where they were assembled together; and they were all filled with the Holy Ghost, and they spake the word of God with boldness.

The Holy Spirit gave power to timid people. Their hearts trembled with fear at the thought of the Jew who crucified the Lord Jesus. Samuel anointed David; the Spirit of God was on him. David fought the lion and bear. You have no power except the Spirit of God comes on you. At the same token, when Spirit departs, then you will be helpless and fearful. Many do not speak in the tongue as evidence of receiving the Holy Spirit. They are confused and do not know how to help new converts. They are not bold since they have refused to receive the Holy Spirit as the Lord spoke. Many are wandering here and there to seek the truth. Pray that the Lord does not allow anyone to go to false prophets and teachers. Ask for discernment and perception.

Ephesians 4:30 And grieve not the holy Spirit of God, whereby ye are sealed unto the day of redemption

1 Thessalonians 5:19 Quench not the Spirit.

You who are speaking and teaching against the Spirit of God since you do not have, be careful of God! There will be a day you will cry. Let the living Lord help you,

Matthew 12:31: Wherefore I say unto you, All manner of sin and blasphemy shall be forgiven unto men: but the blasphemy against the Holy Ghost shall not be forgiven unto men. 32 And whosoever speaketh a word against the Son of man, it shall be forgiven him: but whosoever speaketh against the Holy Ghost, it shall not be forgiven him, either in this world, neither in the world to come.

There is a place where you never want to go called Lake of fire.

Mark 9:44 Where their worm dieth not, and the fire is not quenched.

Do not play with fire, unless you have given the reprobate spirit like King Saul.

2 Thessalonians 2:11 And for this cause God shall send them strong delusion, that they should believe a lie:

Delusion means false representation; illusion; error or mistake proceeding from false views. From the KJV dictionary. This end-time I have seen many roaming in sins. They do not perceive since God gives the lying spirit and they believe, just like the King's saul. Do not let the Lord depart from you in Jesus's name. Amen!

LET US PRAY

Heavenly Father, we pray that please give us your Spirit to live within us forever. We need your Spirit. If not, then we are not yours. You gave your Spirit to teach, lead, and guide us. We want true prophets and teachers. The Bible says many false teachers and prophets say that you have the Holy Spirit without receiving it by speaking in tongues. These are the evil spirits working as a tare in the field of God. Lord, we thank you for your Spirit. We desire it since it gives us the power to witness with signs and wonders. We can do greater work if we have your spirit. Give us your Spirit in Jesus's name. Amen! God bless you!

SEPTEMBER 21

PROMOTION AND DEMOTION!

All hiring, firing, giving positions, and removal happen in heaven. God promoted you in the kingdom or the secular world.

Never say it is because of me. Don't say or think, I qualify for this. Don't take the glory. Keep your vainglory out. It is all because of the Lord! Wicked gets the promotion it is but for a moment. They will go high just to thrust out. Who tries to take the glory? The one who does not know the Lord. They exalt themselves and have a prideful nature, like Satan. In God, we always will have a promotion. Paul was always in prison. God promoted him to the Lord.

2 Corinthians 12:7 And lest I should be exalted above measure through the abundance of the revelations, there was given to me a thorn in the flesh, the messenger of Satan to buffet me, lest I should be exalted above measure.

See how God gave promotion to Paul above all other Apostles even though he killed many Christians? I passed all the tests for the Federal job. Even at finals, a lady was hindering me from passing. The job requirement was to take a written test with 8 machine tests to qualify. The last one was getting harder since the lady behind me was making extra noises to interrupt me from passing. My examiner saw and told me why you did not complain. I did not understand why you were taking longer since you passed 7. The examiner separated me from the other lady, and I passed. With the same token, they fired two others. She intended to prevent me from getting a good-paying federal job. God protected me from a wicked lady by my good examiner. The blessings of God make you wealthy. Our God is amazing. No matter who tries to steal our blessings, He will get rid of our enemy.

Remember, it goes for secular, religious, or spiritual authorities. Religious leaders have no authority to control others lives. One day, God will remove them from their position. On Judgement Day for sure, but also on earth, there is a day of promotion and demotion. Our God is no respecter of people. I started reading the Bible when I was in my teens. I finished the Bible many times. My relation with the Lord is not through any churches, organization, or religion, but by the word of God and the Spirit of God. I went to different churches since my hunger was great. I always learn and receive many gifts of the Spirit and being used by Almighty God. Our God uses us if we seek and do as He asks us to.

Promotion and demotion are from the Lord!

Joel 2:27 And ye shall know that I am in the midst of Israel, and that I am the LORD your God, and none else: and my people shall never be ashamed.

Trusting the Lord, Abraham got the title of the father of faith. He did not give himself a title, but the Lord. We should never give ourselves a title, but let the Lord. A man was called out of his people and nations.

Genesis 24:35 And the Lord hath blessed my master greatly; and he is become great: and he hath given him flocks, and herds, and silver, and gold, and menservants, and maidservants, and camels, and asses.

Lord gives promotion, and He also demotes. How does God do and command? Your attitude, actions, reaction, and relation with the Lord bring promotion or demotion. Do not think you can harm God's people.

Samuel said to King Saul:*1 Samuel 13:14 But now thy kingdom shall not continue: the Lord hath sought him a man after his own heart, and the Lord hath commanded him to be captain over his people, because thou hast not kept that which the Lord commanded thee.*

So now you know God promotes and demotes according to your performance. Keep the commandments of God.

Acts 10:4a And he commanded them to be baptized in the name of the Lord.

Now, do you dare to teach otherwise? Be careful or God will demote you soon. Fear God. Philistines envied Isaac, seeing a promotion from God.

Genesis 26:12 Then Isaac sowed in that land, and received in the same year a hundredfold: and the LORD blessed him. 13 And the man waxed great, and went forward, and grew until he became very great: 14 For he had possession of flocks, and possession of herds, and great store of servants: and the Philistines envied him.

I always wished to be rich with His Spirit. My goal is to be like Jesus and desire to do greater than what He did. I seek heavenly things. The ministry and the will of the Lord are important to me. No one can hurt me if the Lord is with me. God owns all, so can give all.

John 14:12 Verily, verily, I say unto you, He that believeth on me, the works that I do shall he do also; and greater works than these shall he do;

I have known some best and anointed pastors. It caught my attention that those possessing immense gifts exhibit genuine humility. When I see them ministering to people, operating in the nine gifts of the Spirit is mind-boggling. I see the gifts have not made them high and mighty. God does not mind giving them all that they need to lift His name higher. It is the name of Jesus we need to make higher. Once you lift the denomination, organization, or church, you will never see the operation of Jesus.

Psalm 75:6 For promotion cometh neither from the east, nor from the west, nor from the south.7 But God is the judge: he putteth down one, and setteth up another.

1 Peter 5:6 Humble yourselves therefore under the mighty hand of God, that he may exalt you in due time:

God does all, promotion and demotion.

Psalm 78:70 He chose David also his servant, and took him from the sheepfolds:

Do not think your degree, wealth, knowledge, or talent gives you promotions. But the humble, who is ready to take the Lord's command as the highest authority and none else. You live in the wealthiest nation, but God is not with you. Then your life will not progress. All we are is walking mud. Do not think great of yourself, since God sees your heart. Daniel was promoted, but God demoted the false accusers.

Daniel 6:24 And the king commanded, and they brought those men which had accused Daniel, and they cast them into the den of lions, them, their children, and their wives; and the lions had the mastery of them, and brake all their bones in pieces or ever they came at the bottom of the den.

The Lord Almighty prepares promotion and demotion in heaven.

Micah 6:8 He hath shown thee, O man, what is good: and what doth the Lord require of thee but to do justly and to love mercy, and to walk humbly with thy God?

LET US PRAY

Heavenly Father, we thank you for showing us how to walk humbly and do justice. Our action shows our reaction to your command. We are liable for our promotion and demotion. Help us not be like careless Esau or King Solomon. We receive blessings and help us pay attention to hold it tight. We put all our effort purposefully so we can continue in the blessings. Lord, grant us the wisdom to navigate through life's challenges. God, it pleases us your change not. Our God, who is in heaven, watches our actions and reactions. He watches us as we do the right to give Him glory. Our God can give and take it away. So, Lord, we ask for a sincere, clean heart to do as you require of us in Jesus 'name. Amen! God bless you!

SEPTEMBER 22

THE HIGHEST NAME OF JEHOVAH IS JESUS!

Many names addressed to the same God from the beginning. Jehovah God has many names as He played different roles. One God has only one name, which is YHVH, in English, Jehovah. Following are the descriptions and titles for one true God. Always remember that there is only one God. God reveals His nature by acting in various characters. El Shaddai (Lord God Almighty). El Elyon (The Most High God). Adonai (Lord, Master). Yahweh (Lord, Jehovah). El Bethel: The God of the house of God. Jehovah Nissi (The Lord My Banner). Jehovah-Raah (The Lord My Shepherd). Jehovah Rapha (The Lord That Heals). Jehovah Shammah (The Lord Is There) Jehovah Tsidkenu (The Lord Our Righteousness). Jehovah Mekoddishkem (The Lord Who Sanctifies you). El Olam (The Everlasting God). Elohim (God). Qanna (Jealous). El Hakabodh: The God of Glory. Jehovah Jireh (The Lord Will Provide). El Rai: God, seest me. Jehovah Shalom (The Lord Is Peace). Jehovah Sabaoth (the Lord of Hosts). We understand God by His actions and label His name for different needs. Many do not know how and what God can do. God acts for the situation you are trusting for, which makes you overwhelmed.

On earth, we have our name. But when we are babies; we are called a baby. When we grow up, we become fathers, mothers, teachers, doctors, managers, and presidents as we take different offices. Our offices represent our professions, but that is not our name. Same way, the Lord is one. His name is Jehovah, but as He acted in different roles for His creation, He took the relevant title justly. The adjective affixed with His name can understand one of many characters and the nature of one God. Father is not the name of the man, but we can see the relationship he has with the child. God does the same, we being His children. He acted on the situation to provide, deliver, or save. So God took the name which fits for that act. In the end, God took the name 'Jesus'. Jehovah came as Jesus in the New Testament. This name is above all the previous name He was known for. Why is it above all names? All Old Testament names of Jehovah were swallowed up in the name of Jesus. It is a name above all names.

Angels said. *Luke 2:21 And when eight days were accomplished for the circumcising of the child, his name was called Jesus, which was so named of the angel before he was conceived in the womb.*

All the above names dissolve in one name, Jesus. Jesus' name replaces all the above names. No need for a distinctive name when you are talking about His different offices. Jesus is not just a magic name; all authority is in this name. This highest name is called above all names of His Old Testament. Since the name of Jesus can do everything and anything. Jesus is in Hebrew Yeshua or Yehoshua, which means He will save. Yeshua means salvation in Hebrew. That is God Jehovah saves, heals, delivers, etc. Now why in the end, Lord, put on this name? Since this name is the saving name. Saves from what? From what you need to be saved. Delivers from all you need to be delivered from. In Jesus's name, you see the miracle, healing, freedom, and forgiveness of sins.

Act 10:43 To him give all the prophets witness, that through his name whosoever believeth in him shall receive remission of sins How do you receive the forgiveness or remission of your sins?

The Bible says you need blood for the forgiveness of your sins.

Hebrews 9:22 an and without shedding of blood is no remission.

So who shed the blood? Jesus did. Blood has life and if there is a name above all name, saving name, delivering name, but where is the blood?

1 John 5:6a This is he that came by water and blood, even Jesus Christ; not by water only, but by water and blood.

The solution to sin is blood! If you use the name Jesus Christ in Baptism produces the blood. So do not go in the water taking any other name or title Father, Son, and Holy Ghost, but use the name of Jesus Christ. God hid blood under the name of Jesus.

1 John 5:8 And there are three that bear witness in earth, the Spirit, and the water, and the blood: and these three agree in one.

This name Jesus takes away all sins and sicknesses attached to our sins. Try this name. It is a miraculous experience in the water.

Colossians 3:17a And whatsoever ye do in word or deed, do all in the name of the Lord Jesus

Philippians 2:8 And being found in fashion as a man, he humbled himself and became obedient unto death, even the death of the cross. 9 Wherefore God also hath highly exalted him, and given him a name which is above every name: 10 That at the name of Jesus every knee should bow, of things in heaven, and things in earth, and things under the earth; 11 And that every tongue should confess that Jesus Christ is Lord, to the glory of God the Father.

All diseases, sicknesses, oppression, demons, and sins have to bow before the name of Jesus.

Act 4:12 Neither is there salvation in any other: for there is none other name under heaven given among men, whereby we must be saved.

Mark 16:17a And these signs shall follow them that believe; IN MY NAME shall they cast out devils;

Act 19:5 When they heard this, they were baptized IN THE NAME OF THE LORD JESUS. Acts 10:48a And he commanded them to be baptized IN THE NAME OF THE LORD. This Jesus is coming as King of Kings and Lord of Lords. Being His bride, you must take His name into baptism.

Galatians 3:27 For as many of you as have been baptized into Christ have put on Christ.

When you go under the Water, baptize in the name of Jesus you are putting on Christ. How wonderful is the name of Jesus? Satan knows the meaning of the Name Jesus. God revealed the name Jesus as Jehovah God in flesh to save His creation. I love the name of Jesus, and I know it is above all other names.

LET US PRAY:

Our heavenly father; we are grateful for giving the name of Jesus. Jesus is the saving name of Jehovah In the New Testament. We thank you for the blood you shed for our sins. It is the blood of Jehovah God, according to Acts 20:28. Thank you, Lord, for coming to take revenge against the enemy. Restoring a relationship by giving the blood that has life. Our blood is sinful as sin is connected. Your blood is the only solution we had, and you did it. Thank the Lord for the highest name and name above all names. The name of Jesus gives us authority. We love this name, for we have put on your name by baptizing in Jesus' name. God, we confess the name of Jesus; we bow at your name. Thank you for the excellent name of Jesus. Amen! God bless you!

SEPTEMBER 23

LORD, OPEN SPIRITUAL EYES!

Why doesn't one see the Lord? You do not see the Lord unless the Lord opens your eyes. I keep the prophets in my life since their eyes are open to the things of God. In the old times, prophets were called seers. The prophet sees for me; I am seeing the spirit world with a telescope or bird's-eye view of a prophet. Some years ago; the pastor called me out. He said; I see the Angel opening the big door and no one can shut it. I need to see what the Lord has stored for me. Our eyes have limited power to see. There is a spirit activity going around us in the spirit world. The Pastor called me and said I saw many people behind the door; they were not black or white. He asked me, are you going to the Philippines? I did not see this vision, but he saw it since he was a prophet of God. Well, then he received the understanding and right away said that you will go to India. Which I did!

Yesterday someone called me while we were praying at my house. The devil attacked the person five times. As you know, the devil's arrow is to kill, steal, and destroy. He said God protected me each time. We all prayed for him and one person said; I saw a big angel around him. The person was calling from India, and as we told them what one of the prayer warriors saw, he started jumping and dancing. Being a man of God, the devil is trying to remove him from the land of the living. This Spiritual world needs spiritual eyes. Fasting kills the hindrance of flesh and opens spiritual eyes. No one sees Holy angels, Jesus, fallen angels, demons, or Satan around them by natural eyes. That is why God has given us the prophet, who has spiritual eyes to see. The Lord takes care of us through their eyes.

Isaiah 6:5 Then said I, Woe is me! for I am undone; because I am a man of unclean lips, and I dwell in the midst of a people of unclean lips: for mine eyes have seen the King, the Lord of hosts.

So Isaiah saw the seraphim in heaven. The disciples trembled in fear at the thought of facing the elders and priests. Two disciples were walking and met a stranger on the way. They were discussing the crucifixion of Jesus with this stranger. But when the Lord opened their eyes, they saw it was the risen Lord.

Luke 24:31 And their eyes were opened, and they knew him, and he vanished out of their sight.

Many have entertained the Angels since angels look like us.

Hebrews 13:2 Be not forgetful to entertain strangers: for thereby some have entertained angels unawares.

God says, in Ephesians 4:27 Neither give place to the devil.

Spirit world will enter your life, home, or country if you bring things not approved by God. How can your eyes be opened? Just obey the commandment of God, even if you do not understand. The Word of God is Spirit; you do exactly as it says, that will help you enter the Spiritual world. Isn't it so wonderful that if this world obeys the written Word as it is, then we wouldn't have many religions? These religions, denominations, churches, and blind leaders cause us to stumble. Do not follow this blind leader, follow Jesus by obeying His Word.

Luke 9:23 And he said to them all, If any man will come after me, let him deny himself, and take up his cross daily, and follow me.

If you do, then the Lord will do the rest as He did for Paul.

Book of Acts 26:18 To open their eyes, and to turn them from darkness to light, and from the power of Satan unto God, that they may receive forgiveness of sins, and inheritance among them which are sanctified by faith that is in me.

We know the world will go after everything until they find the truth. Many are turning to the Living God since their spiritual eyes are being opened by the true Lord. We have five physical senses and five spiritual senses also to see, hear, smell, taste, and touch the spiritual world. People go into a trance that is a half-conscious state. They see the spirit world. This state of mind comes from the Lord alone.

This happened to Peter when he was fasting in a city called Joppa

Acts 11:5 I was in the city of Joppa praying: and in a trance I saw a vision, A certain vessel descend, as it had been a great sheet, let down from heaven by four corners; and it came even to me:

This state of mind helps us to see spiritual matter. Many times, while praying, I see the spiritual world. It is important since I pray for people on the phone who are far away. Spiritual eyes have no restrictions and no need for a passport or visa. The Lord helps us to see the matter with His eyes. Desire spiritual senses so you can minister to others with perfect knowledge.

The Bible says, *2 Chronicles 20:20b Believe in the Lord your God, so shall ye be established; believe his prophets, so shall ye prosper.*

Keep the prophets; he will see and tell you the matter which concerns you. May the Lord give us true prophets to solve the problems. Many are too smart not to believe the prophets. Do not go to the false. One evening, I came out of the church and it was very dark. The Lord told me to wait. I stopped the car in the parking lot and looked around; I saw people passing by before me in the dark. See, God saw and stopped me from going further. I obeyed His voice and avoided an accident. Our problem is, we act too mature and grown-up. I see many things in the spirit world since I fast and pray regularly. I see from time to time lizards, spiders, skeletons, spirit webs, dogs, tigers, lions, and many forms of evil figures. Since I believe in the spiritual world, I find no problems believing and understanding. I see real people doing different activities while praying. I know God is showing me, so I pray for their needs. Once you find the One true God, then deceiving false gods and goddesses will be over. It appears the spirit of Satan, who likes to take God's creation to hell. Hell is real. Many have seen it; I have seen and heard it as well. May the Lord make us believers of the true God. His name in the New Testament is Jesus. It is the saving name of Jehovah God. He has become the savior. John the Baptist, the forerunner of God Jehovah, said, I saw heaven open and the Holy Spirit came like a dove. Dove was the sign from the Spirit of God to identify the Son of God. The Son of God represents one true God in the flesh. Amen! May the Lord open your spiritual eyes so you can battle against the enemy, who is snatching all from you. Fight this battle with spiritual eyes and take it by force. You have the authority to destroy Satan's kingdom, in Jesus's name. Amen!

LET US PRAY

Lord, to know and serve you is a privilege. Open our spiritual eyes to see the things concerning you. Our God is doing mighty work for those who are following in His footsteps by obeying Him. We know the prince, principalities, and power of darkness rules at this end-time through the government, so it is our job to put on armor and come against it. Our eyes will see the work of God if we follow, as it says in the Bible. May the Lord open the eyes of the blind to see there is a false god, goddesses, hell, and darkness, so they turn to the one true living God! We pray that God, be our eyes to lead us in this pitch-dark world to see. Lord, Your Word is light and lamp in our ways. It is not for argument but to follow, so help us Lord in Jesus's name. Amen! God bless you!

SEPTEMBER 24

BRING THE DEVIL TO CAPTIVITY!

Once you recognize the truth about given power and authority, then you can claim legal ownership of what belongs to you. Once upon a time, man and woman were living in the Garden of Eden. I knew their location and ownership. Only the one crook devil played the trick and took away all the rights. The rights were taken away by breaking a contract with the creator who gave them the place. Disobeying the condition of God caused the evacuation. Now the one who gave all legal rights came on earth in the flesh and paid the price to buy back. His name is Jesus. God restored what Satan stole from us. Earlier was the Spirit God who created all and also this first man and woman called Adam and Eve. May the Lord make you aware of the rights, authority, and power that are given to us. Relationship with the creator was reestablished with His creation by shedding the Blood of the creator. The Creator put on the flesh with the saving name Jesus.

Satan continues the plowing evil plan by changing, twisting, adding, and subtracting scripture. In the devil's zeal, he has raised many false teachers and prophets. The devil does not need a snake body since he has found greedy, jealous, envious, power-hungry, and willing people. Ambitious characters find a position in the religious world. We have many true workers on the field who know their rights with given power. But some are working as opponents called the snake. The snake generation will not allow people to repent and go into the water in Jesus's name for the remission of sins. Baptism in the name of Jesus is a powerful sin-forgiving experience. It is getting back what they lost in the Garden of Eden. The Lord said you would die, which is the eternal death of the soul when you sin. The blood of savior Jesus, that is the highest name Jehovah, speaks I gave my life instead. Savior's blood speaks for those who put on the Christ by baptizing in Jesus's name. Also, the Lord gives us the Holy Spirit by evidence of speaking in tongues. The Great God Spirit comes within to empower us. He gave us His name, authority, and power to live upright and triumphant. If this is the case, then someone has to train you in the army with knowledge of the truth, since the truth has the power to set the captive free.

John 8:31 Then said Jesus to those Jews which believed on him, If ye continue in my word, then are ye my disciples indeed; 32 And ye shall know the truth, and the truth shall make you free.

Are you free or a slave? Are you under the power of bondage, sicknesses, or daemonic operation? Let me tell you, forget all false teaching, preaching, denomination, non-denominations, and organization. Enter today in the Church which is built on rock. Rock is the revelation of the identity of Jesus. Who has the key?

Peter has the key, which he reveals in Acts 2:38. Acts have established the church. It's not the building, but the one who is born of the water and spirit that is... A den where thieves are is what the building is called. In the Book of Acts, you will find the key to opening heaven. We have been given back the power, authority, and rights of the Lord Jesus. No weapon can prosper against people who have discovery of name Jesus, like Peter, Paul, and many others. May the Lord give you the key by giving revelation of Him who came to buy back my and your rights by shedding His Blood.

1 John 3:1 Behold, what manner of love the Father hath bestowed upon us, that we should be called the sons of God: therefore the world knoweth us not, because it knew him not.5 And ye know that he was manifested to take away our sins; and in him is no sin.

Born again knows Jesus since they love and obey His commandment, but not the world. Get a revelation of Jesus as God, robbed of flesh. Most of the false versions of the Bible have removed God and inserted him. Let us see who he is. And why?

1 Timothy 3:16a And without controversy great is the mystery of godliness: God (not he) was manifest in the flesh,

Acts 20:28b to feed the church of God, which he hath purchased with his own blood.

The one God Jehovah became the savior for His creation to save. He brought us back with His Blood. Peter recognized that is why he started blood-bought churches. Peter knew Jesus was the given Son and mighty God to take revenge. The devil screwed up God's creation, but the Lord knows how to redeem it. 2000 years ago Lord started His blood-bought church by His disciples. Lord Jesus said, Believe the teaching of prophets and apostles, I am here to shed blood. I gave the Key to the Apostle and prophet Peter who knew me.

Ephesians. 2:20 And are built upon the foundation of the apostles and prophets, Jesus Christ himself being the chief corner stone.

Peter said *Acts 2:38 Then Peter said unto them, Repent, and be baptized every one of you in the name of Jesus Christ for the remission of sins, and ye shall receive the gift of the Holy Ghost.39 For the promise is unto you, and to your children, and to all that are afar off, even as many as the Lord our God shall call.*

Now 42 verses said they all continue in the doctrine of Apostles and 41 added three thousand 47b: And the Lord added to the church daily such as should be saved.

They baptized these new converts in the name of Jesus. The blood of the Lamb offered redemption for their souls, providing shade. The gates of hell have no power over this church.

Matthew 16:18 And I say also unto thee, that thou art Peter, and upon this rock I will build my church; and the gates of hell shall not prevail against it.19 And I will give unto thee the keys of the kingdom of heaven: and whatsoever thou shalt bind on earth shall be bound in heaven: and whatsoever thou shalt loose on earth shall be loosed in heaven.

When you possess an understanding of Jehovah's manifestation in human form, bearing the supreme and superior name, the devil is compelled to back down. The key to defeating the devil lies in the name's revelation of Jesus.

20 Then charged he his disciples that they should tell no man that he was Jesus the Christ.

Jesus is not Jesus Joseph, but Christ the Messiah is the savior of the World.

SEPTEMBER 24

Jehovah said I am one.

Isaiah 43:11 I, even I, am the Lord; and beside me there is no saviour. 12 I have declared, and have saved, and I have shewed, when there was no strange god among you: therefore ye are my witnesses, saith the Lord, that I am God.

Learn the truth about the revelation of Jesus. Do not let the devil fool you. Bind and break the power of the devil by fasting and praying. Lose all Angles, the Holy Spirit, and lose the captive of Satan by ignorance and lie. It is the most wonderful time to know that you can take it back all by force from the devil. Get violent with the Devil and its army, blind them, and cast them out of the country. Destroy false gods and goddesses with their lies. Heal the sick, remove the false teachers and prophets. Tell the devil, I bind all your agendas, tricks, devices, and lies and send you back to hell. I own the earth, cover the earth, sin, soul, body, and Spirit with the Blood of Jesus. Have the knowledge that you can do all, not a few or some. You must know the power; authority is ours in the mighty name of Jesus. Amen!

LET US PRAY

In the name of Jesus, we have power, authority, and victory. The truth sets us free. Lord, help us love the truth and obey it. Deliver us from the false lie of Satan. We do not accept the lie of the devil, who continues its devices to keep us. Lord, thank you for giving authority to Born Again to claim back what we lost. We refuse to subdue. Help us go into the world and preach the gospel by casting the demons out and healing the sick. Praying in another tongue so the people know we have the Spirit of God within. It is the most privileged time; that we have power through the Spirit of God. We bring the devil into captivity by the authority given to us in the stronger name of Jehovah God, which is Jesus. Thank you for what you did for us, in Jesus's name. Amen! God bless you!

SEPTEMBER 25

YOUR CHOICES DEFINE YOUR TITLE!

It is not your profession, religion, or spiritual title, but your choices that define you in the Kingdom of God. The Lord called a man a traitor or betrayer. Why?

Luke 22:48 But Jesus said unto him, Judas, betrayest thou the Son of man with a kiss?

Judas betrayed God, so he was called a betrayer of the Lord Jesus Christ. He was also called a thief. Why? He stole the money from the bag.

John 12:6 This he said, not that he cared for the poor; but because he was a thief, and had the bag, and bare what was put therein.

Your choices are penniless, then God will title you poor. Your title will let others know what you are. Priest and High Priest in today's term, Bishop, pastors were envious of Jesus Christ.

Mark 15:10 For he knew that the chief priests had delivered him for envy

Matthew 12:34 O generation of vipers, how can ye, being evil, speak good things? for out of the abundance of the heart the mouth speaketh.

The choices of the Generation made them recognized as a snake generation. Deceiver, liar, sneaky can bite you. They live quietly amongst you, but only time will prove what they are. The nature of the person gives them the correct title.

The Bible says your title, position, and calls do not count, but it is your work. God was careless of the title priest, high priest, scribe, and Pharisees. Their choices and work gave them a title in the Bible.

Daniel was called a great beloved. Why? He loved to pray and worked wholeheartedly for the Kingdom of God. He did not back off from the decree of death that was pronounced by the King. What makes God happy; is when you love God unconditionally. That is what He desires from His creation. Can you go to the den of lions knowing that death is at hand? Daniel's choices represented him to receive the title from God.

Daniel 9:23 At the beginning of thy supplications the commandment came forth, and I am come to shew thee; for thou art greatly beloved: therefore understand the matter, and consider the vision.

SEPTEMBER 25

Daniel 10:11 And he said unto me, O Daniel, a man greatly beloved,

We title an individual barren if they don't have children. Why is Jesus Christ the Highest title in heaven, on earth, and beneath since He gave the blood which has life? Jehovah God put on flesh since humanity had sin in their blood. Taking stripes, wearing the crowns of thorns, and suffering mocking gave the highest name. Now, what is your problem since God said that was the only name above all names? In Jesus' name all bow, not some? It is the name of God; He received this title since He emptied Himself.

Abraham was the father of faith. His choice gave him the title.

James 2:22 Seest thou how faith wrought with his works, and by works was faith made perfect? 23 And the scripture was fulfilled which saith, Abraham believed God, and it was imputed unto him for righteousness: and he was called the Friend of God.

So what are you called, gossiper or peacemaker, liar or the man of integrity and truth? Holy and righteous, or the unholy and unrighteous! Your work is important in the eyes of God. My work is more important than any title the secular or religious world gives me. My name is as important as the name of many who were titled by the Lord. Make sure that you know there is a God in heaven who watches you. What you are doing in the world for Him is more important than what you are doing for the church. No wonder the Bible says many will choose Broadway. Many are called antichrist, and many are called sinners.

God picked David, seeing His heart. Now do not get jealous like King Saul and try to kill those whom you fear could replace you. You can only be replaced if you are disobedient to the Lord. Fear God and not people. Please God, not people, pastors, churches, family, or anyone.

1 Samuel 13:14 But now thy kingdom shall not continue: the Lord hath sought him a man after his own heart, and the Lord hath commanded him to be captain over his people, because thou hast not kept that which the Lord commanded thee.

Moses was called a humble man. Why? What is the opposite of the humble? Prideful right? The prideful knows all and cannot obey God. God or others will not pick a prideful person to work for them on earth. Pride cannot keep any positions; they will be removed. They do not know that they are prideful. To be meek is to be humble.

Number 12:3 (Now the man Moses was very meek, above all the men who were upon the face of the earth.)

God needs submissive people who do not add or subtract to His instruction.

I remember many years ago; I had just started attending church and taught what the Bible says. Now I loved the Lord but never heard many things about this faith people were teaching. They taught women are not supposed to wear pants and showed it was biblical. Oh my God, I said. I worked in the post office, so I thought I would wear pants only at work since the job's nature involved much moving.

I found beautiful pants, but this consciousness of mine was so clean since they baptized me, in Jesus's name. Now, those who have not used the name of Jesus in baptism would not understand. When you are baptized in Jesus's name, God gives you a clean conscience. You must experience this. The post office was where I worked. I heard many comments admiring my new pants. I also looked in a mirror and said, I love the way these pants fit. It was perfect for my figure. As I was working, a thought came to my heart, but how am I looking in the eyes of God? And suddenly shame came on me. I felt like I was standing in front of God and felt ashamed of man's garment. Oh Lord, suddenly the Spirit of God took over and covered my whole body. I heard from every cell of my body I love you sincerely. For days, I heard this voice. I decided that very moment I would go home and get rid of all my pants. And I removed all unholy clothes in the sight of God. It is the Lord who dresses us up. I live in America; you find all kinds of clothes but the Lord helps me choose clothes that please Him. Remember, the first lesson to Adam and Eve was to teach them to cover the naked body. The apron does not cover their skin. If we would have continued in the designer God for our apparel, then we wouldn't see raping, molesting, fornication, adultery, and trafficking of bodies for prostitution.

What was the impression or title of Jeremiah in heaven?

Jeremiah 9:1 Oh that my head were waters, and mine eyes a fountain of tears, that I might weep day and night for the slain of the daughter of my people!

The prophet had a burden and was known as a weeping prophet.

It is your choice, attitude, and behavior that will make you known in heaven. Choose the correct lifestyle, and work, and get the best title ever in Jesus's name. Amen!

LET US PRAY

Heavenly Father, we thank you. You desire us to live right in the sight of God. Our God will know exactly what we do and think. It is the blessings from God and not the title or position we hold. We desire to be what you have called and the best by choosing perfectly. May the Lord find us diligent and sincere in the eyes of Him. We try our best to look good or do our best to achieve the title on earth. We please or try to please others and ignore the one whom we must please, that is our Lord Jesus. Many have changed the way and word of God by choosing to please flesh or people, but Lord. Today we decide to choose you and you alone. We want to hear every impressive title from you, and also at the end to hear well done, my good and faithful servant. Make us care for the Lord, not religious groups. We thank you for calling us. We bless your Holy name in Jesus's name. Amen! God bless you!

SEPTEMBER 26

HOW TO SUSTAIN IN DISASTER!

In times of famine, scarcity, earthquake, flood, and various disasters, we must learn how to sustain ourselves. Many times, financial crises come, and we have to know how to sustain them during that time. May the Lord lead us during the time of scarcity. We hear the time of trying is here. We see it all over the world and many natural disasters. But I know even as we will not be put to shame.

Isaiah 54:4 Fear not; for thou shalt not be ashamed: neither be thou confounded; for thou shalt not be put to shame:

God will sustain you in any natural or supernatural disaster. Because our God is called the Savior. He saves, heals, and delivers from all trouble trials. The Lord can do what you ask.

Isaiah 51:7 Hearken unto me, ye that know righteousness, the people in whose heart is my law; fear ye not the reproach of men, neither be ye afraid of their revilings.

God provided the desert place with two fish and a few pieces of bread.

Matthew 14:15 And when it was evening, his disciples came to him, saying, This is a desert place, and the time is now past; send the multitude away, that they may go into the villages, and buy themselves victuals. 16 But Jesus said unto them, They need not depart; give ye them to eat. 17 And they say unto him, We have here but five loaves, and two fishes. 18 He said, Bring them hither to me. 19 And he commanded the multitude to sit down on the grass, and took the five loaves, and the two fishes, and looking up to heaven, he blessed, and brake, and gave the loaves to his disciples and the disciples to the multitude. 20 And they did all eat, and were filled: and they took up of the fragments that remained twelve baskets full. 21 And they that had eaten were about five thousand men, beside women and children.

Lord knows your needs. The Lord also knows how to keep you and provide for you. You will be sustained and helped provided no matter where you are.

God sent the man to the widow, how the widow sustained. I am not thinking of Elijah since the Lord provided him at the brook of Cherith by the revenue.

1 Kings 17:6 And the ravens brought him bread and flesh in the morning, and bread and flesh in the evening; and he drank of the brook.

Now in Zarephath, God had a widow and her son. God sustained her since the Lord used Elijah to stay in her place. She had a handful of meals and a little oil. During this time, she was ready to starve to death. May the Lord help us understand how to support the people of God. It is the blessings to give to the prophets and laborers of God. As you know, they are the most important in the land. I do not believe in medicine, but I depend on healing, miracles, and prophecy which come from the Lord. That is the only way I believe. So in my life, I always find true prophets and teachers. You will never find me in religious churches. God is not there. I learned from my parents and brother to give true laborers of God when they pray for us. Giving to them will sustain me. I never let the true prophet and teachers go empty-handed. It is not our bank balance, food in the barn, or everything we think of, but it is God who knows how to sustain us. I have noticed giving genuine people of God a miracle happens. There are thirties, sixties, and hundreds of folds of blessings. We do not know which one is the best ground.

Now, this widow cooked and served Elijah first and was sustained by God.

1 King 17:14 For thus saith the Lord God of Israel, The barrel of meal shall not waste, neither shall the cruse of oil fail, until the day that the Lord sendeth rain upon the earth 15 And she went and did according to the saying of Elijah: and she, and he, and her house, did eat many days.

So, do you see how the widow and her son survived? They took care of the man of God. It is a must that your blessing is hidden by giving to the man of God.

I know the man of God was sustained by the Ravens, but the woman needed a blessing to sustain herself in the time of famine. Our life has many lessons to learn.

It is a time when laborers are not taken care of. Many think we give tithes offerings and missions and we are done. But what about the people you call for your spiritual needs? They are always there for you, pray for you, and work day and night. They do work as true laborers. Many nails, hair, spas, and wonderful things for a woman to pamper. I see those drug dealers, sellers, liquor, bartenders, and many others get a good tip, but people treat laborers who are working for God worse. You lose your blessings. Nowadays, people have made many churches, organizations, denominations, and projects. Each time, they get good donations to enjoy their life. Many donate the receipt.

Matthew 6:3 But when thou givest alms, let not thy left hand know what thy right hand doeth,

So do not worry about how much you give and where you give, it is between you and God. Anyone who has relied on the help of the Lord's laborers without extending blessings has lost those blessings.

Matthew 10:41 He that receiveth a prophet in the name of a prophet shall receive a prophet's reward; and he that receiveth a righteous man in the name of a righteous man shall receive a righteous man's reward. 42 And whosoever shall give to drink unto one of these little ones a cup of cold water only in the name of a disciple, verily I say unto you, he shall in no wise lose his reward.

I see more and more people depend on me to buy them or give them. It is the time when they have learned to give churches seeing no miracle, healing, deliverance, or any sign and wonder. They live with the impression that we need them for our ceremonies. If not, then they will gang up against us. We live in a society. I live with this truth and am not afraid of threats, lies, and slanderous words. I know that in the last 20 years; the Lord has sustained me, and defended me from the spirit of dogs, tigers, liars, thieves, and the religious power of darkness. He will keep me and sustain me if I stand for the truth. Never worry if you are living and standing for the truth of God. I mean, the Lord knows how to sustain you and bless you. God destroyed the world at the time of Noah, Lot, and the time of famine, where Isaac received hundredfold crops. It is the hand of the almighty God that sustains. Do it the way of God and see what happens to your finances, your farms, your barns, your health, your family, and your country. Learn how and where to invest your money. It is always best to invest in the Bank of Jesus, where you will sustain calamity. In Jesus's name, Amen.

LET US PRAY

Lord, we thank you that people who trust in the ways and voice of God will receive strength like an eagle. They will not faint or weary but receive to go above their problem. The Lord will give them the wings of an eagle to go to the height where they see the problem through the eyes of providers and sustainers.

Our help does not come from anywhere but the Lord if we know how to step in by faith at His command like the widow of Zarephath. Time is bad when we see more and more disasters where there is no place we can hide our food. We see the lava burning the home city; the flood is wiping out the land, and the earthquake is destroying it. But our Lord never runs out of supply. He has multiple supernatural and amazing provisions. May the Lord teach us to give and invest in the right places where we can receive blessings. Show us the fertile ground of God where we can plant our money to sustain ourselves in the time of necessity in Jesus's name! Amen! God bless you!

SEPTEMBER 27

ARE YOU OPPRESSED IN YOUR NATION?

Many are oppressed, depressed, and in agony since they forgot the ways and laws of the Lord.

Psalm 127:1 Except the Lord build the house, they labor in vain that build it: except the Lord keep the city, the watchman waketh but in vain.

So there is a law, commandments, and precepts of God for you to receive help from the Lord. Many think that we believe in God but live like the devil and act like a devil, then they invite the judgment of God. Your protection is in keeping the laws and not finding the best job or having much education. No matter where you go, write the laws and commandments of God in your heart to follow. If you do, then no one can move you or replace you. Remember King Saul, priest Eli, and others who repeated the same mistakes.

Proverb 12:3 A man will not be established by wickedness, But the root of the righteous will not be moved.

Proverb 10:30 The righteous shall never be removed: but the wicked shall not inhabit the earth.

The Lord establishes you if you hearken Him or remove you if you forget the Laws of the Lord. Never think it is someone who causes you trouble. Identify examples in the Old Testament to understand the mistakes or to follow a good example of a successful person. Now, the Old Testament should be a forgotten story, since it is for our example and admonition. So do not ignore the Old Testament. Matter of fact, OT is my favorite part of the Bible.

Judges 3:7 And the children of Israel did evil in the sight of the LORD, and forgat the LORD their God, and served Baalim and the groves.

God sent the King of Mesopotamia to oppress the Israelites, and they served the enemy for eight years. Israelites turned to God and God delivered them by the hand of Othniel and there was rest for 40 years. Again, after forty years, they forgot God and did evil and the Lord sent the King of Moab, and the Israelites served them for eighteen years. Again the Israelites got distressed, and they repented and the Lord in His mercy delivered them by the hand of Ehud and the land rested for 80 years. Ehud died, and they went astray and did evil. King Jabin of Canaan oppressed the Israelites. When they repented and turned to God, God used the prophetess Deborah and Barak to deliver. God used from Ehud to Samson, 13 judges, to save the Israelites when they cried out and repented.

SEPTEMBER 27

Acts 13:20 And after that he gave unto them judges about the space of four hundred and fifty years until Samuel the prophet. 21 And afterward they desired a king: and God gave unto them Saul the son of Cis, a man of the tribe of Benjamin, by the space of forty years.

With the last two judges or prophets, Eli and Samuel were to gather 15 judges by whom the Lord talked, ruled, helped, and rescued the Israelites when they repented. The one common thing was that they repeated the same mistakes as soon as their captain or their judge sent by God died. See how important your leaders are. Picked the right one. Not the one who seems good, but good. There was a difference between Eli and Samuel. God thrust Eli out and the Lord replaced him with Samuel. Some play, perform and live and receive the consequences.

Wake up. You will be gone, replaced, and suppressed in your land. I watch the chaos on every land. People are being raped, killed, and robbed by people who came from other nations. What do you think causes them to be oppressed? Pray that the Lord sends the true teachers to teach us the oracle, laws, and commandments of God. I hear a young girl saying, this is my nation and no one can say anything to me. I can walk, dress, and live, however. Reminder, it is God's earth and follows as thus, says the Lord. May the Lord give us the right commander and chief to enforce the ways, laws, and statutes of the mighty God.

No one owns this earth but the creator God.

Unrighteousness will be removed. Our young children, teens, and adults need the guidelines to live, or God will send the oppressors. We will find the remnant in any era or dispensation who fears God. May the Lord bless us with one who lives right. May the Lord provide righteous and true spiritual leadership. Our nation needs reminders and teachings from the Word of God. The guideline has come from the Lord.

Many spiritual leaders have fallen into a spiritual sleep. That is why we see the people oppressed, possessed, depressed, sick, living, and doing what they are not supposed to do. May the Lord give us a Shepherd whose interest is to lead us beside still water, and feed us the green pastures, which are the word of God. Lord, reassure us of our unshakable protection and stability by faithfully abiding by your commandment. We live in a time when we question, is the man of God from the Lord or a hireling? A wolf in sheep's clothing. I would not even dare to visit some buildings called churches, knowing they have their agenda to destroy the Lord's kingdom. Lord came for what? To restore His creation and pay sins' price with His blood. One Spirit God put on flesh and shed the blood for me.

Now, if you find any religion using the Bible to misguide you, then you will also be defeated. The righteousness of God differs from self-righteousness. I see in Europe, England, and many nations suffering since people come from all over the world to rob. Lord, help us understand natives are replaced by desiring forbidden fruits and Broadway to enjoy their flesh, lust of eyes, and pride. Our job is to keep the commandments of God and not to support the misguiding laws of the land. Many think land allows freedom, so we should enjoy it. But this freedom is a trap of Satan, so stay away. Freedom comes only by abiding by the Laws of God. All others are the same devil coming to all Eves and Adams who are wondering. Individuals in their states who used to shop in the middle of the night are now robbed, raped, and gone through a hard ache. Why? We are repeating the same mistakes. Do not take any freedom from Satan, since he is not free.

Jude 1:6 And the angels who kept not their first estate, but left their habitation, he hath reserved in everlasting chains under darkness unto the judgment of the great day.

2 Peter 2:4 For if God spared not the angels that sinned, but cast them down to hell, and delivered them into chains of darkness, to be reserved unto judgment;

So what do you think? God will let you escape if you do wrong. Change your ways, motives, and lifestyle, and walk in the light of God. Do not find organizations or religions where your lifestyle fits, but find the leaders who lead you the right way. You will be protected. Lord, bless you and your nation with good spiritual, righteous, and holy leaders in Jesus's name! Amen!

LET US PRAY

We resubmit to you, Lord, to the will and ways of God. We humble ourselves and turn from our wicked ways so you can heal our land. It is my duty and calling to keep my nation secured by living a holy and righteous life according to the Word of God. We thank you. Lord, give us righteous apostles, pastors, preachers, prophets, and teachers, called by you. We need righteous leaders to reign in the land. Please give us true and righteous leaders. Please restore and heal the land. Whatever devil has stolen, killed, and destroyed, bring it back as we turn to you. Give us an obedient heart to obey the voice of God. Please restore what we lost and stole in Jesus's name! Amen! God bless you!

SEPTEMBER 28

WITCH, WIZARD, ENCHANTER, MAGICIAN!

No one wants to talk about this subject. But what does the Bible say about the evil workers of the Devil? The Devil has an army to fight against the King of Kings, Jesus. Satan does all works against furthering the kingdom of God. Satan and its followers are called liars. The rule in high places is to bring down God's people. Its Agenda is to accuse the righteous and holy people. The Lord said to Adam the day you will eat the fruit; you die, that is eternal death, not physical death. The Devil came as a serpent said,

Genesis 3:4 And the serpent said unto the woman, Ye shall not surely die: The Devil tells exactly the opposite of what God says. May the Lord help us follow the truth. The Lord commanded witches to be removed. Do you have one around you?

Exodus 22:18 Thou shalt not suffer a witch to live. If you use these witches, you also will be removed from the land.

1 Chronicle 10:13 So Saul died for his transgression which he committed against the LORD, even against the word of the LORD, which he kept not, and also for asking counsel of one that had a familiar spirit, to inquire of it;

Make the Lord your only source to uncover the truth. The Lord will punish other sources. We are limited to the physical realm, but spirits are not limited to the physical and spiritual world. One time, this brother who was working for Jesus was late going home. Many people used to come to his workplace for deliverance from the demons. As he was casting the demon out, the demon said, your wife is coming. His wife parked far away to check on the husband. Brother looked around and said, no she is not. But as she walked in, he saw her. See, the devil sees the surrounding people just like we see at the physical eye range.

Leviticus 19:31 Regard not them that have familiar spirits, neither seek after wizards, to be defiled by them: I am the LORD your God.

Now sorcery is the black magic, enchantment. God forbids diviners, enchanters, and magicians in the Bible. They used satanic power in Satan's church, which is the power of darkness.

Act 8:9 But there was a certain man, called Simon, which beforetime in the same city used sorcery, and bewitched the people of Samaria, giving out that himself was some great one:

These practices are everywhere. Today, during the morning hours of prayer, I saw a witch. I have been praying for the USA a lot. All this evil allegation, the accusation is such a drama. It is hurtful since there is a satanic shameless world that uses witnesses to destroy the good people. As I saw this witch clearly with my naked eyes open, I started binding and destroying its agenda. I hate news but sometimes I have to watch since the Lord wants me to intercede for some people. As I turned on a YouTube news channel, the lady said the allegation about a good man was like a witch hunt. I said I just saw that witch. May the Lord help us understand that the spirit world is real. It is not just going to church and coming home to relax. You, being the church of God, prepare to face your enemy. Get ready by fasting and praying to destroy the devil's agenda. You have the power of the Holy Spirit, truth, and authority. If you do not have the Holy Spirit, then go to a person who can lay a hand to receive it by speaking in tongues. People of God praying and fasting are the only hope for the nations against the agenda of Satan. Satan can destroy you just like he would have at the time of Esther, but she knew what to do. So let us do the same fasting and prayer.

1 Peter 5:8 Be sober, be vigilant; because of your adversary the devil, as a roaring lion, walketh about, seeking whom he may devour:

The Devil has one business to accuse the people of God. You see this in your home and everywhere. The wicked witch or evil man will constantly accuse the family of destroying it. But never worry about the accuser, liar, and wicked. They are living dead. There is no hope for these wicked witches or men in your home or country or at your work. There are instructions in the Bible. Always speak victorious testimony, and say to the devil the Lord did this to so and so, remind the devil, it is the blood of Jesus against you. That means no matter what allegation or accusation you make, I have the righteous blood of Jesus to protect me. The Savior's blood was shed for me to take away all my sins, so hahaha. Never be afraid of the one who makes allegations, just stand on the word. Their end is near.

Revelation 12:10 And I heard a loud voice saying in heaven, Now is come salvation, and strength, and the kingdom of our God, and the power of his Christ: for the accuser of our brethren is cast down, which accused them before our God day and night. 11 And they overcame him by the blood of the Lamb, and by the word of their testimony; and they loved not their lives unto the death.

This devil comes through your relatives or countrymen, or women. Laugh at it. Do not allow them to come into your house since their motive is wrong and will drop demons in your house. Read the Bible, follow instructions, and learn why to keep evil out of the door. I tell you, the accuser will get mad even though they have their evil witnesses, like their wicked daughter. Do not expect any good thing from this wicked. Stay away. If you have to go around them, bind demons from them and break their power. Send Angels before you meet them. Believe me, their end is bad. Trust God. Nowadays, we have many evil men and women. Why? We forgot to pray and fast. More fun, tea party, eating, hunting, celebration after celebration, golfing, you name it. Most labeled pastors do not know how to cast out demons. Some churches would not let me; they would monitor me if I did. It is their monopoly and agenda, not the Lord to work in their den. Jesus was doing it. Why is it so foreign in America to recognize demons and their work? What happens when the country becomes religious and ends Jesus? If we don't allow the Holy Spirit to lead, guide, and do the work, then we see the power of God diminish and lawlessness. Time to wake up. We see the many witches, warlocks, enchanters, diviners, wizards, and magicians walking around us in beautiful clothes and driving beautiful cars. Some are standing on the pulpit and have magnificent churches. But is there anyone who recognizes the forces working behind the kidnapping, raping, an allegation of an innocent, killing, and destroying the good people? All activities are in different organizations and buildings are to bewitch you. I had a dream about India, where the religious groups are rich. No one casts demons out, no one opens blind eyes, lame do not walk, but have big congregations to deceive them. People love to be deceived since someone brainwashed them with false teachings. I dreamed of the spirit of dogs and tigers working with so-called religious Christian people in the state of Gujarat. Be careful. Start praying in your home rather than giving money to support false organizations. It is another form of Satan destroying the kingdom of Jesus Christ. The Bible says to seek the Lord, not sit on the pew. I sought and found Him. They are strongly antichrist. All their denominations and false prophets and teachers work against the Bible. May the Lord send the mighty true teachers and pastors to your home, town, city, and country, and you believe them in Jesus's name! Amen!

LET US PRAY

Oh, Lord, we need you and your power of the Holy Spirit to come against daemonic power. Lord, bless us with the truth as the religious demon has failed your people. Lord, give us true teachers and prophets to come against all this chaos happening in this world. You have given us the authority, power, and your name Jesus; we thank you, Lord. Our God is true, but it is our choice to obey you and your truth. Lord, help us love the truth, prayer, fasting, and your Word more than ever before. It is our Lord who knows how to save, keep, and deliver from Satan. May the Lord put an unbreakable hedge of protection, mighty angels, blood, and Holy Spirit around us, our children, home in Jesus's name! Amen! God bless you!

SEPTEMBER 29

DO NOT DESTROY THE TEMPLE OF GOD!

Now you may think, what am I talking about? I am talking about your physical body. One time the Prophet asked the smoker, would you smoke in the church? He said, of course not, it is disrespectful. So the prophet said let me teach you today what the Lord is talking about. Your body is a temple or church, the building is not a church. He took him to.

1 Corinthians 3:16 Know ye not that ye are the temple of God, and that the Spirit of God dwelleth in you? 17 If any man defile the temple of God, him shall God destroy; for the temple of God is holy, which temple ye are.

That day, this smoker, for the first time, understood that it was wrong to smoke. Many use the body for a drug. God has made our body so He can abide in us as the Holy Spirit. The Holy Spirit is the one God's Spirit. Now if you smoke, drink, commit adultery, fornicate, or do drugs, then you are defiling the temple of God. Many know that on cigarette packages, a warning is written that it causes cancer. Lungs fail and damage happens to the entire body. It is a fact that many who consume cigarettes die with many problems. Over 4,80,000 deaths are yearly in the US only! Listen to the Lord. Now how many die from the drug? Last year alone, it was 72,000. Do we know it is wrong but still careless? Believe in the maker of your body. Use the life manual, which is the Bible. We must believe the Bible over the doctor. We know the Bible is the only accurate information. Time and time we have to use the Bible to prove and show the effects, side effects, and consequences of disobeying the word. Suffering and pain are awful, but their family suffers as well.A cigarette causes cancer; 41,000 die from cancer each year. Now, do you still want to disobey God? God says get rid of the bad stuff or I will destroy that temple which you defiled. What are HIV and AIDS? AIDS is in the advanced stage of HIV. 1 million people died last year in the US alone. 1.8 million died globally. That is 3 deaths every minute. Love yourself. Turn to God. Life can be more enjoyable than death. Life is the gift of God. People do not relate many sins to sickness, but sin causes sickness. I have found this information from a Google search. But I only stand on the word of God. Get wise. Sexual sins are against God's temple.

1 Corinthians 6:18 Flee fornication. Every sin that a man doeth is without the body; but he that committeth fornication sinneth against his own body.19 What? know ye not that your body is the temple of the Holy Ghost which is in you, which ye have of God, and ye are not your own?

Paul was addressing one very serious problem. He warns the fornicator that his body, which is the temple of God, will be destroyed.

SEPTEMBER 29

1 Corinthian 5:1 It is reported commonly that there is fornication among you, and such fornication as is not so much as named among the Gentiles, that one should have his father's wife. 2 And ye are puffed up, and have not rather mourned, that he that hath done this deed might be taken away from among you.

When you defile the temple, which is your body, then the Lord will depart, but Satan will take over. Now Satan's job is to steal, kill, and destroy.

1 Corinthians 5:5 To deliver such an one unto Satan for the destruction of the flesh, that the spirit may be saved in the day of the Lord Jesus.

If a brother or sister in the Lord does wrong, then do not keep company with them.

1 Corinthians 5:9 I wrote unto you in an epistle not to company with fornicators:10 Yet not altogether with the fornicators of this world, or with the covetous, or extortioners, or with idolaters; for then must ye needs go out of the world.11 But now I have written unto you not to keep company, if any man that is called a brother be a fornicator, or covetous, or an idolator, or a railer, or a drunkard, or an extortioner; with such an one no not to eat.

Nowadays, this subject is not much preached, and we see the worst result of death. A believer should never compromise with these sins. Our job is to teach, obey or not is their choice. So remember, we deliver the word of God and not worldliness. Love, the one who tells the truth, embraces the truth. No matter what, we cannot afford all the suffering and in the end, hell. Rather, we straighten up and live a righteous life. God never saves us from sin. God delivers us from sin. Sin separated Adam and Eve. John the Baptist gave the baptism of repentance to mend the broken relationship between God and His creation. Remember the blood in life bought you. Jesus paid the price by giving His blood. He took a stripe, so the blood that came out of that stripe could heal you. He took 39 stripes to heal you, and if you have sinned, it will be forgiven. How easy is it?

James 5:15: And the prayer of faith shall save the sick, and the Lord shall raise him up; and if he have committed sins, they shall be forgiven him.

Seems like an easy good deal. Why not repent of sins? Sin's pleasure is for a moment and then eternal suffering. Repentance is the way called turning from sins. If you immerse in the water in the name of Jesus, there is the blood of the lamb is under that name. The Blood of the Savior will wash away all sins. It is free. May the Lord give us wisdom.

1 Corinthian 6:9 Know ye not that the unrighteous shall not inherit the kingdom of God? Be not deceived: neither fornicators, nor idolaters, nor adulterers, nor effeminate, nor abusers of themselves with humankind,

Get the power of the Holy Spirit, which will give you the strength and power to fight against all temptations of darkness. May the Lord help us not to fail God again. His blood can clean any deep sins and make us whiter than snow. Also, your soul will inherit the eternal place. May the Lord give you wisdom and understanding to turn to Him.

Hebrews 3:6 But Christ as a son over his own house; whose house are we, if we hold fast the confidence and the rejoicing of the hope firm unto the end. 7 Wherefore (as the Holy Ghost saith, Today if ye will hear his voice, 8 Harden not your hearts, as in the provocation, in the day of temptation in the wilderness:

Do not neglect God; He did everything to bless, deliver, and defend by giving His precious life. God manifests in the flesh to shed the blood. Do not reject the name where the blood is hidden. When you go under the water, use His precious name to wash your sins in the blood. You will receive the Holy Spirit; you will speak in another tongue to receive the power to fight Satan. Amen. May the Lord Bless you and give you an abundant life. Amen.

LET US PRAY

Lord, we come before your altar. Knowing we have sinned, and the wages of sin is death. There we have blood to wipe away all sins. Thank you for filling us with the Holy Spirit to fight the devil and temptations. Our Lord, you are a good God and have shown unconditional love in this end time by coming in the flesh to shed the blood. The truth possesses an overwhelming strength that can liberate us. Give us the truth and help us renounce religion. Lord, send true prophets and teachers to the lost to guide them. Remove confusion from us. Put love for truth. You deserve all glory, honor, riches, knowledge, wisdom, understanding, and praise, in Jesus's name. Amen! God bless you.

SEPTEMBER 30

I COME TO SEE THE LORD!

I do not care about the building, people, clothing, hairstyle, music, lecture but the Lord. Searching the Lord in operation by healing the sick, setting people free, and raising the dead. I do not go to prayer gatherings just as a religious routine. I will not get hooked up with the false fake ways, customs, and routines of Satan. The Lord destroyed all kinds of routines, even the Sabbath day. Now you can rest since the Lord is setting people free and healing if you let Him. Follow the ways of the Lord and not any ritual routine of Satan in the name of religious churches, denominations, and organizations. May the Lord not just set you free, but keep you free. He can if you allow Him. Learn to seek, then wait till he shows the way. I know He can if we allow him to do great. Get rid of your agenda; it will not work but destroy the work of God.

May the Lord help you depend on Him.

When you go to church, think about what is your motive. Many times I forwarded wonderful messages. I read their irrelevant opinions; they found fault and criticized me. So the critic goes to church to criticize. They hooked the one who criticizes a powerful demon of religion. The devil remains indifferent to their chosen-to-meet spot, as the demon within them finds satisfaction and solace, and remains hidden within their corporeal vessels.

No one is going to cast him out from the body since the one who preaches does not know how to fight the spiritual battle. Nice message to manipulate and win them into their kingdom. The devil laughs and says, welcome to my world will save you from the word of God.

Religion organizations oppose the truth and have won millions not to believe what thus saith the Lord.

Now, when I was visiting different denominations or non-denominations, I was looking for God. I heard some man of God preached good, anointed messages and sang and taught true or partly true. I said I wished to have these people in India. Nowadays, many have the Holy Spirit, and they are doing miracles. Some of them perform miracles. God saved many who are living to the truth and obeying the book. I am not trying to start any religion but the one already established by prophets and the apostles, as the word of God says. I am putting bricks on their foundation. The apostle and prophet built the church in the Book of Acts as the foundation. Now you can build in Galatians, Ephesians, Corinthians, Asia, Europe, Australia, and throughout the world on every continent. May the Lord help us not to start another organization, denomination, or non-denomination. We do not go to church to criticize but to see the Lord. He said the gates of hell will not prevail.

ELIZABETH DAS

I look for the saints gathering in Jesus' name where demons come out, fire comes down to burn the devil and its work. Demonstration according to the word of God, is greater work.

John 14:12 Verily, verily, I say unto you, He that believeth on me, the works that I do shall he do also; and greater works than these shall he do; because I go unto my Father.

This is my first and foremost search for a greater good. Do not unite with the religious group who think they are the best. Labeling a different name to their organization could be wrong, but the Lord. I am looking for a greater work. People who allow the Lord to work through the Spirit. I like the work of the Spirit, by the Spirit of God coming to you.

John 14:14 If ye shall ask any thing in my name, I will do it.

Yes, I go to a fellowship to see God doing, moving, healing, the blind see, the lame walk, and cancer patients need no chemo. No need to interfere with doctors and the immense building of hospitals.

The Spirit of God finds the problem, so no need for MRI, X-ray, ultrasound, or diagnostic most expensive procedures. No need for surgery since the hand of God moves through the hand of disciples of God who built their churches on a rock. Rock is the revelation of who Jesus is. Rock is the revelation of Jesus as Jehovah's Savior.

We see His hand moving through the believer to set the captive free. I have been watching the AMI live services in Johannesburg, South Africa. People fly there from all over the world to see the hand of God moving through the man of God to do greater work than this.

No one sees the Lord, but the sign and wonder confirms His presence.

Mark 16:20 And they went forth, and preached every where, the Lord working with them, and confirming the word with signs following. Amen.

I go to the church where the Lord is working through a disciple who is called by God, not by organizations.

Mark 16:15 And he said unto them, Go ye into all the world, and preach the gospel to every creature. 16 He that believeth and is baptized shall be saved; but he that believeth not shall be damned. 17 And these signs shall follow them that believe; In my name shall they cast out devils; they shall speak with new tongues; 18 They shall take up serpents; and if they drink any deadly thing, it shall not hurt them; they shall lay hands on the sick, and they shall recover.

When I was working with one brother Min, I saw him talking to the demons in people and then He commands the demon to get out. It was the most amazing time of my life. But I still did not stop from there, but looked for something greater than this. After a while in Dallas, I got bored and said, Lord. I need more. The box of the religious organization where I started looking for more. I said Lord you lead me, so He took me to another place where the pastor walks to you and prays, casts out demons, heals the sick, prophesy, informs, comforts the broken, and heals their wounds by giving them the word of knowledge and prophecy, and so forth.

I said, but I still want more. Now let us see where He is taking me next. I am seeking, asking, and knocking. No stopping, closing, and staying! Keep going and going. May the Lord help us believe in God. He said what He meant.

One late night, a young college girl called me. She said the demon was not leaving her room. She opens the door for the demon to watch the wrong site on the internet. Be careful. If you open that scene, he will come and will destroy you. This can happen if you are not looking for the Lord. Look for the Lord, drag yourself out of that comfort zone of a building called a church, pew, and denomination. God is not there. God is where you never can imagine. I came across God in areas that people often criticized. Do not let denominations, non-denomination, or organizations bewitch me or you. Thank God, He showed me mercy since I was looking for Him. Isn't that so wonderful? Our God is beyond amazing, performing miracles, healing, delivering, and working wonders. Look for this Jesus who has not changed and will not. May the Lord give you a sight of a greater vision to desire and behold the wonderful work of God. Look for it and you will find it. Amen! Happy blessed journey.

LET US PRAY

Lord, it is our job to seek, to see what you have stored for us. Give us hunger, courage, and boldness to flow in the Spirit to find the place where you are working.

The Lord works through the one who allows Him. Many are traveling far to see the work of God. I am so glad that some on earth are doing the mighty work of God. We believe you, please send us the true teachers. Where you are, there are liberty and miracles. You only work through us with your conditions and not ours. Many have started churches in conditions where you are not there. Thank you, Lord. Help us reconnect again on our knees, so we can connect again. No matter what we say, it is very easy to see you move among us if we surrender. Let us be your children, knowing you will do greater through us. Our Lord is faithful in Jesus's name! Amen! God bless you!

OCTOBER

OCTOBER 1

GOD BEAUTIFIES MEEK WITH SALVATION!

Everyone likes to look beautiful! People get a beautiful look when they get saved. I am a first-hand witness. For years, I have observed when a person's sins are washed away and receive the Holy Spirit, which has a glow on their face. What I mean is that when the person repents from all his sins, sins are washed away by being baptized in the name of Jesus and receiving the Holy Spirit, that person looks graceful. This person does not need to change the beauty products she uses, but by the touch of the Lord, she or he is beautified. God comes in their body, which God has made for Him to stay. This body is God's Holy Temple. When a person commits fleshly sin, this temple gets defiled.

What are fleshly sins? Let's see what the Word of God says,

Galatians 5:19b fornication, uncleanness, lasciviousness, 20 Idolatry, witchcraft, hatred, variance, emulations, wrath, strife, seditions, heresies, 21 Envyings, murders, drunkenness, revellings,

1 Samuel 16:7 But the Lord said unto Samuel, Look not on his countenance, or on the height of his stature; because I have refused him: for the Lord seeth not as man seeth; for man looketh on the outward appearance, but the Lord looketh on the heart.

Fleshly sins reflect on a person's face.

People do not have joy when they are not happy.

The possessive and envious people will have bone disease. They will die getting uglier and skinnier. Their skin tone turns dark or pale. I have seen these people whose beauty vanishes away. Depression, worry, and hatefulness are manifested on their faces. Makeup and face surgery do not help.

When a person turns from evil ways by repenting, washing sins in the water in Jesus' name, and receiving the Holy Spirit, will bring change within. I remember one prophet; his past life was terrible. He sat on the gutter, in and out of jail. He looked ugly because of his sins. When he turned to the Lord, Jesus came into his life, and he looked radiant. When the Lord comes, then He renovates His dwelling place. Our body is His temple. His hand formed it. The face shines and the features change. Ladies who walk with the Lord have a beautiful glow on their faces. I visit the convalescent home where I meet many ladies. The Ladies who are Christian have beautiful shiny countenances.

Once in India, a Hindu classmate of mine told me she could tell in an enormous crowd who is a Christian. I asked her, "How?" She replied, "There is a light on their face." People care so much about their outer look. I grew up in India. I never knew all this makeup. We just cleaned up our bodies and combed our hair, and that was all we did. Some ladies, who are converted to Christianity, said their coworkers noticed they looked gorgeous after their baptism. One of these ladies, named Gigi, said, "Everyone told me I look beautiful after her baptism." See, God created all things beautiful.

Ecclesiastes 3:11 He hath made every thing beautiful in his time:

Beauty comes from heaven. All Job's daughters were beautiful.

Job 42:15a And in all the land were no women found so fair as the daughters of Job:

God does not make ugly but makes ugly beautiful. I learned a woman who has anger, jealousy, or pride has the harshest look. It is a person's insight that brings outer appearance. Inner ugliness peeps through the face. If people know the truth, then they will not be deceived by Satan.

Searching from Google, it shows that in the year 2003 per analysts at Goldman Sachs the estimated worth of the global beauty industry, including skincare products $24 billion, make-up $18 billion, and haircare $38 billion.

— It is growing at up to a 7% rate a year. It is more than twice the rate of the developed world's GDP. Plastic surgery, cosmetics, and dermatologists make billions of dollars a year. A lost human does not know that the devil is playing with their mind and selling the product by convincing they will look beautiful. The Devil also makes people feel ugly and worthless. My friends, do not believe in Satan; You need a dermatologist named Jesus.

Who made your body? Jesus, not Satan, who is messing with your body. How long are you going to live on this earth? All these plastic surgeries and beauty products will harm you. Who cares for you? Only The Lord! Satan will point out your eyes, nose wrinkles, and little details that no one cares about or notices. But you need to change your thinking. Come in God's presence, worship the Lord, read His Word and follow it, pray and fast. Believe me, you will look beautiful. Inner beauty will shine through your face.

Speak to yourself, I am beautiful!

Psalm 140:4 For the LORD taketh pleasure in his people: he will beautify the meek with salvation.

You are the bride of Jesus, and He wants you to look beautiful, not according to the world's standards. Remember, God has made your body and every detail in the body. Satan is the ugliest creature. He makes you feel what he is. All unholy fallen angels are carrying out Satan's plan to make you feel ugly. No, you are beautiful!

Proverb 16:31 The hoary (grey) head is a crown of glory if it is found in the way of righteousness...

When the Lord comes within to deliver you from drugs, alcohol, jealousy, envy, pride, anger, lies, and deceit, you will look beautiful. That is the Lord's job and not anyone's. How long will your beauty last after spending thousands of dollars on plastic and cosmetic surgery? Some are not happy with eye color, skin tone, or whatever. You need to come to the great beautician, Lord Jesus. Come in His presence as Moses did.

Exodus 34:30 And when Aaron and all the children of Israel saw Moses, behold, the skin of his face shone, and they were afraid to come nigh him. 35 And the children of Israel saw the face of Moses, that the skin of Moses' face shone: and Moses put the vail upon his face again, until he went in to speak with him.

The devil is deceiving you by introducing all these eyes, faces, and skin products. We never used all this before. Then why now? As we walk away from the presence of God and believe the deceiving introduction of Satan, we deceive ourselves. Devil deceivers like to steal you and your money from the Lord. God will try your faith on earth. You stand believing and doing what the Lord says. Rest assured, your light will be so blinding that even the devil will tremble in fear and hastily retreat from the luminosity that radiates through you. Remember, the devil was the most beautiful creature of God. When he sinned, he became the ugliest creature. Look around his images of skeletons, ugly, scary, right? Yes, and guess what? He wants you to look like one. God has made you in His image. You do not need help from Satan. Just say I look like my father Jesus; I am beautiful. I made it in His image. Jesus made me beautiful. And I am beautiful inside out.

2 Corinthians 4:16 For which cause we faint not; but though our outward man perishes, yet the inward man is renewed day by day.

Godly aged people look beautiful, even in old age.

Psalm 92:14 They shall still bring forth fruit in old age; they shall be fat and flourishing;

LET US PRAY

May the Lord of heaven give a heavenly touch to beautify us. We are the image of God, and the Lord knows how to make us beautiful. We are His future bride. Lord, Help us keep our self-spotless, without wrinkle and blemish for Him. No one but the Lord knows how to take care of His house and temple, which is our body. Lord, we bring ourselves to your altar as a living sacrifice. We trust you. God made us in His beautiful image. We love you and are praying for you! In Jesus' name. Amen! God bless you.

OCTOBER 2

FINISHED WELL!

We all start, but how we end is most important. Every wedding day is so joyous, but do they finish? And if they do, then how? It is more than something you see in the beginning. It is an important role you have to play when you are going into the race of your life. Think about your life as a race. How did you take each trial, how did you react, and what was the outcome of each trial? When Jesus said it is finished.

John 19:30 When Jesus therefore had received the vinegar, he said, It is finished: and he bowed his head, and gave up the ghost.

He started his life with modesty, being born in a lowly manger and raised by the Carpenter family. There is no significance to His life. But the purpose of life and to make the best out of it are life gaining and crown winning. When Jesus died as a blasphemer, according to the Priest and High Priest who did not know the God walking in flesh. May Lord help us have the right role and not the role of the murder of the truth and God. How sad for those who got positions and powers for self-gain. Our God put on the role of servant and lived and walked as a servant.

Philippians 2:6 Who, being in the form of God, thought it not robbery to be equal with God: 7 But made himself of no reputation, and took upon him the form of a servant, and was made in the likeness of men: 8 And being found in fashion as a man, he humbled himself, and became obedient unto death, even the death of the cross. 9 Wherefore God also hath highly exalted him, and given him a name which is above every name: 10 That at the name of Jesus every knee should bow, of things in heaven, and things in earth, and things under the earth; 11 And that every tongue should confess that Jesus Christ is Lord, to the glory of God the Father.

We all have a call on our life. We must pay attention that once we are baptized in the precious and most powerful name of Jesus Christ, we are in the army of God. No matter what it looks like, we have the victory. We battle in victory. We must know the adversary's devil comes to devour the people of God. Matter of fact, the devil wants to destroy the creation of God. Life trial brings a very crucial time. We will see no way out but wait on the Lord. The Lord who made the way for the Israelites will be with us to do the same.

I was in a wheelchair for a couple of years, and because of the pain, I lost my memory. Words cannot express the agony I was in. I have never taken medicine in all these years. During that time, I did not know the healer Bro. Min exists in this world. But I just had a promise from God that He will bring me out of this long fiery trial. The word of God and the voice of God I trusted.

Proverb 4:12 When thou goest, thy steps shall not be straitened; and when thou runnest, thou shalt not stumble.

I was never curious or questioned God how, but was holding on to the promises. I trust God with all my heart. God, the creator of heaven and earth, gave me a promise. It took years and is still not completely out of it, but I know for sure that God will perform His promises. I do my missionary work having faith in the Lord. I trust in God for my health, finances, and ministry hundred percent. It is not an easy rosy road, but victorious. I do not want to believe after complaining, mourning, and groaning, but before I receive the promises. The Lord said and will work out.

Hebrew 10:37 For yet a little while, and he that shall come will come, and will not tarry. 38 Now the just shall live by faith: but if any man draw back, my soul shall have no pleasure in him. 39 But we are not of them who draw back unto perdition; but of them that believe to the saving of the soul.

Nothing is impossible with our God. It is not a mere empty promise if you keep your faith. Hold on to His word while facing mountains; the flood, no food in the house, losing the job, children being evil, spouses leaving, and many wars around your promises. The scene you can change by speaking your faith to it. Get rich in faith. Get to know your God by seeing His mighty work throughout the Bible. The devil is a liar. Satan has seen heaven; He knows how beautiful it is up there. But he creates the worst pictures. He is a prince of the air and controls the world with his evil plan. But laugh at the devil, remind the cross, show the scripture, and say it is finished. I got my life back.

What happened in the Garden of Eden is done away with Lord Jesus. We lost then, but now the blood speaks better than the blood of animals. Perceive you have more power than the devil. Take charge and command to get out. Bind and rebuke him. Command him to lose your life, finances, family, and country. Break the power of the devil, demons, and fallen angels in the name of Jesus. The day I went into the water, it covered me with His blood. Life is in the blood of Jesus. He paid wages of sin in full. How great it is to know the truth and see the devil put its tail between its legs and run. I have encountered the devil many times and seen them defeated. Not just for me, but for all to whom I minister around the World. God showers us with blessings and grace. The devil is still getting hold of those having the form of godliness and denies the truth. But on the day of judgment, they will not find a way out. Permanent departing to darkness.

2 Peter 2:20 For if after they have escaped the pollutions of the world through the knowledge of the Lord and Saviour Jesus Christ, they are again entangled therein, and overcome, the latter end is worse with them than the beginning. 21 For it had been better for them not to have known the way of righteousness, than, after they have known it, to turn from the holy commandment delivered unto them. 22 But it is happened unto them according to the true proverb, The dog is turned to his own vomit again; and the sow that was washed to her wallowing in the mire.

My dear brothers and sisters, don't think you are smarter than God and have started your mission and made God's blood non-effect by removing the name of Jesus in baptism. Be careful. There is hell where there is no light, all there is torment. Our God did all, and this is the last and the best provision for your and my life. You may feel it is too much, my problem is hard to bear, cannot take any more. Wait on the Lord, He will come and strengthen you, cry out to Him. He will not give you more than you can bear. Do you feel alone? A reminder, He will never leave you or forsake you. He will see you through; it is not my promise but the Lord's. Finish well, there is a crown waiting for you. There is a gold street, and your Lord has created a mansion just for you. Finish well, yes, you can. Blessing.

LET US PRAY

Lord, we thank you for the word of faith. Faith will not bring shame. Faith in God moves the mountain, so shield our faith. Help us, Lord, to stand on over five thousand promises. It is the Lord who can do beyond our imaginations. Our God is reliable and wonderful. No matter what and how it looks, He will give us peace, victory, a solution, and salvation. May the Lord hold our right hand while going through miry clay. He will not let our feet slide. God does not sleep and slumber. Have faith in the Lord. Finish our race like a courageous, bold man. God is going before us to keep us in Jesus's name! Amen! God bless you!

OCTOBER 3

TESTIMONY!

What is the testimony? Why is it necessary? What is it to do with the devil? What is it to do with God's creation? Testimonies are proof or evidence. A written, spoken statement that something is true. The Bible testifies to the One true God. The word of God is the only accurate record of God. You can try His word without altering it and will accomplish what it promises. Just do not dilute, add, or subtract to it.I attended the Pentecostal assembly in the 1980s. I heard them testifying about the goodness of God. Later, the time of testimony disappeared, giving an excuse that it takes too much time. During testimony, people jumped out of their seats to testify. They reveal the legitimacy of the truth of the word. It made people bounce out of their seats and dance, cry, and trust in His precious name and His precious Word. Understand, testimony should not be in for the wall of the buildings but should be everywhere. I testified at my work. My co-workers were on the edge of their seats, eager to uncover the details of my life during that extraordinary situation. I was a living testimony everywhere I went. My interest was to proclaim the name of Jesus. And let people know God is real. His name in the New Testament is Jesus. Jehovah is called Yeshua in the New Testament, which is Jehovah's Savior. He has all the characteristics of the Old Testament plus by giving his blood became a healer, deliverer, and savior. Lord restored the loss of the Garden of Eden. You will understand if you know the meaning of the name Jesus. He is the Son who Isaiah says, the mighty God, the everlasting Father. Long-awaited Jesus.

John 1:45 Philip findeth Nathanael and saith unto him, We have found him, of whom Moses in the law, and the prophets, did write, Jesus of Nazareth, the son of Joseph.

Jesus was the Word manifest in the flesh. Jehovah's Spirit put on flesh for our redemption. To let the devil know I am here, to take back what you stole in the Garden of Eden. It is a new story, only if you identify the Blood hidden behind the name of Jesus and your testimony. You receive testimony by allowing the Lord to take over the reign of your life. It is not about Daniel, Moses, and David, but a greater story than what we read in the Old Testament. How beautiful it is that now we have a loving God living in us called the Holy Spirit. Our story should be new every day. Remember, Jesus said I make all things new and I prefer new. We should have every day new victories, healing, provisions, and amazing experiences altogether. My heart overflows with gratitude for the extraordinary life God has bestowed upon us. Do not preach the ordinary Jesus; He is love; He forgives. Let your testimony be worldwide, written on every billboard, every history, every home, on televisions and media. The media should release your testimony to the world. God is traveling, living in our shadow, our clothing in our spoken Words.

Luke 7:16 And there came a fear on all: and they glorified God, saying, That a great prophet is risen up among us; and, That God hath visited his people.

Luke 5:26 And they were all amazed, and they glorified God, and were filled with fear, saying, We have seen strange things to day.

Matthew 9:8 But when the multitudes saw it, they marvelled, and glorified God, which had given such power unto men.

The people should preach and announce our story.

The testimony is the report or the accurate statement given by others about God. Practice the unadulterated word of God. To obey the Word of God as it is. No one but your life testimony should be the actual picture of God's power. You are the living evidence of God's greatness. Wherever nation or place you live or travel, you will create the story by facing situations, sicknesses, demons, authority, and darkness, by trusting God. It is the report you will tell, and it is the story others will testify. The God of Abraham, Isaac, and Israel is moving and living in us. They took away testimony from the building called the church since it was destroying the kingdom of darkness. Satan disposes of what destroys his kingdom. I will purchase false teachers and prophets at the price they demand. The devil offered millions of cash, take it, but no testimony. Why?

Revelation 12:11 And they overcame him by the blood of the Lamb, and by the word of their testimony; and they loved not their lives unto the death.

Adam and Eve lost their blessings by eating forbidden food. Don't sell your blessings given by the Lord. Be careful speaking against God's anointed.

Psalm 105:15 Saying, Touch not mine anointed, and do my prophets no harm.

If you do then, there will be a demonstration of it. God will show up and show off to take care of the case on behalf of the anointed one.

Esther 5:14 Then said Zeresh his wife and all his friends unto him, Let a gallows be made of fifty cubits high, and to morrow speak thou unto the king that Mordecai may be hanged thereon: then go thou in merrily with the king unto the banquet. And the thing pleased Haman, and he caused the gallows to be made.

God's people will overtake the enemy. A story will be in your favor. Your testimony will have the power of rescuing and overcoming. The story of the enemy will be your story. The enemy will plot against you and will become a victim. It will turn against them. Learn the way of God for the magnificent result. Fear, worry, and anxiety have to depart from you, and let God show up to magnify His glorious name. Your story is about to change; your victory is coming, and the Plan of the enemy is about to destroy. You are going higher, you will be the head, above, highly favored, and first. Receive the testimony, read it, and make it yours.

Esther 6:13 And Haman told Zeresh his wife and all his friends everything that had befallen him. Then said his wise men and Zeresh his wife unto him, If Mordecai be of the seed of the Jews, before whom thou hast begun to fall, thou shalt not prevail against him, but shalt surely fall before him.

The Lord of heaven said, lo I make all things new, give you new victory, healing, new provisions, and deliverance. Your life becomes ordinary to extraordinary. You will testify, I was poor and now I am rich; I was a thief, but now I give. I was a slave, but now Free. Once I was sick and now healed, lame and walk, deaf and now hear, blind and now I see. My testimony in the book "I did it His way" declares how wonderful our God is. Your testimony's record stays on earth forever. Have a great testimony today. Amen!

LET US PRAY

Heavenly Father, our life changes the day we meet our maker. Our life takes an unusual mode. Our life became what he planned before I was born. Lord, you become our way through the truth and life. Lord, we surrender to you to be our master. When we see lion bears, storms, floods, and fire, we speak the name of Jesus to see the mind-blowing testimony. When we see the enemy on each side, we speak the name of Jesus and will see the enemy run away seven ways, drawn in the water, and destroyed. Lord, our testimony can be created by keeping your word as the shield, light, and sword to destroy the enemy. Testimony is the blood against Satan. Help us, Lord, to do what it takes to create our story never heard before, greater than ever in Jesus's name. Amen. God bless you!

OCTOBER 4

UNKNOWN WAY, HOLD HIS HAND!

Many times, we do not know what's happening. Where are we going? What are they saying? But the Lord is the leader, and He is our Guide. The Lord speaks if we hear. He helps us if we allow it. Help us act and react right in our sight when we feel lost. Because many times we have an unknown road, and we do not know the direction. We do not know what decisions to make. But let your spirit lead and guide us, Jesus. Help us, Lord! The road of our life is unknown to us. Life opens up every day, every morning, as we open our eyes. It reveals bit by bit. Let your Spirit make our life a beautiful flower. Beautiful roses! As you bring the sun to shine in our lives, let it give a beautiful breeze and aroma to many who think life is not worth living. Help us incline our ears to know where to stop, go, turn, and run. Lord's ways could be higher, lower, or. Help us, since life is unknown to us. Make it known to us through your Spirit. So we see the blossom in our life. If you see life as a book, and someone is writing your story, then you will be careful. But it is you, with the help of God or you in flesh with Satan's hand, that will bring the two different endings. May the Lord help you understand that life is unknown to you and me. Life has many stages, life has unknown parents and unknown places from the day we are born to the day we die. The Story will make someone happy or sad. It will remember or will burn away in hell. It can make a difference in heaven and on earth. May the almighty who sent you on earth lead your unknown way. It is not an accident that you are here. God Almighty plans for your success. If you let Him lead you through your path, then put your hand in His hand. He knows the way and all the way if you let Him.

Jeremiah 10:23 O Lord, I know that the way of man is not in himself: it is not in man that walketh to direct his steps.

Someone knows that today is their last day on earth, then they will say something best, do something great, and change the course of life. But it is unknown to them. It is the plan and span of life unknown to you. Open your Bible. It is an incredible and enlightening source of knowledge for your unfamiliar way of life. If you want to find every detail, find an altar and say, Lord, I give my life to you, take it all. Do as you please. People are called pilgrims on the earth. We all are pilgrims on the earth. Some make wise decisions to have the Lord be the guide to take them on the journey every day. Our Lord has made no wrong turn, never got lost, or never found confused. May the Lord be the only one in charge of your life. Not even your wife or husband. Have you ever been a visitor to other nations? You know how it feels, so think correctly and go every morning meeting Him and giving your life in His hand. The Lord's goodness envelops you and transports you to a realm of altered reality. You may say, yes, I have written all that I have to do. Rather, say, let me do everything the Lord has written according to His plan. May our life on an unknown path be known and revealed as the flowers or caterpillars meet the butterfly. In life, there are many surprises every day at every stage. From baby to childhood, teenage, young, adult to going down it is all new life unknown road. It will shock and surprise you. Our life has no steady ways, but the Lord is steady, safe, and all-knowing. He will if you put your hand in His hand. It is the most unpredictable way, but the most beautiful way. It will take you places. Just put on a seatbelt. You are flying over, or riding up and down, the mountain of your life. With the Lord as your anchor, you can rest assured that safety and security will be by your side. It is great when they reveal the unknown way by hearing and seeing beyond. I use the word of God to reveal to me the path and plan of God. It is the prayer connection to the Lord to help me find the unknown path.

Every morning brings new grace and mercy, which is the anchor. Travel bit by bit life we live, no hurry to decide. It will open up on every stage you go and every day as you proceed. May the Lord strengthen you through your unknown way. Joseph was in prison.

Genesis 39:20 And Joseph's master took him, and put him into the prison, a place where the king's prisoners were bound: and he was there in the prison.21 But the Lord was with Joseph, and shewed him mercy, and gave him favour in the sight of the keeper of the prison. 22 And the keeper of the prison committed to Joseph's hand all the prisoners that were in the prison; and they did there,he was the doer of it.

Joseph allowed God to take him to the new road. They sold him as a servant in a foreign country with an unknown language.

When God sent me to Texas from California, I came first and was alone but having God with me; I found favor and His mercy. As you know, the adversary has a very discouraging way. But if you just trust the Lord, He knows how and when to defeat the enemy. Just give it to God. Do not see tomorrow, just wait for the finished road, the end of your trip. When Joseph was up next to the Pharaoh, that road he never saw in the jail. While all his brothers were selling him, Joseph saw himself as a helpless slave. Unknown road, He kept God as His guide and anchor

Isaiah 26:3 Thou wilt keep him in perfect peace, whose mind is stayed on thee: because he trusteth in thee.

Proverb 23:18 For surely there is an end; and thine expectation shall not be cut off.

My Lord's truth is your shield and buckler while going through this unknown journey of life. Let the Lord be your guide through the storm, darkness, and uncertainty, and you will find solace. Any time you think you are smarter than God, or you put trust in other than God and His Word, you take it down in your heart, you will lose down the road.

LET US PRAY

Heavenly Father, we come before your altar knowing that life has many difficulties, but life can also bring a steady road if we give it to you. Jesus is the only director of our life. We do not, but He knows all. May your faith be in His ways and paths. He knows the way to green pastures. He knows the quiet way on the bank of the river. It is not you, but the Lord alone can take you. Just another side of the mountain. There is a beautiful city where you can rest. It is the way where the security of angels is given. May our Lord help us through the beautiful, unknown life journey till we finish. May our God be the guide till the day we depart to the heavenly place where we have never been and do not know how to reach there. Our God is the only one who knows how to take you there. Put your hand like a little child in His hand, hold fast and He will take you there in Jesus's name Amen God bless you!

OCTOBER 5

GOD IS UNDER HOUSE ARREST!

The Lord cannot move into His house. You are His house. It is an organized kidnapper who has kidnapped God in His house and arrested Him.

How did it happen? The thief, greedy, jealous, envious, and prideful, took over and voted the Lord out and arrested His Spirit. I have heard some organizations, denominations, and non-denominations wouldn't let you listen to anything or anybody but them. Read and study only what they publish to brainwash but not other good literature. They wouldn't even let you hear what God says. They say what fits their standard. May the Lord help us. Religious leaders have murdered the truth. It is the same old serpent under a different mask, deceiving God's creation. As time passes, we remove truth and compromise little by little. Later, Satan creeps in and removes the Lord, and establishes his throne.

One church invited me when I was visiting India. The main pastor sat on the pulpit with his legs crossed, prompting from the back the Preacher what to do. A student speaker started praying. The pastor said, no. The student pastor stopped and started reading the Bible as the main pastor asked. Where is God? Where is the Holy Ghost? No where near these people. It is all man-made Satan-led collaboration. It is a shame. No one can say one word or they will kick you out. No one cares what God has to do or say for His creation. We see a church building and cross and go there. It is painful when we see this happen to God. God weeps and hurts for His creation, but He is under house arrest, helpless. What thus saith the Lord has no importance, but a religious leader. Leaders in a long robe with a cross on a ribbon hanging around the neck have power over all.

Religious leaders took over God's offices and nothing you could do or say about it. You come sick, then go somewhere to the hospital. We do not allow Jesus to work here to heal, deliver, and set hurting people free. Religious leaders will train communities like dogs and tigers to bite you if you say anything against the organization or leaders. No disciple can cast out a demon, heal the sick, and baptize in Jesus's name to wash away sins. We have all that you need, a false teacher's false prophets-prophetess to misguide people. Jesus is home arrested and we are in charge of His office. A lady was praying in her tongue in the Pentecost church and a church member took her to the bathroom and asked her to be quiet. The unbelievable situation is happening in the churches since you are a church, not a building. The people who held the position have had their rules and regulations, follow them, or get out of the door. All they have is lies and religion. The Lord is under house arrest.

OCTOBER 5

They do not worship the Lord to show up to set people free. They cannot deliver, since no prayer. No gifts of the spirit are in operation to take care of the problem. To find the doctor for help. Many organizations do not know what Jesus is all about. They shot the Lord out a long time ago. They want nothing to do with His work but theirs.

A man went for baptism, and the pastor said, we do not baptize here since the government does not want that. Are you working for the government or Jesus? I replied they do not baptize in Jesus Christ's name since they are the antichrist. May the Lord remove this thief from everywhere. Open your eyes and do not support or listen to them. Open your Bible and learn to take care of God's business. Don't you know who sold God, and the house arrested Him? Not Roman, but high priest and priest. Many women and men are working for Satan, with no spiritual growth. It is the hardest place where demons are in every home. The new religion and new man-made corrupted laws replaced the truth of the Bible. No wonder we do not see the world get excited about Jesus. No one even believes Jesus can deliver since they are an alcoholic, bound with a cigarette, or drug, demon-possessed, and having authority. 2000 years ago, the Lord walked free, but the Romans arrested Him under the influence of toxic religious leaders. The same toxicity is here today. Now it is the same situation. Where is power? There is an influence of the position and power of woman and man, but not the Holy Spirit. The power of religious organizations has arrested God.

Years ago, in the 90s, I was traveling to India; and wanted to find a place where I could pray. I went to the nearby church building and asked the watchman to let me pray there. I prayed till I felt I was full of Spirit and all attacks lifted. The next time I asked them to let me pray, they said the pastor did not want anyone to pray in this building in Ahmedabad city in India. No wonder why their houses have demons, movies, adultery, alcohol, divorces, illnesses, and problems. Prayer is not allowed, but only on Sunday, and one midday, they open the shop for business.

Matthew 21:12 And Jesus went into the temple of God, and cast out all them that sold and bought in the temple, and overthrew the tables of the moneychangers, and the seats of them that sold doves, 13 And said unto them, It is written, My house shall be called the house of prayer; but ye have made it a den of thieves.

After Jesus died, He was not in the building but in you. If you rebuild what He overthrew, then it is called the house of the thief! Satan is a copycat! He replaces the truth to start its activity. May the Lord open your eyes.

Isaiah 66:4 I also will choose their delusions and will bring their fears upon them; because when I called, none did answer; when I spake, they did not hear: but they did evil before mine eyes, and chose that in which I delighted not.

The Word becomes flesh to dwell with us. That word will judge you. If it is me, I will be extra careful about whom I follow. The best thing to do is to let the Lord work in and through me. I want God to be free to move me and guide me so I can magnify Him. I desire, Lord, to be free who makes the world free.

John 12:48 He that rejecteth me, and receiveth not my words, hath one that judgeth him: the word that I have spoken, the same shall judge him on the last day.

The Priest and High Priest arrested our Lord, the one whom He gave the charge. Later, they gave Him the death penalty by crucifying him. We again crucified him by the one who uses the Bible just for personal gain of money and power. Straightforward business! Turn the congregation against those who are casting demons out and preaching the truth. How does the Lord become their slave, and they become master? Simple, when the religious leaders know all but God. These leaders have a lust for flesh, lust for eyes, and pride in life. The Lord has no chance to find work or place in their city, country, denominations, organization, and near them. Isn't that a shame? Do we see every corner of churches, but nowhere, Jesus? He cannot work since He is under house arrest by His people. My Lord, open your eyes to run from false teachers and prophets. Find God on your knee by praying and fasting. You can free Jesus from the false religion jail, false conferences, teachers, and prophets. You preach Jesus by opening blind eyes, a deaf ear, lame walks, and demons come out in His name. Just let Him be free. Amen, God bless you.

LET US PRAY

Heavenly Father, we come before you, knowing you are not free in the building they called churches. The credit goes to the religious societies and denominations that have arrested you. Open everyone's eyes to see you walk city to city, town to town to cast out demons and heal the sick. Our religion, in the name of Christianity, has brought many curses. We know that the truth is to set us free, but we arrested your spirit again to stop your plan. We have rejected you by rejecting the Spirit of God. Let God raise the army, who can fight so you are free to heal, deliver, provide, and much more. The Lord has done all to free us. We want to be free and stay free. The religious denomination and blind leader have destroyed all your purposes. Give us true teachers and prophets, so we experience freedom, in Jesus's name! Amen! God bless you!

OCTOBER 6

REDEEM BY FULFILLING CONDITIONS!

The Bible is full of wonderful promises. Many did what the Lord called them for and saw the fulfillment of the promises. Now, given all promises do not mean they entitle you to it. Even all things available in the store don't mean you can buy them. You need money to buy it. To buy, you need the correct currency as well. I want this does not mean you can have it. Many people are hungry and starving. Why? They lack money to buy food. Same token God has given promises, but you must follow, as it says. Ask help from the Holy Spirit to reveal hidden promises and teach how to receive them.

By the same token; perceive why you are going to church and there is still chaos all around. What is missing? A Christian home, city, or country is suffering from a satanic attack. Why? Find what we must do to recover. Yesterday, I prayed for a lady at my house. Many demons came out of her body. I saw the surrounding darkness. I am glad the lady was humble enough to let me pray when I offered her. Lady said I saw a weird-looking red figure with a horn on the forehead. Praying the second time, she saw another green ugly demon come out. Of course, she saw with spiritual eyes. You can see if your spiritual eyes are open. Demon posses can see the spirit world since demons are the spirit. Lady started crying since she felt much better. How did it happen? It happened since I pray and fast according to the word of God. Now, you are members of the church, and diluting the word will not work. It does not mean the Bible is false. The Bible is the accurate word of God. You need to follow the word as it is. The humble disciple asked a wise question to the Lord about why they couldn't cast out the demon. Additionally, you can question whether the provided biblical promise does not produce. Now do not go to the lost church authorities. The title meant nothing. Many are lost.

Matthew 17:19 Then came the disciples to Jesus apart, and said, Why could not we cast him out? 20 And Jesus said unto them, Because of your unbelief: for verily I say unto you, If ye have faith as a grain of mustard seed, ye shall say unto this mountain, Remove hence to yonder place; and it shall remove; and nothing shall be impossible unto you. 21 Howbeit this kind goeth not out but by prayer and fasting.

The fall cometh by pride or arrogance.

Proverb 16:18 Pride goeth before destruction, and a haughty spirit before a fall.

Proverb 8:13 The fear of the LORD is to hate evil: pride, and arrogancy, and the evil way, and the froward mouth, do I hate.

Proverbs 29:23 A man's pride shall bring him low: but honour shall uphold the humble in spirit.

The opposite of pride is humility. If you are the victim of pride, you will not handle promotion, honor, and elevation. You will come down as you go up. Make sure with all diligence do soul searching to get rid of pride, arrogance, and evil as soon as possible. Let your leaders proclaim the fasting, whole as nations. Not as religious leaders water down fasting by introducing Daniel's diet as. Please follow the fasting recorded in the Bible. Handle your promotion well.

2 Chronicles 7:14 If my people, which are called by my name, shall humble themselves, and pray, and seek my face, and turn from their wicked ways; then will I hear from heaven, and will forgive their sin, and will heal their land.

Do you see why we have many problems on the land? We have a part to do for God to perform the scriptures. Many times I prayed, and people got healed and got excited. A few days later, when the devil comes back, they do not know what to do. You need faith in God rather than the pain. Pain left in Jesus's name does precisely what I did: it works. I put oil, lay my hand, and command pain to leave. It goes out the door. Do you do this? If not, then do not expect to heal. You also can use elders for prayer if they follow Jesus.

James 5:14 Is any sick among you? Let him call for the elders of the church; and let them pray over him, anointing him with oil in the name of the Lord:

Are you calling who? Spiritual elders or doctors? Please do not call anyone who does not know what to do. We are so accurate in the secular world to establish our career, to achieve promotion. We replaced God for the few years of establishment on the earth. In the beginning, the Lord gave us accurate oral instruction, then He gave us the Torah to serve the Holy God. All things are possible if you believe. Believe in exact information and not a fraction. If you perceive the result of your action, then you will do it the best and right. But since you do not know the outcome, you gamble and compromise.

At work, someone questioned me about my hair, jewelry, and clothing, so I explained I follow biblical instructions. I dress up like a lady. I use the cloth to cover my body. Lord showed Adam and Eve. My hair is how ladies' hair should be and jewelry I do not need. God's accepted lifestyle is not what the world accepts. It is hard for someone to even believe it is a sin to dress up like the world. Lady coworker said God is love so He will forgive me if I do not follow God's instruction. Satan knows the Word of God better than you and me. He targets the instruction of God little by little. The world does not define or design my life. My life will receive a reward by doing what is right in the sight of God. God has a book of life; God wrote the names of those who care for His instruction to follow. The Lord will send people to hell if their names are not in the Book of Life. So if you believe this is true, won't you do it? The King of Babylon was judged and thrust out when he used vessels of the Holy Temple of God. What makes you think you are exceptional?

Daniel 5:25 And this is the writing that was written, Mene, Mene, Tekel, Upharsin. 26 This is the interpretation of the thing: Mene; God hath numbered thy kingdom, and finished it. 27 Tekel; Thou art weighed in the balances, and art found wanting. 28 Peres; Thy kingdom is divided, and given to the Medes and Persians. 30 In that night was Belshazzar the king of the Chaldeans slain.

Why is it so hard to obey seeing God's care? Why can't we recognize the truth and the power of the truth? I noticed many religious authorities are working for Satan. Many women go around and help Satan establish the kingdom. They think they are right. I see their life as a mess; life has no progress, but right now they have little position, little power, and little recognition by the religious authority. They do not care what thus saith the Lord. Do not worry about tomorrow. May the Lord protect us from this deceitful man, a woman in power and position. Open your eyes and ears, and open your Bible with the correct word. Learn the Character of

Jesus who is our role model and do it as He did. Let the Holy Spirit be the teacher, the guide to empower you for this temporary, lifelike shadow. May the Lord give you all wisdom and knowledge in Jesus' name. Amen!

LET US PRAY

Heavenly Father, we come before you, knowing all you have said is for our significant benefit, with great interest in our life. Our heavenly father opens our eyes and ears to see the truth of the Word. Your Word is, above all your name, Satan and its followers, called religious groups, target it. We want to follow you and not be deceived by the followers of religious groups. We know no weapon formed against us can prosper. No power of darkness has power over us. We are confident in God's goodness and the magnificent deeds He has undertaken for His creations. Following your words, it has mentioned will and has brought us to the expected result. We want to experience the hidden blessings of the Word by following it. We know the Lord has a narrow road, so we choose to meet you, Lord, in Jesus's name. Amen! God bless you.

OCTOBER 7

TREASURE HIDES IN THE BIBLE!

The Bible is an amazing book. The writer of the Book is the creator of heaven and earth. He needs someone to teach accurately. With no personal interpretations! God-seekers find the treasure. The treasure is not for all who are called but passes all the trials. Trial and test prove your capability and potential for taking responsibility. God prefers one who knows Him, so they can represent Him precisely. The Lord wants to establish His kingdom to defeat Satan liar, deceiver, stealer, killer, and destroyer. Keep the commandments and instructions of God and keep His ways. So you can face any storm, trouble, trial, and opposition. God will let you find His treasure. May the Lord give you an understanding of who He is.

God is the owner.

Deuteronomy 10:14 Behold, the heaven and the heaven of heavens is the LORD'S thy God, the earth also, with all that therein is.

Do not focus on little, focus on all that you desire. We live in such a blessed time. Many times we see places and feel, Wow! I wish I could live in these nations. Why does no one want to move to a third-world country? No one wants to be poor or in want. It is nothing but scarcity and lack. Even Rich cannot get everything since it is not available.

Genesis 1:28 And God blessed them, and God said unto them, Be fruitful, and multiply, and replenish the earth, and subdue it: and have dominion over the fish of the sea, and over the fowl of the air, and over every living thing that moveth upon the earth.

God is an owner of all and can give all if you walk in His conditions. Find the scriptures on how you can turn into rich, have abundance, and have no lack. It is possible. Think about the countries that used to be ordinary and how they became great nations. They found the rich God who gives. Many so-called gods will make nations poor, making worthless customs never come out of debt. Many cultures have the custom of giving a girl a dowry. The birth of the girl is a nightmare. In many countries, they mistreat the girl child. People work day and night, instead of digging through the word of God for their needs. I have seen people work many jobs and are still in debt. Don't have time for the children and later find them victims of bad things, later in jail, and in the end, killed. Dig into the word of God, and find the way to be rich. Rich in spirit, financially rich, and all that can bring wealth into your home.

Proverb 24:4 And by knowledge shall the chambers be filled with all precious and pleasant riches.

King Solomon was wise and full of knowledge. King Solomon asked for knowledge. Knowledge increases wealth.

1 King 10:23 So king Solomon exceeded all the kings of the earth for riches and for wisdom.

Deuteronomy 8:18a But thou shalt remember the Lord thy God: for it is he that giveth thee power to get wealth,

Many poor people, families, and nations find Jesus to have provisions, riches, knowledge, and wisdom.

Revelations 5:12 Saying with a loud voice, Worthy is the Lamb that was slain to receive power, and riches, and wisdom, and strength, and honour, and glory, and blessing.

How great is our God? Our God wants nothing from you, but He will give you your needs and much more since He has it.

Ephesians 3:20 Now unto him that is able to do exceeding abundantly above all that we ask or think, according to the power that worketh in us,

God has all the above. If you want it, just follow the way of God. Your country will be blessed and will never beg.

Deuteronomy 28:12 The Lord shall open unto thee his good treasure, the heaven to give the rain unto thy land in his season, and to bless all the work of thine hand: and thou shalt lend unto many nations, and thou shalt not borrow. 13 And the Lord shall make thee the head, and not the tail; and thou shalt be above only, and thou shalt not be beneath; if that thou hearken unto the commandments of the Lord thy God, which I command thee this day, to observe and to do them:

Lord's knowledge is beyond us. If we follow Him wholeheartedly, then He will give us. May the Lord make us rich in every way. In health, wealth, power, position, knowledge and wisdom, and so on. People who think they are very smart, intelligent, and know all will never learn. They will go poor, and cannot be anything. So when you come to God, come as a student.

Micah 6:8 He hath shewed thee, O man, what is good; and what doth the Lord require of thee, but to do justly, and to love mercy, and to walk humbly with thy God?

Walk gently and not be high-minded. I came to the US almost 40-plus years ago. I have many friends who remember Old America. Even people in their 60s said when we were younger; that the USA was not this rich. A 90-year-old good friend told me we did not have all that we see today. America sought God; they sent a missionary, to help the poor. They blessed Israel. When you bless the people of God, you will be blessed. We must always bless prophets and laborers of God.

Numbers 24:9b Blessed is he that blesseth thee, and cursed is he that curseth thee.

Philippians 4:19 But my God shall supply all your need according to his riches in glory by Christ Jesus.

The key to being wealthy is in the Word of God. People of God will always be wealthy. A nation that serves the Lord will be wealthy. Many sell drugs, pearls, diamonds, and gold, but they are not becoming wealthy.

If you learn the way to be rich through the word of God, then you will be rich. Wealth will multiply. The devil who steals, kills, and destroys will be removed from your territory since God will put a hedge of protection around you.

Job 1:10 Hast not thou made an hedge about him, and about his house, and about all that he hath on every side? thou hast blessed the work of his hands, and it increased his substance in the land.

Why did Job have all this? The Man who is righteous like Job will be blessed and wealthy. A nation whose laws are righteous will also be wealthy. May the Lord give you the key to wealth, knowledge, wisdom, and riches in Jesus's name. Amen.

LET US PRAY

Heavenly Father God is not only rich in heaven, but also He made earth very rich for the God seeker and God-fearing people. Fear God and walk in His path to receive all wealth and blessing. The blessing of God will keep the wealth of the Lord. Heavenly Father, we know there is nothing impossible if we humbly come and walk right in your sight. May the Lord give us the true teachers and prophets who know how to bring us to the promised land. Lord, we cannot come there. We need your help. Lord, teach us your way and desire to continue in it. Our God never wanted us to be poor but rich. We know we hold the key, so the Lord gives us the wisdom to open the hidden treasure. Lord, give us a generous heart to receive overflowing in abundance. We need the key to open all hidden treasures around us, in Jesus's name. Amen. God bless you.

OCTOBER 8

THE BATTLE BELONGS TO THE LORD!

The battle over our souls, lives, children, and what belongs to us. But if we have the Lord, then He will fight our battle. It is His responsibility to fight for us if we surrender to Him. The Lord has many angels who will be in charge to come against the plan and strategy of Satan. Satan targets and declares war against God's children and God's creations. May the Lord help us understand that an unseen enemy has a plan to steal, kill, and destroy what belongs to us. This war has an enemy who is unseen by our naked eyes. It is a spiritual being coming against us to block, stop, and hinder. Only Jesus can protect us if we obey, follow, and believe in Him.

One time I was in the post office and a co-worker lady, who was not even a Christian, looked up in the air and said there was something in this place. She said, I come here and feel oppressed. It is the place where I worked for almost 20 years. It is the place where I had a major battle, a major victory, dreams, and visions. I learn about powerful demonic operations and how to battle. The Lord asked me not to take that job. But I thought God wanted me to have this job since I had 100% in written and machine tests. I just started learning the biblical truth and did not understand the spiritual world.

Most organizations, denominations, and non-denominations do not know about the spiritual battle. They fight in the flesh. People will attack you in the group using their power of position. They use bad words and hold grudges. Their mentality is I will do the worst if they do wrong to me. That is called retaliation. Wicked will fight with a gun, knife, hand, or indirect persecution. But this battle of ours is not the battle with flesh and blood but against the prince, Satan. Fallen angels are called principalities and the demons are dead lost spirits. These cause mental, physical, and emotional pain to humankind. All have a distinct part or role to play in God's creation. They are called territorial demons. A familiar spirit is the demons of your family who died. The wandering demons want to fight. It was the time I was going through many battles since I was learning the truth. As you know, I hate religion. Religions, denominations, and organizations are the blockers, stoppers, and hinderers of the truth of God.

Our God wants to be in charge of your life if you let Him.

Exodus 14:14 The Lord shall fight for you, and ye shall hold your peace.

1 Samuel 17:47 And all this assembly shall know that the Lord saveth not with sword and spear: for the battle is the Lord's, and he will give you into our hands.

Unseen enemies are all around you, and you must look to God for help.

Many times, the enemy holds grudges for the generations since they do not know they have been poisoned. The Word of God is true. It can bring you out of the lie of the enemy. His truth is our shield and buckler. The truth can set us free from the opponent's power, plan, bondages, and whatnot. May the Lord teach us how to battle in prayer on our knees. Our knees have forgotten how to battle. In this world, we have trained the Army, Navy, Marine, and military so that we don't worry. We have the best machinery, so we forgot to pray to God who brings us victory. I have very little knowledge of the battle since I do not have a TV. One time, a person was upset that I was not involved in the Battle of the Nations. So when the Lord moved on me, I prayed and they won the battle. I saw the yellow ribbon on every tree. But the man was fleshly, not understanding that I move by the Spirit and not by his feelings. He wanted me to be involved since his blood was boiling with emotion. He put the flag and brought the flag to the church. I wish He would have put people on fasting and prayer. Any battle needs the Lord. Every battle starts with the devil.

War is against our youth, our children, marriages, wealth, health, prosperity, you name it. The person who is deeply connected to the spiritual realm understands the significance of prayer and fasting and is profoundly attuned to the subtle movements of the spirit, will be the one to emerge victorious in the battle. May the Lord make you a warrior on the knee, to come against all daemonic operations over the land, state, county, city, and home. May I suggest to you, please pray, pray as you have never prayed? Play shofar, release the word of God in the air, and make it clear to the enemy that our warfare is not carnal but mighty through God.

2 Corinthians 10:4 (For the weapons of our warfare are not carnal, but mighty through God to the pulling down of strong holds;)

Stand looking in the air, stretch forth your hand, and bind Satan. The power and authority of Satan, fallen angels, and demons destroy in the name of Jesus.

One particular lady has done all this. The drug demons of her family were out the door. The family is free now. A Lady in Asia testified that there are no ambulances, witch doctors, and fights in that town since she anoints and prays early in the morning. Go stand in all directions, first bind, then command those demons to leave, break the power of it. May the Lord go before you to prove to you how mighty He is. It is a spiritual battle. Use the Word, which is spirit, as you speak with authority. Word is God. God is Spirit. So as you speak the Word, those words will create what it meant to create.

No weapons formed against me can prosper. It will perform the same. All weapons of the enemy will collapse. All power of darkness will be destroyed. See, the power is in the Word of God; the Word is above all His name since the Word is God.

John 1:1 In the beginning was the Word, and the Word was with God, and the Word was God.

The Lord fights our battle rather than us by our fists or carnal flesh. The very work of Satan can be reversed back to Him only if you know how to.

Ephesians 6:10 Finally, my brethren, be strong in the Lord, and in the power of his might.

Deuteronomy: 32:30 How should one chase a thousand, and two put ten thousand to flight, except their Rock had sold them, and the LORD had shut them up?

The Lord must go before you and teach you what to do to win the battle. May the Lord declare when to fight. Let all be done under His guidance and He will destroy the enemy's might and power. Let me advise you to bring your battle to His altar and pray. Use anointed oil over the area where your battle is. If it is an office, city, or home, use anointed oil and destroy it. I play shofar to destroy demons' power. Send the correct word of God and let it swing against the enemy to destroy. May the Lord help you today to connect with Him on your knees and give you perfect peace and victory.

I proclaim victory over all battles. In the victorious, mighty name of Jesus. Amen! God Bless You!

LET US PRAY

Heavenly Father, we come to you and bring all our battles to the Altar of God. Show our fingers how to fight. Give us the correct word of God to consume the enemy. Blind the Devil and consume it with your spirit. It is the battle against the enemy to destroy all its strategies. We have the power, but many do not know how to use it. We lack the knowledge and so we perish. But Lord, we want to give you glory, honor, and praise by winning every battle of sickness and oppression. Help us against powerful forces flooding the nations at this end of time. Move in our hearts and teach us truth through the Word, since we depend on you. You go before us; we follow you. You hide us from the enemy. Let your name be the strong tower. We have the Name Jesus above all names. Thank you, Lord, God bless you, Amen!

OCTOBER 9

CELEBRATE JESUS!

Being Christian, we should celebrate victory every day. We see the world celebrate unique achievements. They achieve their performance, and they celebrate. We Christians should be at that level to celebrate Jesus. When Esther became the queen, she used her power and favors to help her people. Being sold to the slave was ok but being sold for slaughter was not ok. She said I would give my life to my people. She knew so many things likely to put her life in jeopardy. One of them was fasting. Babylonia did not know she was a Jewish slave. Being the queen, she also has to follow the rule of the king. She cannot go in and out to meet the King. Many things were not favorable, but she took the risk of rescuing her people. Because of her wise act of rescuing her people, the World celebrates the victory of Purim.

Esther 9:17 On the thirteenth day of the month Adar; and on the fourteenth day of the same rested they, and made it a day of feasting and gladness.18 But the Jews that were at Shushan assembled together on the thirteenth day thereof, and on the fourteenth thereof; and on the fifteenth day of the same they rested, and made it a day of feasting and gladness.19 Therefore the Jews of the villages, that dwelt in the unwalled towns, made the fourteenth day of the month Adar a day of gladness and feasting, and a good day, and of sending portions from one to another.

This is the time many countries celebrate Halloween, and people in some other countries dance before idols. During this season, much idolatry and adultery. We see the world is suffering today. They slaughter Christians everywhere. We must rise and proclaim fasting and prayer for suffering Christians. Today someone sent me a message. Please pray for my sister. Her husband beat her up for believing in Jesus. Last year, the antichrist group beat one pastor up for sharing the gospel. He lost some memories. He won them to Christ, who harmed him and forgave them. God works in their heart if we forgive and pray for them.

So He asked me to pray for these people. We Christians must celebrate many, many victories over Satan. We must rise as present-day Mordecai and Esther to come against persecution happening in different places in the World. Would you rise to pray and fast when you see our Christian brothers and sisters being killed and persecuted?

Esther 4:1 "When Mordecai perceived all that was done, Mordecai rent his clothes, and put on sackcloth with ashes, and went out into the midst of the city, and cried with a loud and a bitter cry;"

This is what we must do before we get the victory. We need to become a present-day Esther to rise and proclaim fasting.

Esther 4:15 Then Esther bade them return Mordecai this answer, 16 Go, gather together all the Jews that are present in Shushan, and fast ye for me, and neither eat nor drink three days, night or day: I also and my maidens will fast likewise; and so will I go in unto the king, which is not according to the law: and if I perish, I perish.

Remember, you need a reason for celebrations. Celebrate your life, achievement, and victory over the battle. Christian should celebrate victory over the devil all the time. Isn't this obvious? We will watch the devil put to the worst defeat. Time to rejoice and dance when we see slaves get freedom. Same way, nations celebrate the day of freedom. Hebrews were slaves under Pharaoh in Egypt for 430 years. When the Lord delivered them from slavery, they celebrated. Later, Egypt tried to get them back, but The Lord was on their side.

Exodus 14:7 And he took six hundred chosen chariots, and all the chariots of Egypt, and captains over every one of them. 8 And the Lord hardened the heart of Pharaoh king of Egypt, and he pursued after the children of Israel: and the children of Israel went out with an high hand.

Lord, is called the way maker, made the way in the ocean.

Exodus 14: 27 And Moses stretched forth his hand over the sea, and the sea returned to his strength when the morning appeared; and the Egyptians fled against it; and the Lord overthrew the Egyptians in the midst of the sea. 28 And the waters returned, and covered the chariots, and the horsemen, and all the host of Pharaoh that came into the sea after them; there remained not so much as one of them.

Our Lord can give many celebration days like this if we go to Him and cry out. Do not bury your privileges, deliverance, healing, promotions, and victories over the enemy. Chapter 15 of Exodus celebrates the victory over the enemy.

Exodus 15:1 Then sang Moses and the children of Israel this song unto the Lord, and spake, saying, I will sing unto the Lord, for he hath triumphed gloriously: the horse and his rider hath he thrown into the sea.

Our Lord is incredible! He wants to give us nothing but victory and defeat for the enemy. Victory to those who allow God to fight the battle. It is time for us to wake up. We need a worldwide revival. We need worldwide delivery like Moses, Joshua, Esther, and Mordecai. May the Lord wake us up and do what it takes. Call fasting and prayer, cry out for the land, losing the battle. May the Lord use you as a distance warrior to send the powerful prayer missiles. Target the enemy. Target those witches, warlocks, the devil, fallen angels, and rulers of the nations to let them know; that I am coming in the Name of my God. He is our banner. He will win. Look up, your redeemer draweth nigh. Fear gripped the hearts of the Israelites when they faced Goliath. But David, a shepherd young boy's blood, boiled up as he heard someone speak against their God. David said who are these unclean lips talking against my God?''

1 Samuel 17:45 Then said David to the Philistine, Thou comest to me with a sword, and with a spear, and with a shield: but I come to thee in the name of the Lord of hosts, the God of the armies of Israel, whom thou hast defied. 47 And all this assembly shall know that the Lord saveth not with sword and spear: for the battle is the Lord's, and he will give you into our hands.

That day, David killed Goliath, and they rescued the Israelites from the Philistines.

1 Samuel 17:52 And the men of Israel and of Judah arose, and shouted, and pursued the Philistines, until thou come to the valley, and to the gates of Ekron. And the wounded of the Philistines fell down by the way to Shaaraim, even unto Gath, and unto Ekron.

We can also celebrate once we know how to. May the Lord give you many celebrations in the coming year, in Jesus' name. Amen.

LET US PRAY

Our heavenly Father, we celebrate for every breath we take. To see another day is for another victory.

Help us celebrate Jesus, not for good only but also for bad, since we know all things happen for those who are called for you. We ask you to bless us every day and give us the strength to carry on our life as victorious children of God, in Jesus's name. Amen! God bless you.

OCTOBER 10

REASON TO CHOOSE RELIGIONS!

Why do people choose religions, churches, denominations, and organizations over Jesus? Why did Eve and Adam Choose fruit over Lord's Commandment? To satisfy the lust of eyes, flesh, and pride of life. Why do people choose the king over, Lord Jehovah God?

1 Samuel 8:4 Then all the elders of Israel gathered themselves together, and came to Samuel unto Ramah, 5 And said unto him, Behold, thou art old, and thy sons walk not in thy ways: now make us a king to judge us like all the nations. 6 But the thing displeased Samuel, when they said, Give us a king to judge us. And Samuel prayed unto the Lord. 7 And the Lord said unto Samuel, Hearken unto the voice of the people in all that they say unto thee: for they have not rejected thee, but they have rejected me, that I should not reign over them.

The Lord warns of the cruelty and harshness of the King toward them.

Listen to their answers.

1 Samuel 8:19 Nevertheless the people refused to obey the voice of Samuel; and they said, Nay; but we will have a king over us; 20 That we also may be like all the nations; and that our king may judge us, and go out before us, and fight our battles.

The Lord did all for us as our Father. In the end, He came to redeem us from hell by paying the price of sin. He paid in full for our sins by shedding His blood. Life is in the blood, so He gave His Blood to redeem us from hell. Now it is the same, we reject His blood. Are you curious about how we reject His blood? Let me show you how. We deny Jesus as the only God Jehovah manifested in the Flesh. Satan did a great job by removing God by inserting He.

1 Timothy 3:16 God was manifest in the flesh, (instead, it says, He was revealed in the flesh,)

Good job devil. Many, like Adam, Eve, and the Israelites who rejected God by asking for a king, are here today. That spirit continues living on earth, rejecting the plan of God in every era. It is the flesh that rejects the Lord. Human flesh and spirit work contrary to each other. May the Lord give us a heavenly sight with desire and visions. Love your soul more than flesh. The flesh is only living for 70 or by strength in the 80s.' It will be back to dust. No matter what God did for us, we choose religion over God. God has given humanity one power, which is to choose life or death and blessing or cursing. And we choose wrong all the time. No matter what, we reject the one who has the best interest in our being. God desires to bless you by giving us abundance. Our God is benevolent, and He only brings about positive outcomes. May the Lord put the love for self in our hearts. We must love ourselves since there is a life after this earthly limited life. When you do not know, then please ask God what to choose.

The United States was where I came to seek God. I sought God with all my heart, mind, soul, and strength. I found the truth; it was hidden. God asked me to be baptized. As I came out of the water, I got remission of sin by using the name Jesus. Under the name of Jesus, there is precious cleansing blood hidden. The name of Jesus is above all names. I wrestled with uncertainty, unsure whether to proceed with baptism in the name of Jesus, given my unfamiliarity with supporting scripture. The false teachers bewitched me. I needed deliverance from the false teaching of baptism. I honor and glorify the name of Jesus, acknowledging His worth.

I embraced the challenge, showing unwavering bravery and a lack of fear of being abandoned. I was never afraid of rejection. No one can blackmail me, since I sold out to God with my reputation, like Mary. Hey, God is real, and He fights our battle. I am never alone. He is with me. He is greater than anyone. As they baptized me in Jesus's name, I came out free from the power, grip, and heaviness of sins. No matter what, I was ready to pay the price.

It is easy when we join religious groups. You will not be crucified, but I was not afraid of the crucifixion of self. The soul needs protection against the devil, false teachers, false prophets, and our flesh. I stood up for the truth and started preaching against the enemy. Many generations have been misguided by baptizing them by the title father, son, and Holy Spirit. They argue, saying that Jesus said Father, Son, and Holy Spirit. Who wrote the Bible? The only God, Jesus, no one but Him. The enemy gives another lie. Our Lord possesses an extraordinary talent for shielding the truth from those who wander astray. Find out how they practiced the name of baptism in the book of Acts and the history of the former church. It is the only record you believe.

The gates of Hell cannot prevail. The Liar devil said it is ok, believes Jesus, and uses the title. I dislike the blood coming on you when you are buried in baptism in Jesus' name. I dislike seeing you put on Jesus. The blood makes me work harder. So all set, now the man-made organizations, denominations, and non-denomination have complete power over us. It will allow your flesh to live as pleases you and not God. Make sure you are fair to the soul. The body will be dust, the spirit will go back to God, but what about your soul? It will suffer forever. I remember the religious leaders, how they gave flower garlands and welcomed the people who came from abroad. Why? They love your money and not the soul. Under-covered enemy of your soul.

2 Corinthians 11:13 For such are false apostles, deceitful workers, transforming themselves into the apostles of Christ. 14 And no marvel; for Satan himself is transformed into an angel of light. 15 Therefore it is no great thing if his ministers also be transformed as the ministers of righteousness; whose end shall be according to their works.

We know the Lord is good and has given some

Ephesians 4:11 And he gave some, apostles; and some, prophets; and some, evangelists; and some, pastors and teachers;12 For the perfecting of the saints, for the work of the ministry, for the edifying of the body of Christ:

Remember, God warned us against false teachers and prophets. So love yourself. Banish the fear of rejection and the dread of being alone from your mind. I am always alone, but never alone. I have God all the time. Our God is wonderful. He has created angels for our services. Last, God sent me to the church in Dallas, which was far from my city. I watched and listened to what I was taught. Now you say how we can be bewitched or poisoned? By those who are not seeking God and His will. Fasting and prayer connect us with God. Many are so lost that you would rather not go there. You will get religious diseases. Believe me, Jesus was the cure for that demon of the jealous, envious, power-hungry, greedy authorities. But rather than receiving the cure, they gave 39 stripes and crucified Him.

You might say how sad, I wouldn't do it. You wouldn't know that you are one of them if you were sitting under false teachers and prophets. So go back to the Bible and receive the Holy Spirit as I poured it out on a day of Pentecost. You will be led, empowered, guided, and taught by the Holy Spirit only if you give Him liberty. Remove religions and start a relationship with your maker by repenting and baptizing in Jesus' name to wash away your sins. Receive the Holy Spirit by speaking in tongue. Amen!

LET US PRAY

We thank you, Lord, for not giving up on us. Our God is outstanding and deserving of abundant praise. Our God has given us the blood for our sins. Help us not to reject it by rejecting the name of Jesus in baptism. Lord, help us love the truth to be set free. It is the only way we can get our relationship back to what we lost in the Garden of Eden. Put love for you more than religion. We know religion is substituting a relation with a living God. We know it is the form of godliness without the power of the Holy Spirit. The truth possesses an unparalleled strength to deliver, heal, and liberate us. Please put love for you in our hearts. If we love you, then you will reveal and manifest yourself as you did to Paul, Peter, and many others. We desire a new beginning in Jesus's name! Amen! God bless you!

OCTOBER 11

RAISE GOD'S GIVEN CHILDREN FOR GOD!

Many selfish parents use their children for their benefit. If they have problems with others, then they will use their children's mouths against them. Isn't it so sad? Why are children evil? Listen to their private conversations with children's ears. You will be surprised. God has blessed you with children. But please don't ruin their life. God gave you the responsibility to educate children in righteousness. Equip them with the sacred teachings, so they can flourish and prosper in any location across the globe. Many parents use them for their nasty ways and evil purposes. Some mothers raise their children against their fathers and in-laws. Is it going to work? A wicked mother raising her daughters in a nasty way for her benefit, but not for their future marriage and children. The wicked mother milks her daughter for the support of the family. This wicked daughter will not be appropriate to her husband or her in-laws. She will be the thorn in the side. There will be a war in the family. A curse will sprout in the family. My Lord, give us the perception before picking a wife. You pray and fast and let God do Him the rest. God designed the family to multiply. It is for His service and not your personal feelings and evil plans. Your thoughts are most dangerous to you and your children. Let us just follow the plan of God.

Psalm 127:3 Lo, children are an heritage of the Lord: and the fruit of the womb is his reward. May the Lord give you His wisdom to raise the children.

Many wicked people raise their children just like them.

Psalm 58:3 The wicked are estranged from the womb: they go astray as soon as they be born, speaking lies. We have the sinful blood of Adam. We know good and evil, not innocent anymore. If we don't teach the truth, then children will manifest sin as they grow older. God gave you the responsibility of your children. Raise them right, and correct them when they need correction. They can receive blessings but depend on their parents' raise.

Proverb 23:13 Withhold not correction from the child: for if thou beatest him with the rod, he shall not die.

Teach them the Word of God, the commandment of God, practice, and give them the truth. Ultimately, these children have to stand in the world. When you do right to them, then they will not end up in jail, prison, on drugs, alcohol, gangster, rapist, and much more. What you put in their ear will sprout. You poison with your wickedness, or you plant the life-giving word of God in their ear, it will produce. Parents raise children. If they are bad, go look in the mirror, and blame yourself and not your neighbor.

OCTOBER 11

Deuteronomy 6:7 And thou shalt teach them diligently unto thy children, and shalt talk of them when thou sittest in thine house, and when thou walkest by the way, and when thou liest down, and when thou risest up.

Many parents take responsibility for their education, but not for the word of God. Sunday school is not enough. God is a provider and will provide if we raise God-fearing children. Teach children how to practice the Word of God.

Joshua 8:35 There was not a word of all that Moses commanded, which Joshua read not before all the congregation of Israel, with the women, and the little ones, and the strangers that were conversant among them.

Joshua 1:8 This book of the law shall not depart out of thy mouth; but thou shalt meditate therein day and night, that thou mayest observe to do according to all that is written therein: for then thou shalt make thy way prosperous, and then thou shalt have outstanding success.

Their success is assured through the dedicated practice of Word. They will be head, never tail. They will be above and never beneath, and first and never last. Success is a natural outcome for children who receive a good upbringing. Knowing right from wrong, Joseph told the woman that I could not sin against God. Sin is against God. Breaking the laws of God is a sin. The wages of sin are death, that is the punishment in hell.

Genesis 39:9 There is none greater in this house than I; neither hath he kept back any thing from me but thee, because thou art his wife: how then can I do this great wickedness, and sin against God?

Honoring God by keeping His commandment, God promoted Joseph next to the Pharaoh. It is the Lord who gives the promotion. Parents do not poison children with evil. Do not teach them to be haters, liars, adulterers, and fornicators. Who taught Joseph the laws of God? His parents. Moses, the mighty man in Egypt, rejected the throne. Why? He knew he had a real God. He revered God by fearing Him. God used Moses to deliver the Hebrews from the Egyptians. May the Lord give you wisdom on how to raise your children. It is a tough world, but your job is to teach the word of God. Many great people like Paul, Matthew, Andrew Simon Peter, and people whom Jesus picked to be His disciples. They were raised by the mother to serve God and not the organization, denomination, non-denomination, or synagogue. Do not raise them for your belly, wicked, alcoholic, and one who can work for you. Most selfish, ignorant parents do that to their children. They are responsible for their soul if it burn in hell. May the Lord give you love for your children to raise them right.

God promises He will bless, provide, and keep you if you keep His commandments, statutes, laws, and precepts. The Lord owns them, so take care of them. Many have done the most wonderful job of raising, and I admire them.One of them was the Ruth Moabites. God had to bring the great-grandmother from Moab, who valued God. Ruth Moabite loved the ways of God. She was not born and raised in it, but she chose to serve the living God by learning from her mother-in-law. Mother-in-law Naomi was her teacher; she taught the laws of Jehovah God, and she followed and never bargained.I had the most wonderful parents who raised us confident, courageous, and true to the Lord. I loved their lifestyle. We shared everything with Mom and she always advised us. She was not just an ordinary pastor's daughter, but a mighty righteous woman who did right and taught us right. May the Lord give us mothers whose interest is in children's soul welfare. May the Lord give us mothers like Jochebed, Mary, Ruth, Naomi, and many like them. These mothers are accurate in teaching children the Word of God and not the ways of the World. God bless righteous parents.

LET US PRAY

Our heavenly Father, we thank you for the children you have given us. It is our responsibility to train and teach them the oracle of God. Our responsibility is to show them the way of God. God gives us a sense of responsibility with wisdom, so we do our best. Our children are the head and not in prison, alcoholic wicked. Let us be day and night praying, Mother, to keep them in the right direction. The mother who stays on the knee keeps their children from the hand of Satan and its tactics. We want fearless children of lions, fire, trial, and trouble, but to be valiant, courageous, and blessed by the Lord. In Jesus' name! Amen! God bless you!

OCTOBER 12

REPETITION MAKES US PERFECT!

Repetitions of action have a goal to improve. If you want to improve, you must practice. Not a few times, but continue every day. When I read the Bible every day, it gives a unique understanding each time. My mom said that when I read the Bible all over again, I find something I did not get last time. True, reading the word and practicing it gives us a greater understanding. Our God has given the life-changing, life-giving Word. Our God does not want us to stagnate or be paralyzed. We keep our hand or any part of the body in one position, then it becomes difficult to maneuver. But keeping moving is the key. Same way, when we practice the word of God, it becomes easy.

1 Timothy 4:8 For bodily exercise profiteth little: but godliness is profitable unto all things, having promise of the life that now is, and of that which is to come. 9 This is a faithful saying and worthy of all acceptation.

People of God must continue reading the word, meditating, and practicing. If you know the word, then you will know how to apply it when it's required.

Psalm 19:7 The law of the Lord is perfect, converting the soul: the testimony of the Lord is sure, making wise the simple. 8 The statutes of the Lord are right, rejoicing in the heart: the commandment of the Lord is pure, enlightening the eyes.

Doesn't this sound good? Who wouldn't like to be perfect, wise, right, with joy in the heart, and pure? All are to receive if we know the laws, statutes, commandments, and testimony of God. It is the Lord's provision that on earth we practice not the law of the nation but the Law of the Lord. Paul was an expert in the Torah and needed some correction of understanding. I have seen many Muslims pray five times a day. Christian practice if they like. The Bible says.

1 Thessalonians 5:17 Pray without ceasing.1 Timothy 2:1 I exhort therefore, that, first of all, supplications, prayers, intercessions, and giving of thanks, be made for all men;

Psalm 63:1a O God, thou art my God; early will I seek thee:

That means getting up early in the morning and seeking HIM. The Bible says I will pray morning, noon, and evening. So as you enter each part of the day, you are entering with prayer. Do you practice this? Three times was in the Old Testament, but now we pray without ceasing.

Psalm 55:17 Evening, and morning, and at noon, will I pray, and cry aloud: and he shall hear my voice.

Daniel 6:10 Now when Daniel knew that the writing was signed, he went into his house; and his windows being open in his chamber toward Jerusalem, he kneeled upon his knees three times a day, and prayed, and gave thanks before his God, as he did aforetime.

Persistent prayer made it easy for Daniel to go into the lion's den. Daniel practiced and had a spiritual muscle. Practice gives us spiritual muscles. The Lord has given us the Word of God, and we have to practice it in everyday life. When people practice not to lie, it is easy for them not to. Once you know the truth, then you do it. If you do, when the trial or trouble comes, it will not harm you since you are practicing what is right according to the truth. David continued practicing the truth.

1 Samuel 24:4 And the men of David said unto him, Behold the day of which the Lord said unto thee, Behold, I will deliver thine enemy into thine hand, that thou mayest do to him as it shall seem good unto thee. Then David arose and cut off the skirt of Saul's robe privily. 5 And it came to pass afterward, that David's heart smote him because he had cut off Saul's skirt.

They classified David as ten thousand, but King Saul was a thousand. The man who can kill ten thousand, for him to King Saul, was the piece of cake. But He said

6 And he said unto his men, The Lord forbid I should do this thing unto my master, the Lord's anointed, to stretch forth my hand against him, seeing he is the anointed of the Lord.

A man who practices the word of God is perfect in his lifestyle. You can achieve the best medal, and prizes, be first, above and head. Practice that makes you perfect.

Judges 20:16 Among all this people there were seven hundred chosen men lefthanded; every one could sling stones at an hair breadth, and not miss.

1 Chronicle 12:2 They were armed with bows, and could use both the right hand and the left in hurling stones and shooting arrows out of a bow, even of Saul's brethren of Benjamin.

How were they so accurate? They practiced, and they became the hairline accurate. Who gets all the trophies? The one who practices. If you live and practice the word of God, then you will be the best Christian. Christianity is the everyday practice for the best result. If you miss, you lose the life game. Once lost, get a chance again if they repent. Repent and Baptize in Jesus' name and try again. Practice warfare on your knees with fasting. We must practice the righteousness of God to come against Satan. Learn which sword to swing against the enemy, and then you will cut Satan off. All done in faith. It will bring you glorious victory. Following biblical fasting and prayer will lead you to success.

The winner does not need to learn to sling but learn to pray as Jesus did. It is there in the word of God. One time at work, a lady asked me to pray for her friend who also was working in the Post Office. She knew I practiced Christianity. I always lay my hands on people when they come for prayer. She asked for prayers many times and experienced healing. But this time she said just pray for my friend. He couldn't sleep for months. He is now taking the highest doses of medication. So I said Okay. As I started praying, I started hearing someone clapping or screaming in my ear. I felt strange. I kept praying, not understanding why I was experiencing spiritual unrest. Once I came home from church and was resting in bed. With my eyes closed, I saw the demon walking out of the wall from head to side. Instantly, I bound the demon and broke its power, and perceived it was broken. I couldn't understand it at that very moment. So, in prayer, I asked the Lord what happened. Lord said it was the warfare you did for the man you were praying for. The next time I met the lady, I asked her to check on her friend. She said he was sleeping well at night without medication. A week later, he came to my department to thank me. Later, I gave Him the Chinese/English parallel Bible. See, we must practice our assignment. If we do, this hospital will close, and people will know that Christianity is real. I learn from this battle by praying for him. Let us practice; repetition makes us perfect. Amen!

LET US PRAY

Lord, help not to forget to cast out demons, heal the sick, raise the dead, cleanse the leopards, and then preach Jesus. We forgot to continue this Gospel with signs and wonder. We forgot to practice what you asked us to do everywhere we went. Help us be familiar with the assignment that you have given us. Our job needs practice to be perfect. Without that, we will have religions. We must follow you, knowing Jesus is the same yesterday, today, and forever. May the Lord give us the wonder-working power to continue every day what it takes to be a perfect Christian. Our life is the light, a lamp, an example of many lost in this world. You have ordered, and we are not living in it. Forgive us, Lord, we want to turn and do right in Jesus's name! Amen! God bless you!

OCTOBER 13

HAVE YOU PREPARED YOURSELF?

It is both ways, the one who delivers the message and the one who comes to receive what God is delivering must prepare. God needs the vessel to use.

2 Timothy 2:20 But in a great house there are not only vessels of gold and of silver, but also of wood and of earth; and some to honour, and some to dishonour.

When God is using you, He also gives you favor. I see many being used by the Lord and also honored by the people. Especially in the African Nation! They reverence pastors, preachers, evangelists, etc. There is such a hunger and thirst in them. Of course, some hypocrites also criticize. They are like priests and High Priests, jealous, greedy, arrogant, and prideful. Hypocrites were upset with all that Jesus did. So we have the same situation today for the same spirit. Many cannot recognize God working through this mighty prophet and the people of God. They hinder the work of God. It will never bless them since they cannot recognize God in them.

God only uses the vessel prepared for Him and Him only. Peter, Paul, John, and many others prepared for the lord. And their shadow, clothes, and touch, God used to heal people. Why? Because they walk close to God, pray, and fast that the spirit of God is in it. Spirit dwells in the cloth, shadow, and everything that they touch. Isn't that great? God uses us if we prepare ourselves. I always honor the genuine man of God. True prophets and teachers have the authority to bring blessings.

Matthew 10:41 He that receiveth a prophet in the name of a prophet shall receive a prophet's reward; and he that receiveth a righteous man in the name of a righteous man shall receive a righteous man's reward.

Now the one who never wins one soul has many problems. They cannot reverence anyone but the one who believes in the man of God accepts and receives healing. But a critic will lose the blessings. Prepare yourself to receive the blessing. God's people are valiant. Don't come to see the man but the man of God. I am crazy about the anointed man of God. They have power and authority. Many never received healing or deliverance since they do not reverence the anointed people of God. There is a difference between people and anointed people of God. God uses them and if you can't accept them, it means you are not accepting blessings. Jesus took stripes 2000 years ago, but you cannot get healing since you have no respect for the people of God whom He is using today. You are not respecting God by not respecting true prophets and teachers. May the Lord change your mind. Get rid of your critical nature.

OCTOBER 13

Roman 13:1 Let every soul be subject unto the higher powers. For there is no power but of God: the powers that be are ordained of God. 2 Whosoever therefore resisteth the power, resisteth the ordinance of God: and they that resist shall receive to themselves damnation. 3 For rulers are not a terror to good works, but to the evil. Wilt thou then not be afraid of the power? do that which is good, and thou shalt have praise of the same: 4 For he is the minister of God to thee for good. But if thou do that which is evil, be afraid; for he beareth not the sword in vain: for he is the minister of God, a revenger to execute wrath upon him that doeth evil. 5 Wherefore ye must needs be subject, not only for wrath but also for conscience sake. 6 For for this cause pay ye tribute also: for they are God's ministers, attending continually upon this very thing. 7 Render therefore to all their dues: tribute to whom tribute is due; custom to whom custom; fear to whom fear; honour to whom honour.

I look for the anointed person called by God. If not, then I leave and drop them off right away. People of God prepare themselves to meet God and then meet His creation. The Lord was the God in the flesh, preparing Himself before He met His creation. Once you allow yourself to be controlled by fake, false prophets and teachers, then they will train you to speak against the real one. People said Jesus did all good.

But Pharisees and priests said,

Matthew 12:24 But when the Pharisees heard it, they said, This fellow doth not cast out devils, but by Beelzebub the prince of the devils.

Does God need any approval from this critic, greedy religious authority? They never knew God. They made the house of God a den of thieves. So sad! When I go abroad or here in the US, God uses me mightily, and much healing and deliverance happens, but the one who does not know God gets jealous. I do not understand why people are so bewitched by false teachers. They bewitched congregations with their false teaching. I have nothing to do with them. I will not be a partaker of false teaching. God, in His mercy, has given us the Word of God and given every detail. But remember, each word of God needs revelation. I work around the world; it is easy for one who is a new convert to believe in Jesus. It is hard for a bewitched religious Christian to believe the truth. I warn them to get away from the false teachers and prophets. Beware! They will use the Bible and twist the word by representing it to fit their false doctrine. Doctrine means teaching, instructing, or explaining. It is easy for the new converts if they come from other religions since they are not misguided. We can prepare them to preach the kingdom of God. Since they have ears to hear and eyes to see clearly. They also get blessed with many great encounters with God. For them, every day is a new day, a new walk, a new revelation. Lord shows up in their life as they call on His name. May the Lord send us true individuals, like Moses, Joshua, Paul, John, and many others, as we pray. People are tired of going to church. Many are losing their congregations. People lose interest and trust in the Lord. May the Lord put love for Jesus, perception, and discernment of spirit. Remember, we are called to go out and preach, not sit on the pews or benches. Lord overthrew the table and came out of the temple. You are His church. That is why He created you.

1 John 4:1 Beloved, believe not every spirit, but try the spirits whether they are of God: because many false prophets are gone out into the world.

The genuine people welcomed the anointed people of God. No need to waste time with an infidel or skeptic. To work for God, you need to hear from God. I work for God. People come for counseling, so I have to get an answer from God. I cannot answer what I feel. This is not my business; I am not religious. When I prophesy or tell the physical problem or about daemonic deliverance, I have to first prepare myself. I cannot meet people without contacting God first. My prayer life starts before 4 am. I meet the Lord. I fast, so I completely mortified my flesh. The Lord talks to me as clearly as I am talking to you. So remember, the people of God have prepared for the service of God's creation. It is the disciplined life, the closer walk with Him. The communication channel has to be open and must obey God's voice. Amen!

LET US PRAY

Heavenly Father, we pray for the loyal people of God who come into your presence to serve your kingdom. This is the kingdom's services and not self-services. If they have you and if you are working with them, then they know how to help. It is God reaching the creation through the chosen holy vessel of God. If we all prepare then, we have a perfect world. But we know it is not. Lord, we are here for your services. We must prepare to do what you have assigned. You did everything wholeheartedly, and we testify to the result. If we do the way you will do, we also will see the greater as you said. Lord, the problem is we are busy and lost in the world. Many are five fools, not preparing. So Lord, help us be five wise, ready, and prepared to meet you in Jesus's name. Amen! God bless you!

OCTOBER 14

HAVE YE RECEIVED THE HOLY GHOST?

The Blood of Jesus purchased the New Testament Church. Is powerful since it has the power of the Spirit of God. The Holy Spirit is the God in us.

One God, who is Spirit, comes to us.

Acts 19:2 He said unto them, Have ye received the Holy Ghost since ye believed? And they said unto him, We have not so much as heard whether there be any Holy Ghost.

People have not heard and some haven't received the gift of the Holy Spirit. It is God's given gift of His Spirit.

The Bible says in. John 7:39 (But this spake he of the Spirit, which they that believe on him should receive: for the Holy Ghost was not yet given; because that Jesus was not yet glorified.)

This Holy Ghost's power comes on us to enable us to witness our city and the end of the World. We cannot witness signs and wonders without it. Many say the day you believe you received His Spirit. The Bible does not agree with this doctrine of a demon. Jesus has instructed His disciple and also the future disciple, like many others and me. Only the chosen one will follow Jesus's instructions. He said to follow the apostles' and prophets' teachings. They laid the foundation.

Acts 2:42a And they continued stedfastly in the apostles' doctrine

We have to open the book of Acts where you will find the doctrine of the Apostle. Follow their doctrine, which means teaching to continue the book of Acts. New Testament Church purchased with God's blood. The Lord paid the price with His blood. Now simply baptize in Jesus' name to wash away sins. Jesus hides His blood under the name of Jesus.

Acts 20:28b to feed the church of God, which he hath purchased with his own blood.

God purchased His people with the blood of Jesus. Jesus is the Old Testament God in the flesh. This Church is powerful enough to defeat the devil since it has the power of God called the Holy Spirit. Jesus said to His disciples do not depart from Jerusalem until you receive the Holy Spirit. Do not work without the Holy Spirit. You will be powerless, do not deliver the Powerless Gospel. Jesus instructed them after the resurrection.

Luke 24:49 And, behold, I send the promise of my Father upon you: but tarry ye in the city of Jerusalem, until ye be endued with power from on high.

After the resurrection, The Lord reminded them again, not to go fishing, wait, I am sending you the Holy Spirit. Again, give them the address where to wait.

Acts 1:4 And, being assembled together with them, commanded them that they should not depart from Jerusalem, but wait for the promise of the Father, which, saith he, ye have heard of me.

The Holy Spirit will be a teacher and guide, and will empower you. The Holy Spirit enables Samson and David to destroy spiritual darkness. Also helped Daniel stand against trouble. The Holy Spirit is the best teacher if it comes to you.

John 14:26 But the Comforter, which is the Holy Ghost, whom the Father will send in my name, he shall teach you all things, and bring all things to your remembrance, whatsoever I have said unto you.

Jesus was with them, then came in them. The disciples followed the instructions of Jesus. On the day of Pentecost, they received the Holy Spirit.

Act 2:4 And they were all filled with the Holy Ghost, and began to speak with other tongues, as the Spirit gave them utterance.

Before departing, Jesus instructed of some signs to recognize His disciple are;

Mark 16:17a c And these signs shall follow them that believe; they shall speak with new tongues;

So if you see someone is not speaking in a tongue, they are not disciples. The new tongue in Greek is glóssa, which is the language you will speak without learning at the university. The church in Samaria was born of water but not born of Spirit. Peter and John came to Samaria to lay hands to receive the Holy Spirit.

Acts 8:15 Who, when they were come down, prayed for them, that they might receive the Holy Ghost: 16 (For as yet he was fallen upon none of them: only they were baptized in the name of the Lord Jesus.)

The Holy Spirit needs to fall on His people, whose name is written in the Book of Life. God chose them before the foundation of the world.

Ephesians 1:4a According as he hath chosen us in him before the foundation of the world,

If God did not choose you from the foundation of the world, then you will not receive the Holy Ghost. If you do not have the Holy Spirit after baptizing in Jesus's name, then you must receive it.

Romans 8:9c Now if any man have not the Spirit of Christ, he is none of his.

1 Thessalonians 1:5a "For our gospel came not unto you in word only, but also in power, and in the Holy Ghost,

OCTOBER 14

Receiving the Holy Ghost is the most wonderful experience. You lose control of yourself and God takes control. The tongue is the unruly member and God takes over it. I have received the Holy Ghost and cannot explain this marvelous experience. Seek the Spirit of God, then you will say, Wow! Now I understand why the Devil is saying you have it, even if you don't. The devil has built most of the religious organizations on false doctrine. They discontinued the Book of Acts since they rejected God to come to give them power. How are you? Stiff neck, Antichrist? Powerless? I have heard and seen people receiving the Holy Spirit Baptism. The foreigners are witnesses since they understand the language. Just like a day of Pentecost. Many Jewish nationalities of Jewish understood, but not the ones who spoke.

1 Corinthian 14:21 In the law it is written, With men of other tongues and other lips will I speak unto this people; and yet for all that will they not hear me, saith the Lord. 22a Wherefore tongues are for a sign, not to them that believe, but to them that believe not:

Why do people reject the Holy Spirit? We have always rejected God in each dispensation. In the end, the same situation. We do not want the Holy Spirit the way the Bible wants us to receive it. The mentality is that I want my way, not God's.

Acts 10:44 While Peter yet spake these words, the Holy Ghost fell on all them which heard the word. 46a For they heard them speak with tongues, and magnify God.

So Peter knew how people receive the baptized with the Holy Spirit. I had some coworkers come to my house and as I prayed over her and her little daughter, they both received the Holy Spirit and spoke in tongues. Next Sunday, they brought the other little daughter, and she also received the Holy Spirit. She went to school and the Holy Spirit took over and started speaking in tongues. She told her mom, Mom, the Holy Spirit came to me in my classroom. I was speaking in tongues. Many people have received the Holy Spirit in my house. Be like a little child. Then they were all baptized in Jesus's name.

Isaiah 28:9 Whom shall he teach knowledge? and whom shall he make to understand doctrine? them that are weaned from the milk, and drawn from the breasts.

LET US PRAY

Lord, we thank you for the Holy Spirit. It is the greatest gift when it comes within. The Holy Spirit is around us since your spirit fills heaven and earth. It comes within us when we receive the gift. It gives us power. Thank you, you said I will not leave you comfortless, I will come to you. Thanks to those who allow you to dwell in them. You are a gentle God who knocks on the door of the heart. If we open, you will come. Let today every heart open to receive the Holy Spirit by evidence of speaking an unknown tongue. We do not understand this language but helps us pray or intercede in prayer language. I thank you for filling me with your spirit. Fill those who desire, seek, and ask in Jesus's name! Amen! God bless you!

OCTOBER 15

THE ACCUSATION AND ALLEGATION ARE THE OLD TACTICS OF THE DEVIL!

The devil, known as a liar, continues to use his old trick of fabricating lies against the righteous. It's just the same as always. Wherever you travel, the devil employs his team to convince others he possesses it all. Really? He makes promises he can't keep and uses intimidation tactics. The loser known as Satan, the Devil, is utterly defeated. The positive update is that he won't ever succeed. He makes it his mission to bring misery to the lives of the righteous. The one who knows the Lord will find it ineffective.

When you know the Word, God, and the truth, you can turn the Devil's accusations into blessings and praises. Once you realize how to overcome all of Satan's schemes, you'll be filled with excitement.

While many know how to get out, some are unaware. Knowing and obeying are two separate situations. Although we are uncertain of the result, knowing the Lord can provide us with solace and faith during the trial.

Many are the afflictions of the righteous. Not some or little, but many. We do not know the number since it says many.

Psalm 34:19 Many are the afflictions of the righteous: but the Lord delivereth him out of them all. 20 He keepeth all his bones: not one of them is broken.

The Bible comforts His children:

Psalm 94:13 That thou mayest give him rest from the days of adversity, until the pit be digged for the wicked.

At work, a Christian friend asked me why evil has no trouble, but Christians have many. The Lord promises us in the above scripture; that He is digging for their sudden calamities. They dominate in every endeavor, their achievements shining brightly, but one day their success will come to an end.

During our many trials, we must get hold of peace by doing right in the sight of God.

Isaiah 32:17 And the work of righteousness shall be peace; and the effect of righteousness quietness and assurance forever.

OCTOBER 15

Get the Joy of the Lord, it will be your strength.

Once you learn what is your portion in the Lord, then an enemy will be like a barking dog, shallow water making much noise. And righteous are like steel water runs deep.

As the devil grows like grass, but is soon cut down.

Psalm 37:1 Fret not thyself because of evildoers, neither be thou envious against the workers of iniquity. 2 For they shall soon be cut down like the grass, and wither as the green herb.

It is true; they do not live half of their life. Go look in the cemetery at what age they die. They die early. The devil uses evil people and has no power to deliver them from the Lord. God is mighty, and the devil is a loser.

The accuser, Satan, keeps a close eye on every step of your journey.

Psalms 37:32 The wicked watcheth the righteous, and seeketh to slay him. 35 I have seen the wicked in great power, and spreading himself like a green bay tree.

Job is the best example of it. He was the righteous man accused by the devil, but the end was praises and blessings. Double for the trouble. Uncountable blessings flowed to his bosom. Remember, blessing comes from the Lord, and it can come only if you keep the righteous laws, commandments, and precepts of the Lord.

My mom worked in the hospital as a nurse. When they expanded to the hospital, they reported her as a righteous and truthful lady to the new management. I have seen my mom's entire trial; she stood like a tree planted by the river. Mom never lost the battle. She was a mighty prayer warrior and kept the word in her heart. A woman of faith.

Psalm 37:39 But the salvation of the righteous is of the Lord: he is their strength in the time of trouble. 40 And the Lord shall help them, and deliver them: he shall deliver them from the wicked, and save them because they trust in him.

Many times we wonder why these wicked are ruling, putting allegations and accusations against the righteous and nothing happens to them. Wait, trust the Lord. The devil is a liar. The enemy will be defeated.

Proverb 2:22 But the wicked shall be cut off from the earth, and the transgressors shall be rooted out of it.

Think of Jesus. What happened to Him? He said I came to my own, and my own crucified me. The one in charge of His work got rid of Jesus.

Jesus was triumphant over the devil by paying blood for us. The devil just helped Him in fulfilling the plan of God. Without the devil and his accusation, you will not get blessed. You won't have victory if you do not have an opponent. You would never see the fulfillment of the promises of God if you do not see the tactic of Satan against you. Joseph, David, Daniel, and many more were promoted while going through the distress, running away from the sword, the enemy, but knew the way out. It took courage to stand for truth and unwavering faith. We all know the devil has, but for a short time, he is a roaring lion.

Revelation 12:12 Therefore rejoice, ye heavens, and ye that dwell in them. Woe to the inhabiters of the earth and of the sea! for the devil is come down unto you, having great wrath, because he knoweth that he hath but a short time.

Put on an all armor of God, the breastplate of righteousness, gird up loin with truth, the helmet of the salvation of hope, take also the shield of faith, and go forward with shoes preaching the gospel of peace.

Swing the Word as a sword, knowing it is appropriate.

May the Lord provide the faith and trust to quench the fiery dart. Many fail themselves, getting weary and complaining. I remembered a good Christian lady who did not want to read the Bible and pray. Her battle gave her much emotional trauma. She lost faith. That is why Jesus said to pray and tarry for one hour. When the battle reaches the point where you feel like I am losing, that is the point you are winning if your faith fails not.

The devil always makes much noise; he does not know any better. His tactic needs God's counterattack.

Hosea 4:6a My people are destroyed for lack of knowledge:

Get knowledge of God and find your rights, authority, and power given to you. Learn how to defeat the devil just like Jesus did when Satan came against Him. Learn and use what the Lord wrote in the Word of God. You can come out of Satan's accusation and allegation very rich, and successful with all praises if you know how and what to do.

Many took their enemies' position. David replaced King Saul, and Samuel replaced Eli. It is the game of Satan and if you know the condition, the commandment of God, you will be above, first, head, and highly favored. Angels will minister to you as they did to Jesus. You will gain the hedge of protection. It is a spiritual battle that cannot be fought with the fist, but by the Word of God. Amen.

LET US PRAY

Lord, when the enemy comes like a flood, then Lord raise your standard. You have promised us that water will not overflow us; the fire will not burn us.

We serve the God who has power over fire, lion, water, weapons of Satan, and the fearful sight. With the Lord, all things are possible. God gave all power to you in heaven, earth, and beneath the earth. It secured our soul in you; you have carved us on your palm, and no one can remove us. We have a hundred percent eternal security, so the Lord has mercy on us. The God of Israel never slumbers or sleeps. He will never be without sources and resources. We serve the convenent keeper God. His word is good, so we thank you for keeping us in your wings. Your name is a strong tower that puts their trust in you. We thank you for helping against the tactic, accusing allegations of a devil in Jesus' name! Amen! God bless you!

OCTOBER 16

MYSTERY OF CHRIST!

Mystery means a puzzle, riddle, secret, or something that a human cannot explain or understand. Mystery means hidden or secret things not obvious to the understanding (from Lexicon strong). The Bible is the written word of God. God spoke and about 40 people in different eras or ages at different places and took dictation. It took 1600 men years to complete the Word of God. Now we have a complete Bible. The Bible has 66 books. But the New Testament spoke about Jesus. It did not mention gentiles in the Old Testament as a partaker of Jehovah God except for the descendants of Abraham's promised child.

God is a mystery in the New Testament since Jesus Christ came into the flesh. If you know the answer to this riddle or puzzle, then mastery is revealed. Only the Spirit of God can reveal the mystery. God revealed first to Peter. That is why the first Church, which is your body, was started by Him. Peter had the key to opening the kingdom of Heaven. The kingdom of heaven can only be open if you know the mystery of Christ, that is God Jehovah in flesh as Jesus. Otherwise, you are not called, but you called yourself. The second was to Paul, whom the Lord met at Damascus Road, and it solved the church (we are the church) problem. Once you know the mystery of Christ, then Jews and Gentiles will never have the same problems.

Colossians 1:26 Even the mystery which hath been hid from ages and from generations, but now is made manifest to his saints: 27 To whom God would make known what is the riches of the glory of this mystery among the Gentiles; which is Christ in you, the hope of glory:

Christ has given us hope by giving us access to the blood by baptizing us to wash away our sins if we use His name, Jesus Christ. People will not use the name of Jesus Christ if they do not understand the mystery of Jesus Christ. Who is Jesus Christ? In the past, Jehovah had many names for acting and doing the work. Jehovah said I was so and so. Over they gave ten powerful names to one true Jehovah God. One true God has over 72 names. But the Mastery is in Jesus' name Jesus, the highest name, name above all Jehovah's name. Jehovah put on the flesh and gave blood for His creation and solved the problem of sins. Blood has life, and He gave life by shedding His Blood.

1 Timothy 3:16a And without controversy great is the mystery of godliness: God was manifest in the flesh,

Now the Devil did not like 'God was manifested in the flesh,' so he changed 'he' instead of 'God'. Now you will try to know or understand the oneness, but the devil's dirty game will not allow it. The devil changed the Bible, so you cannot solve the puzzle or riddle of Jesus Christ. Jesus Christ said, who has seen me has seen the Father. you need the revelation by the Holy Spirit. Jesus was walking God in the flesh. He asked all disciples, only Peter knew the mystery.

Matthew 16:17 And Jesus answered and said unto him, Blessed art thou, Simon Barjona: for flesh and blood hath not revealed it unto thee, but my Father which is in heaven.

Father is spirit so He can reveal, but His part of spirit put on the flesh is Jesus Christ. It cannot be revealed. Paul killed many. Nowadays, many Christians are killed around the world. Why? Since a murderer does not know the mystery of Christ. Once they know, it will solve the problem. It takes the Spirit to reveal. I explained the mystery of Christ to a family who was baptized in the name of Jesus.

Since I moved to the US, I have never had to deal with the Gujarati Bible. But one night the people whom I was showing in English scripture found out it was the missing verse in the Gujarati Bible. I couldn't believe the evil work of the devil. These people will not solve the mystery. The Word of God is Spirit since Spirit God wrote it.

1 John 5:7 For there are three that bear record in heaven, the Father, the Word, and the Holy Ghost: and these three are one.

This verse was not in the Gujarati Bible and later I found out it is not in most of the Bible except KJV. So how will this person get the revelation while teaching? May the Lord punish the devil. I am not the partaker of this false transcript of the Bible. After that in each Bible study; I requested to open their Bible, so I could show them the devil changed their Bible. And they agreed, yes, we need to get rid of this corrupted copy of the devil's version Bible. God used one scripture to reveal the mystery of the truth to me. I couldn't wait, since God did not reveal it to me. I was baptized in the Name of Jesus Christ and had the most powerful experience of forgiveness of sins but never saw Jesus as Jehovah's God. Once in a Bible study, it was revealed to me. That day, the puzzle of Jesus Christ was completely over. Not only Paul but many have the same problem accepting Jesus as Jehovah's savior by reading the corrupt scriptures. Also, learning from the false teachers and prophets who have no revelation of the Mastery of Christ.

My revelation came from *Isaiah 43:10 Ye are my witnesses, saith the Lord, and my servant whom I have chosen: that ye may know and believe me, and understand that I am he: before me there was no God formed, neither shall there be after me.11 I, even I, am the Lord; and beside me there is no saviour.*

The condition is that if you love God more, then the devil's indoctrinated denomination will reveal to you. The spirit of God can reveal the mystery. Do you care about your soul? Do you care for other people's souls? False teachers, pastors, and denominations are sending many to hell. Why? If you have no revelations of the mystery of Jesus Christ, then you will not know the truth of Christ. How can you or anyone baptize in Jesus' name if the spirit of God does not reveal it?

Ephesians 3:1 For this cause I Paul, the prisoner of Jesus Christ for you Gentiles, 2 If ye have heard of the dispensation of the grace of God which is given me to you-ward 3 How that by revelation he made known unto me the mystery; (as I wrote afore in few words, 4 Whereby, when ye read, ye may understand my knowledge in the mystery of Christ) 5 Which in other ages was not made known unto the sons of men, as it is now revealed unto his holy apostles and prophets by the Spirit; 6 That the Gentiles should be fellowheirs, and of the same body, and partakers of his promise in Christ by the gospel:

May the Lord give you a revelation of Jesus Christ today.

Paul said. *Colossians 2: 8 Beware lest any man spoils you through philosophy and vain deceit, after the tradition of men, after the rudiments of the world, and not after Christ. 9 For in him dwelleth all the fulness of the Godhead bodily. 10 And ye are complete in him, which is the head of all principality and power:*

Thank you, Lord, for revealing the greatest mystery of Jesus Christ; God was walking on earth to shed His blood and give an example. He purchased the soul of obedience through His blood. I am one of them. Praise God!

LET US PRAY

Lord, thank you for revealing the mystery to those who love you. It is no mystery if we allow the Spirit of God to reveal. What a joy that we know is the hidden treasure of Christ. We carry in an earthen vessel. May the Lord save many by washing their sins in the name of Jesus, where the blood is hidden. Thank you for being our lamb. Thank you for taking away the sins of the world by shading your blood. There is no forgiveness without shedding the blood, and you did it for your bride. It is the mercy of God, since many have chosen the narrow way. We will continue the book of Acts. The acts of a miracle, sign, and wonder, healing will continue by the one with whom the mystery God has revealed in Jesus' name! Amen! God bless you!

OCTOBER 17

GOD IS CONCERNED ABOUT WHAT CONCERNS YOU!

If you or we go to God concerning any issues, questions, problems, and situations, the Lord will take care of it. My Lord attends to all your worries and cares about your well-being. It is the very thing you need to take to the Lord. He is qualified for all that is impossible. The Lord said nothing was impossible for me. But when you see your home, families around, and the situation in a city-state, country, or around the world, are you concerned? Does Your heart get heavy? Do you cry out for someone missing, a sick child? Are you concerned about the situation that others are going through in other nations?

Much just concerns what touches them. I have heard and seen the attitude of the people saying; it is not my problem. How about it becomes yours when you see it?

The Lord in heaven said, Love others as you love yourself. Love others, how? I have seen many family members working against each other. Especially when you have jealous family members or people who come by marriage. How sad! It's the enormous snake you live with. Even your known people will not wish well for you. I have seen, and I still do not believe but I have no choice. A few of my friends acted funny and were angry at me. I was shocked and surprised. I worriedly turned to God for guidance. He showed me they are very jealous, envious, and prideful. This kind of person hates it when you go higher. So be careful while sharing matters. If this is your brothers, sisters, friends, neighbors, or any who came by marriage, pray for self-protection and pray for them. Help but keep them at a distance. You wouldn't believe this, but you have to. All that you do is good for them since you are good, but all they will return will be shocked or surprised. May the Lord help you believe how the Lord sees. The Lord sees the heart and what they are and not what you think and believe.

Our concern should agree with the Lord. We may appear, but the Lord has the facts. Get concerned for all who are bad, evil, wicked, lost, and unworthy. It is your concern for the soul, situations, and concerns that will become God's.

It is the time we must get up and pray, and learn to go back to basics. Going to church will never change the situation, but going to God will. Going to God is a forgotten matter. We had a family altar, then I saw my mom pray, and I saw my father kneel and pray. Some of the family members will pray on their own. I always prayed. I loved to pray. One of my college friends who was Hindu said, I read your birth date number. People are very religious. She said when I was reading this article I was thinking of you. You are what your number says. Well, we Christians do not believe this. She said it was not a horoscope. It is the nature of people born on certain dates by Germans. I still do not believe that. Lord Jesus can change us if we repent, baptize in Jesus's name, and fill with His Spirit.

I believe God gives the burden to the soul if we ask for it. God will give a burden to the nations and people. My concern is for children around the world. I pray every day. I cut all the missing children's photos and prayed for protection. We must give our children homework to pray for something. It is our job to teach them to connect with God rather than games and the Internet. We are losing them in the world. Some have lost them forever. They do not know where they are. When they are going through something, they look for the gun rather than God. When they have a problem, they take their lives rather than take from it on the knee. See what we have raised. We mocked our parents. We think it is old-fashioned. But I rather see my parents praying than sitting at the bar, doing my nails, and hair, or watching a movie. These old-fashioned parents have kept the nations, people, and families safe, sound, and saved.

Lord came since He was a concern for His creation, confused, entangled in the trap of sickness, and disease, oppressed by the devil, and heartbroken. His concern made the God of the universe, who created heaven and earth come down to resolve the problems. He gave the Holy Spirit, so we get the power to do the same. The Lord of Heaven worked so much.

Mark 3:20 And the multitude cometh together again, so that they could not so much as eat bread.

Mark 6:31 And he said unto them, Come ye yourselves apart into a desert place, and rest a while: for there were many coming and going, and they had no leisure so much as to eat.

We cannot afford to be indifferent; we must be genuinely concerned about the crises we face as entire nations and as individual families. We must find a solitary place and kneel and pray.

Get concerned, and bring the matter to the Lord. I always see the dream, and visions and hear the audible voice of the Lord. For much time I would share or intercede and would fast if it was needed. Fasting every week and long fasting is our lifestyle. Nevertheless, we are willing to go above and beyond if needed.

Luke 5:16 And he withdrew himself into the wilderness, and prayed.

Mark 1:35 And in the morning, rising up a great while before day, he went out, and departed into a solitary place, and there prayed.

Luke 6:12 And it came to pass in those days, that he went out into a mountain to pray, and continued all night in prayer to God.

Lord was concerned for all that was going on. He was in flesh and all flesh must come to God. Jesus was in the flesh, and did all that flesh must do.

Psalm 65:2 O you that hears prayer, unto you shall all flesh come.

We are in flesh and flesh limits that is exactly what Lord Jesus the God who manifested in flesh was teaching and giving us an example. Lord Jesus also set an example.

1 Peter 2:21 For even hereunto were ye called: because Christ also suffered for us, leaving us an example, that ye should follow his steps:22 Who did no sin, neither was guile found in his mouth:

May the Lord help us weed out all business, wasting time, and following false churches, organizations, pastors, teachers, and authorities.

Jesus said follow me, carry the cross, rejection, and suffering which comes while following Jesus. May the Lord make you concerned for those who are helpless, hurt, and need help from heaven. Our concern will make God concerned. If you call on God, He will answer by fire. You can take it by force or fire. Get concerned, and the Lord will do the impossible possible, water in the desert, in Jesus's name. Amen.

LET US PRAY

Heavenly Father, we come to your altar, knowing you are you and our God has directed us. It is the way, truth, and life through Jesus and no other way. We see many so-called gods and goddesses have shown a different way. It is the concern we have for past sins and curses, for the present and future. We have security in the Blood of the Lamb Jesus. The blood of Jesus speaks better than the blood of Abel. The blood of Abel was crying out from the earth since blood never dies. Blood has life. Today we stand covering self-sins with the blood of Jesus. Hear us what we ask for, knock and seek you for. Let your blood wash, not our sins only, but wherever we plead over as well. Our heavenly Father gives us the burden, concern, and desire for all and what concerns you and us. Your concern becomes ours. We desire the life of Jesus, so the world can be a pleasant, safe, beautiful place to live. Children can move safely and soundly. Our security is in you, Lord. Our hedge of protection comes from heaven as we kneel and bring to you. In Jesus' name. Amen! God bless you!

OCTOBER 18

THE MIND IS A DEVIL'S WORKSHOP. GOD WORKS WITH HEART!

Life starts in the heart. If you read and live by the word of God, your life will match the designers' plan. God is the designer of our life. The only true God, Jesus Christ, created us. He also has given a prescription of His Word on how to live Holy, righteous, and true. If you live according to the word of God, then you will be as.

1 Peter 2:9 But ye are a chosen generation, a royal priesthood, an holy nation, a peculiar people; that ye should shew forth the praises of him who hath called you out of darkness into his marvellous light;

God knows our being and has given instructions to be successful, fruitful, Holy people just for Him. We keep the word of God in our hearts since the heart is the origin of life.

Psalm 119:11 Your word have I hid in my heart, that I might not sin against you.

We keep God's law in our hearts. *Psalms 37:31 The law of his God is in his heart; none of his steps shall slide.*

Take a step by keeping His laws. The true teachers and true prophets do accord to the Word of God. The nation of these people will shout for victory. If the nation has the Law of God, taught from childhood, then those nations will produce people like Daniel, Joseph, Moses, and many righteous. The Lord promotes. God gives knowledge to those who walk in the way of His laws. Keep the law not on lips but in a heart to follow.

Proverb 4:20 My son, attend to my words; incline thine ear unto my sayings. 21 Let them not depart from thine eyes; keep them in the midst of thine heart. 22 For they are life unto those that find them, and health to all their flesh. 23 Keep thy heart with all diligence; for out of it are the issues of life.

Your heart decides your matter. Life is not the one that boasts or speaks big matters. Life hides in your heart. The Bible warns us that the heart is deceitful. Also, warn that the heart is unknown to the person. If you are taking time and planting words and praying over this seed, it will flourish. No one can predict but the hidden heart, which only God knows. Lord, see your heart. If He sees a clean good heart, then He will use them. Many are enthusiastic and will do anything to go up. They will bribe, lie, cheat, and compromise with the word of God. King Saul was one of them. He, being rejected, tried all the way to destroy the David whom the Lord had elected. Both had an act: one was trying to go up a ladder, but another was just trying to do what pleases The Lord. No matter what, one who pleases God proves they know God. You do not have to kill your sister or brother or anyone better than you. If the Lord accepts the person, then change your ways and do the right for God to accept you.

First God, then your passion! Many have put on the fake robe of religion to go higher. They want to promote themselves by pleasing people, authorities, and power. Religious ambition will do anything just to have praise, power, and position. May the Lord help this self-seeker opportunist. As they go higher, they slide back quicker. The devil works on our minds. When I was younger, we could not read magazines, novels, no movies and there was no TV, so it was a plus for us. We see the prince of the air come through the back door. In the old times, people never went to a movie. They prayed, always revived, read the Bible, and lived a holy life. During the olden times, the prince of air TV, movies, shows, music, and destructive elements did not influence society. The church I went to in the 80s taught us not to watch TV. That kept the garbage out of our minds. There was no TV in India when I left for the US in 1980. Praise God! I am thankful for that. Sin is infecting our society, family, and country with TV.

The flesh enjoys the garbage relayed from the media. The perverted Devil started church lives a little better than Hollywood. It is the mentality that accepts us as we are. Change the Bible, because we have minds set like Eve. We want to try if it looks good, tastes good, it gives us total control, that is called the pride of life. At this time and age, do not tell the truth. Wrong data is processed in our mind already and the mind is corrupted. If you have put all the garbage in your mind, then the product will be what you see today. It is the product of Satan, unruly, high-minded, truce-breaker, lawless, unholy, ungodly, adulterer, and power-hungry people. Satan is the first covenant breaker. Now his agenda is to make everyone like him. He has many producers, directors, stars, singers, musicians, movie makers, and name it, working for the mind-altering transcript. If you enjoy that devilish mind-harming, life-destructive product to infect your mind, then never expect a clean home, society, and country. It needs a sweeper and reformer censor board to put a stop, block, close, or boycott it. Keep teaching and restricting children from evil in their lives. Our society cannot rely on parents alone since the influence comes from the prince of the air. It works on your mind. How difficult it is to bring them back unless you get into the Word of God.

True prophets and teachers taught and trained you, and then society has hope. Life has many influences, but if you have a heart full of the word of God, have fewer chances to be ruined. Life is short, so stop window shopping with a slew foot devil. The devil has many honey-dripping salespeople who know how to strike you down. May the Lord give us the wisdom and knowledge to hold on to the word of God. A deadly mind-blowing prince of air TV has changed the world. It can be the best tool if God uses it. But the devil uses it to destroy our minds. Nowadays, there is no difference between night and day shows. Media teaches how to steal, rob, do witchcraft, put spells, and name them. Society had many problems in the past, but pornography has made children insecure in their own families. How? Putting Satan's idea in mind. Do not fill your mind with garbage infecting enemy flesh. Injecting it with a corrupt series of thoughts makes life uncontrollable. Stop watching mind-contaminating life destructive dirty shows and start reading the Bible. It will do good for your spirit, health, and soul. May the Lord help us love ourselves. No one but you can secure your soul. You have the power to put a stop to the devil and be the door for the Lord. Amen!

LET US PRAY

Lord, help us make the right choices since we live in an advanced world. We not only have a TV, but the world is in our hands. Help us perceive since we have mind-blowing information and life-destructive experiences. It is our job to keep the word of God in our hands and not this little life-destructive devil's cell phone. We carry it wherever we go. TV, tablets, and other devices have become babysitters. We have the worst addiction; and world-controlling power, choices are ours. It has destroyed the world. Many accidents,

OCTOBER 18

and tickets, and many are behind bars just because of the distracting phone. Our God has given us the life-saving and soul-protecting Word of God in the Bible. Lord, help us open it and read and know it. Help us hide it in our hearts. It will protect our life as we live by it. It is the Lord's instructions for His creations to keep us from evil and appearing evil in Jesus's name.

1 Thessalonians 5: 22 Abstain from all appearance of evil. In Jesus's name. Amen! God bless you!

OCTOBER 19

YOUR WORD IS THAT POWERFUL!

The Spirit of God brought all into existence by speaking to it. God said let there be light, let there be a firmament amid the waters and it was. He said, let the waters under the heaven be gathered together unto one place and let the dry land appear and so it was on the command of His word. Let the earth bring forth grass, the herb-yielding seed, and the fruit tree-yielding fruit after his kind, and it appeared. Let there be lights in heaven's firmament to divide the day from the night, and let them be for signs, and seasons, and days, and years, so it was: Our Word designs, builds, produces, as it has the power to bring forth what you say. Please watch what you say!

We see and enjoy what is around us, which also came into existence by speaking to it. And let them be for lights in the heaven's firmament to give light upon the earth: Let the waters bring forth abundantly the moving creature that hath life and fowl that may fly above the earth in the open firmament of heaven. And God created great whales, and every living creature that moveth, which the waters brought forth abundantly, after their kind and every winged fowl after his kind, Let the earth bring forth the living creature after his kind, cattle, and creeping thing, and beast of the earth after his kind:

God said it was good. All came to existence by the Spoken Word of God. You have power in your tongue. Life and death are in the tongue. Choose your word carefully, because it will bring that into existence.

Another day, God asked me to call this person and ask her to sit outside and read the Bible out loud. She said I prayed loud but not Bible reading. May the Lord help us see what happens when we read the Bible out loud over places. Try it. No matter who you are, it is the Word of God. God honors His word and promises. Many read words quietly, so no one knows the word. I request you to play the Bible on speaker so non-Christians can hear. This will be good for India since they have the liberty to do so.

I was at the hospital to pray over an Indian man. He suddenly went into a coma and his father-in-law flew from India to visit him. I always go with the Word of God, which is the Bible. Only one could visit. Seeing no one inside the room, I went in and started reading the Bible. I saw this father-in-law peeping through the glass door, so I asked him to come in. I asked if he would read the Bible out loud. He agreed to do so. On the next visit, the elderly father-in-law said I had never read the Bible, but the Bible is fascinating. He requested another copy of the Bible. I right away bought him a rainbow Bible.

Never take your spoken word carelessly. It will happen as you have stated. Words have the power to determine your destiny, so pick the right word for yourself and others. Early morning at prayer time, Sister Pena said, yesterday I had an accident, but I thank the Lord for it.

OCTOBER 19

1 Thessalonians 5:18 In every thing give thanks: for this is the will of God in Christ Jesus concerning you.

I was glad for it because standing on the word of God redeems the promises. She was a little injured and had no medical insurance. We prayed to the Lord to touch and heal her. It is a joy to see the fulfillment of the word as you speak. You are creating the remedy of healing, deliverance, and miracles by claiming it using the word of God.

When I go shopping, I speak positive words like I will find a good deal and all I need. God has for me, so take me there to shop. He will give me a good price and it always happens. Many said it never happened to them. Learn the word technique. The promised word of God needs a faith ingredient to quicken it. If you speak the Word by faith, it creates what you are expecting.

God spoke for light and darkness did not come. So you speak what you desire and see what happens. Discover what and how people speak and the result of it. When they speak negatively, there is a negative effect. Words are powerful, either negative or positive. It is your thinking, knowledge, and confidence in God that will cause the production.

Daniel 11:32b the people that do know their God shall be strong, and do exploits.

Read the Word; the Word does the work. A miracle only happens when you speak what you desire.
By the hand of Moses, God did many miracles knowing Moses's understanding of Him. By the same token, the Hebrews were afraid when they saw Egyptians pursuing them. Moses comforted the Hebrews by speaking the Word.

Exodus 14:13 And Moses said unto the people, Fear ye not, stand still, and see the salvation of the Lord, which he will shew to you today: for the Egyptians whom ye have seen today, ye shall see them again no more forever. 14 The Lord shall fight for you, and ye shall hold your peace.

The Lord honors what you claim. You are the one who brings the matter into existence by speaking. 28 And the waters returned and covered the chariots, and the horsemen, and all the host of Pharaoh that came into the sea after them; there remained not so much as one of them.

How beautiful! Do not scream, cry, and fear, wait on the Lord for salvation, which is healing, deliverance, and salvation is on the tip of your tongue. It is the God who has given His Creation the authority to claim, redeem, and give life to each promise. Do you know your creator? Look at His might and power. Do you know His knowledge, wisdom, riches, and glory? If not, then you will never progress. You cannot get what you desire. Lack of knowledge is a dangerous enemy of humans. You will die hungry, sick, oppressed, possessed, and hurt because of a lack of knowledge. May the Lord fill our tongues and lips with the spoken words of God. His Word needs the boosting of your faith. It has mountain-moving power and life-saving strength. Word has a supernatural mind-boggling creative force.

I pray for people on the phone and watch the result beyond their imagination.

Teach others the Word and use the Word in your conversations. The Word will open others' eyes when it fulfills.

Isaiah 55:10 For as the rain cometh down, and the snow from heaven, and returneth not thither, but watereth the earth, and maketh it bring forth and bud, that it may give seed to the sower, and bread to the eater: 11

So shall my word be that goeth forth out of my mouth: it shall not return unto me void, but it shall accomplish that which I please, and it shall prosper in the thing whereto I sent it.

What is the problem? Why don't we see the works of God in operations? Honestly, people do not know how to claim the promises of God. It came out of God's mouth and not yours or any humans. Believe and declare to see establishing the Bible's promises.

I have seen many speak like I am poor, don't have money, cannot give, etc. Believe me, they are still poor, do not have, and always lack. Same token, one who always speaks positive words, has an extraordinary story. I am using President Trump's words, very positive, 'big,' 'great again' etc and we see the marvelous result. I pay attention to His word with faith has brought significant results in the USA. Our Word needs the knowledge of the almighty before you speak with confidence. Open the Word of God, and learn it by applying it to the situation. Pray to the Lord to bring the Word back to home, in school, in our nations, and individual lives. You are the one who can and will do your part to bring the word back on earth in Jesus's name! Amen!

LET US PRAY

Heavenly Father, the creator of all we see and feel, we give you glory and honor. Your knowledge is beyond our imagination, but give faith in what we want to bring to existence. Our faith needs knowledge, so Lord, please supply it. What a wonderful God you are! We thank the Creator for sharing all that He owns. Thank you for giving us access to your expert knowledge. Your Words are the treasure. To know the Word is to know treasure, riches, and power. Lord, we claim the healing by speaking it to existence. Not only that, we want to be the witnesses in the Word. Now, through the blood, we gentiles have access to the same privileges. Thank you for the blood, which is hidden under your name. It cleanses our sins if we go in the water by pronouncing the name of Jesus. The name of Jesus has swallowed up all the Old Testament names of Jehovah. This name "Jesus" has the blood of the Lamb; the redeemers' blood has life-giving power to all who obey the word of God in Jesus' name! Amen! God Bless You!

OCTOBER 20

LET PEOPLE HEAR HEAVENLY TALK!

Have you ever overheard someone calling your name and when you looked around, found no one? Many people have heard the Voice of God.

Samuel heard his name three times.

1 Samuel 3:8 And the LORD called Samuel again the third time. And he arose and went to Eli, and said, Here am I; for thou didst call me. And Eli perceived that the LORD had called the child.

He went to Eli three times, thinking he called him. Eli perceived it was God. Eli taught Samuel and us how to respond to the voice of the Lord.

Job 33:14 For God speaks once, yea twice, yet man perceives it not.

The Lord calls whom He wants to talk to. The Bible says the voice of the Lord only comes to those who hear them.

1 Samuel 3:1 And the child Samuel ministered unto the LORD before Eli. And the word of the LORD was rare in those days; there was no open vision.

The Lord talks to those who hear Him. Eli was not listening to God, even when he was positioned by God. Eli, the high priest, God should talk to, but he was disconnected from God by putting someone and something before God. Now God found someone who honors God. Remember, you are not called to fill up the gap but to perform the job diligently and sincerely. Once I had a call from a lady. She said I heard you praying in my ear. During that time, she was in jail. Do not judge a person by the past. This lady was a prophetess. She did something wrong before the Lord saved her. They put her behind bars for a few months. During her shower, another elderly woman mentioned hearing me. See, if you are praying for someone, they will hear you even at a far distance. People mentioned I heard someone talking to me. See, the demons have a voice without a body. You can talk to demons like you are talking to God. When you go to a psychiatrist for help, they will prescribe you medicine if you talk about hearing voices and seeing spirits. Medicine will make you drowsy. We know the channel that we have to enter. To enter the spiritual world, we must enter by the Holy Spirit.

Jesus said. John 14:6 Jesus saith unto him, I am the way, the truth, and the life: no man cometh unto the Father but by me.

If your channel is with the wrong media, then you will connect with Satan's world. Once, someone called and said, she channels an evil spirit on the computer which she shouldn't. She felt and saw evil. She was afraid. I said let's pray; After we prayed, the evil spirit left. My question is why are you channeling with the wrong people and the wrong media? All are available does not mean you have to connect. You will hear them since the spirit world is the real world. My prayer is we should all channel with the Lord. What happens if we do? All will see the glorious light, and hear the voice of the Lord; we will see the supernatural movement, voices, and visions in operation.

We need many Daniel, Joseph, Moses, and Joshua today. Why aren't we connecting with the Lord? We connect to the building called the church, choir, preaching, and hold positions offered by the organization's systems. The one position I like is to connect to God on my knee with fasting. It's the best connection, and it works! You will see heaven open, earthquake, healing, deliverance, name of a person, birth date, and addresses will be given when you pray and minister. May the Lord show us what we need to see and hear to bring transformation into our lives. If people can hear me thousands of miles away, then it is easy to reach any banned nations with the gospel of God. The Gospel needs to be preached. First, pray to God to fertilize the ground, then preach. Many can hear you if you pray for people in jail, in prisons, in Satan's churches, in China, India, or anywhere in the world. God knows how to translate the message into their languages. The gift of the Word of knowledge and wisdom kicks in. May the Lord give us the mind of Christ. If we pray for others and help them hear God, the Holy Angels will work for us. God created angels to minister to the needs of His creation.

Hebrews 1:13 But to which of the angels said he at any time, Sit on my right hand, until I make thine enemies thy footstool? 14 Are they not all ministering spirits, sent forth to minister for them who shall be heirs of salvation?

Learn different categories of angel so you know which one to ask for. They do work for us. They cooked for Elijah.

1 King 19:7 And the angel of the LORD came again the second time, and touched him, and said, Arise and eat; because the journey is too great for thee. 8 And he arose, and did eat and drink, and went in the strength of that meat forty days and forty nights unto Horeb the mount of God.

In the night, Joseph heard the voice of God giving Him instruction.

Matthew 1:20 But while he thought on these things, behold, the angel of the Lord appeared unto him in a dream, saying, Joseph, thou son of David, fear not to take unto thee Mary thy wife: for that which is conceived in her is of the Holy Ghost.

We also can do much in spirit if we allow the Spirit to lead, guide, and teach. I have prayed, and people have felt the power of God at work, in the hospital, and at home, and situations have changed. Send the messages by the Spirit. Send a message to the unknown through the channel of God.

Acts 16:9 And a vision appeared to Paul in the night; There stood a man of Macedonia, and prayed him, saying, Come over into Macedonia, and help us.

God sent His Word to heal the diseases. Lord Jesus does not have to be present physically in the room, city, or place. He sent His Spirit to 120 disciples on the day of Pentecost and later to all who seek. They all spoke unfamiliar languages but were known to the pilgrims who came to Jerusalem for the ceremony. See, God was talking to those Israelite pilgrims in their languages. Pray to the Lord to give you the supernatural ability to speak to others in their language to convey God's message to them. The work of the Spirit is greater than what you can imagine. Surrender and allow God to take control. When you pray, pray to claim His Word. It produces audible, visible, tangible, and much more. If demons influence a man and a woman, they can hear the voices of demons and have nightmares and fear. How much more can we do if we are filled with the Holy Spirit? We can do greater. Spirit speaks and performs miraculous work. Send the Spirit of God to places like North Korea, prisons, or anywhere you wish. And see the transformations it brings. Your channel should be the Lord and not another medium. Sickness will flee, a chain will fall off, and angels will do their work through your spoken word over places, people, and situations. We live in the dispensation of God where He is using us, but His Spirit is doing the work through us. Spirit is doing all if you have received the Holy Spirit. I am impressed by recognizing the voice of the Lord. It reaches the places where I cannot, in Jesus' name. Amen!

LET US PRAY

Please speak to our hearts, Lord. Let us speak in faith to the withered hands, dead people, and sick to bring them back to life. Let deliverance and healing take place at the sound of our voice. Pray that Living God is in operation. Operations of God is much higher level than any other media. There is the voice we hear through the media like tv, phone, books, people, and the internet. But as we connect with a living God, we will see an extraordinary outcome. You cannot imagine, but once it becomes physical, you will see to appreciate it. Our God spoke; therefore, we have to speak. Ezekiel spoke to the bones and saw the nation come back to existence. Once the nation was wiped out from the map but brought to existence by the spoken word of prayer. Channel up with the prison by prayer. You will see the power of God work by the simple words spoken by faith. It is the work of the Lord done for you as you asked, knocked, and sought by channeling the Spirit of God. As you channel with TV, Wi-Fi, and internet connections the same way connects to God to see the healing, deliverance, and salvation through the Lord's Spirit. Amen! In Jesus's name. God bless you!

OCTOBER 21

RECEIVER OR REJECTOR!

God says great things for the one who is the receiver of the words and His ministers. But it is against the one who rejects the word of God. The rejecters of the truth are the losers. The rejection of God's instruction is not just the loser of benefits, but cursed as well. The loser always can be corrected if they change their thinking and attitude.

1 Thessalonians 4:8 He therefore that despiseth, despiseth not man, but God, who hath also given unto us his holy Spirit.

Teaching the word of God is very important. That is establishing the kingdom of God. Stand on the Immovable ground of the word of God. Success will be yours if you make the decision to stand tall, dedicate yourself to practice, and abide by the rules. It has life-giving power and success. It has many more benefits hidden in it.

Think about Eve and Adam before falling into sin; God was visiting them and walking with them. No sweating, all blessings, blessings to move around in the garden of Eden. They were protected, never to worry about an attack by an animal. The ground gave the best fruits without sweating. Men and women had never experienced the curse.

Isaiah 5:24 Therefore as the fire devoureth the stubble, and the flame consumeth the chaff, so their root shall be as rottenness, and their blossom shall go up as dust: because they have cast away the law of the LORD of hosts, and despised the word of the Holy One of Israel.

As they rejected the voice and commandments of God, the Lord kicked them out and they were on their own. Eve and Adam were the first rejectors of God. The Kings, like King Saul, King Solomon, and other Israelite kings in history, were noble until they went against God's commands. As they rejected the voice of God, then they were cursed. No matter what it looks or how it feels, remember to receive God's word and obey. The Lord will show you the portion of the planned picture as you allow Him to paint for your life each day.

Life is a gift given by God with conditions. Pay attention to obey the Lord's plan, which you enter by keeping His covenant. All covenant keepers lived and enjoyed the blessings of God and left an inheritance from the Lord.

Abraham left an inheritance to His generation, the land of Israel, the king came out of His bosom, and much more.

David was a receiver of God's command with the willingness of the heart. David received the blessings of the eternal throne. The Messiah, the redeemer of the world, was promised to come to this world from His bosom. Wherever you go, remember that you can have all that you want by doing attachments of dos and don'ts. These dos and don'ts are designed by God not to harm but will keep you on a straight and narrow path leading to the eternal Kingdom. God does not need one who is smarter than Him but obedient to follow His instructions. One must be submissive to the ways of God. Amen!

Proverbs 22:29 Seest thou a man diligent in his business? he shall stand before kings; he shall not stand before mean men.

As we are dealing with our daily business, we proceed with care. In the same way, how much should we be with things for God? My heart overflows with gratitude to the Bible. I receive the commandment, laws, and statutes to have an abundant life. The Lord can give the abundance of life to the receiver of the word without adding and subtracting.

King Solomon served the Lord and became the receiver of the blessings of God. It is the one who becomes the rejector of the Lord and dies lost.

I meet the true prophets and teachers with an open heart and mind to receive the word. The prophet is the most important in my life. I believe I can prosper only if I have the true prophets. The direction and advice he gives come directly from the Lord. Who can be better than the Lord? No one! The Lord assigns and recognizes the prophet.

If you are going to visit one, make sure you receive every word that comes out of His mouth for you. I always pray, before going to the prophets, that God speaks to him about my situation. He will deliver a prophecy if you receive it.

I have visited many prophets. I always asked God to please give Him the word for me. I receive it but also tape to remind myself. I write it down right away if I have no recorder with me.

It is a serious business. I visited the church when the man of God came to me before church started and said; you have a back problem and I will pray for you when the Spirit of God moves on me. Once the prophet told me I would travel soon to another country for missionary work, and I did. He said do not worry about the money God will provide and He did. The prophet is the mouthpiece of God to speak to us.

I am so glad for the God-given prophets. In a prophecy meeting, the Prophetess asked me, 'Do you know me?' I said no; she said, let me tell you what God is telling you. He is using you for prayer.' Lady prophetess told me in another meeting, 'I see prayer in you; you are the mother in the Lord.' Now that time, a lady pastor was sitting next to me; she is my friend, and she said she is my mentor. My friend and I never met or spoke to this lady prophetess.

I now go to various prophetess meetings. There was a prophetess who told me to continue attending the congregation where God asked me to go. My heart raced with fear as I realized the location was not safe. I kept going there since she prayed against the fear. Same time, another prophet from the state prayed and spoke. "Fear not, my child. I am with you." I went for many years till God moved me out of that place. How nice!

When you go to fellowship, meet God before you enter the gates. Ask God to speak to you and receive His word. He will speak to you. I always go for a personal message. Yes, there is a message for all to receive, but I like it when they call me out by my name and tell me my message from the Lord.

1 Corinthians 14:3 But he that prophesieth speaketh unto men to edification, and exhortation, and comfort. 4b he that prophesieth edifieth the church.

Look for the true prophet. Once you receive the prophecy, hold fast, even if it takes some time. No matter what, it will happen. The Prophecy regarding Israelites was after 430 years. It happened to Abraham after 30 years for the promised child. It is the word of God and not the voice of a man.

Isaiah 55:11 So shall my word be that goeth forth out of my mouth: it shall not return unto me void, but it shall accomplish that which I please, and it shall prosper in the thing whereto I sent it.

Be a receiver and hold tight. Hold fast the word you receive from God as a prophecy for your life. Amen!

LET US PRAY

Lord, we know the Word of God will do well if we do it. The Bible is a book we learn by exercising. If we do the word, then the word does better than magic.

It shows the power of the word in and through us. Let the World of God fall in our clean and good ground of the heart. Lord, we receive your word and give it to the next, and next, generation as it is. Pay attention to teaching, so they are the receiver and partaker of the blessing sprouting through it. Our forefathers saw the blessings of receiving the word; we reap that blessing. Help us receive the word to continue in blessings. Our God is good and does great to those who love and receive Him as their personal God. We have God-given parents, but we want to experience God to continue our journey with Him. Our heavenly Father, we pray today you help us. We not only teach our children, but teach this generation to follow this Bible. We pray they receive it for themselves and live blessings for the next in Jesus' name! Amen! God bless you!

OCTOBER 22

THE BELIEVER RECEIVES WHAT THEY CLAIM!

God said, let there be light, and there was light! A lady said if I touch the garment, then I will be whole. And she was whole by touching. The Bible clarifies that with a man it is impossible, but to God, all is possible. Have you heard Christians say I am a believer? Why? If one has faith in the Lord Jesus, yes, they are a believer. You can quicken or make the Word alive by doing as it instructed.

Matthew 19:26 But Jesus beheld them and said unto them, with men this is impossible; but with God all things are possible.

God created us in His image and blessed us. Gave all power through the Holy Spirit and authority in Jesus' name. Do you believe in it? Believers can move God if they align with the Word. The Lord has power, and He has given it to us if we believe. Many have testified that the Lord said it, so I believed it. Believers mean someone who believes and submits to something. When Christian says I am a believer, it means they believe in God Jesus as Lord and savior. How much and how far? If you say you believe in God is not good enough to convince anyone or even God. Can you prove what, in reality, you believe? Faith will be tested and tried. Let's see how you stand.

If the man said I believe. How and what do you believe in?

Luke 7:7b but say in a word, and my servant shall be healed.

The result of what you believed will back your belief up.

10 And they that were sent, returning to the house, found the servant whole that had been sick.

People in the old times believed in prophets. They used to call them Seers; God gave them the office.

1 Samuel 9:6 And he said unto him, Behold now, there is in this city a man of God, and he is an honourable man; all that he saith cometh surely to pass: now let us go thither; peradventure he can shew us our way that we should go.

When you attend a meeting or greet a believer, watch if their lifestyle matches with the Lord's word. Life should flow by the Holy Spirit if you believe and obey the Lord. The Bible is God's book for those who want to believe. It needs a believer to operate with power and faith. God picked disciples and gave them authority. On His departure, He sent the power through the Holy Spirit.

Do you believe you have *2 Corinthians 4:7 But we have this treasure in earthen vessels, that the excellency of the power may be of God, and not of us.*

In earthen vessels which are our body, have the Holy Spirit. If you have the Power of the Holy Spirit, then you can cast out demons, raise the dead, and heal the sick. I do not have a fear of believing in the word of God.

This morning I prayed for the lady who had neck pain. I asked her to put anointing oil with her right hand on her neck. Immediately, this lady believed. She did not go to the doctor but asked me to pray. I prayed, and she was healed. How simple? Why are you making it so complicated? Believe in making it happen. If people say, I do not believe I can be healed, so she wouldn't.

Mark 6:5 And he could there do no mighty work, save that he laid his hands upon a few sick folk, and healed them. 6a And he marvelled because of their unbelief.

We exhausted our time when people were debating different medical insurances, didn't we? We believe in knee replacement, heart transplant, and many pain-giving surgeries. It is very expensive and inconvenient. Why do we not preach or practice what is available by speaking it to existence? Why do we become unbelievers? We do not go to the Seer given by God. We go where there is an unbeliever preaching or teaching. I asked for prayer from only those who believe in the power of God. I get many calls, emails, and texts for the prayer request. They know what I believe. The one who does not believe has hope in tangible things putting in their mouth or seeing a man in front of them talking. I do not. I believe in the Lord and His Word. Each Word of God is exceptional today. I believe in God, who said all things are possible. What happened to modern so-called believers?

Jeremiah 2:11 Hath a nation changed their gods, which are yet no gods? but my people have changed their glory for that which doth not profit.

Believe in God for healing and deliverance. It is available to you in the Bible. Let me tell you, come out of the building where you are held captive and seek God. God is not in the building, but if you seek, He will lead you to the one who has gifts and wouldn't sell. If you do, then the shepherd boy will be crowned, and the slave will be the mighty man in the courtyard of the King. He will be ten times better than witches, warlocks, magicians, and astrologers. Believing is the key on your side to opening the treasure.

Many say I believe, but do you witness the outcome of what you believe? I prayed for many people; the one who believes and sees the results, even though they are idol worshipers. God is not a respecter of people. Believe in God, that is what it needed.

The Man said send me your word. The Lady of Phoenician who asked for deliverance for the daughter was not a Jew. It convinced them that Jesus could heal, deliver, and set free. They convinced the Lord in a way far better than today's Christians. Today's Christians are the best customers of doctors and pharmacies. How can you believe they are believers? Maybe they are, but not in Jesus's stripes, deliverance, or power in His name. God gave forgiveness for sins through His name in water baptism. If they believe, then we will have all been baptized in Jesus' name. Instead of believing the powerful blood hidden behind the name, they become theologians and false teachers of the Bible by rejecting and teaching others to reject the Word.

Therefore, we can say that many claim they are believers; but by checking their lives, they are unbelievers of the Word of God. They will not believe the word without tangible results.

When you attend church, who are you listening to? The one who has the best music, a nice church, a wonderful message, and no power to heal and deliver. Watch for the signs and wonders. If there are not, then they are not believers. They know of God, but do not know God. Which category do you fall into? Believer or unbeliever? If you are a believer, then show me the evidence. I am blind now, I see; I am whole; I walk.

Yes, I have the book out there called. 'I did it His Way.' I am getting many recommendations and offers as the best book. It is not the story, but the true-life testimony called a memoir.

When we see the Lord coming in the cloud, what will happen to the unbeliever? Going to church never makes you a believer, but standing on the Word does. I am surprised while dealing with a believer and finding out they are not by the evidence of their practice. How sad that we see the world is making more unbelievers rather than believers by attending the religious gatherings they called churches. They do not know God. In the New Testament time, Jesus' 120 disciples turned the world upside down. If we were the same product of that disciple, we would not find hospitals, witches, warlocks, and magicians in our generation. Counterfeit Satan has stolen money, life, and health by establishing a different religion. Follow Jesus, go out and do what the Lord said, and understand the word. You are the proof of a Believer or unbeliever by your actions. Amen!

LET US PRAY

Lord, we thank you for God, who said nothing is impossible if we believe. We believe what you said in the Word. We want to walk in the light of your written promises to yield the light by proving that it is God who said it and meant it. No weapons of the enemy can prosper, as we believe. We believe believers can cast out demons and heal the sick through the name of Jesus. The name of Jesus is the name above all Old Testament names of Jehovah God. That is why the people of God are called Jesus only in the New Testament. Jesus only since we know the power behind the name of Jehovah's savior. Demons believe the name Jesus and tremble, so Lord, we believe only the name is Jesus is powerful. Amen! In Jesus' name. God bless you!

OCTOBER 23

TALK TO GOD IN HIS LANGUAGE!

God has a language that you find in the Word of God. God has instructions in the Bible for attitude, and clothing style for all and every occasion. The Lord taught us a language that we should use. David has spoken some words while entering His presence. God had all the attention to Him.

Psalm 100:4 Enter into his gates with thanksgiving, and into his courts with praise: be thankful unto him, and bless his name.

We must learn the language of thanksgiving even if we are during a financial battle, health, or any crisis. Remember, David had nothing but the battle. David taught us the language which brings victory, forgiveness, and blessings from the Lord. Dancing when coming out of trouble victoriously, but entering the new trial, they forget the language of the Lord. Some never learn and end up in the same place. Many can't handle the problem since they never learn or know the Lord. Learn to keep freedom, victory, blessing, and healing by learning the language to talk to your creator. Remember the reaction of Hebrews when Egyptians beat the Hebrews up? They got freedom and were in little trouble; they started compiling. You think wow; this person will never forget their difficult time and be grateful to the Lord forever. Hear what language they use, seeing little trouble coming to them.

Exodus 16:2 And the whole congregation of the children of Israel murmured against Moses and Aaron in the wilderness:

Exodus 15:24 And the people murmured against Moses, saying, What shall we drink?

See, God keeps a record of your language and the words you use. Please learn the language to use while speaking to the mighty God who is called merciful, just, and holy. Be careful when you walk by His footstool. Earth is His footstool. Do not use whatever words, it will make the Lord angry. What kind of language do you use with your boss? Do you talk nicely and politely to your spouses, parents, children, or neighbors? You use kind and polite words for them. Then why don't you learn to talk the proper way with the knowledge of who He is? When you have trials, trouble, war, or chaos, please talk to the Lord where He can intervene. The language of art moves the Lord to deliver, heal, save, provide, help, and give more than you ask and think.

Numbers 14:22 Because all those men which have seen my glory, and my miracles, which I did in Egypt and in the wilderness, and have tempted me now these ten times, and have not hearkened to my voice;

OCTOBER 23

Let us see how the ear-pleasing languages of people made God move to favor them. Listen to the language of the blind man when he heard Jesus was passing by,

Luke 18:38 And he cried, saying, Jesus, thou Son of David, have mercy on me. People rebuked the blind man and asked to be quiet, but he kept asking to have mercy, Look, the language of the person changes the heart of God. 41 Saying, What wilt thou I shall do unto thee? And he said, Lord, that I may receive my sight.

The Lord healed His eyes, restored his sight.

Your language has to melt the person's heart when you need favor, mercy, or help. Speak to God by exalting Him to move on to your situation with compassion. Graceful language is the key to getting help.

Matthew 8:2 And, behold, there came a leper and worshipped him, saying, Lord, if thou wilt, thou canst make me clean. 3 And Jesus put forth his hand, and touched him, saying, I will; be thou clean. And immediately his leprosy was cleansed.

Listen to the language of these needy people, that favored them to receive help. God is the same yesterday, today, and forever. Has not changed and will not change. So may I advise you? Learn the language to win the person. Do not tear but restore. If I have to meet someone, I try to give them little gifts and do something just to please them. You will find their favor. Your language should be the most wisely picked for God, even though you have sinned against Him. When David fell into adultery and murder, God confronted David. When the prophet Nathan came with a message from God, David did not raise his voice or justify or hide his sins, but.

2 Samuel 12:13 And David said unto Nathan, I have sinned against the LORD. And Nathan said unto David, The LORD also hath put away thy sin; thou shalt not die

Again, David sinned against the Lord by numbering the troops. Hear his language, and how he approached the Lord's throne. He enters the throne room by asking for mercy, confessing the fault, and sin, and accepting that he was guilty. Always confess your sins and ask for forgiveness. Cain, King Saul, and Esau would have had another chance if they would have confessed their sins. If you sin against God, then only God can forgive you if you confess.

Chronicles 21:8 And David said unto God, I have sinned greatly, because I have done this thing: but now, I beseech thee, do away the iniquity of thy servant; for I have done very foolishly.

His sins were pardoned by giving the offering of wheat for a meat offering, a burnt offering, and a peace offering. God pleases when you use the language of God, but are displeased by the language of your flesh. React by knowing God as God. Recognizing God as all-powerful, almighty, having the office of the creator. Prepare before approaching the throne. Many fell before the altar since they did not know how to prepare themselves and use the language of the Lord. God is not man, He said I change not. God is God.

May the Lord give us the power of the language even when we communicate with each other.

Proverbs 18:21 Death and life are in the power of the tongue: and they that love it shall eat the fruit thereof.

Proverbs 13:3 He that keepeth his mouth keepeth his life: but he that openeth wide his lips shall have destruction.

I have seen people who have no communication skills, have no control over the flesh, and harm their families. Many marriages and families are destroyed by not having the correct vocabulary. Lord, help us use the right expression. Some are kicked out since they do not have the correct words to speak. May the Lord give wisdom to those who have this problem. May the Lord wash their tongue with the blood of Jesus and anoint them with the Holy Spirit. Lord, give everyone a wise heart. Out of the abundance of heart mouth speaketh. Guard your heart, guard your ears and eyes. A deadly thing can enter your heart and will harm you. We know our God as the merciful, holy, righteous, and wonderful father. Learn how to approach the throne of God with the right, wise, and correct word in Jesus's name! Amen!

LET US PRAY

Heavenly Father, we know our language has much to do with our thoughts and feelings. Let us think like you and act like you. We know God pleases us by the language we speak. You said nothing is impossible; all things are possible. Lord, it is our approach to continue believing in you. You are the source if we learn the correct language. Help us think before we open our mouths. Language is a superb weapon. It can bring healing to families, marriages, and even countries. Dialects can bring God's attention. Our expressions by language can take us to the top, heal the heart, and bring us out of judgment. Our language shows us exactly what we are. Lord, give us humble and God-fearing language when we talk. Lord, give us the wise heart to understand the time we are passing through. And help us use the language to establish and prosper in Jesus's name. Amen! God bless you!

OCTOBER 24

PRIVILEGES OF CALLED AND CHOSEN!

The Bible says. Matthew 22:14 For many are called, but few are chosen.

God gave the trials to all who are called by Him. One who passes trials comes out as pure as gold. They are clean, holy, and righteous. They are called chosen. It is like a person who applies for a position with many applicants. The hiring authority will pick one who qualifies and meets the conditions for the job. The person who is chosen needs to be qualified. God said follow me. Do not follow organizations and pastors, but God named Jesus. If you do, then.

1 Peter 2:9 But ye are a chosen generation, a royal priesthood, an holy nation, a peculiar people; that ye should shew forth the praises of him who hath called you out of darkness into his marvellous light;

The people of a nation must choose their leaders who enforce the laws, commandments, and statutes of God, then God will bless that nation. We see chaos in life, counties, and nations because they do not have the ways of God.

Pray the Lord also sends spiritual authority for guidance.

Ephesians 4:11 And he gave some apostles; and some, prophets; and some, evangelists; and some, pastors and teachers; 12 For the perfecting of the saints, for the work of the ministry, for the edifying of the body of Christ:

When the authority is listening to the will of God, produces a generation of saints, a disciple of God, and the Holy, peculiar people and nations. But the authority is like a viper, thief, jealous, and greedy and will train the generation of adulterers and vipers. You are living under your privileges if you are obeying the so-called religion but the Lord. Jesus said follow me, that is for you, me, apostles, prophets, evangelists; pastors, and teachers. If all of us follow Jesus, then we can be above, head, first, and highly favored and blessed. Look for the authorities who fear God and not people. God called us for Himself, to further His kingdom. Prepare every morning to hear and obey your daily assignment by surrendering and obeying God. We have the plan of God already ready, just have to tap into it.

Ephesians 2:20 a And are built upon the foundation of the apostles and prophets,

So look for what the apostles and prophets have taught in the Bible. You do not need to go through anyone once we repent and baptize in the name of Jesus and have received the spirit of God by speaking in tongues. We have access to the holy of the holy place. We do not need the Priest or the High Priest. When we listen to preaching, make sure it is the Word of God.

Acts 17:11 These were more noble than those in Thessalonica, in that they received the word with all readiness of mind, and searched the scriptures daily, whether those things were so.

Don't be led by false teachers and prophets.

1 Peter 2:5 Ye also, as lively stones, are built up a spiritual house, an holy priesthood, to offer up spiritual sacrifices, acceptable to God by Jesus Christ.

While praying, I remembered I was in His throne room. I can tell my answer is on the way. We get desperate in testing and trying times. One of those times when I was losing my mom. I asked God; I did not want to see my mom depart. Help me Lord, and He said to go on such-and-such a day. So I booked the ticket to reach that day. My mom passed away the previous day. See, we can talk to God about our personal feelings and personal guidance. He is a compassionate God and understands you more than anyone.

One time I was going through a fiery trial, and I asked God, "Why wasn't I getting healed?" He told me, "It is the process of time. It will be a day that you will walk and later you will run. It will take time since this is a long trying time, but you will come out as gold. I have God, I walk with him, and I talk with Him. Our problem is that we do not go to God.

John 1:12 But as many as received him, to them gave he power to become the sons of God, even to them that believe on his name:

David, Daniel, Joseph, Jacob, Paul, Peter, and many others had the privilege of calling on God, their father. You can also go to Him, and He will lead and guide you. Walking with Jesus and keeping His statutes and commandments is the key to continuing the relationship. God gives us first and we must offer Him back to receive the blessing over the remaining. In this dispensation, we don't have a temple, so give to true apostles, missionaries, pastors, prophets, and evangelists working as laborers in the field of the world. Support to those casting demons out, healing the sick, teaching home to home. Give to those going around the cities and country as a worker of Jesus. Give to the poor, naked, and hungry.

Proverbs 3:9 Honour the Lord with thy substance, and with the firstfruits of all thine increase.

His promises are greater.

Philippians 4:19 But my God shall supply all your needs according to his riches in glory by Christ Jesus.

Remember, many so-called gods and goddesses have many rituals, ceremonials, traditions, and customs that will always keep you in bondage. But Jesus gives. Gave His life, took diseases, and promised heaven for the one who is born again. The most privileged people are the people of God. When individuals turn to God, the first experience we have is peace, joy, and comfort. We have the Holy Spirit to teach and guide us. We are called the blessed of God. Christians have protection against Satan, diseases, darkness, and poverty. Their land is fruitful. Our God blesses our land, fruits, trees, crops, birds, animals, and all we have. The nations that fear God are different. All want to move to a rich nation, so they can have what they desire. Many people whose gods are not real may have money, but things are still not easily available. No matter what they say, they are wandering from nation to nation for food, a job, and a better life. Just go find the roots of blessings. It is the Lord who is called the King of kings and Lord of lords. May Lord open the blinder of eyes and deafness of the ear. Be the model of Christ to prove that your God is real and true. Our shadow, presence, spirit, and life should be the light in the darkness. Our God will keep the difference between believers and non-believers. Many nations have witnessed that Jesus blesses the nations who believe in Him. The owner and sustainer of His people and the land.

Isaiah 1:19 If ye be willing and obedient, ye shall eat the good of the land:

Poverty is not the portion of God's people. I was talking to some people who have recently turned to Jesus. They said the first thing we noticed was that our salary had not increased, but we had all that we needed. Even built a new house, freeze, phones, motorbikes and, you name it. Before we brought little and had nothing, but now it is a different story. We wake up hungry but never sleep hungry. Our provisions are always there. Our privileges have the condition; we must Love our Lord with all our heart, mind, soul, and strength.

Deuteronomy 11:27 A blessing, if ye obey the commandments of the Lord your God, which I command you this day:

Heaven is waiting for you and me who are born again. We have an eternal home. Isn't that nice? I am so excited that God has given us what we need and our future is bright for eternity. May the Lord Bless you.

LET US PRAY

Heavenly Father, we are so privileged to be called your children. Having the Lord Jesus as our God, we have comfort, peace, strength, healing, angels, and much more for our protection and needs. May the Lord change the hearts of those who have not experienced the mercy and goodness of God. To know Jesus and walk with you is the greatest privilege. Don't let us go astray by idols, so-called gods, and goddesses who cannot see or hear. Lord Jesus, we thank you for creating the earth for your creations. Your Word is true. We do not depend on science or technology. We can heal in Jesus' name. In your name, we have authority over the situation. We come against the devil and its tactics in your name. In Jesus's name, we have all we need. Our God is a blessing. God has blessed us with a sound mind. Lord Jesus has protected us from Satan, who comes to kill, steal, and destroy. He has nothing impossible and loves us enough to give His life, which is in His blood. We are grateful for giving your life to us, in Jesus's name! Amen! God bless you!

OCTOBER 25

WHO IS JESUS?

Is He Jehovah? Are you Jesus only? Do you believe that if you have seen Jesus, you have seen Jehovah God?

1 Corinthian 2:8 Which none of the princes of this world knew: for had they known it, they would not have crucified the Lord of glory.

Yes, the crucified Jesus was the Jehovah who came to bruise Satan under His feet by shedding His blood. When Jesus went up, heaven received Him as the King of Glory. He entered the Holy of the Holy place in heaven with every drop of the blood He shaded for our sins.

Psalms 24:7 Lift up your heads, O ye gates; and be ye lift up, ye everlasting doors; and the King of glory shall come in.

This is not an ordinary battle, but a battle over yours and my soul. It is for all and not just the descendants of Abraham. It is the God Jehovah who said I purchase you by my blood.

Acts 20:28b to feed the church of God, which he hath purchased with his own blood.

Who purchased with His blood? God! One God, who put on flesh, had a secret name given by the Angels. It is the name above all previous names of the Old Testament of Jehovah. The Bible has mentioned 956 names and titles of God. But in the end, this true God who robes in flesh said, "Now, my New Testament name is Jesus".

John 5:43a I am come in my Father's name,

Jesus means 'Jehovah Savior', Hoshea Yehoshua Yeshua. The Hebrew verb Yasha means to deliver, save, or rescue. So, if you are called Jesus only, they are telling you the truth. Jesus is the name above all previous names of Jehovah. The long-awaited Jehovah was walking on earth.

Isaiah 35:3 Strengthen ye the weak hands, and confirm the feeble knees.4 Say to them that are of a fearful heart, Be strong, fear not: behold, your God will come with vengeance, even God with a recompence; he will come and save you. 5 Then the eyes of the blind shall be opened, and the ears of the deaf shall be unstopped. 6 Then shall the lame man leap as an hart, and the tongue of the dumb sing: for in the wilderness shall waters break out, and streams in the desert.

Isn't that true why people call us Jesus-only people? Yes, we are not the devil only, but Jesus only. One day all have to confess and bow before the Name of Jesus.

Philippians 2:10 That at the name of Jesus every knee should bow, of things in heaven, and things in earth, and things under the earth;11 And that every tongue should confess that Jesus Christ is Lord, to the glory of God the Father.

The Old Testament declares the same for Jehovah God, knowing the future name of Jehovah will be Jesus.

Isaiah 45:22 Look unto me, and be ye saved, all the ends of the earth: for I am God, and there is none else.23 I have sworn by myself, the word is gone out of my mouth in righteousness, and shall not return, That unto me every knee shall bow, every tongue shall swear.

It is the saving name for all His creation, since this name Jesus has the blood of Jehovah hidden.

Philippians 2:9 Wherefore God also hath highly exalted him, and given him a name which is above every name:

See why the devil may not use the name of Jesus in baptism? Since baptism is for forgiving sins and if you speak the name of Jehovah's saving name, Jesus, it will wipe away your sins in that name. There is blood hidden in that name, Jesus.

1 John 5:8 And there are three that bear witness in earth, the spirit, and the water, and the blood: and these three agree in one.

Where is the blood? Without blood, no forgiveness of sins. New Testament water baptism is for the forgiveness of sins. Disciple John explains where the blood is.

1 John 5: 6 This is he that came by water and blood,

Even (even =kai= which is) Jesus Christ; not by water only, but by water and blood.

People who do not want to use the name are the ones who have no revelation about who Jesus is. If you have no revelation of Jesus, then you are not the church purchased by the blood. You discontinue the church in which Jehovah came in flesh to buy back His bride. You are a rejecter of the name. The Name of Jesus has nothing to do with you. The one who rejects the name of Jesus does not know the father.

1 John 3:1 Behold, what manner of love the Father hath bestowed upon us, that we should be called the sons of God: therefore the world knoweth us not, because it knew him not. 5 And ye know that he was manifested to take away our sins; and in him is no sin.

The one who does not believe the Spirit of God put on the flesh is called an antichrist. We have a majority of churches started on false doctrine.

1 John warns us not to believe every spirit. Many, not few, but many false prophets have gone into the world and started churches to deviate you from following Jesus. How do you know that these false prophets will not believe Jesus Is Christ, the Messiah, the Savior, the Son of God? The last living survivor John the Beloved warns them and us,

1 John 4:2 Hereby know ye the Spirit of God: Every spirit that confesseth that Jesus Christ is come in the flesh is of God:3 And every spirit that confesseth not that Jesus Christ is come in the flesh is not of God: and this is that spirit of antichrist, whereof ye have heard that it should come; and even now already is it in the world.

The book of John said the Word was God (Word=God) and manifested in flesh John 1:1, 14. Now his first later explains clearly

1 John 5:20 And we know that the Son of God has come, and hath given us an understanding, that we may know him that is true, and we are in him that is true, even in his Son Jesus Christ. This is the true God, and eternal life.

The term Son of God meant God in the flesh, not the son of Joseph. Jesus confessed He was the Son of God. It was very offensive and was punished with death for blasphemy. On the confession, they crucified him. It was blasphemy since they were sure that he was a son of Joseph and not God in the flesh, that is the Son of God. One God follower Jew tried stoning Jesus on His confession of being the Son of God. Jewish terminology, Son of God, meant God in the flesh. Jesus's name was no problem, but saying the Son of God was. It made Him God, not the second person of Satan's teaching.

John 5:18 Therefore the Jews sought the most to kill him because he not only had broken the sabbath but said also that God was his Father, making himself equal with God.

May the Lord give you revelation today of this wonderful name, a name above all His names. And I confess I am Jesus only. Amen!

LET US PRAY

Lord, we thank you. We call Jesus only people. It is the name we bow;

we baptize for the forgiveness of our sins. We know the power of the name since the demon trembles and obeys. It is the name that was hidden for ages. I am so glad that you gave me the obedient heart to baptize to wash away my sins in your precious name. Lord, let my family be baptized in the name of Jesus in water baptism. I wondered and was amazed to see the surgery of my heart, conscious and removing the heaviness of mountains of sins. We want others to know the highest name of Jehovah God for this New Covenant. All covenants are the blood covenant, but this last one is with His blood. Thank you for putting on flesh and shedding blood. We have no words to say thank you. Lord, we bless your Holy name in Jesus's name. Amen! God bless you!

OCTOBER 26

NOT HOW YOU BEGIN, BUT HOW YOU FINISH!

It is said that the ending is important rather than the beginning. We know the Lord had said, "No matter how dark your sins are, if you repent, wash your sins in the blood of Jesus in water baptism, it will wipe your sins out and you will become clean. How nice!

The thief on the cross met the Lord and said.

Luke 23:40 But the other answering rebuked him, saying, Dost not thou fear God, seeing thou art in the same condemnation? 41 And we indeed justly; for we receive the due reward of our deeds: but this man hath done nothing amiss. 42 And he said unto Jesus, Lord, remember me when thou comest into thy kingdom.

The fear of God is important. The thief didn't justify His sins but confessed. He recognized the man on the cross with power and authority. We must recognize the authority and power of God to enter His court. He has all the power. Lord Jesus has the power to forgive our sins so that we can enter heaven. Wages of sin are death. The thief on the cross finished well since he recognized God next to him and did what it took.

43 And Jesus said unto him, Verily I say unto thee, today shalt thou be with me in paradise.

All who were in Egypt started their life as a slave. When they cried out, God set them free. What family you are born into is not as important as how you end up. You can escape from your title as poor, slave, gentile, lost, thief, liar, murderer, Hindu, Baptist, Catholic, Pentecostal, Mormon, Jehovah's Witnesses, or any other. It is in your hands to find a way out. Moses's family was a slave; David was a shepherd boy, not even recognized by the family.

1 Samuel 16:11a And Samuel said unto Jesse, Are here all thy children? And he said, There remaineth yet the youngest, and, behold, he keepeth the sheep.

So David did not end his life keeping his few sheep. He sought God, and God found His heart right with Him. Serve God with all your heart. Peter confronted all who crucified or assent to crucify,

Acts 2:36 Therefore let all the house of Israel know assuredly, that God hath made that same Jesus, whom ye have crucified, both Lord and Christ. 37 Now when they heard this, they were pricked in their heart, and said unto Peter and to the rest of the apostles, Men and brethren, what shall we do? 38 Then Peter said unto them, Repent, and be baptized every one of you in the name of Jesus Christ for the remission of sins, and ye shall receive the gift of the Holy Ghost.

See, you did wrong, but do not go to the grave with all your sins. Before leaving the earth, get forgiveness for your sins. It is the way out of hell, slavery is not your portion anymore. When you recognize sins, then repent of your sins. And Go in the water in Jesus's name to wipe out all your sins. Wages of sin are death in hell. Remember, all have sinned. May the Lord give us His name and bless us with the gift of repentance.

Proverbs 14:12 There is a way which seemeth right unto a man, but the end thereof are the ways of death.

Always remember, none of us are born sinless. All have sinned, and that is the reason Jesus came to give the blood. Blood has life, and He gave life for our sins. Thieves on each side of the savior. One mocked the Lord, and another repented. They were just a step away from hell and heaven.

Paul is talking about the most liberal country of Corinth.

1 Corinthians 6:9 Know ye not that the unrighteous shall not inherit the kingdom of God? Be not deceived: neither fornicators, nor idolaters, nor adulterers, nor effeminate, nor abusers of themselves with mankind, 10 Nor thieves, nor covetous, nor drunkards, nor revilers, nor extortioners, shall inherit the kingdom of God.

God has called sinners to accept the invitation and take the required steps before departing the earth. Do not live under curses, sicknesses, bondages, and in darkness, but.

11 And such were some of you: but ye are washed, but ye are sanctified, but ye are justified in the name of the Lord Jesus, and by the Spirit of our God.

Wash your sins in the water using the name of Jesus. The name of Jesus has blood. Receive the Holy Spirit to give you the power to continue in the truth. May the Lord help us accept the truth. Truth has the power to set you free. All who love the truth will find it. The name of Jesus' baptism is fought against. Why? The Devil don't like the blood; he hates the blood which is life. Blood is the key for the Gentile or Jews to know the role of Jehovah in flesh for the end time. It is the eternal redemption plan of God for His creation. Many who have experienced the saviors' blood can testify that it is the most powerful water birth experience. No matter what, if you cry out to God and say, I am looking for a way out of hell. The Lord is merciful if you seek for the truth to be free from sins, sicknesses, and hellfire. All your toil will be over. There are many so-called customs for the forgiveness of sins, but none has the blood of Jesus. But we have the beautiful name of Jesus, where the Savior's shed blood is hidden. May the Lord Jesus bless us with wisdom like the thief on the cross next to him. That is to know who Jesus is like a thief on the cross, Peter, Paul and many others. If you do not have a revelation of Jesus, then you will start another confused denomination or organization.

Psalm 107:6 Then they cried unto the LORD in their trouble, and he delivered them out of their distresses.

I read a book written by a North Indian Evangelist. The man found scriptural truth in Jesus' name baptism and started preaching on it. He was in the theological college and questioned Jesus's name in baptism. The seminary kicked him out. But he saw it in the book of Acts, so he continued to look for someone to baptize him in the name of Jesus. Finally, the Lord led him to this missionary who had the truth, and he baptized him in the name of Jesus. He did not need the degree to misguide him. After that, there was a revival in the northern part of India. Even though religious authorities spoke against him, the Lord was with him. Many miracles happened. It has set many free. Many find the truth and do nothing to spread it for the furtherance of the kingdom. It is not about Broadway but the narrow way. It is the finding and keeping the truth. I am only interested in the truth.

Matthew 15:14 Let them alone: they be blind leaders of the blind. And if the blind lead the blind, both shall fall into the ditch.

The follower of Jesus finishes well. Many are called, and few are chosen. Just a few? God compares the time of Noah with His second coming. How many saved, just eight? We have contaminated the earth with sins. Standing alone is okay, but I want to finish my race safely. I want to hear the word 'well done,' entering the pearly gate to meet my savior. The whole intention of life is to enter through the door of physical death for the eternal rest of my soul. Amen!

LET US PRAY

Lord, we are lost, have mercy on us. The blood of Christ saved sinners. We are grateful for the blood.

The animal's blood does not need to be shed anymore. We have the priceless blood of the savior. Blood is priceless and valued so little by many. We who are saved know how important the name of Jesus is in baptism. We are grateful for pardoning the sins of a thief. The world did not pardon him, but the Lord gave him eternal life. Our concern is eternal life. We want to enter eternal rest. There is no rest in hell. We need your anointing to preach the truth till the end. It is worth living even if eight righteous get saved. Our God preached until the last breath He took on earth. Never late to turn to you to hear the plan of salvation. We want to be a preacher of truth. The truth will and has set people free from hellfire, sicknesses, oppression, and diseases. We thank you for the truth, in Jesus's name. Amen! God bless you!

OCTOBER 27

PLANT THE WORD AS A SEED!

The Bible speaks about the seed. The seed is the Word of God and as you speak the seed sprouts.

When you speak of the Word to others and they respond by believing and obeying the Word you will see the power manifesting in you and in those who believe. Many do not repent so the word will not grow in bad soil. Your heart is where your life begins.

Mark 7:20 And he said, That which cometh out of the man, that defileth the man. 21 For from within, out of the heart of men, proceed evil thoughts, adulteries, fornications, murders, 22 Thefts, covetousness, wickedness, deceit, lasciviousness, an evil eye, blasphemy, pride, foolishness: 23 All these evil things come from within, and defile the man.

The heart must be grounded and needs to be pure. So we must repent and stop living in sin. Jesus Christ did not have to repent because HE was a sinless God in the flesh.

So as you start walking in righteousness and remove all wickedness from your heart begin planting the word of God and it will grow. If you pray and practice the Word of God you will see the power of the Word.

1 Peter 1:22 Seeing ye have purified your souls in obeying the truth through the Spirit unto unfeigned love of the brethren, see that ye love one another with a pure heart fervently: 23 Being born again, not of corruptible seed, but of incorruptible, by the word of God, which liveth and abideth forever. 24 For all flesh is as grass, and all the glory of man as the flower of grass. The grass withereth, and the flower thereof falleth away: 25 But the word of the Lord endureth forever. And this is the word which by the gospel is preached unto you.

Long ago one of my friends from work shared a testimony of the power of planting the seed in her heart. Her husband tried to persuade her to make a call, but she was hesitant as she felt it was not the right thing to do. Since she was now a Christian she refused to do it so her husband, who was a drunk, got up to beat her. In trying to defend herself this scripture came to her mind and heart and she spoke 1 John 4:4b greater is he that is in you (that is in her), than he that is in the world. She then heard a big blast and her husband was thrown against the wall like a ball. She knew it was an Angel. After that incident, he never tried to harm her.

There is power in speaking the Word of God. Out of the abundance of the heart the mouth speaketh. So feed your heart and mind with God's word, the Bible. In doing this it will come out of your mouth. Your job is to plant the word in the good soil of your heart and weed out any bad things that have sprouted.

Jesus is the Word in the flesh. He wrote the Word of God, when He spoke blinded eyes were open, and missing limbs were healed. All He did was speak the Word. Do you see why the Lord did what He did? I know that speaking the Word brings a great anointing. One day I needed to buy some tablecloths. I said Lord I hate to go to the mall but you know directly where I need to go so please lead and guide me there. I went to the same place where the tablecloths were.

What we have in our hearts is what we will speak. If we have any fear, anger, jealousy, pride, or anything that is not good it will also come out. It is our responsibility to put HIS Commandments in our hearts.

Deuteronomy 6:6 And these words, which I command thee this day, shall be in thine heart: 7 And thou shalt teach them diligently unto thy children, and shalt talk of them when thou sittest in thine house, and when thou walkest by the way, and when thou liest down, and when thou risest up. 8 And thou shalt bind them for a sign upon thine hand, and they shall be as frontlets between thine eyes. 9 And thou shalt write them upon the posts of thy house, and on thy gates.

The first commandment is first since in this world people have many gods and goddesses. Well you know what God says then the devil says just the opposite.

Deuteronomy 6:4 Hear, O Israel: The Lord our God is one Lord: 5 And thou shalt love the Lord thy God with all thine heart, and with all thy soul, and with all thy might.

This is the very first commandment. What do you have in your heart? The First Commandment or some false doctrine? The false doctrine has targeted the very first commandment. Job well done devils.

The scribe asked the first question.

Mark 12:28 And one of the scribes came, and having heard them reasoning together, and perceiving that he had answered them well, asked him, Which is the first commandment of all?

See the answer. This is what Jews always planted in their heart. God cannot become two or three.

Mark 12:29 And Jesus answered him, The first of all the commandments is, Hear, O Israel; The Lord our God is one Lord: 30 And thou shalt love the Lord thy God with all thy heart, and with all thy soul, and with all thy mind, and with all thy strength: this is the first commandment.

These are the fundamental words as a seed we must plant. If we have questions we must go to the author of the book. His name is Jesus. If you have questions about his identity go to Him. He said, do not change the word but keep it as I wrote. This revelation comes by His Spirit, not by flesh or blood. Meaning that it does not go to someone who has murdered the first commandment and agreed with the devil, who knows more than God. It is your soul and your salvation. God hid the truth from one who doesn't love the truth. The devil steals the planted word if you are not guarding your heart by obeying the Word. If there are further questions study the Word from a true uncorrupted copy of the Bible, which is the KJV.

Word planting on the clean fertilized ground will produce good saints. May the Lord guide us to never agree with the multitude that follows false teachers and prophets.

Someone questioned why born-again Christians Baptized in Jesus' name have a hard life. False teachers and prophets are trying to scare people away from entering the narrow path. We enter through the strait gate which means restricted. You are not on a broad way. Jesus and all his disciples kept the Word in times of trouble. Although the Lord brought them out of some. No, the Lord brought them out of them all. Remember that our job is to plant the truth. Wait till the Word sprouts and the devil's mouth will shut. When you heal the sick, cast out demons, and raise the dead it's not that important, but God writing your name in the Book of Life is more important than anything. I play the audio Bible 24/7. I want nothing but the Word of God in my heart. Amen!

LET US PRAY

Lord, you are amazing all the time. We are the most privileged to have the Word from you. It is not man's word, but God's. Help us read, study, and meditate to find direction in life. We want to be called a Holy, righteous, and royal generation. It is the Lord who has called us from the darkness to His marvelous light. Your Word is light in us. Any lamp we have is your word. Help us Lord to do what the Word says. Help us believe as your word says. Your word is the only surety we have. It is a blank check not to keep but to fill it in to cash it. We can fill your word with our name, our children's name, and whoever's name. It is good all the time for any situation or any circumstance. Our hearts overflow with gratitude as we witness the manifestation of the Word in human form. Many have experienced power in the Word. Let God live in our hearts as the Holy Spirit. You fill the world but come and live in us. We thank you for the Word living in us, in Jesus's name! Amen! God bless you!

OCTOBER 28

THY KINGDOM COME ON EARTH!

God rules in heaven. He created the earth and gave authority to man to guard, manage, and keep the earth in order. If you perform God-given duties then the Lord will do His part. But if you don't, then you will lose all power and authority. Now the Lord had to fight the devil who deceived a careless woman and man. May the Lord show you a big picture of the kingdom and how it runs under the sovereign God. The Lord has given you a vineyard to take care of. Where are you wondering, watching, and talking? At the forbidden places? May the Lord help us be extra careful to guard our steps, eyes, and life. Our choices in life will bring a horrific or great reward. Many have taken direction without a director. Many have misguided themselves without a guide. You cannot live without the director of your life.

Our life has great meaning if you find it. Hold on and keep going to the mark of the cross. Paul found the King, allowed Him to be his ruler, and poured his life into the kingdom. We do not know God or know so little to believe anyone who talks about Jesus. We jump in the boat thinking it is going to heaven. Make sure the boat has the Holy Spirit as your guide.

Our God can bring the kingdom of heaven to earth if He has an obedient listener like Moses and Abraham. Obeying and submission are the keys to your success. One true God created you and me, but before that, He created the place for you and me. God loves to be the king and savior but the one who chooses Him as the king is us. It is our responsibility to let God be the ruler, provider, and savior of the earth. Earth manger is human and God has given us free will with very few restrictions. A little restriction was just to check them out whether or not they were to obey. Many times I wish God would have made us like a robot. But our loving God gave us free will to choose whom we want to serve. God or ourselves. Our self will lead or be misled by the earthly trap. Take heed of God's instructions and stay away from Satan's detractive plans. Our good God wanted to walk and talk with us for our welfare. Our welfare was His responsibility. But we wanted God out by breaking one law. Forbidden was His and ours test. The Lord said, can you choose me as your sovereign God to take care of you? We always have some laws on the land. They enforce some laws if we choose to disobey. God gives us all, the devil traps us by making us fall into the trap. The Devil is disobedient and shows us the same. When God says thou shalt not, then the devil says you must try and just do it.

Our God can do what He promised to His creation. But does He find one who knows how to follow His instructions? Does He find one who hears and does it? If the Lord finds one King who obeys, then He can send in His kingdom again on earth. Our God needs someone who can hear and obey. How would you like it if you owned a company, and no one listened to you? You cannot continue doing business. If we refuse to obey the rulers of our house, then it will be chaos.

God is looking for someone who is looking for Him to be his boss, master, guide, and God. It was free will in the Garden of Eden then and is still free will today. Many miss understanding the love of God. He loves all sinners, but not their sins. Our sins separate us from His role as King in our life. You know or do not know, once you transgress, God will reject you from relation.

He allowed listeners in obedience to represent Him against every opposition. The Lord cannot bring His kingdom without citizens who respect and revere Him.

Our God wants you and me to listen to His voice. He wants them to know that His kingdom in heaven can come on earth. The wealth of knowledge, blessings, protection, riches, honor, wisdom, power, and strength from the Lord will be yours. May our Lord help us so the divine plan of God can work today which did not work in the garden of Eden. Check yourself and say, Lord, help me, I want your will to be done on earth where I am living and in which you have given me power to rule.

Genesis 1:26 And God said, Let us make man in our image, after our likeness: and let them have dominion over the fish of the sea, and over the fowl of the air, and over the cattle, and over all the earth, and over every creeping thing that creepeth upon the earth. 27 So God created man in his own image, in the image of God created he him; male and female created he them. 28 And God blessed them, and God said unto them, Be fruitful, and multiply, and replenish the earth, and subdue it: and have dominion over the fish of the sea, and over the fowl of the air, and over every living thing that moveth upon the earth.

Do you want dominion back? It is still possible if you go back to the Lord. Block other voices you are listening to and stop following what you think is right. May the Lord guide us as we seek Him and grant us faith to surrender, unafraid of any worldly authority. There are positions in His kingdom that he can give. He does not need a coward, rebellious, or disobedient person to build His kingdom. King Jesus knows many rebellious, religious, and disobedient people building their kingdom. But with God, you must listen, obey, and submit. No further questions. He will take you to your expected end. Isn't that nice? The ones who heard and obeyed God were the wealthiest and most blessed people. God was their King.

Genesis 13:2 And Abram was very rich in cattle, in silver, and in gold.

By obeying God, Jacob's children became wealthy.

Genesis 30:43 And the man increased exceedingly, and had much cattle, and maidservants, and menservants, and camels, and asses.

Nothing can stop their crops from multiplying even by famine.

Genesis 26:12 Then Isaac sowed in that land, and received in the same year an hundredfold: and the LORD blessed him. 13 And the man waxed great, and went forward, and grew until he became very great:

See, we want all, but we do not want God as King. If we do, then His kingdom will be established in us. Land may have many difficulties with too much rain or no rain, tornado, hurricane, earthquake, or lava, but God says if you let me, I can help. God knows how to provide and how to bless. Let the Lord be the ruler of your life. He wants His kingdom here on earth, but He needs someone who allows Him to do this. Many reject God not knowing, but today surrender to the Lord and see how good He is. He has become my King and God. For almost 20-plus years I have not worked and still see miracles and provisions. Many great things have been done by him in my life. His provision, healing, protection, and blessings have been bestowed upon me. He has made me rich with His indwelling Spirit. He has good taste in Him. Today, please allow Him to be your king. He wants to take you to your expected end. Allow His kingdom to come on earth. Amen!

LET US PRAY

Heavenly Father, we thank you for your desire to be ruler and king over our lives. Thank you for giving us the gift of life. Help and strengthen us to let you be the king over our lives. Our Lord is good, His desires to bring His kingdom on earth as it is in heaven only if we allow it. It is we who allow Him to be the master of our life. Our God, we desire your kingdom to come. Lord, find us worthy and faithful. May the Lord give us His Spirit to guide and lead. Our God is a sustainer of our soul. May Our Lord send His word to all who desire and want His kingdom in their life and country. Lord, have your way, let your will be done on earth as it is in heaven. In Jesus' name. Amen! God bless you!

OCTOBER 29

ARE YOU BLOOD BOUGHT?

Blood has life. Your life is saved by someone else's life. Which means someone had to shed their blood to save your life. Remember, to save you from the death penalty caused by sin, it will cost someone, that is in the blood, their life. Wages of sin are death. God said the last plague was to kill the firstborn of the Egyptians. The night that God was going to kill the firstborn, He asked, go kill the lamb. The Lord brought you by the blood of a lamb.

Exodus 11:1 And the LORD said unto Moses, Yet will I bring one plague more upon Pharaoh, and upon Egypt; afterwards he will let you go hence: when he shall let you go, he shall surely thrust you out hence altogether. 4 And Moses said, Thus saith the LORD, About midnight will I go out into the midst of Egypt: 5 And all the firstborn in the land of Egypt shall die, from the firstborn of Pharaoh that sitteth upon his throne, even unto the firstborn of the maidservant that are behind the mill; and all the firstborn of beasts.

This was the death penalty pronounced by the Lord in the firstborn of the Egyptians. To rescue the Hebrews, the Lord asked them to take a lamb and kill it. So God gave the blood of the lamb for the life of Hebrews.

Exodus 12:21 Then Moses called for all the elders of Israel and said unto them, Draw out and take you a lamb according to your families, and kill the passover. 22 And ye shall take a bunch of hyssop, and dip it in the blood that is in the bason, and strike the lintel and the two side posts with the blood that is in the bason; and none of you shall go out at the door of his house until the morning.

This is a fact that if you are not bought by the blood, you will face the death penalty and be called to eternal death instead of eternal life. Now do you understand why God covered the sins of Adam and Eve by killing the animal?

Genesis 3:21 Unto Adam also and to his wife did the LORD God make coats of skins, and clothed them.

Blood saves the lives and souls of the sinners. May the Lord give us an understanding that sin will cost the soul punishment in the lake of fire. You do not want to suffer in the fire of hell, especially if you do not want to go there. Every year, the priest did a costly blood-shedding ritual to rescue a soul.

Leviticus 17:11 For the life of the flesh is in the blood: and I have given it to you upon the altar to make an atonement for your souls: for it is the blood that maketh an atonement for the soul.

OCTOBER 29

Shedding the animal blood was not enough to get the forgiveness of the sins running in our bloodline. The animal blood sacrifice ritual was only good for one year. We need human blood to rescue humanity from the eternal death of the soul. We can survive on earth by shedding the blood of an animal, but it has no power to rescue the soul from the eternal punishment of hell.

Hebrews 10:8 Above when he said, Sacrifice and offering and burnt offerings and offering for sin thou wouldest not, neither hadst pleasure therein; which are offered by the law;

Sinful human blood is not good enough to pay the price of our sin, which is eternal death. We need sinless blood. God said I would put on flesh and get the blood myself.

Hebrews 10:7 Then said I, Lo, I come (in the volume of the book it is written of me,) to do thy will, O God. God came in the flesh.

1 Tim 3:16 became the lamb to shed the blood.

John 1:29 The next day John seeth Jesus coming unto him, and saith, Behold the Lamb of God, which taketh away the sin of the world.

This Lamb had you and me in mind to rescue our soul. Knowing the blood of an animal cannot.

Hebrews 10:4 For it is not possible that the blood of bulls and of goats should take away sins.

Do you understand the glorious plan for the dispensation of God, also called a dispensation of grace? We have the blood of God Almighty and not the animal. If you reject the blood of Jesus, then you have no salvation. Think twice or thrice before you reject the name of Jesus in baptism. Why? Since God hid blood under the name of Jesus.

1 John 5:6a This is he that came by water and blood, even Jesus Christ; not by water only, but by water and blood.

The water baptism must have the name of Jesus Christ for the blood. What did God do for His church or bride? He gave His blood. Our sins cost Him His life. If Adam and Eve would not have done what they did, then there would've been no need to shed the blood. May the Lord give you an understanding that the result of our sins needs someone to shed the blood.

Acts 20:28b to feed the church of God, which he hath purchased with his own blood.

God purchased you and me with His blood by manifesting Himself in the flesh. So where is the blood? God hid His blood under the name of Jesus. As you go under the water, speaking God's saving name, Jesus, it will become blood to wipe away all sins. Jesus is the saving name of Jehovah's savior. You must take this name when you go into the water for the forgiveness of your sins. If you do not take the name, then there is no blood. And if there is no blood, then there is no remission of sins.

Matthew 26:28 For this is my blood of the new testament, which is shed for many for the remission of sins.

Peter, being a Jew, rescued the sinner from the savior's blood. No more animal blood! Hallelujah! The very first church started was bought by the blood of Jesus.

Acts 2:38b Repent, and be baptized every one of you in the name of Jesus Christ for the remission of sins. 41 Then they that gladly received his word were baptized: and the same day there were added unto them about three thousand souls.

Samaria washed their sins in blood by being baptized in Jesus' name.

Acts 8:16 they were baptized in the name of the Lord Jesus.)

The first time a heathen or gentile received the forgiveness of sins.

Acts 10:48 And he commanded them to be baptized in the name of the Lord.

The sins of John the Baptist's disciple were cleansed by the power of Jesus' name.

Acts 19:5 When they heard this, they were baptized in the name of the Lord Jesus.

The humble disciple, John the Baptist, had to go twice under the water. But they did it right. I was first baptized by the sprinkling of water, which is not baptism. By obedience, I was baptized a second time, hearing the voice of the Lord asking me to be baptized in Jesus's name. I learned how powerful that experience was. No wonder the devil fights the name of Jesus. You know now. It is the blood that is life that the devil is fighting against. Run from those who do not take this saving name of Jesus while baptizing. They are grievous wolves. Amen.

LET US PRAY

Holy Jesus, heavenly father, one spirit true God, thank you for coming into this world to shed your blood. Thank you for being the sinless Sacrifice for me and the entire world. All who have gone under the water by taking the Name of Jesus have the blood. We know Jehovah God becomes the lamb to take away the sins of the world. Lord, we allow the name of Jesus into the water for the remission of our sins. We know father, son, and the Holy Ghost are not the names, but just the title of the one true God. We thank you for giving a revelation of Jesus. It is the only saving name for our souls. Our one true God gave blood. It is for all who accept the life-giving blood. May the Lord make us the partakers of this great Gospel preached by the disciples who had your revelation. Lord, thank you for rescuing us from hellfire. It costs you your life by the shedding of your blood. We are indebted to the heavenly Father in Jesus's name. Amen! God bless you!

OCTOBER 30

GET TRANSPARENT!

Transparent means crystal clear, and unambiguous. When someone says something that you know is true, you'll never have to question them because they are speaking the truth.

When you go to the Altar of God, you have to be transparent. Be clear while confessing your sins to God. He already knows them. The moment you confess, God knows you recognize Him and His position. You recognized God as a judge who knows all. He will forgive and have mercy on you. God knows we are dirt and have many flaws. We cannot be perfect. Go to the mercy seat of God.

Hebrews 4:16 Let us therefore come boldly unto the throne of grace, that we may get mercy, and find grace to help in time of need.

One who does not know God will worry about society, people, and others. Worry about God, who knows where you are, what you have done, and what are the consequences of sins. The big people repent, not the little ones. They always make others responsible for their wrong acts. Big people know that I only have to worry about the prominent judge who knows all. When we sin, the one who is going to punish us, in the end, is God, our creator. So why worry about others? It is senseless. Our job is to confess our faults, our sins, and our trespasses. I do not believe that we go to any human when we sin against God. We go to others when we have a fault but not the sins.

We see the sins of families, self, and sin ignorantly. All sins need to be addressed here on earth. We live in a time of sinners pointing at others instead of confessing and repenting. I have seen those who do wrong and blame others. They are ignorant. These people do not know God. Now they will have no way out of hell since they do not want to confess.

Our God wants us to be transparent to Him. When you sin, you have a way to blot it out.

Proverbs 28:13 He that covereth his sins shall not prosper: but whoso confesseth and forsaketh them shall have mercy.

Have you seen people who confess and continue in sin? That is not boldness but carelessness. Wages of sin are eternal death. If you address sin and take a necessary step, then you have a way out. We all have sinned. No one is perfect. So, confess and be baptized in Jesus' name to wash away your sins?

Heaven is not for the sinner but for the saints. His bride took the name when they went into the water, in Jesus's name. Hasn't the creator of heaven shown us the way out?

Song of Solomon 1:3 Because of the savour of thy good ointments thy name is as ointment poured forth, therefore do the virgins love thee.

Micah 6:8 He hath shewed thee, O man, what is good; and what doth the Lord require of thee, but to do justly, and to love mercy, and to walk humbly with thy God?

Your way must be the righteous way to God.

By reading the Bible, we have the word to recognize right from wrong. We live in a time and day that people do not know what is right from wrong. Many confess sinful life without restitution. Confess your sins to God for forgiveness and it will cleanse you from the sin. Complete turning from sin has salvation. God can restore you to your original status.

Psalm 32:1 Blessed is he whose transgression is forgiven, whose sin is covered. 2 Blessed is the man unto whom the Lord imputeth not iniquity, and in whose spirit there is no guile.

So get sincere. Do not be afraid. God has a redeeming plan for you. God will restore you if you turn from your sins. Restoration is only for the one who says it as it is.

The difference between King Saul and King David was that David was transparent, but Saul was not. King Saul cared for people and feared them. He was not true, and it cost him his throne. By the same token, King David's approach to the throne was for mercy. David only cared for God because he knew God. He said I am naked before you; you know all. So I need mercy. We should go directly and become transparent by confessing our sins. God did not thrust him out of the throne, nor did He, his children. Matter of fact, Messiah came through his bloodline. Do not fear people, position, or security. Once you speak the truth, you are protected.

Have you heard of some court cases? Don't you wonder why criminals have to waste others' time and money? Putting the government system through trouble is a waste of time and money. Now some cases are ridiculous. Some are habitual liars. Once you confess, the judge might have mercy on you.

I know some people who are habitual liars. All they tell are lies. It is self-harming and brings down their reputation. Lord, help us be truthful. We know liars have no hearing in heaven.

2 Corinthians 5:10 For we must all appear before the judgment seat of Christ; that every one may receive the things done in his body, according to that he hath done, whether it be good or bad.

You have a chance on earth to escape from the judgment of God. Get right with God, do right, and get transparent. I noticed in America, people are transparent. They will speak of any sin of the family or others in the open. There is no business for the gossiper. When you hide, then the gossiper has something to talk about. You will hear the juicy story. Once you tell the truth, there is no need to fear. God will guard your back.

Revelation 21:8 But the fearful, and unbelieving, and the abominable, and murderers, and whoremongers, and sorcerers, and idolaters, and all liars, shall have their part in the lake which burneth with fire and brimstone: which is the second death.

Our God is merciful. You fear God and Him alone. Why?

Matthew 10:28 And fear not them which kill the body, but are not able to kill the soul: but rather fear him which is able to destroy both soul and body in hell.

Why so many sins? We forgot to introduce God and to speak about hell and heaven. The things that matter to declare are not declared. We must be transparent about our sins so people understand the value of confession, restitution, and repentance, which is to rescue the soul. Jail and prisons are temporary, but the punishment of hellfire is eternal. Live transparently and the devil will not have any dominion over you. Never be afraid of man, but of the Lord our God only. Amen!

LET US PRAY

Heavenly Father, we thank you Lord that you are good and greatly to be praised. There is forgiveness. That is why we come before your altar of mercy. You have the power to transform the transparent one. Our heavenly father we give you glory and honor for being a merciful judge. Thank you for the promises of cleansing if we confess. What a great God who has a remedy for sins. Our sins have many side effects. Many are sickly, oppressed, possessed, and in hell. It needs boldness to confess. You have mercy if we come boldly to your throne room. We introduce the great creator to the people on earth. He also gave us the chance to be free from all our trespasses and charges. Our God is good and will never change. So come to God boldly, and say, Lord, I am here, forgive me. We write our sins in a paper by confessing and, as we burn this paper, you also blot it out. We thank you for giving us many chances in Jesus's name! Amen! God bless you!

OCTOBER 31

CHECK SHORT CIRCUITS IN YOUR SPIRIT!

The word of God is good all the time. You will bring a short circuit of your blessings if you don't make God your priority and serve him as He desires you to. May the Lord help us in this situation. Learn the way of God for him to release the blessings. That is the correct way to go. When you are facing trials, trouble, sicknesses, demotion, hurt, pain, calamities, and curses confront the self where the root is.

The Bible says. Deuteronomy 32:39 See now that I, even I, am he, and there is no god with me: I kill, and I make alive; I wound, and I heal: neither is there any that can deliver out of my hand.

Our God is good. His words are pure and holy. One who puts his trust in the word testifies that there is no flaw in it. Lord kills and heals so prepare your heart.

Psalms 18:20 The LORD rewarded me according to my righteousness; according to the cleanness of my hands hath he recompensed me.

Many think God is hard, unmerciful, and has no compassion. My question to them is do you love and care for yourself? Do you identify where you are falling short? The Lord can give you laws, statutes, and commandments, but who is responsible to follow and keep them? Look in the mirror. You are liable for your actions.

Deuteronomy 28:47 Because thou servedst not the Lord thy God with joyfulness, and with gladness of heart, for the abundance of all things; 48 Therefore shalt thou serve thine enemies which the Lord shall send against thee, in hunger, and in thirst, and in nakedness, and in want of all things: and he shall put a yoke of iron upon thy neck, until he have destroyed thee. 49 The Lord shall bring a nation against thee from far, from the end of the earth, as swift as the eagle flieth; a nation whose tongue thou shalt not understand; 50 A nation of fierce countenance, which shall not regard the person of the old, nor shew favour to the young:

God has laws. We must listen, observe, and follow them or we will cause ourselves to miss out on the blessings. Let us find some of these kinds. Look what Moses did. God said,

Numbers 20:8a Take the rod, and gather thou the assembly together, thou, and Aaron thy brother, and speak ye unto the rock before their eyes; and it shall give forth his water,

God said to speak, correct? Let us see what angry Moses did. *11a And Moses lifted up his hand, and with his rod, he smote the rock twice: and the water came out abundantly,*

God said to speak and Moses struck the rock twice. Let us see how he short-circuited the blessing of the promised land.

12 And the Lord spake unto Moses and Aaron, Because ye believed me not, to sanctify me in the eyes of the children of Israel, therefore ye shall not bring this congregation into the land which I have given them.

Listen carefully. Your judgment should be in accord with your response to the book, not according to the false teacher who taught you. The Bible says, let them hear who has an ear. Do you have an ear?

Numbers 4:15a And when Aaron and his sons have made an end of covering the sanctuary, and all the vessels of the sanctuary, as the camp is to set forward; after that, the sons of Kohath shall come to bear it: but they shall not touch any holy thing, lest they die.

There is a duty that a priest must perform. But we have both false and true prophets. We must find and follow the right one.

2 Samuel 6: 6 And when they came to Nachon's threshingfloor, Uzzah put forth his hand to the ark of God, and took hold of it; for the oxen shook it. 7 And the anger of the Lord was kindled against Uzzah; and God smote him there for his error; and there he died by the ark of God.

It does not excuse the king, find dos and don'ts to escape from trouble. Keep in mind that the Bible says Jesus is the same yesterday, today, and forever. May the Lord help us keep the word of God in our hearts, so we do not sin against Him! Our sins cause us agony, pain, and heartache. We are not above the Word of God. Carelessness is hurting. Even if you are upset, angry, sick, or in any situation, be wise. The Lord has a fire, and He will rain down on you. No weapon formed against you can prosper only if you are keeping the statutes of God. You are the above, head, first, and highly favored if you keep following Jesus in good or bad, in the fire, in the lion's den, and all circumstances of life. Your God can keep you if you keep the Word.

Psalm 119:89 Forever, O Lord, thy word is settled in heaven.

Isaiah 40:8 The grass withereth, the flower fadeth: but the word of our God shall stand for ever.

Understand the power of ignorance and obedience in the Word. As our knowledge increases, we get shy in reading the Bible. I had lunch with a few beautiful elderly ladies. They were serving God in their ways. One of them was bubbling in the Holy Spirit. I was listening and observing them. As I got to know them, I joined them in their conversation. I was so glad I was there. Many fight for their religions, but I never do. Many have a connection with their false teachers, pastors, or prophets. I am only connected with God by prayer and reading the Word. If you have this problem, then you will pull them into your religion. I know the truth sets us free. The Bible says God's word is true. How nice! The very strict and word-keeping pastor has fallen into sin. I have seen the judgment of God on them and their family. I have seen them doing what they were taught. But if you read the Word, it has not changed.

From the beginning, I remember telling myself that I would listen to the leaders if they were doers of the Word. If they follow the Word to a certain degree, then I will listen to that part only. I am seeking the truth. It will go well if I have the truth. If not, then it will bring a short circuit in my life, which I do not want. Who would like that anyway? We must seek God and not things. Do you understand the KJV Bible is for you and me? Do not pick or choose any other translations. It is your success or short circuit. It will never change, so pick up the clean, pure, and sound word of God's copy of the Bible. If you do not know, then let me inform you that the KJV is the correct one. It is our responsibility, not pastors, prophets, and teachers. They will get their reward, but I am responsible for my soul. Amen!

LET US PRAY

Lord, the word of God is not in heaven or another side of the world, but it is in our language at the hand distance. Help us be mighty diligent and accurate in what we read and obey. We know all words of God are from you. No human influence on the Word of God. You breathed, which will never change. Heaven and earth will pass away, but your word will stand. That shows us how accurate, sincere, and diligent we should be when we study the word of God. No personal interpretation is needed but the submission. We are grateful for the example of both one who did exactly and the one who missed. But we want to know and do as it says. We know the word of God is not to argue, debate, or make money. It is to follow without adding and subtracting. So the Lord helps us to allow the Holy Spirit to teach, lead, and guide us since the Holy Spirit breathed this Word. We want to be blessed in abundance, so help us remove all that can bring a short circuit in our life In Jesus's name! Amen! God bless you!

NOVEMBER

NOVEMBER 1

WHAT KIND OF CHURCH DOES GOD WANT?

God made it known that He wants the church to persist, just as His disciples had established it.

Matthew 16:15 tells us, "He saith unto them, But who says ye that I am? 16 And Simon Peter answered and said, Thou art the Christ, the Son of the living God. 17 And Jesus answered and said unto him, Blessed art thou, Simon Barjona: for flesh and blood hath not revealed it unto thee, but my Father which is in heaven.18 And I say also unto thee, That thou art Peter, and upon this rock I will build my church; and the gates of hell shall not prevail against it.19 And I will give unto thee the keys of the kingdom of heaven: and whatsoever thou shalt bind on earth shall be bound in heaven: and whatsoever thou shalt loose on earth shall be loosed in heaven.

" Simon Peter built the Church, having a revelation of Jesus. The revelation of Jesus is called the Rock. The Rock is knowing who Jesus is. Jesus never told them who He was, but He asked them what they thought of Him. Simon got a revelation from the Spirit, answered of knowing His identity, and was correct. Simon established the foundation of the first church on the Day of Pentecost. After this, many so-called churches were built to their belief and did not have a revelation of Jesus as one God in the flesh. Many Satanic churches have crept in by establishing them on corrupted teaching. But the church which was started in the Book of Acts is still going on, and the gates of hell will not prevail against it. Our God is marvelous and intentional in His care for His one church. Even when Paul and Peter were alive, the devil tried to corrupt God's church.

1st Corinthians 1:12 says, "Now this I say, that every one of you saith, I am of Paul; and I of Apollos; and I of Cephas; and I of Christ. 13 Is Christ divided? was Paul crucified for you? or were ye baptized in the name of Paul?"

Many say I am Catholic, Presbyterian, Methodist, Baptist, and many, many denominations and non-denominations. Entering the so-called church has become a breeze for Satan. Last night I had a call from California, and this brother shared a beautiful message from God. Now in her 60s, a South Korean woman, who received a divine calling at 19, shares her message across the globe. Jesus told her that all these denominations, non-denominations, and organizations are created by humans. I'm completely separate from them. Some men or women have established them. Moreover, spread the word that out of all Christians, only 15 percent are saved. She witnessed both heaven and hell, where people experienced extreme joy in heaven and intense suffering and pain in hell. Regrettably, individuals are putting in a lot of effort for their religious groups and institutions. It is important for us to preach the same message as the early church, which was established by the Apostles and prophets. The gates of hell will not overcome it, as God proclaimed. Jesus said in.

John 3, "Jesus answered and said unto him, Verily, verily, I say unto thee, Except a man be born again, he cannot see the kingdom of God. 5 Jesus answered, Verily, verily, I say unto thee, Except a man be born of water and of the Spirit, he cannot enter into the kingdom of God. 11 Verily, verily, I say unto thee, We speak that we do know, and testify that we have seen; and ye receive not our witness.

Additionally, during our discussion, the brother mentioned that Jesus told a woman that those without the Holy Spirit won't enter Heaven. I said, wow! God is sending this lady everywhere to give the message to receive the Holy Spirit. I am so glad someone is obedient to God, giving His message to the wor's message to the world. While being sent by God, she seeks His guidance on what to say. Throughout her entire life, she has journeyed to every continent and various other countries. Under the disguise of false denominations, non-denominations, and organizations, God and His teachings have been buried. Their tactic is to scare people into thinking that if they don't join our club, they won't find a spouse. Who will bury you and stay connected to you? This question should be directed to Jesus, Paul, and Peter, in my opinion. Although we enjoy seeing miracles and healing, the highest priority is saving souls.

Jesus said in Luke 10:20, "Notwithstanding in this rejoice not, that the spirits are subject unto you; but rather rejoice because your names are written in heaven." Every work started by the disciples of Jesus asked questions: have you received the Holy Spirit?

Disciples did not say, you accepted Jesus so you have the Holy Spirit; that is the lie!

Acts 2:4 tells us, "And they were all filled with the Holy Ghost, and began to speak with other tongues, as the Spirit gave them utterance."

So they spoke in tongues as a sign of receiving the Holy Spirit.

Acts 19:6 says, "And when Paul had laid his hands upon them, the Holy Ghost came on them; and they spake with tongues, and prophesied."

Now, if they receive the Holy Spirit by just believing, then John and Peter wouldn't have any need to go to Samaria, right?

Acts 8:15 tells us, "Who, when they have come down, prayed for them, that they might receive the Holy Ghost: 16 (For as yet he was fallen upon none of them")

The Holy Spirit was received by these people who were not part of the Jewish community. How? You do not see the Spirit, but the Spirit talks through your tongue in an unknown language.

Acts 10:44 reads, "While Peter yet spake these words, the Holy Ghost fell on all them which heard the word. 45 And they of the circumcision which believed were astonished, as many as came with Peter, because that on the Gentiles also was poured out the gift of the Holy Ghost. 46 For they heard them speak with tongues, and magnify God.

" This is what Jesus was talking to Nicodemus about in John, Chapter 3. Truly, this is what Jesus is telling us today. The evidence of receiving the Spirit is the Spirit will give you a new language. I received the Spirit of God in the 1980s. God filled me as I was worshiping in the church.

Roman 8:9 says, "But ye are not in the flesh, but in the Spirit, if so be that the Spirit of God dwell in you. Now if any man have not the Spirit of Christ, he is none of his."

Amen! Receive the Holy Spirit by evidence of speaking in another tongue.

LET US PRAY

Heavenly Father, our hearts overflow with gratitude as we acknowledge Your divine communication through Your obedient and chosen messengers. It is the hunger and thirst within us that attracts God. Many have received and I can witness that there is nothing like the Holy Spirit. It is You who comes to us. It is You who dwells in us in the new covenant church which you purchased with your blood. Help us believe and receive Your Spirit. We know you want to indwell in our body, which is your temple. Come, Holy Spirit, as our guide, teacher, and father, to give us the power to stand against Satan. Lord, we welcome the Holy Spirit as a powerful tool to witness. By receiving the Holy Spirit, we have citizenship in heaven, in Jesus's name! Amen! God bless you!

NOVEMBER 2

THE ONLY AUTHORITY YOU PLEASE IS GOD!

es, if you please the father, creator of the universe, then all is well. It is important to recognize how short time we are here on earth. Our God has shown us the way to please Him. I desire to please God and not anyone. Those who are evil, deceitful, and corrupt wield authority and occupy positions of power, but we must remain steadfast in our faith in God. We do what pleases Him, regardless.

1 John 3:22 And whatsoever we ask, we receive of him, because we keep his commandments, and do those things that are pleasing in his sight.

The bottom line is to please God. It is the only thing we have to be mindful of. When God manifested in flesh, He had one thing in mind. That is to please God. Why? Because He wanted to show us the correct way. Following the Lord Jesus is no problem because He lived right. Our problem is we look around and try to please people around us. We must know our job is to please God. Many want us to please them or to do as they desire, which is good, but when it hinders our walk with God, then we must refuse. You either please God or man or yourself. No matter what it looks like, learn to please Him alone. Do not choose your spouse to please, like Eve and Adam over God. You know the result. Some please the children and raise them as snakes. Love will correct the children. Learn to stand for the truth that is the greatest love. Using a rod of iron to correct children is pleasing in the eyes of God. Obeying the commandments of God pleases Him.

Hebrew 11:5 By faith Enoch was translated that he should not see death; and was not found, because God had translated him: for before his translation he had this testimony, that he pleased God. One who serves the Lord in all situations is the one who pleases God.

Matthew 6:24 No man can serve two masters: for either he will hate the one, and love the other; or else he will hold to the one, and despise the other. Ye cannot serve God and mammon.

Mammon meant wealth. I have seen many go to work even when they are sick because they receive money that they can count, touch, and spend. But for God, they are tired, busy, have appointments, and have many excuses. See the difference; Mammon, which is money, is valued by man more than God. I remember when I was working; I decided I would fast three days and night once a month without food and water. Each month of the year, I get three days in a row of holidays. But some months of the year I have to take extra leave so I can fast for three days and night. My whole life was around my fasting, prayer, and God. I make sure that I fast. Each week I fasted for two days. I always did biblical fasting with no water and no food. My life is all about God and nothing else. I never craved money. I know keeping God first, the money will come. The day God took away my job, He said you work for me, and I will take care of you. It was not my idea to quit a good-paying Post Office job, but the Lord took it away.

Romans 8:8 So then they that are in the flesh cannot please God. 5 For they that are after the flesh do mind the things of the flesh, but they that are after the Spirit the things of the Spirit.

Nowadays, different religious authorities love congregations to please them rather than Jesus. How sad! I've witnessed numerous spouses prioritizing each other over God. It is ok as long you are not displeasing God. But when you step on God's commandment to please the people whom you either fear or are connected with, such as authorities or families, then you are not worthy of the Kingdom of God. Keep in mind you must know the Word to please the Lord.

Hebrews 11:6 - But without faith [it is] impossible to please [him]: for he that cometh to God must believe that he is, and [that] he is a rewarder of them that diligently seek him.

I did not have many friends since most of them went to church and would compromise. Some of them will please friends, family, and themselves. Many would lie for a little favor; I wouldn't. I want to please God and God alone. Choosing a narrow road means following God. We cannot fit into the world, the worldly style, or ways. That is why we do not have many friends. No problem, now we have a friend named Jesus. He suffices to provide, help, and bless. Some compromises for the children. Parents allow children in what pleases them and not what pleases God. It is okay if it is not hindering your walk with God, but if it is, then you have to shun it. I have seen many who like to please others rather than God lose out with God. Fear is another factor in not pleasing God. The woman thinks they have to submit to their husbands. If he is a liar, wicked, and wants you to do something dishonest or unethical, then you shouldn't. There will be friction between you both, but so be it. The devil got into a tussle with us, but we would win if we did not compromise. To please God or people is an either-or relation. No one else but you can decide.

John 8:29 And he that sent me is with me: the Father hath not left me alone; for I do always those things that please him.

Jesus said, follow me. If you please the world, then you will lose salvation. Remember, this world will pass away. So do not worry, you will lose nothing. Rather, you spend eternity with the Lord by doing right in His sight. When disciples followed Jesus, there was much opposition from the religious leaders.

Acts 4:18 And they called them, and commanded them not to speak at all nor teach in the name of Jesus. 19 But Peter and John answered and said unto them, Whether it be right in the sight of God to hearken unto you more than unto God, judge ye. 20 For we cannot but speak the things which we have seen and heard.

Our God is real, and He does not require much from us. I have seen in other religions that their gods and goddesses demand much. People who believe in false gods and goddesses will do all the rituals. Some will even kill others. How sad! God's commandment is not grievous. Obeying Him brings nothing but blessings. So Pleasing God has an eternal reward. Decide today to please God and Him alone. Never compromise with the world in Jesus' name. Amen!

NOVEMBER 2

LET US PRAY

Lord, you compare our life span with flowers and grass, which will perish soon. Our life expectancy is from 70 to 80. Could you help us do what is right in your sight? God, you have given us a life-giving commandment. If we please God, we have a reward, but if we fear or choose to please anything or anybody will cause us to fall. Lord, many who pleased you saw the reward on earth and will receive an eternal reward as well. May our Lord give us the heart to love Him! Love will keep us on the correct path. Our God, who loved and did all that it took. So help us, Lord, to do as you gave the example. Help us follow you, Help us carry our cross. Make us righteous in your sight. Make us wise and diligent to know right from wrong and choose right. Our life has choices to make, and we want to make right and wise choices, in Jesus' name. Amen! God bless you!

NOVEMBER 3

ONE GOD IN THREE ROLES OR THREE GODS?

The knowledge of God is the most revelatory ever. This knowledge comes only by revelation given by the Spirit of God. Why? From the beginning, God wants relations with His creation. At this end-time, He has given us the choice to love or reject Him. In the beginning, there was one commandment to live or die eternally. It's the same law today. If you love me, I will tell you who I am. I am Jesus, the humble God, who walks among His creations. He never announced to be a King of kings or Lord of Lords but made Himself known as a lamb or a servant. By the same token, some recognized Him as a prophet, or coming Messiah, or the Son of God. Many never understood the hidden meaning of the name Jesus given by Angel. That name was kept secret for the ages. If anyone asks today, tell me who Jesus is. You might have many answers from each individual. It will reveal the mystery of God to some who love and keep His commandments. It shows that Jesus is not obvious to know or understand except to intervene in the Spirit of God. Why do we need Spirit intervention to know Jesus? Who can identify a person but themself only, right? Like you know who you are. In the gospel of John,

John 1:23 He said, I am the voice of one crying in the wilderness, Make straight the way of the Lord, as said the prophet Esaias.

So John Baptist said I came to repair the broken bridge. Sin caused a broken relationship in the Garden of Eden. John prepared the way for Jehovah God to reach humanity.

Very first Commandment *Deut 6:4 Hear, O Israel: The Lord our God is one Lord:*

Malachi prophesied about John the Baptist. John Baptist preached the repentance of sins with baptism to remove sin. Sin caused the broken relationship between the creator and creation.

Malachi 3:1 Behold, I will send my messenger, and he shall prepare the way before me: and the Lord, whom ye seek, shall suddenly come to his temple, even the messenger of the covenant,

Now the Role of Jehovah as Son of God, Messiah, or Christ meant God in flesh. God has no son, but He had the second role as a redeemer.

NOVEMBER 3

Is 61:1 The Spirit of the Lord God is upon me; because the Lord hath anointed me to preach good tidings unto the meek; he hath sent me to bind up the brokenhearted, to proclaim liberty to the captives, and the opening of the prison to them that are bound.

Is 9:6 For unto us a child is born, unto us a son is given: and the government shall be upon his shoulder: and his name shall be called Wonderful, Counseller, The mighty God, The everlasting Father, The Prince of Peace.

The Old Testament introduces the Son as a mighty God and everlasting father. The second role of Spirit God, as a male child manifestation of Jehovah God in flesh. Jesus said He was the God in flesh.

John 14:7 If ye had known me, ye should have known my Father also: and from henceforth ye know him, and have seen him. 9 Jesus saith unto him, Have I been so long time with you, and yet hast thou not known me, Philip? he that hath seen me hath seen the Father; and how sayest thou then, Show us the Father?

This explains the Spirit God came into the flesh to buy back what we lost in the Garden of Eden. Jesus paid through His Blood which has life. Jehovah God and Jesus, as in the third role of the Holy Spirit:

John 14:18 I will not leave you comfortless: I will come to you. 28a Ye have heard how I said unto you, I go away, and come again unto you. 23 Jesus answered and said unto him, If a man love me, he will keep my words: and my Father will love him, and we will come unto him, and make our abode with him.

Jehovah God, in this third role, comes as the Spirit to dwell in us. One day, this role of the mediator will be over.

1 Corinthians 15:24 Then cometh the end, when he shall have delivered up the kingdom to God, even the Father; when he shall have put down all rule and all authority and power. 25 For he must reign, till he hath put all enemies under his feet. 28 And when all things shall be subdued unto him, then shall the Son also himself be subject unto him that put all things under him, that God may be all in all. See, everything will be over in the end.

1 John 5:7 For there are three that bear record in heaven, the Father, the Word, and the Holy Ghost: and these three are one. One Spirit God has three roles.

If one God then you need one throne,

Rev. 4:2b a throne was set in heaven, and one sat on the throne. 4a And round about the throne were four and twenty seats:

Revelation 21:5a And he that sat upon the throne said,

1 King 22:19b I saw the LORD sitting on His throne, and all the host of heaven standing on His right hand and on His left. Only one God is King.

1 Timothy 6:15 Which in his times he shall shew, who is the blessed and only Potentate, the King of kings, and Lord of lords;

Jesus is the King of Kings and the Lord of Lords since He is Jehovah God in the flesh, coming to rule over all. If Jesus is separate then, He cannot say He is Lord, King over Jehovah.

Revelation 19:16 And he hath on his vesture and on his thigh a name written, King Of Kings, And Lord Of Lords.

What's gone wrong today is not having the revelation. People who believe in three gods, which is polytheism, mean many gods. The oneness of God was not a problem with the Jews in the Old Testament, but it was a big problem when He put on flesh in the New Testament. It is strictly revealed by the revelation. One condition is to love God and second, the manifestation of Jesus comes by Spirit and not flesh and blood. One who walks in the Spirit has no problem, but the one who walks in the flesh does not know Jesus. Many believe Jesus is a distinct entity. But Heaven does not declare Lord Jesus as another God or second God of the Trinity. Hands up and sit back. The only way you know Jesus is,

John 14:21 He that hath my commandments, and keepeth them, he it is that loveth me: and he that loveth me shall be loved of my Father, and I will love him, and will manifest myself to him. He will manifest to you.

Do you realize God has a strainer to keep out who is not created for heaven? These are those in the flesh who see one God as three separate entities. The chosen sees as one true God by revelation through the Spirit. The Author of the Bible is One God. Two types of people introduce Jesus. One who has the revelation of one God and others without revelation sees them as three separate entities. Have revelation straight from the Spirit of God. In 325 AD, the Nicaea conference helped the Devil to establish its plan to divide and rule. The devil who knows there is one God divides it in three and removes the blood by removing Jehovah God's highest name, Jesus. The Bible says;

James 2:19 Thou believest that there is one God; thou doest well: the devils also believe, and tremble.

LET US PRAY

Heavenly Father, the one and true God, came in flesh to redeem us through His precious blood. Lord, your Word is spirit and we need your Spirit to explain the truth. Our love makes a difference. Our heavenly father we have all scriptures here and there. Help us how to connect them. Thank you for revealing yourself to us otherwise; we would not have known you. God is a mystery and only your Spirit can reveal. Let the Lord introduce us himself rather than we introduce you. Our God has an unbroken system. So we submit to you as our creator, savior, guide teacher, and redeemer. When it is all over, you will be one again. In Jesus' name. Amen! God bless you!

NOVEMBER 4

ALL PROMISES COME WITH THE TRIAL!

Prepare to meet the trial before redeeming the promises. Have you seen achievement without passing an exam? If the mountain is so smooth, no one can climb it. God makes our trials in heaven, which we have to pass on earth. All tribulations have a way out. No matter where you go, there will be some kind of trouble and trials. Unique trails are prepared for you and me. Our God tries to make us pure and holy. God makes a trial package for us before we see the promises taking physical form.

I meet many people from all over the world. All go through some kind of trial. No matter what, you can only win on your knees. When you defeat the devil on your knees, you will have victory. That is to defeat the devil in prayer.

When I travel to a country, I know I am going to meet the devil of that country. I go on a mission with fasting and prayer so that I finish what I am sent for.

God's chosen people must learn how to battle with spirits. Many battles are just your thoughts. When you see the situation getting bad right away, you think negatively instead of using the right word of God. Say, I give my situation to God and He will take care of it. Dismiss the worry and fear in the bigger picture without giving them a second thought. Once you learn applications of the Word of God over the situation, it becomes easier. Do you know why? Each time when the Lord does supernatural things, it will lift your faith higher. No Mountains are too high, and no ocean is too deep for God. For he made them all. The Engineer of this world has the power to rearrange this world by speaking to it. Living in advanced technology, we can believe in many things. One who lives by faith cannot believe anything but the Lord.

In my case, I could not believe the doctor. I have never used medicine and do not know what a doctor can do. I always ask saints to pray when I am sick to get healed. Always learn through the Holy Spirit.

God promises all things are possible! You receive it by speaking it to bring it into existence. If you start a company and you are the CEO of the company, how will you handle your company? If I am the CEO of my life company, I want to make sure I have no evil and negative thoughts to take over my life. My life has to be led by the Spirit of God and my helper is the Angels of God.

I was going through trials of physical injury. The Postal Doctor started messing up my case, so they sent me to a referee doctor. The lady who took me there said this doctor would do good to you. Well, he was a referee doctor, so I thought he would. After taking physical exams, he left the room with an attitude. I received his report stating; that he resolves the work-related injury and dismisses my case. So I was upset and prayed bitterly against the doctor. In my vision, I saw this doctor lose his mind and see him in an insane condition. I know I was angry and bitter. Understanding my prayer would harm the doctor, I said, Lord, do not let this happen, and I forgave him. I saw the doctor's condition was completely insane; I was that angry. After I calmed down and forgave him, then God spoke to me. God said this doctor had done well for you. I asked how. Lord told me that for retirement I needed my case resolved with the post office, I have to find the personal physical problem to get a disability retirement.

Well, the referee doctor said the cause of my debilitating condition is my blood problem. My physical problem gave me retirement. I was sick, but for disability retirement, work-related injuries needed to be resolved. I did not know that. It was a journey with continual obstacles in the way. Think about this, I never went to a doctor, so how can a physician write a report on my physical problem? I went in prayer and the Lord said, gather all the reports you have collected these past few years of injury and send them to the physicians. I never went to physicians, but for this retirement, I needed a personal physician. As the Lord instructed, I sent all the reports to my physician, and he signed the retirement paper.

Isn't God so good? He teaches us what to do if we ask. It had been the hardest physical and mentally stressful journey before I retired. Lord promised me you would walk and run, but before reaching that promise, I had many battles. We think it is an easy road. No, rougher than you can imagine. No matter what you say, no trials are without pain. All trials have a battle and all trials can give you victory if you know the way maker. If you know how to connect with God. Most people say they know God. But to know Him personally, in your trials, in your situations, you need some training, guidance, teaching, and help. Find one who is a true teacher, an expert warrior, filled with the Holy Spirit, and loves the Lord. I can do it if I have the guidance of the Holy Spirit.

I get many calls for prayers. Some I do not know personally. Even though I know them; I have not seen them for a while. With growing children, they changed a lot. Another day early morning, I was praying with my friend. I saw her older daughter in my vision, so I prayed for her. I asked my friend if there was any problem with her daughter. My friend said that her daughter is a people pleaser. I said that is not the only problem she has. But the older daughter is shorter than her younger sister. She said yes, that is why she is very sad. My friend said, my younger daughter is taller than the elder. I said, can I pray to God to make her taller? She said, yes. I said ok, and I prayed. God can solve any problem if we pray. Now I haven't seen her, but the spirit spoke about the problem. The Word of God has promised that. "If you believe, all things are possible." Then why would you not believe it? Christianity is nothing but the game of faith.

Your faith can increase if you know and practice the word in your daily life. Watch what happens if you speak to the situation. Now Christians quote the scripture. Have you tried speaking the word of God to your situations, problems, and trials?

I have some black colored shoes and needed a different color. Because of my back condition, I can wear only certain brands of shoes. One afternoon, God spoke to me to go to Ross' store. I went and started looking, but found nothing. I asked the Holy Spirit for direction. He took me to the shoe department. I saw exactly my style and the brand I wear. To my surprise, I found the blue, and the price was way down. I picked it up. Ross never carries that brand of shoes but sees how God operates. Maybe the angel brought it for me.

I am blessed since I trust His leadership. To receive the promises of God will face trials. Through the trials, it will result in marvelous testimony to tell. Since it is your life-changing story, people will believe it as you tell it. This is where you bring God's glory. Who would not like to believe in this amazing God? I believe, and I testify about my life story. You can try Lord Jesus. Trials will be there, but when you try, you will be clean and pure like gold. It is a way of life. Successful people have gone through not one but many trials before reaching promotions. A package of promises has hidden problems, trials, and tribulations. After solving and resolving, you can pick up your promise. Amen!

LET US PRAY

Lord, trials will write many stories if we faint not. Faith is a muscle and needs exercise to keep it strong.

Let our life give you praise. We want to live by your laws and commandments to achieve perfect peace. Life is short, but full of trials and troubles. Trusting you, the Lord will bring us out of all. Promises are there but have many hindrances, so teach us to apply your Word for each problem. God, you are faithful; you have shown us your example and come out victorious. Help us stay on our knees to receive direction, instructions, and wisdom for all we go through on earth. It is the way of life you desire us to live. The victory of our life can show others to live in perfect peace and harmony in God's plan, so the Lord helps us in Jesus's name. Amen! God bless you!

NOVEMBER 5

WAKE UP MY PEOPLE!

Many Years ago, early in the morning, I was praying by the altar. I saw the Pastor of the church, got up from the corner seat of the pulpit, and pushed me. Was he a pastor? No, it was the fallen angel who wanted to rule there. The pastor was not present there. Satan assigned fallen angels to fight against the congregations, prayer warriors, and leaders. Our position is not to show up with a beautiful hairdo, in the best clothes and songs, but to come with putting on the armor of God. We have a battle against Satan and its army, capturing the sinner's soul, and we are here to set the captive free. We have battled against the devil who wants to bring and introduce evil. I saw Satan's target is on true pastors, authorities, the wives of pastors, and authorities. Remember, Eve. It is the same today. You stay focused and do not worry about yourself and your surroundings, but fight. Wake up and pray.

Jeremiah, Elijah, John Baptist, and many others who stood for the truth have suffered. You will too. Get rid of the creeping, wicked ways of Satan. Satan will persecute you but hold on to God. Pray fast, and get delivered from the glamouring attraction. Wake up and pray for the spiritual leaders. Even people who are called by God can get corrupted or sidetracked. Please pray and fast. You may be present time Daniel, Esther, Joseph, or yourself who has stood for the truth. God will use you if you do not fail God. Get delivered from all false teaching. Toss out adding and subtraction where you feel suffocating. You stand and do what is right, even if you have to standalone. We have many weak men like Ahab. Many were distracted, like King Saul, Jeroboam, and King Solomon.

When you see wrong-spirited authorities taking over, hit your knee and pray, cry out. Satan will persecute you using wicked authorities. These are deceptive demons, since they have the form of religion. We have a mission from God, but when it changes from God's mission to ours; then we are on the wrong side. Dive into the spirit world by fasting and praying to know the unseen activities of Satan, fallen angels, and the demonic world. Prayer and fasting help us see the spirit world. You will see and hear about spiritual activities. Watch those spiritual authorities operate by following the ways of God. God gives them instruction, and the mind-boggling power operating by them. These operations of God take effect with true Christianity. I am sure you understand what I mean. The Bible is not a living word in the life of religious authorities. It is a dead word in their mouth, even they teach and preach, shout and scream. We need to experience anointing, and anointing breaks the yoke.

Why and what do you expect when you attend church? Of course, to solve problems, family issues, and many difficulties and be delivered, period. You need deliverance; Death is canceled and demon activities within, around, on, and against you are destroyed. If you go to a chapel to meet a pastor or spiritual authorities for deliverance but they do not know how to help you, then there is no need to go there. No need to trust them instead of trusting God. Remember, the building is not a church, but your body is the church. Get connected by repenting, baptizing in Jesus' name, and receiving the Spirit of God. Jesus will come and dwell in you to guide, teach, and empower you. Please allow Him. Go on fast, pray, and start seeking His face. If you do that, then the Lord will lead you and guide you. I know God has many ways to help. Nothing is impossible, but all things are possible with God. If you believe this, then you can bring a revival today. You can be the present-day disciples of Jesus.

Our problem is that we have no time. We are too busy. Self-made destructive plans and problems have entangled us. We are complacent. No desire to resolve but perfect acceptance of the condition. How sad! I am not accepting any of that package of Satan, return to the senders.

Every day, I wake up and hit my knee. All night toiling, praying that the strategy of Satan against me has to go back to the ocean and be burned in hell. God said do not get violent against each other, but find where the devil has its seat. He lives in the water; His seat is in the north and now stands on the pulpit. Nonstop activities in a religious building, an untiring effort, made Satan's goal of destruction successful. We get tired, comfortable, fall asleep and we do not care to seek, ask and knock. Help us, Lord. Today's activities are so worldly, helping the devil and hindering God. Satan's good ideas replace all spiritual movements.

Satan's congregations are killing, blood sacrificing and at that time, we are giving candies to each other. Why do our children not go on the street to preach? The Bible says to teach your children. What are you teaching to celebrate all daemonic Satan's festivals? One after the other, we are joining Satan's business and forget what we are called for. Christians should be known for casting demons out and healing people by touching the clothes or shadows of God's anointed people. Now all Satan's books out there teach witchcraft and communicating garbage on the computer. Demonstrating how to kill the babies, poison people, and steal. Do not hear misleading voices. Wake up, we still have time. Instead of opening the door for yoga, eastern religions, and ungodly performances, we must seek God and follow His footsteps. What happens if we get violent with Satan? No one on earth will be possessed, oppressed, or influenced by the devil. Do you remember many teens who used to run away from the house? I remembered God revealed to me the demons were pulling my feet, literally snatching me out of the house. So I started binding and rebuking what demons were doing to me and others. This kind of Satan's work does not need your advice or counseling; it needs your prayer and fasting to deliver your children from the destructive hold of Satan. When you see the daemonic operation, then get the word. Start using the word light, sword, and lamp. Take authority and destroy evil strategies against the target. Jesus said tarry for one hour. Jesus wrestled in the middle of the night and destroyed the devil's activity in the night. Angel supplied strength when he prayed.

We go to sleep since we are tired. We wake up tired, get vitamins, exercise, and try to stay in shape. Satan has introduced exercises that open the door for Him. We drink coffee and tea to wake up. But to pray, we are tired. We feel you are talking to the air. What an evil time! People have more faith in authorities whom they see as religious actors and actresses than Jesus. Wake up, get a hold of God, and do it right. Our God needs someone who can go against worldly religious activities to destroy the plan, work, and operation of Satan. The devil introduced the religion of Halloween. People have spent 9 billion dollars in 2018. Now think about where we are heading.

I have no time for this. I am awake, on guard. The armor of God is protecting me against Satan. Let us pray more, connected with God. Religions are powerless since no fastening. Would you like to join the social club? Wake up and go back to basics. First, pray, pray without ceasing. Fast, so you have the power to cast out demons and heal the sick. Know your God by meditating on the word and applying it. The real world is an unseen spiritual, not the physical, what you see. The Kingdom of God needs spiritual giants to take back, restore, and take revenge on the enemy. It is the greatest time if you learn and know God and His ways. Wake up, turn back, and live victoriously in Jesus's name. Amen!

LET US PRAY

Heavenly Father, we come to you knowing you have given us the power of the Holy Ghost. It is to lead, guide, and teach. How wonderful if we use and allow it in our lives. Lord, help us stay full with your spirit since it is not by might, nor by power, but by thy spirit. We need to exercise the word of God, trusting that intervening in the Spirit of God can destroy the devil's plan. We know that is God Himself. Your Spirit is the empowering force against the strategy of Satan. God is good, yesterday, today, and forever. Help us, Lord, since we have a weakness to walk away from you. Pull us back, hold us close, keep us under your wings and the Blood In Jesus's name. Amen! God bless you!

NOVEMBER 6

KNOWLEDGE NEEDS AN APPLICATION!

You may be a scholar, yet do not know how to use knowledge practically. My mom worked in the Hospital. She shared many work experiences with us. She said some doctors won an award for writing a thesis. They have done the research and are good in theory, but putting the patient in their hand might be risky. However, many doctors are great in surgery but never won an award. That is true since she saw some surgeons ruin many cases, and the ratio was high. So the ones who were good at writing were not good at surgery. So many patients preferred certain doctors for the surgery. I would not blame them. Would you?

So the one who knows how to apply the theory is an excellent surgeon. When you hear the preaching and teaching from scholars, but life does not match with their preaching, then no one will believe. I want the application rather than preaching and teaching. The product is wonderful only if your life shows it. The product will sell if it has evidence to back it up. God, the creator, proved to be a creator by demonstrating many cases. Jesus claimed to be a resurrection and life. He proved it; He resurrected Himself on the third day. Can you prove what you are preaching? I wouldn't believe it if there was no support or evidence.

John 11:43 And when he thus had spoken, he cried with a loud voice, Lazarus, come forth. 44 And he that was dead came forth, bound hand and foot with graveclothes: and his face was bound about with a napkin. Jesus saith unto them, Lose him and let him go.

Jesus created us, so He knows how to fix us. Only Jesus can fix our body parts and no one else. Of course, if He gives authority, then He will let us.

Matthew 8:16 When the even was come, they brought unto him many that were possessed with devils: and he cast out the spirits with his word, and healed all that were sick:

Matthew 4:24 And his fame went throughout all Syria: and they brought unto him all sick people that were taken with divers diseases and torments, and those which were possessed with devils, and those which were lunatick, and those that had the palsy; and he healed them.

The proof of what He did is in the Bible. We must learn the application of the Word by following Him alone. You can talk in the real world, but the proof will justify your statement.

Many attend buildings where organizations, denominations, and non-denominations meet; they hear loud exciting messages but no evidence. Don't just scratch your head, but ask where the evidence is.

All this is available if you find the route through the truth by following Jesus.

John 8:30 As he spake these words, many believed on him. 31 Then said Jesus to those Jews which believed on him, If ye continue in my word, then are ye my disciples indeed; 32 And ye shall know the truth, and the truth shall make you free.

So if you take any other route but Jesus Christ, then you will find the form of religion without power and evidence. It forms organizations, denominations, and non-denominations. See what difference the truth makes?

When I go out to preach or teach, I preach with evidence that He is the same yesterday, today, and forever. Someone took another way, which is the way of destruction. Do not believe, go back and be the disciples of the Lord Jesus. I sought denomination ways that did not work. Seeking God, I found the way of the Lord Jesus. It worked. I experienced it is easier to be delivered from drugs, alcohol, and lies than religious demons. Religious denomination, or even non-denominational, is a stronghold. Following denominations, you are working against the Bible. I always loved Jesus. In my family, we have a lot of religions. We all were searching. I never claimed to be a member of religious churches. Seek God through the marvelous way of trying to find Him. He will put some problems or trials where you need the hand of the Lord. Religious churches will bring hopelessness. So problems, trials, tests, sicknesses, and a situation come in the way to bring us closer to God.

I only depended on God for healing and deliverance. I have never taken medicine. Looking back, God has healed me in a variety of ways. I told God that I am so glad that you have many ways to heal and help. You visit the doctor; he might give medicine, but it will have many side effects. When God heals, there is none. How beautiful is that? Not only that, but He also forgives any sin connected with sickness.

I admire one who operates in the spirit and one who depends on God for their situations. They are the witness if they go to Jesus. May the Lord provide us true prophets and teachers who preach the kingdom with evidence, signs, and wonder.

Moses also asked how they would believe that you have sent me. Lord asked him to cast the rod which was in his hand,

Exodus 4:3b and it became a serpent; and Moses fled from before it. 4 And the LORD said unto Moses, Put forth thine hand, and take it by the tail. And he put forth his hand, and caught it, and it became a rod in his hand:

A second miracle if they do not believe first,

6 And the LORD said furthermore unto him, Put now thine hand into thy bosom. And he put his hand into his bosom: and when he took it out, behold, his hand was leprous as snow. 7 And he said, Put thine hand into thy bosom again. And he put his hand into his bosom again; and plucked it out of his bosom, and, behold, it was turned again as his other flesh.

NOVEMBER 6

We must prepare before we talk about Jesus. Many know scripture very well, doesn't Satan also? He steals, kills, and destroys. Your knowledge needs the recipe to bring it to life. Talks can be good, but evidence will attract people to believe and trust. It is a worldwide invitation.

Nowadays, the one who is called by God does amazing miracles. They receive information from the Holy Spirit. They receive knowledge supply from the throne of God. As you know, God is the one who should be your director. If you have tried a religious organization, and it did not work, then you have to seek Him. It is in the prayer room on your knee. Encountering God makes all the difference. Not the label of pastors, preachers, apostles, or missionaries. If you visited the chapel and it did not resolve the problem, it means you have gone to a religious organization. Know the Bible, and start applying it to your life and situations. May the Lord ignite the word by initiating your faith! I obey what the true prophet, or Holy Spirit, asks me to do. If the Spirit asks me to dance, or go say something to someone or lay a hand, or anoint, or buy someone something, I just do it. The application will show you the powerful outcome of the Word. Jesus will get the glory if you keep faith in Him alone and not in your religion. Amen!

LET US PRAY

Heavenly Father, you said to follow me. Help us follow worry-free. Help us surrender, knowing you are about to do world-class miracles and healing. Knowing you are about to transform someone's life out there. The only way God works, and no other, is total faith in you. Our God is good and will do the mighty, only need the willing vessel. Lord, I surrender. Use as you desire, as pleases you. God in heaven looking on earth who is seeking, asking, and knocking. He will help and show this world great things. Not God, but we have to change. We have found the way away from Him. Lord; you are good and will never change. Change us, transform us into your image. Transform us, so people see Jesus working in and through us. It is never-ending work. The Lord has worked for all of us. God needs the tool willing to work. May the Lord find many laborers to work under His instruction and condition. We want this world to know that He is the same forever in Jesus' name. Amen! God bless you!

NOVEMBER 7

NO ONE BUT THE LORD JESUS CAN FIX IT!

Humans can make and fix many machinery and things, but certain things are only God. In India, to be barren is shameful. Sometimes the witch doctor asked to kill someone's baby for them to conceive. Lord said I can open the womb. Only God can fix it.

Genesis 30:1 And when Rachel saw that she bore Jacob no children, Rachel envied her sister; and said unto Jacob, Give me children, or else I die. 2 And Jacob's anger was kindled against Rachel: and he said, Am I in God's stead, who hath withheld from thee the fruit of the womb?

Only God opens the womb. Only God gives life. According to the New Testament, God gives authority to His Spirit-filled saints to speak of life over the dead, but the devil can only kill and destroy.

Many people have asked me to pray so that they can conceive. I prayed, and they conceived a baby. I talked to one lady. She said I did everything that the witch doctor asked me, but with no result. One time, I visited a church, and they prayed over me to conceive the baby, and I did. I was reading the Bible and also crying out to Jesus as they asked me to pray, and I got a free baby. She said, I spent money on the crock, goat to sacrifice, and meal grain offerings, but it did not work. If you have any problem, learn to go to Jesus. Lord Jesus said nothing is impossible for me. God keeps something in His hand, so we stay connected with Him. God wants to stay connected with His children just like parents do.

Deuteronomy 32:39 See now that I, even I, am he, and there is no god with me: I kill, and I make alive; I wound, and I heal: neither is there any that can deliver out of my hand.

Only the Bible talks about the creation, the creation of man and woman. The Bible says God gives every breath of life to all we see on earth: humans, birds, trees, water, and sea creatures. He also created unseen angels, archangels, etc.

Genesis 1:27 So God created man in his own image, in the image of God created he him; male and female created he them.

Only God can do creative work. God has created many angels and spiritual beings to help, but the creation is in the handiwork of God. Today, we have the most disturbing world blaming each other. Politicians, governments, kingdoms, and power-hungry will try to overthrow the pertinent helping power. If we pay close attention to history through the light of the word of God, we can figure out it is the kingdom of darkness fighting against the kingdom of Light. Do not blame each other, do not put your trust in the one you pick to rule, but look up and cry out to God for help. Do not forget that only God can fix your problem, whom our religious authority has forgotten. When Jesus walked on earth, His people couldn't recognize their Messiah, king, and God.

I have seen no cause or root of the problem in a political party but in God's people. Religious authority has caused this world's heartache by not remembering the way of God. Let us repent, kneel to pray, cry out, and ask God to give us a spiritual leader to teach the ways, and the truth, of God. A shepherd to lead us beside the still water, be the shepherd to our soul. I believe this world and country will find peace, healing, and deliverance from all problems. Our problem is we are too smart. We know all and do not need God to get by. As long as we look religious and do not change. We dislike waiting until He shows us the way.
We cannot solve any of the problems. Do not trust man or woman, but the Lord. Pray, repent, turn from wicked ways, and seek God for all your needs.

Reminder, Esther, King David, King Asa, Joseph, Daniel, and many others went to God to fix the problem. These all had prominent positions and were intelligent, wise, and strong people. Where did they look? They all looked up. Not down here, but up. Repent, turn, and seek God. Seek God for help in the troubled times of our nations. Ask God to send the best-anointed people who know the Lord. Stand to intercede in gape for our nation.

I love good and truthful authorities, but my trust is only in God. I pray to God for them. Remember, God said I change not. Nowadays, you meet people who lie, deceive, steal, and much more. Keeping the religious label of different organizations but having no repentance and transformation. So, who are their leaders? They are like the people who couldn't recognize God when He walked in flesh. I fear God for them. I say Lord have mercy on them. They do not know what they are doing. Help them. May the Lord forgive and grant them grace and mercy.

God help us hit the knee and cry out for the blind and deaf leaders. We will see the supernatural move of God.

Joshua 10:11 And it came to pass, as they fled from before Israel, and were in the going down to Bethhoron, that the LORD cast down great stones from heaven upon them unto Azekah, and they died: they were more which died with hailstones than they whom the children of Israel slew with the sword.

All around us is nothing but trouble, a fearful sight. Our authority will fail, and the army will fail, but not God. Cry out to God. Now, as the coming of the Lord is closer, we see more and more faithless people. They struggle to believe in miracles, healing, and supernatural operations. God knows how to bring you out and deliver you from the slavery of Egypt. He can declare you free and you will be free. Seek God, time to seek His face, He alone can help. We tried and tried and it is not working. Pray the Lord to bring the Bible into our lives, in our children's lives, and in government authorities. The only way the problem can be fixed. How many times have I heard this scripture from the pulpit?

2 Chronicles 7:14 If my people, which are called by my name, shall humble themselves, and pray, and seek my face, and turn from their wicked ways; then will I hear from heaven, and will forgive their sin, and will heal their land.

When they quote this scripture, I feel like asking them when they are going to follow it. When? It is time for you to wake up. I never see fault or cause of the chaos because of the leader of the country but in religious leaders. They have fallen asleep and cannot wake up. We have adopted different ways, songs, lectures, and money collections, over prayer. How sad! We have made the nations prayerless.

Luke 6:12 And it came to pass in those days, that he went out into a mountain to pray, and continued all night in prayer to God.

Why are we so prideful to kneel and pray? Pray that God sends us humble authorities to lead, so we can win. I only belong to God's church. Matter of fact, I know I am the Church. Repent and pray. Please pray only God can fix the problem in Jesus' name. Amen!

LET US PRAY

Heavenly Father, we know it is all our fault. We are too proud and arrogant, forgetting how to be humble. Claims to know all and forgot the ways of God. We see the chaos, but we have made ourselves numb to the problem. We are lost and raising a lost generation. Help us do the right and do what you want us to do. Send us the authority like Moses, Joshua, and King David. We want you to be our authority to guide us to promise land safe and sound. Lord, it is our responsibility to cry out, ask, and seek. Today we bring our broken and divided nation to your altar. Please fix it. Send us spiritual leaders in Jesus' name. Amen! God bless you!

NOVEMBER 8

THE PLANTATION BRINGS PLENTY!

We always expect a lot. We think we deserve all, but heaven's business does not work that way. God of heaven has a law. If you follow the law, then it works. I love to give but sometimes I have met the thief who stole my money. Remember, it is still good to give since our God knows how to return double. If you think people robbed you or stole from you; you do not want to give any more for a good cause. No, that is wrong judging. I have met many who stole from me and spoke nastily about me. Will it stop me from doing good? No, I know better. The word of God supports what I know. I will keep giving. Giving is planting.

God says: Joel 2:25 And I will restore to you the years that the locust hath eaten, the cankerworm, and the caterpiller, and the palmerworm, my great army which I sent among you.

See, it will destroy all this devour, but the Lord will give us double back. May the Lord comfort your heart. We are on earth and meet all kinds of people. They speak senselessly and try to hurt, but remember, our God sees all. He compares a widow with a rich man; the Lord weighs and values more than what the widow gave.

There is a place, people, and ground where you need to plant your money. I tithe and pay my offering, but I also know where I get the best interest to plant extra. I give the laborer and sowing the places continually.

First, you make sure that you give wholeheartedly.

Luke 6:38 Give, and it shall be given unto you; good measure, pressed down, and shaken together, and running over, shall men give into your bosom. For with the same measure that ye mete withal, it shall be measured to you again.

Just give! My parents lived around Hindus. In India, we know a particular caste as a giver. My parents said they were rich; they had so much since they gave press down, overflowing. Of course, if you have seen the giving, you will believe God is not a respecter of people.

Luke 6:30 Give to every man that asketh of thee; and of him that taketh away thy goods ask them not again.

We know some people are just takers but still give them. I believe as long as you are not a taker, then it will come back to you.

Deuteronomy 15:9 Beware that there be not a thought in thy wicked heart, saying, The seventh year, the year of release, is at hand; and thine eye be evil against thy poor brother, and thou givest him nought; and he cry unto the Lord against thee, and it be sin unto thee. 10 Thou shalt surely give him, and thine heart shall not be grieved when thou givest unto him: because that for this thing the Lord thy God shall bless thee in all thy works, and in all that thou puttest thine hand unto. 11 For the poor shall never cease out of the land: therefore I command thee, saying, Thou shalt open thine hand wide unto thy brother, to thy poor, and to thy needy, in thy land.

When you see beggars, hungry, and naked, please give, it will do good for you. It is your plantation for a reward.

When you go in the presence of God, never go empty-handed. When someone visits us and we know they are laborers for Jesus Christ, we always give. If the laborers come to my door, I always bless them. It doesn't matter whether I use them.

The Bible says; Deuteronomy 16:17 Every man shall give as he is able, according to the blessing of the Lord thy God which he hath given thee.

If God has given you much then, you are required to give much. It is the key since many fail there. They think we give the church, but what about the one you use for prayer or spiritual need and just walk away without blessing them? You are losing the blessings of the laborer. Don't miss out on thirty, sixty, hindered, or unlimited blessings by blessings to the laborer. You do not know what you can receive, since God will give it.

Luke 10:7 for the laborer is worthy of his hire.

Many have missed out on being a laborer. If you are a laborer for the Lord, trust Him for provision. I always give my testimony since God asked me to work for Him. He told me I would take care of you, work for me. It does not mean that I have all. For many times I struggle, but I wait on God. One who called me for His service promised to take care of me. The hidden secret, you must know who promised you. Will He fail? No, once you learn to wait on God, you will know His faithfulness. I love to serve Him fearlessly since He has never failed me.

Psalm 41:1 Blessed is he that considereth the poor: the Lord will deliver him in time of trouble.

Read these scriptures over and over. God is faithful, He honors His Word if you believe and act on it. He depends on you and me. Many look at the poor and say God bless you and walk away. You lost your opportunity to bless the poor. The Lord watches our reaction to how we treat the poor and needy. Please give to the poor. I love to give widows and visit convalescents with little gifts to bless them. Blessings are better than money. Would you like to get nothing, stay poor, and say I am blessed? No, you are not. Blessing means to pick up something and give.

Proverbs 22:9 He that hath a bountiful eye shall be blessed; for he giveth of his bread to the poor. 22 Rob not the poor, because he is poor: neither oppress the afflicted in the gate: 23 For the Lord will plead their cause, and spoil the soul of those that spoiled them.

The consequences are more than you can afford. Do something for the needy. Word plantation has the best reward. Go out and do something for people who are homeless, poor, needy, fatherless, widows, and old folks. That will be a big plantation if you are truly seeking blessings.

NOVEMBER 8

The Lord is showing how to receive blessings. If you make dinner or supper, call not who can give you back.

Luke 14:13 But when thou makest a feast, call the poor, the maimed, the lame, the blind:14 And thou shalt be blessed; for they cannot recompense thee: for thou shalt be recompensed at the resurrection of the just.

When I travel to poor nations, I make sure I take plenty to give. I believe this blessing will travel to eternity.

I meet different people and see their lifestyles. God bless one who gives generously beyond measure. It surprises me to see how much God has blessed them because of their generosity. Once you know the word of God, and plant it as a seed, you will be blessed and never be without. Your children will be blessed as well. My mom's brother had a job where he met many poor people. Mom said that her brother always carried a bag of clothes on his bike. I never met his daughter but heard that she is well off. Lord took care of her, even though she lost her parents at an early age. So remember to share, giving is receiving. You make room by giving so God can bring you more. God will trust you and give you more if you are planting as He has asked.

LET US PRAY

We thank you, Lord, for giving us first. We want to continue in your blessings, so help and teach us where to give. Let our eyes never close when we see the need. Thank you for allowing us to give. If we do, then this world will be a better place. Lord, we know there are many poor children, widows, and homeless, so touch every heart to do something for them. Our God gave and taught us to give. You gave yourself. Teach us to give ourselves to the kingdom of God. Our God is a giver. Heathen accuses us when we give to the poor, widow, and naked, but our Father taught us to give. The missionaries and Christians are the best of the best. We are blessed since our parents gave us. We want to learn how and where to plant, to see the greater blessing not just in our lives but in our nation, our fields, fruits, crops, and animals. Teach us to plant according to your word in Jesus' name. Amen! God bless you!

NOVEMBER 9

PICK THE SPIRITUAL WIFE!

The wife is called another half and another half of yours can make you whole if she is wise and right. Many kingdoms, kings, men, countries, and the world have been destroyed because of the wrong help. Our world can blame Eve for the death penalty for sin. Flood came because she was looking at and desiring the forbidden of God. The salesperson called the devil and got her into the trap. Your trap is ready since the devil is a sycophant. The devil is the yes and Amen for your destruction. The devil always looks good since he has the asp, poison and you will experience it after you fall into the trap. Observe the lives of Adam, King Solomon, King Ahab who was married to Jezebel, and King Jehoram who was married to Athaliah, daughter of Jezebel. The destructive plan kicked in the Northern and Southern kingdoms of Israel by this mother and daughter. The nation's southern and northern regions went to desolation and captivity in the end.

Never seek peace by compromising with the heathen, bringing them in by marriage. It will open the door for Satan, as King Solomon did. Satan will flood in. Seek God in all situations, ask for His help, and He will.

The woman is the powerful weapon to bring blessings or curses to your life, country, and people of God's kingdom. It is the most dangerous decision to allow them to work in God's kingdom if they are heathen.

King Solomon was not a warrior but was called a wise man. By marrying the heathen king's daughters to seek peace brought calamities to His kingdom.

1 King 11:1 But king Solomon loved many strange women, together with the daughter of Pharaoh, women of the Moabites, Ammonites, Edomites, Zidonians, and Hittites: 2 Of the nations concerning which the Lord said unto the children of Israel, Ye shall not go in to them, neither shall they come in unto you: for surely they will turn away your heart after their gods: Solomon clave unto these in love. 3 And he had seven hundred wives, princesses, and three hundred concubines: and his wives turned away his heart. 4 For it came to pass, when Solomon was old, that his wives turned away his heart after other gods: and his heart was not perfect with the Lord his God, as was the heart of David his father. 5 For Solomon went after Ashtoreth the goddess of the Zidonians, and after Milcom the abomination of the Ammonites. 6 And Solomon did evil in the sight of the Lord, and went not fully after the Lord, as did David his father. 7 Then did Solomon build a high place for Chemosh, the abomination of Moab, in the hill that is before Jerusalem, and for Molech, the abomination of the children of Ammon. 8 And likewise did he for all his strange wives, which burnt incense and sacrificed unto their gods. 9 And the Lord was angry with Solomon because his heart was turned from the Lord God of Israel, which had appeared unto him twice,

The problem is in hearing. The Bible says to hear who has an ear. Everyone has an ear, but one who hears and obeys has an ear. Listen to God and His instruction. Satan will use a wicked woman to tear you down,

NOVEMBER 9

and you will die to lose. Your kingdom with your family will be taken away, and your family will be destroyed.

Never worry about gaining the vote and your position. If you believe in and trust the Lord, he will give you protection, promotion, and prosperity.

Not trusting the Lord is the reason for internal and external chaos. King Solomon was being attacked by the next-door king. Jeroboam came back from Egypt to rise against Solomon's sons. Now, if King Solomon had kept the faith, then he would never have seen the kingdom divided. The kingdom became northern and southern, not trusting God. Put your trust in God Jehovah; He is all-powerful. Wise King Solomon took his eyes away from God. He feared the surrounding nations and worshiped his queen's gods and goddesses.

Joshua 23:10 One man of you shall chase a thousand: for the LORD your God, he it is that fighteth for you, as he hath promised you. Take good heed therefore unto yourselves, that ye love the LORD your God.

Only if you follow His commandments and laws. You will find protection if you keep the ways of God.

Some men marry a woman who has money or can do some housework. Let us see how Abraham asked to pick the wife for his son. Abraham was in the country of Canaan, whom God rejected. So he asked the eldest servant of the house.

Genesis 24:3 And I will make thee swear by the Lord, the God of heaven, and the God of the earth, that thou shalt not take a wife unto my son of the daughters of the Canaanites, among whom I dwell:4 But thou shalt go unto my country, and to my kindred, and take a wife unto my son Isaac.

Jacob served His uncle for 14 years to get a wife.

Genesis 29:18 And Jacob loved Rachel; and said, I will serve thee seven years for Rachel thy younger daughter.

Why? This woman you marry will take your eyes away from the living God. Very dangerous if you do not find a spiritual wife.

Esther was a spiritual daughter and was raised by Mordecai, listening to his every instruction. She overthrew Satan and destroyed the enemy. The enemy comes one way and runs seven ways. Our God has a system to approach, so prepare. You are the daughter of Zion. Do not worry about your nose, the color of your hair, makeup, and look. Look up, He has made you gorgeous, pray and fast. You are the present-day Ester, Mary, and Ruth. May you be the kingdom seeker, not worldly power and position seeker. Our God has called you to rise above. Put on the armor of God and take the weapon of God to defeat the enemy. The enemy is going around like a roaring lion to a devourer, but you can defeat it on your knees. Pray without ceasing, first pray. Our job is not to act like a silly woman, Eve, Queen Athaliah, or her mom Jezebel, who put on makeup and a hairdo before they threw her down as food for the dogs.

Our God is looking for a bride who is not looking around to fail Him and His plan, but one who is ready and willing to serve Him. The church is the bride and remember; we are a church, not the building.

Ephesians 5:27 That he might present it to himself a glorious church, not having spot, or wrinkle, or any such thing; but that it should be holy and without blemish.

He is looking for a wise bride.

Matthew 25:6 And at midnight there was a cry made, Behold, the bridegroom cometh; go ye out to meet him. 7 Then all those virgins arose, and trimmed their lamps. 10b the bridegroom came; and they that were ready went in with him to the marriage: and the door was shut.

This is the most crucial time for the called, chosen, repented, and washed in the lamb's blood. Prepare yourself by receiving His Spirit to meet your groom. He is on the way to receiving His bride. Time is near for the faithful wife of Jesus to work for Him on earth and eternity in heaven. Amen!

LET US PRAY

Lord, we are grateful that you have called and chosen us for the kingdom. We know the kingdom of God suffers violence, so makes us mighty warriors like King David to take by force what belongs to us. You have given us the power. Help us pay attention to using it. Help us look up and keep our eyes focused on you. We battle in victory. You have defeated the enemy. Our Lord and Maker are coming to receive His bride. We are the church, His bride. Let us pray, fast, and prepare. Let the Lord find us without blemishes, wrinkles, and spotless to meet our groom. Soon we will go for eternity to abide with you. Help us, Lord Jesus. Find us worthy to be received in heaven in Jesus' name. Amen! God bless you!

NOVEMBER 10

DO NOT LET YOUR DREAM DIE!

We dream many times throughout our lives. God talks to us in a dream. But remember, when you have many dreams, that also means the spirit is disturbing your mind. When I have many dreams, that means I have to command that evil spirit to get out. Do everything to get rid of the demon. Put the Bible under the head as a pillow, anoint the head and house with oil, lay a hand on the head, and speak in tongue. Take God-given authority of binding and breaking the evil spirits and their acts of killing, stealing, and destroying. Lose the Holy Spirit, God's warrior, ministering, and guardian angels in Jesus's name.

Ecclesiastes 5:7 For in the multitude of dreams and many words there are also divers vanities: but fear thou God.

Today I want to talk about the dream God gives for the future. God reveals the future promises or plans in dreams.

Many destroy the plan revealed in dreams by getting ahead or being irresponsible or impatient. The God-given promise comes later but is still on time. We used to sing that He is an on-time God. Remember, there is a God in heaven that is real and powerful. If He is revealing to you something through dream, vision, audible voice, or through prophets, then get serious. It is not a time to mess around with your life.

Acts 2:17 And it shall come to pass in the last days, saith God, I will pour out of my Spirit upon all flesh: and your sons and your daughters shall prophesy, and your young men shall see visions, and your old men shall dream dreams:

God's direction reveals the future agenda and also gives warnings in the dream. We must pay closer attention to the dream by filtering the false one. Ask God to give you discernment and interpretation of the dream. The dream is very important, so pay devoted consideration.

Matthew 1:20 But while he thought on these things, behold, the angel of the Lord appeared unto him in a dream, saying, Joseph, thou son of David, fear not to take unto thee Mary thy wife: for that which is conceived in her is of the Holy Ghost.

Heaven releases information that you are wondering about or concerned about. Lord Jesus has revealed many plans in the dream. I always try to write my dreams down. Many think they would remember, but they don't.

Please write it down. God solves the mystery in the dream. Remember, God sent Messiah Jesus Christ, but the devil tried to destroy Him. Remembering God is a keeper of His promises if you follow His protecting plan. Thank God for those who obey the order of the Lord given in the dream.

Matthew 2:13 And when they were departed, behold, the angel of the Lord appeareth to Joseph in a dream, saying, Arise, and take the young child and his mother, and flee into Egypt, and be thou there until I bring thee word: for Herod will seek the young child to destroy him.

We had the Messiah, the Son of God, Christ, since someone took the courage to take a step to save the life of the baby. Praise God! When there is a warning, take action, please.

Genesis 28:12 And he dreamed, and behold a ladder set up on the earth, and the top of it reached to heaven: and behold the angels of God ascending and descending on it.13 And, behold, the Lord stood above it, and said, I am the Lord God of Abraham thy father, and the God of Isaac: the land whereon thou liest, to thee will I give it, and to thy seed;18 And Jacob rose early in the morning, and took the stone that he had put for his pillows, and set it up for a pillar, and poured oil upon the top of it.

How necessary was that to seal that place with the Holy Spirit? I seal all your promises given by God with His Spirit in Jesus' name. It will come to pass if you faint not. God is about to do great and mighty for you and your loved one. Just stay consistent, and remind yourself of His promises.

I had a dream of preaching in a Muslim country. Ever since, I have kept the map and I pray over Muslim nations. In my dream, I was a little scared, but in the same dream, I was preaching with boldness. Thinking Muslim, we think of opposition, but if I prepare my way, by fasting and praying, things will happen.

In real life, dream big, that is okay. Keep in mind that there are no limits to what you can accomplish, just like the boundless sky. Live a limitless life. Dream Big. It is not impossible for God who said all things are possible if you believe. Just do not get weary, keep trying, keep hoping and your constant effort will do something great. I pray over all your work. May the Lord Jesus bless and multiply your handy work.

I see dreams and visions and hear the audible voice of God. Interpretation comes as I open my mouth and speak. Open your mouth to support positive words. If you dream, then say I believe it and it will happen. God bless all promises and plans given to me and you in a dream. Remind yourself of a dream. Tell God that you still believe in it. How nice if you say, but do not press God.

Daniel had many dreams with God-given knowledge to interpret.

Numbers 12:6 And he said, Hear now my words: If there be a prophet among you, [I] the LORD will make myself known unto him in a vision, [and] will speak unto him in a dream.

God gave promises to me through the dream in the year 1984. It has not happened yet, but my job is to hold on to it. Abraham had a promise, and he believed in God for it. The God who said will perform it in due season. With God, nothing is impossible, but God has the season for all. May the Lord help us understand he is the great God. Our God can do anything and everything if you fail Him not.

One dream was a warning about Hinduism coming to the East Coast. Lord explained Hindus are consistent. They worship idols for ages. God revealed to me how to pray for Hindus, that is asking God to put love for Jesus in Hindu hearts. So I ask you not once thrice, but pray every day for this God-telling prayer request.

Many of you are out there wondering about your dream. Wait, do not lose your dream by losing hope or being discouraged by seeing no progress. He does not need a reminder or your help. He just wants you to believe and wait. Do not go to heathen, witch doctor, palm reader, or any other media for interpretation, Daniel Chapter 2 is a piece of evidence that magicians, astrologers, or Chaldean could not interpret the dream. But Daniel, a wise man who did interpretation as given by the Jehovah God. Joseph saw in a dream his brothers and mother-father bowing to him. Life took a sad turn on a long, troubled road. He never saw him being accused by a woman. He never saw himself in prison as a slave and in a prominent position in Egypt. The Lord showed him only a symbolic dream. It does not show all the hindrances in your dream, but they will come. May the Lord give us many interpreters of dreams.

God still talks to His creation, who walks with Him and obeys His voice. Amen!

LET US PRAY

Our heavenly father, who is in heaven, communicates with us. Our dream is the unique way of God releasing specific information, warnings, and plans with promise. You are a source of wonder and we are filled with gratitude. We want to dream, but yours only. We want to dream with the knowledge to interpret the dream. Thank you for the examples of how people accepted the dream. Even the one who is the ruler of the heathen nation does not know true God takes heed and precaution. It is a breathtakingly beautiful and extraordinary manner in which God acquires information. Your dream has saved many lives and nations with wise rulers. We thank you for the rulers who rule with information from heaven. We thank you to those who seek to understand it. Thank you for all the promises given in dreams, in Jesus' name. Amen! God bless you!

NOVEMBER 11

DAMAGE OF THE PRAYERLESSNESS!

The danger of prayerlessness. I heard one preacher say that the Lord spoke to him, "pray or die."

That means you must pray without ceasing. It is dangerous if your life has no prayer. I am not talking about the prayer on food, before going to sleep, or when you wake up and pray a little.

1 Timothy 2:1 I exhort therefore, that, first of all, supplications, prayers, intercessions, and giving of thanks, be made for all men;

1 Thessalonians 5:17 Pray without ceasing.

The same God gave the preacher the key to life. Pray or die. May the Lord give us an understanding of prayerlessness. My life is all about prayer. I feel like I am a prayerholic. If I have to fly early, I am up at midnight or in the middle of the night to pray for at least two hours. I am not coming out of my house without prayer. No food is ok, but no prayer is impossible.

Do you hear the news? I mean bad news and hear about seeing the sicknesses. Do you see the suicide, do you hear the child abuse, kidnapping, and molesting? Look at shooting and killing. Do you see internal-external chaos? Do you see people dying at an early age, possessed, oppressed, divorced, and elder abuse? The list will go on and on and on.

Let me remind you, that is because of the prayerlessness of God's people. Imagine the Lord has a system, which is called the calling system, from earth to heaven, which is called the calling system, from earth to heaven. Someone has to call on God who can do all since He is all-powerful, and He said nothing was impossible. Now, this connection is only available for the righteous. Make sure you are repented and born again, God-fearing people.

You say, "I prayed", but prayed after the accident happened. You would have stopped the kidnapping, suicide, stealing, killing, raping sickness, or any damage on earth by praying. All damage results from prayerless people. Do not say it is one person's job.

Since the Bible says:

Psalm 65:2 O thou that hearest prayer, unto thee shall all flesh come.

NOVEMBER 11

Are you made of flesh? Yes, then you must pray. Jesus in the flesh prayed as well. No flesh is an excuse.

Any time you see a problem, it shows the need for prayer. Angels are jobless since no calls are coming from the earth for their trouble. God made angels to serve, help, or fight for humans. A creator is the King of Kings. He does not need to be coming out to take care of the creation. God sends mighty angels and they do what He commands them to do. Creation has limited power. Humans cannot hear or see the spiritual world. But by their cry, by their petitions, by their prayer, God sends help through angels. Let me remind you; God has many archangels or generals over angels. Angels work under the General called Arch Angels to minister to us on earth. But they can come only if someone calls them. For example, in flesh, God prayed, and they strengthened before going through the great trial of crucifixion.

Luke 22:43 And there appeared an angel unto him from heaven, strengthening him.

Have you heard much prayer, much power? Yes, try it. There will be heavenly traffic to rescue, help, heal, and deliver to all of us. If there is a man to pray to, then there is a God to answer. God has a good hearing if you talk to Him. If You are not talking to Him, then do not expect. If you say God is real, mighty, and all-powerful, which is true, it does not mean that He will take over and take care of needs and situations. He does not come uninvited. Invite Him. He will come. Stay connected by continued prayer; it is the only best security system in the world.
Sins of prayerlessness

The job of a man of God is to pray day and night.

1 Samuel 12:23 Moreover as for me, God forbid that I should sin against the Lord in ceasing to pray for you: but I will teach you the good and the right way:

I watch Prophet Alph Lukau. All I hear about him is that he prays day and night. The heavenly realm is what he sees. He was in Paris but called his church people to say that someone was doing witchcraft in his church. He sent someone to remove it as God showed him where the stuff was.

Now the churches are falling apart, and people are possessed. The congregation is dying, under the bondage of sickness, demon oppression, and sicknesses. Why? Because of prayerless authority. Thieves, greedy, have entered the religious world. No matter what anyone says, we know the mission of Jesus is still the same, but we do not see it because of a lack of prayer. He came to heal the brokenhearted, heal the sick, and cast out demons. It is rare; we do not see the supernatural sign and wonder. It has become unfamiliar to people.

You go to the top of the mountain or terrace to pray. Jesus went up to the Mount of Olive to pray. Moses was up there to get connected with the Lord. But David was on a terrace to look around and fell into sin. Go up, do not look around, but look up, kneel, and cry out. You will notice the difference.

This morning this evangelist called me. He said I have to preach at the conference, but I am sick. I prayed and His sinus opened up, his chest pain gone, and before hanging up the phone, he said I could breathe. Yesterday this lady minister called, very down, and as I prayed, she said I am a hundred percent fine. A minister needs help and if I am not connected with God, it cannot happen. They will stay sick, hurt, in pain, and hahaha, the devil will win.

Another day, this pastor from another state called, he was under attack. So I started teaching him how to destroy all the witchcraft attacks. I taught him how to counter-attack. All this happens when you get connected with the Lord. Why do some pastors resign, and why do some fall into sin? No prayer, they are so busy, like Martha. Be like Mary. Every moment you pray. Don't just watch the Christian channel, but channel up with the Lord. The TV is not prayer; TV is another distraction to keep you from prayer.

I pray in the name of Jesus that all this prayerlessness disappears. Pray in every season instant, pray without ceasing. And do not call everyone for your problem, but call Jesus.

I have seen my mom always praying. Her prayer has brought us home safe and sound. Her prayer has kept us from trouble and trial. I had never seen my mom sitting anywhere but at home or at work. I see people in the mall, at a nail salon or spa, at movies, sightseeing, on cruises, vacationing, in a courtroom, in prison, jail, or visiting someone, in the bar, on drugs, with another man, and name it. All this happens because of no connection with God. How about prayer for 24 hours? Lift your case to the Lord and heaven will come down on earth to help, rescue, and do what it takes to help the creation. May the Lord take away our prayerlessness in Jesus' name! Amen!

LET US PRAY

Only Jesus, we thank you for giving us an example of prayer. We know the God, who answers prayer, heals the sick, raises the dead, and commands the demons to get out, does not need to pray, but He prayed since He was in the flesh. May Lord Jesus encircle us with a sense of security and solace, showing us how to pray as you did. You said follow me. Help us not to follow all prayerless religious authority but to you alone. Our connection is very important for our welfare. Our God has given us a well-paid phone which He named Prayer. Isn't that the most beautiful? He has provided all networks and Wi-Fi and has a service plan unlimited. I appreciate the simplicity of this free connection to Jesus' private number. Thanks to this facility, we can get help, and provide for needs and problems. In the name of Jesus, we bind and break prayerlessness. We are called to stay connected, so give us the spirit of prayer. We can rest easy knowing that as long as we call upon Jesus' name, we are protected. Amen! God bless you!

NOVEMBER 12

FOLLOW THE EASY INSTRUCTION OF GOD!

Now we have many denominations, non-denominations, and organizations, since people have found different recipes for God. One God has One Bible and One Way to go to heaven. The Bible is a book to show you how to secure your life on earth and navigate to heaven. It's a no-brainer if you adhere to Jesus' teachings.

Luke 9:23 And he said to them all, If any man will come after me, let him deny himself, and take up his cross daily, and follow me.

Specific but simple instructions given by God!

John 14:6 Jesus saith unto him, I am the way, the truth, and the life: no man cometh unto the Father, but by me.

Isn't this the simple, accurate instruction to do? Why do we follow all other ways and forget Jesus? All these denominations or non-denomination have their ways and not Jesus. So friends, open the Bible and do yourself a favor to stick to the one who said follow me. Have mercy on your soul. Your soul is under your care. Do not trade your soul for a little favor. Don't be careless on your part. Have fear of hell. It is a matter of eternity. I want to do what it takes to come to heaven through Jesus. Who is the door? Jesus is the door to heaven. I am not worried if someone likes me or not about what I stand for. I am a pilgrim, here today and gone tomorrow. Many think God does not care as long as you believe and have a simple faith. Just going to church will save you. No place in the Bible says you're saved if you are sitting on a pew and paying tithes and offerings. Your security is the Word if you follow the way Jesus prescribed to Nicodemus.

The Bible is a map of the kingdom of Heaven. If you want to get there, then let us travel together.

First, check what the Bible says.

Acts 4:12 Neither is there salvation in any other: for there is none other name under heaven given among men, whereby we must be saved.

The Name Jesus has the power to save us. It is a saving name. Name Jesus saves us from sicknesses, and delivers us from demons. It also forgives our sins if we use it in water baptism, which is the greatest of all.

Acts 10:43 To him give all the prophets witness, that through his name whosoever believeth in him shall receive remission (forgiveness) of sins.

The name Jesus is important for entering the pearly gate. No angels will let you in if you do not have the name of Jesus. Nowadays people say do not talk to 'Jesus only people'. Please do not talk to us since we have the saving name, Jesus. It is the name above all previous names of God Jehovah. Be careful! Do not listen to the devil who has made many organizations, churches, and mainline churches. They will threaten you with rejection. You do not need lost authorities of lost churches. You need the name of Jesus to enter the kingdom. Your residence is in heaven and not on earth.

God hid this gospel from the lost organizations, denominations, and non-denominations, just to let them know Jesus never came for them.

First, we must need a revelation of Jesus' identity like Peter and Paul had. He is the God Jehovah in the flesh to shed the blood. The creator walks on earth to redeem creation through His blood. Search the scripture. Do not join any congregation.

Acts 17:11 These were more noble than those in Thessalonica, in that they received the word with all readiness of mind, and searched the scriptures daily, whether those things were so.

Colossians 1:14 In whom we have redemption through his blood, even the forgiveness of sins:

Do you ever wonder why such a big difference today and then? 2000 years ago, a true Jesus brand disciple turned the world upside down. But today, they are powerless, hopeless, oppressed, possessed, and sick. It is a so-called Jesus brand Heaven does not recognize.

I was staying away from some of them who were labeled with different brands, putting Christ to shame.

Romans 2:24 For the name of God is blasphemed among the Gentiles through you, as it is written.

2 Peter 2:2 And many shall follow their pernicious ways, by reason of whom the way of truth shall be evil spoken of.

If someone tells you, Jesus only, then answer them 'yes, we are Jesus' only people'. Many have left the name and found many other confusing, confounding doctrines where they do not have to repent or change lifestyle or work for God's kingdom but theirs.

Jude 1:4 For there are certain men crept in unawares, who were before of old ordained to this condemnation, ungodly men, turning the grace of our God into lasciviousness, and denying the only Lord God, and our Lord Jesus Christ.

Jesus approved Peter to build His church on the revelation he had of Jesus Christ as the Son of God and as the Messiah. You continue building on it. Do not start any other churches or denominations if you don't have a revelation to Jesus. All other foundations are without the chief cornerstone, Jesus.

Once upon a time, I was one of them. But I was seeking the truth. By obeying, I experienced the power of the Blood when I went into the water in Jesus' name.

Exceptional experience! I followed instructions Jesus, saying Believe the prophets and apostles whom I have given the key to.

Ephesians 2:20 And are built upon the foundation of the apostles and prophets, Jesus Christ himself being the chief cornerstone;

Thousands of Jews followed.

Acts 2:38 Then Peter said unto them, Repent, and be baptized every one of you in the name of Jesus Christ for the remission of sins, and ye shall receive the gift of the Holy Ghost.

Church in Samaria: Built on Jesus' instruction to Peter, Acts 8:16 (For as yet he was fallen upon none of them: only they were baptized in the name of the Lord Jesus.)

Heathen or gentile added to the church by washing sins in the blood hidden under the name of Jesus.

Acts 10:47 Can any man forbid water, that these should not be baptized, which have received the Holy Ghost as well as we? 48a And he commanded them to be baptized in the name of the Lord.

Disciples of John the Baptist were baptized again. They were alive in the dispensation when the blood of Jesus was available to wash away their sins. They had the baptism of repentance, but not the forgiveness of sin.

Acts 19:5 When they heard this, they were baptized in the name of the Lord Jesus. 6 And when Paul had laid his hands upon them, the Holy Ghost came on them; and they spake with tongues, and prophesied.

Are you following the easy instructions of Jesus step by step or found another deceptive way to get you out of the plan of salvation? It is still available. Many are following the broad ways of the devil. Check their fruit. Turn back from the dangerous broad road taking you to a hot burning, dark, screaming, torment in hell. There is no door to escape. Seek, ask, and knock. You will find it! Amen!

Hebrews 2:3 How shall we escape, if we neglect so great salvation; which at the first began to be spoken by the Lord, and was confirmed unto us by them that heard him;4 God also bearing them witness, both with signs and wonders, and with divers miracles, and gifts of the Holy Ghost, according to his own will?

LET US PRAY

Heavenly father, that all your ways are blessed, secured, and with all benefits packages. Thank you for giving us your name and invoking baptism. We are blood-bought Jesus-only people. Heaven, earth, and under the earth will bow to the King Jesus. We thank you for never letting me be ashamed of this name, Jesus. The way of Jesus is full of grace and mercy, showing to them who love you. We love you and are not ashamed to call Jesus-only people. You are the King of kings and Lord of lords. We will reign if we follow the ways of God in Jesus' name. Amen! God bless you!

NOVEMBER 13

PERMANENT LOSS OVER MOMENTARY GAIN!

One who seeks power dies without it. Isn't that a shame? There is a right way and a wrong way. The right way will take you to your expected end. As you know, the way will have many obstacles, oppositions, and conflicts, but hold on to God. It has an unimaginable result. You may feel you might die without, but hold on to the Lord. He is faithful.

Psalms 37:25 I have been young, and now am old; yet have I not seen the righteous forsaken, nor his seed begging bread. 28 For the LORD loveth judgment, and forsaketh not his saints; they are preserved forever: but the seed of the wicked shall be cut off.

The Lord slew Er, why?

1 Chronicles 2:3 And Er, the firstborn of Judah, was evil in the sight of the Lord; and he slew him.

Your character is not what you appear to others. Be right in the sight of God. Your character will decide what you are when no one is watching. What did you do with the chances and opportunities you had? The Lord is watching you all the time. You live for God and not for others. Many have rights when they live in a conservative country, but as soon as they fly to free nations, oh my God. The real will come out. They put modest clothes out the door and put on provocative clothes. Do you know what is lacking today? It is the teaching of the truth. We see our society and declare what happened. Our society has the most corrupt and power-hungry individuals who do not care but money and power. If you choose me as your boss, I will do what you like, but don't care about your soul. That makes the home, business, or country lawless.

Joab killed a more righteous man than him.

1 King 2:32 And the Lord shall return his blood upon his own head, who fell upon two men more righteous and better than he, and slew them with the sword, my father David not knowing thereof, to wit, Abner the son of Ner, captain of the host of Israel, and Amasa the son of Jether, captain of the host of Judah.

The pleasure of adultery is momentary, but lost is forever.

1 Chronicle 5:1 Now the sons of Reuben the firstborn of Israel, (for he was the firstborn; but forasmuch as he defiled his father's bed, his birthright was given unto the sons of Joseph the son of Israel: and the genealogy is not to be reckoned after the birthright. 2 For Judah prevailed above his brethren, and of him came the chief ruler, but the birthright was Joseph's:)

Do you think what resulted in the past won't happen in the present or future? God said I am the same yesterday, today, and forever. We need to get into the word of God to learn His nature and righteousness.

Another example of the careless minister,

Leviticus 6:12 And the fire upon the altar shall be burning in it; it shall not be put out: and the priest shall burn wood on it every morning, and lay the burnt offering in order upon it, and he shall burn thereon the fat of the peace offerings.13 The fire shall ever be burning upon the altar; it shall never go out.

Being in the priest's office, you must be careful. Many standings on the pulpit bury their mistakes. Nowadays, teaching the truth is unholy.

Leviticus 10:1,2 10 And Nadab and Abihu, the sons of Aaron, took either of them his censer, and put fire therein, and put incense thereon, and offered strange fire before the Lord, which he commanded them not.2 And there went out fire from the Lord, and devoured them, and they died before the Lord.

The consequence is the same. You and I have to pay attention to it. Our God-given instruction cannot be altered. God says I change not. Do not tempt God. You will lose. If this happens today, we give some kind of excuse, since we do not know the judgment of God. We are living in a time where you can say anything from the pulpit and it is ok. This resulted in unbelievable brokenness, hurting and damaging society.

What is our problem? We see what we want to see and hear what we want to hear. If we are sick, get medicine instead of making it right by repentance. Follow false teachers and prophets since that is the best for an easy life. Do not make a permanent decision over a temporary situation.

The mentality is, who cares for your soul? Religious and secular leaders only care about their position and power. God can give you all if you trust and follow His instruction.

In the insult of not having children, Sarah pressured Abraham to get Haggar, which the Egyptians housemaid. Abraham knows better, despite that, he harkens the wife. Do you know about the difficulties that Israel, chosen by God, is encountering? Our problem is we do not focus. No matter where you go, never try to protect yourself from the fear of pressure from society, people, and family. Stand up for what you believe. Satan will try to make a fool out of you of your trade-off. When you hear from God, then He knows you and your situation. Under pressure, many try to prove it by their action. God gives courage if you stand.

Deuteronomy 31:8 And the Lord, he it is that doth go before thee; he will be with thee, he will not fail thee, neither forsake thee: fear not, neither be dismayed.

We see the peer pressure on our children and no support of prayer or no moral support fails them. It is our responsibility to be there and help. I used to pick up my nieces and nephews and sometimes their friends. Children are vulnerable and need our support. I have no problem helping them since there is a battle out there.

The End-time generation has been misguided. I question why they are acting and talking so uncivilized. Desiring a higher salary, position, and power makes them act like a moron. I believe someone who stands firm, not worried about money, position, and power, will get it all. Many seem like they have lost their minds. How much money is a lot? What position of power is permanent or gives you a good night's sleep? Pray for this generation, even some in their 60s or 70s having no perception or discernment. Wait till you face the Judge of the earth. What argument or appeal will you have then? Doesn't this all show that a bunch of cowards or foolish people are going for little favors, money, positions, and benefits? May the Lord give good, honest, and true teachers and prophets to all of us. Who can stand to enforce the laws of God? Please pray for this generation; they are lost and misguided. If you are one of them, please turn and find the truth in the Bible. The Bible is the book for creation, like you and me from the creator. You will find peace, comfort, and all that you need. Life is only once to live and then there is a judgment. May Lord help and provide us with sound minds and wisdom to make the right decision in Jesus' name. Amen!

LET US PRAY

Heavenly Father, your word says you can give wisdom freely if we ask for it. We ask for not only wisdom but also perception and discernment in our daily lives. It is a onetime shot on earth and has eternal consequences to bear. May the Lord help us be the best at what we are called for. This is our show, our time and we play our life knowing there is a future. We do not think of ourselves only but of our children and theirs. Our life has scars, blessings, or curses according to the decisions we make. Lord, help us make the right choices, since all opportunities are not from you. Our life has permanent effects on others. So help us, Lord, to act and think right, and choose to accord with your will in Jesus's name. Amen! God bless you!

NOVEMBER 14

LORD, ENLARGE MY TERRITORY!

What is the meaning of enlarging territory? It's an area or land which does not belong to you. When you ask God to give what is not yours,

He will. I love to ask God to expand my ministry. I pray for what I have not achieved or beyond me. Have you seen people live in the same hut, same place, and do the same work? Why don't you ask Jesus to increase and expand your territory? Ask God to give you knowledge and wisdom for adventure in new fields. Nothing is hard for God. Your territory is not limited to land but includes knowledge, wealth, a genius mind, and name it. Look at the technology, mind-boggling. Who would have imagined the time we are living in? It is simply someone who believed in enlarging the territory.

Famous prayer in the Bible:

1 Chronicle 4:10 And Jabez called on the God of Israel, saying, Oh that thou wouldest bless me indeed, and enlarge my coast, and that thine hand might be with me, and that thou wouldest keep me from evil, that it may not grieve me! And God granted him that which he requested.

Jabez knew God and dared to pray for it. Today, pray to the Lord who said ask, knock, seek and He will do accordingly. So I pray the Lord enlarges your territory in Jesus' name.

When the artist, mechanics, computer engineer, or performer starts not knowing that he or she will reach that height. So when you start, you do not know your next, but the next will take you to a height that you never imagined.

2 Samuel 22:37 Thou hast enlarged my steps under me; so that my feet did not slip.

When I was working in the post office, my physical battle started. I did not know where it would take me. I only knew it was healing. If I get sick, I call the church and pray to be healed. Not getting healed left me wondering. I did not know where God was taking me through this new trial.

One day, I heard a clear voice of God telling me, "You will never come back here." I was amazed. I knew physical injury plus a postal office battle were difficult, but I had God.

When the day came, a miracle happened. After I had disability retirement because of my blood condition, He did a miracle and I walked. I was not completely healed but was walking short distances. Lord Jesus said, work for me and I will take care of you. I didn't have a computer, so I bought one. Because of unbearable pain, I had a memory loss, I couldn't read to remember. Pain is a killer.

I thought about making the audio of my books. Now I am a perfectionist. I see all these worldly people do their work to the best of their abilities. Why not do the work of God and do it in the best way? So I asked a friend's son who was kind enough to teach me the recording by providing me with editing software. I know money was an issue, but I had a credit card. I used a credit card and thought it was worth it.

I started working on recording. With pain, I couldn't sit continually, but on and off. Many times, I forget the recording procedure and go back to the notes. I forgot to read Gujarati perfectly. I attended the English church and most of the dealing was with an American. I didn't have to deal with Gujarati much. I do not believe in giving up or giving in. It took 1 year to finish four pages but did so well that people asked how beautifully I read and spoke. The Day I put my CD to play, my house was filled with Shekinah glory. It is the thick cloud where God lives. I saw Jesus smiling in that cloud. Hallelujah! Now I make movies and videos, and have a YouTube channel. I am using technology to reach out to the world. I dislike doing the same old things.

Satan has many tricks and techniques to control and steal our time, money, and life. The Devil uses God's given knowledge, wisdom, and talent to make money and convince others he is good.

God uses people who are nothing, nobody. He starts from scratch and makes them from a shepherd boy to a psalmist to worship God and a King, from a prisoner to the ruler of the nation, from slave to freeman, from poor to wealthy, and much more.

Isaiah 43:18 Remember ye not the former things, neither consider the things of old.19 Behold, I will do a new thing; now it shall spring forth; shall ye not know it? I will even make a way in the wilderness, and rivers in the desert.

Yes, hallelujah! I love to have new things every day. If we know the Lord, believe in His wisdom, in His might, in supernatural, His miracle-working power, then we can put our trust in Him. The hit and miss is not God; God is not for the one who thinks they can do all, all-knowing mentality and over-smart. God is for the humble.

1 Corinthians 1:27 But God hath chosen the foolish things of the world to confound the wise; and God hath chosen the weak things of the world to confound the things which are mighty;

One who thinks they are smart can do all that will ruin the plan of God. God has the written script just needs actors and actresses to play the role to show the world His supernatural power. The world will see the master plan of God and be in Ah, think what happens here. How does the slave's own the nation? How does the slave have a worldwide business? Because the Lord enlarged their territory.

Your humble beginning can be enlarged if you pray and ask God to bless it. Only the Lord can bless and enlarge. We see some businesses known in the world and we think about what happened here. It is the Lord who expanded and enlarged their territory.

Learn to ask God for the blessing over your work.

I remember I used to go to sleep early while growing up. Never finish my homework. I was scared to death, knowing I won't pass. I prayed to the Lord to help me study, and He did. I did well in school. I Studied and did not sleep. I knew that was God since before opening my book and leaving for school; I asked God to help me. I noticed my score in subjects was getting higher and higher. God is good.

Nothing is impossible for God. The Lord owns the earth, riches, wealth, ruby, diamonds, and all. Go to Him. He will give you what you ask for. Places like the US used to be empty land. The pilgrim who knew Jesus started praying. In some years, America became one of the best countries. Friend, if we know our God, then it is a different story. It will be a story about David, Moses, Esther, Mordecai, and many more. He is in the blessing business who depends on Him, trusts in God's plan, and believes in obeying and submitting. How great would the result be if we give all to God? Experience of great out of nothing, from free to the slave, from slave to king, poor to rich, and much more. Only if you are humble. Humble, can pray, and submit to God. Barren prayed and gave birth to the greatest prophet who anointed the first two kings of Israel. All is the game of humility and willingness to give God, the Master, the artist Jesus, to make an amazing life story out of you, in Jesus' name. Amen! God Bless you!

LET US PRAY

Heavenly Father, your word says you have the power to make all things new. Make us new again.

Instead of: Embrace the passing of the old and envision a magnificent new future. Let our life be a testimony. Let people see barren to conceive and give birth to a father of nations. It is the Lord who can increase us as an uncountable star. Knowing God, I pray to the Lord to remove every pride, lie, hindrances, stopper, and blocker from us. Lord Bless all our handy work so the world sees and is amazed. Give us that intelligent mind to do what is impossible for us. The hand of God helps us to reach the unreachable mountain. Bless the land where we are right now to produce the saints, prophets, teachers, and mighty laborers of God to reconnect us to Jesus. Enlarge our reaching and preaching points in Jesus' name. Amen! God Bless You!

NOVEMBER 15

WHAT MATTERS THE MOST?

At every age of our lives, something matters to us the most. But ask the dying person what matters the most to them. Life matters to each person differently. We can analyze by the Word of God what matters to you the most. Many characters in the Bible are perfect examples of this. Some have never seen life from God's perspective. Some live spontaneously, not knowing your life has a long-lasting effect. Yet, we all see differently, but the result you face will make you think twice if you get a second chance to live on this earth. Let us face reality; we all will face the consequences of not paying attention or paying less or no attention to those we should have given more. May the Lord give us the wisdom to do right. I said wisdom. Whether you know or don't, your action will have an automatic outcome. You may say, I am sorry for my actions. Doing right would have given you a long life, but your wrong action is cutting it short.

When I was studying, my exam was very important, and I always thought if I did not score, then I wanted to end my life. How silly of me? In India alone, 135,000 disappointed students commit suicide every year. Now, this is very sad. They think a college education is their life. Many are so pressured with the look, marriage dowry, love affairs, family problems, and name it. The problem becomes like a mountain. We see life differently, having contrasting gods. May the Lord give us eyes to see obstacles through His eyes. When things do not go our way, then that limits our thinking. We forget God has promised a brighter and better future. The only condition is to drive your life under the radar of God's word. Your promises can cash if you have the right mind with God's calculator. We know the life span is only 70 to 80 and it will end. So in-between, we think carefully to keep what matters to our soul rather than the lust of eyes, flesh, and pride of life.

May the Lord give us the wisdom of preferring what matters the most to God.

Acts 20:24 But none of these things move me, neither count I my life dear unto myself, so that I might finish my course with joy, and the ministry, which I have received of the Lord Jesus, to testify the gospel of the grace of God.

Eve was looking at the tree as it bloomed with beautiful fruits. It must be eye-catching and flesh-pleasing. The things that should have mattered were her soul only.

The day you eat, you will die.

Genesis 2:17 But of the tree of the knowledge of good and evil, thou shalt not eat of it: for in the day that thou eatest thereof thou shalt surely die.

NOVEMBER 15

Questions, what matters to a person, are decided by the choices they make in picking.

I lived in India and met many people of a different cast. India was very conservative when I left the country. Many had a different way of looking at life. Many lost out by choosing the wrong actions.

Compare the situation through the word of God, and you will think differently.

Hebrew chapter 11 is an example of how the people saw their lives. The earthly success, promotion, position, and wealth were not as important as the plan of the Lord. They fixed their eyes on God so that nothing in this world would have bought them.

Hebrews 11:13 These all died in faith, not having received the promises, but having seen them afar off, and were persuaded of them, and embraced them, and confessed that they were strangers and pilgrims on the earth.

1 Chronicle 29:15 For we are strangers before thee, and sojourners, as were all our fathers: our days on the earth are as a shadow, and there is none abiding.

One who knows the real meaning of life will not make silly choices. They will not look for fun, live in leisure, and die like fools. The world is so mixed up that we do not know what is right and wrong. The devil has entered the home, congregations, schools, and government. People say, Oh, it is just fun. Why do you need so much fun that your soul has to suffer for eternity? My parents, and probably some of yours too, are very meticulous in teaching us right from wrong. We have some family members, like Eve and Adam. Careless, silly woman and man, looking for eye-pleasing, good for the flesh, and pride to look like others. Pray for them; they bring the devil into our house.

In this present day, we have many like King Saul, Eve-Adam, Jeroboam, King Saul, and many silly people who did wrong, showing the result of what matters to them the most. But remember, we are individuals, and we have an individual soul. Learn right and keep it in your heart. You can make a difference, like Joseph, Paul, John, the Baptist, John the Beloved, and many who were known for their integrity and sincerity. Earthly life did not matter to them. They were not afraid of physical death in life. Nothing was the matter except they held onto the truth. Some people try to fit in the crowd, but it does not matter to the prudent. They were called the people of God, who kept faith in the word of God. The Surroundings kept changing as the apostles traveled from country to country and city to city. Language and people were different, but their eyes were fixed and they made their minds up to follow the Lord. Never cared for their surroundings as they kept going and preaching. It did not matter what the future would hold, since the Gospel was the most important to the people of God.

Have you seen one Bible and many divisions? Having one God, many are lost. If you have many ways of salvation, then you have picked and chosen your ways and not Jesus'. If you have one God, one baptism and the only way is Jesus, then where are you looking? He said follow me, pick up your cross. So what is our problem? People live what matters to them the most. Forbidden Fruit, 30 coins, hunger for power, greed, adultery, killing the brother like Cain. It is all where you are looking. What matters the most to your eyes, flesh, and pride? Our God came and showed us the way, and said just follow me. He never said to follow a pastor, and change lifestyle as you live in a foreign country. Now you are married and following your husband, listening to your silly wife, or changing since you have children, then you are going astray. What matters to you the most? All will pass away but the Word of God. May I say pay more attention to where you are taking your soul? What is your problem? What matters to you the most? May the Lord help us so we don't call a fool, lost, careless, blind, deaf, greedy, and generation of the viper. What should matter is the cross, our salvation, and our God. This will change your destiny from hell to heaven, darkness to light, and screaming to everlasting joy. Amen!

Hebrew 11:16 But now they desire a better country, that is, a heavenly: wherefore God is not ashamed to be called their God: for he hath prepared for them a city.

LET US PRAY

Lord, we humbly express our gratitude for guiding us through your example. The thing that matters to you the most is seeing your hurting creation. Your mission was to help, set free, deliver, and preach the Gospel of salvation. Help us do what you asked us to do. It is our time. Do not let us take the shortcut or put it aside, since in every generation we have found something different from what you said and we must stay away from it. You have given us your word to read, know, and follow. Our God's goodness is astounding, as He cares for us deeply and went to the extent of shedding His blood for our sake. We matter to Him the most. He did not care about His life. Jesus emptied Himself, knowing what it takes to correct all our mistakes of the past. Help us open the Bible and find the way you have shown. Lord, help us that nothing matters to us but you. You're the way and the truth, in Jesus's name. Amen! God bless you!

NOVEMBER 16

WHO HAS OCCUPIED THE HOUSE?

You are the house built by God. God built or created your body.

Genesis 2:7 And the LORD God formed man of the dust of the ground and breathed into his nostrils the breath of life; and man became a living soul.

Isaiah 64:8 But now, O LORD, thou art our father; we are the clay, and thou our potter; and we all are the work of thy hand.

God made us and has ownership of our bodies. God is the creator, and no one has the legal right. If the house allows someone, then they can come. Our job is to maintain our bodies made of flesh. Renovate, keep it clean, and take care of it so it does not fall apart. The flesh has weakness and vulnerability to allow the wrong tenant. You are just a manager or controller of the house made by God. Manage it with the right mind and good intentions for the soul. The Lord has given us the information and power to manage it well. Sin separates us from God, but blood brings reconciliation between the builders and His house. Builder Jesus Christ made us so He can live in and have fellowship with us.

1 Corinthians 3:16 Know ye not that ye are the temple of God, and that the Spirit of God dwelleth in you? 17 If any man defile the temple of God, him shall God destroy; for the temple of God is holy, which temple ye are.

Your connection with God will keep your body clean and holy. Holy God cannot live in the unclean body. Do not defile your body by consuming wrong things, sinning, and allowing anything that can defile you. Our body can stay healthy if God lives in it. By the same token, if Satan comes through sin, will steal, kill, and destroy by harming the body. It is shameful that we do not remember or want to know how we are created and the purpose of the creator. We go to one who knows nothing about our bodies, that is doctors. With our lack of knowledge, arrogance, belief in lies, or disregard for truth, we find ourselves living in a state of sickness, unhealthiness, possession, oppression, and disappointment. We rather go to the doctor, spend money, or eat medicine with many side effects but wouldn't repent.

Who occupies the Body makes a big difference. What I mean is Satan comes to kill, steal, and destroy and will do the job, as its title says.
Matthew 12:43 When the unclean spirit is gone out of a man, he walketh through dry places, seeking rest, and findeth none. 44 Then he saith, I will return into my house from whence I came out; and when he is come, he findeth it empty, swept, and garnished. 45 Then goeth he, and taketh with himself seven other spirits more

wicked than himself, and they enter in and dwell there: and the last state of that man is worse than the first. Even so shall it be also unto this wicked generation.

The devil said I would return to my house. If the demon lives in the body, all they need is comfort. The demon doesn't suffer hunger or thirst, and it becomes the master of the house. That is why if you have a demon of alcohol, drugs, cigarettes, gambling, or stealing, then you must get rid of it.

I had a brother who used to smoke. He was hospitalized in Plano Hospital. The demon of cigarettes acted up when I was there with him. He kept asking the nurse; I want to smoke, give me cigarettes. His lungs had carbon dioxide. If he smokes, then there is no way to survive. I am glad I was there. I can say the Lord was there to rescue him. He kept asking the nurse and me for a cigarette while I was commanding demons to get out. I non-stop commanded the cigarette demon to get out. As I commanded in the name of Jesus, it left him. Later, when he was discharged, he saw the little butt of the cigarette and thought this little cigarette was controlling him. No, it was the demon who was controlling, not the cigarettes. Friend, they cannot help medically all these possessed people. You need to take them to one who can cast demons out. Jesus came to set us free. Our body is not for this evil spirit, but for the Lord.

Hebrews 3:6 But Christ as a son over his own house; whose house are we, if we hold fast the confidence and the rejoicing of the hope firm unto the end.

The House cannot stay empty. Fill the void with the Holy Spirit, so the evil spirit will not come back. Go to one who lays hands so you receive the Holy Spirit. Many come to my house for the Holy Spirit, and I pray for them to receive it.

Acts 19:2 He said unto them, Have ye received the Holy Ghost since ye believed? And they said unto him, We have not so much as heard whether there be any Holy Ghost.

If you have not received, as the Bible says, then go find people like John and Peter. Do not go to the religious false teachers and prophets but to the spiritual. They will lay their hands on you.

Acts 8:17 Then laid they their hands on them, and they received the Holy Ghost

Many times, Christians have a false belief that a demon cannot come or stay in our bodies. A demon can come, but you have to know how to get rid of it. What do you think of all these illnesses? Most of them are demons. Cancer is a demon. Learn how to cast it out. Jesus gave us power and learned to use it. If not, then it will take your life and enter another member of your family. What about a heart attack? Kill Generation after generation! Use the power in the name of Jesus against generational curses. Lady said my mom prayed that we never get diabetes, none of them have diabetes. Pray and say I am not inheriting any sicknesses. Do what it takes and never let them occupy your body. You have the power. Learn from Jesus how He cast out demons. You look in the mirror and say, 'Get out of my body.' Lay a hand over your head and say to leave, I command you to come out of my body in the name of Jesus.

You clean yourself, no one but you.

2 Corinthians 7:1 Having therefore these promises, dearly beloved, let us cleanse ourselves from all filthiness of the flesh and spirit, perfecting holiness in the fear of God.

Matthew 17:15 Lord, have mercy on my son: for he is lunatick, and sore vexed: for ofttimes he falleth into the fire, and oft into the water.18 And Jesus rebuked the devil; and he departed out of him: and the child was cured from that very hour.

Another type of demon was deaf and dumb.

Luke 11:14 And he was casting out a devil, and it was dumb. And it came to pass, when the devil was gone out, the dumb spake; and the people wondered.

One of my friends who converted to Christianity told me she was helping one of her friends and, while praying, she was non-stop crying. Her friend was out of her mind, but the next day she was normal. A friend said I thought she was faking. I said, 'No, you prayed and cast out the demon'. She said, 'I know I was crying but didn't know why. 'Many who are active Christians do not know that they have cast out demons. We do not see spirit but behavior and action. So It is our job to command the demon to get out of our and others' bodies as well. Do it yourself to see the result. You realize you have wasted the time not working as Jesus has asked. Amen!

LET US PRAY

Heavenly Father, we thank you that our body is your temple. That is your residence. We invite you to come to our body and abide in us. We thank you. You do not live in a man-made building, but God made the body. It is the place where you live, talk, lead, guide, and teach. You also empower us with your spirit in us. Not by might, nor by power, but by thy Holy Spirit. It is the most powerful experience when we receive the Holy Spirit. We thank you for coming and living in our body. Our body is the temple or your church. We can do many mighty things with your spirit. You promise you will come and live and do great through us. Holy Spirit, you are welcome in this house in Jesus' name. Amen! God bless you!

NOVEMBER 17

ACTION ALERT!

God categorizes us by our actions, not what we communicate, but our actions. Fruits are the action. The action is what you are; God connects acting with what you have in your heart.

Many are just good talkers. They can win you by the way they talk. The devil is one of them. Many liars, thieves, and wicked people are the best talkers. But in the end, we discover, oh no, they cheated, lied, and harmed us. Be careful. God gives us a test to prove what we are. If there is any adultery, then he will give you power, position, and the opportunity to prove what you are.

David and Joseph both proved their moral standard by their actions. Joseph honored God by keeping the commandments, and David fell into adultery. See, the action has proven both. You are innocent unless proven. It is a law that no one can put you behind bars until evidence proves so. Many times I have seen men or women who were accused of doing something, but by bringing evidence, they were convicted or set free.

Jesus said 'den of thieves'. How sad! Another day I met my friend; she is a minister of the Word of God. We studied the word. She asked me, would you sell anything in the church? I said no, the Holy Spirit wouldn't allow me. She said; I dislike people selling stuff in the church. Let's keep the place for prayer.

Matthew 21:12 And Jesus went into the temple of God, and cast out all them that sold and bought in the temple, and overthrew the tables of the moneychangers, and the seats of them that sold doves, 13 And said unto them, It is written, My house shall be called the house of prayer; but ye have made it a den of thieves.

Lord Jesus labels them a thief. Their actions caused Jesus to label them a thief. Have you noticed that nowadays, the country does not want to teach what is right? No Bible, no word of God, no truth and light. It is the time money buys wicked rulers. Satan rules in high places. Our school will teach one-day witchcraft and other religions. They took the Bible out, and they took prayer out. Don't be surprised by the kid's actions, shooting, killing, gangs, fornication, drugs, and alcohol. We label their misbehavior by watching the action. Our actions label our generation. If you find people like Noah or Lot, then the Lord will label them righteous and will rescue them from the problem.

So be careful how God sees and how humans see. Don't care for humans' judgment but for the Lord.

Psalm 7:11 God judgeth the righteous, and God is angry with the wicked every day.

NOVEMBER 17

God said the faithless generation. Some say we have many believers in our country. Jesus says faithless generation. Jesus sees where they put their trust. When they have a problem, do they go to God or fistfight, gunfight, or sword fight? May the Lord give us wisdom, perceptions, and courage to speak the truth.

1 Corinthians 2:15 But he that is spiritual judgeth all things, yet he himself is judged of no man.

We need the spirit of God to guide, teach, and lead in all the right ways.

1 John 2:20 But ye have an unction from the Holy One, and ye know all things.

In the beginning, we knew Solomon as the wisest king. In the end, they labeled King Solomon as a lost man. There is a righteous God in heaven who knows the truth about us. No power conspiracy or bribe can change His judgment. So live as the Lord is watching you and not people. You teach your children to speak, live, and act right. One day, they will bless you. Do not raise them as your puppet, liar, your mouthpiece. It is the game of a mother or father who is a monster and raises one just like them. These people bring calamity and judgment.

Let us check some wonderful titles given in the Bible and see what their actions and reactions were.

Barnabas *Acts 11:24 For he was a good man, and full of the Holy Ghost and of faith: and much people was added unto the Lord.*

Now Godly people label Ruth as a virtuous woman because of her actions toward the mother-in-law: Do you have a daughter-in-law? How would you label her?

Ruth 3:11 And now, my daughter, fear not; I will do to thee all that thou requirest: for all the city of my people doth know that thou art a virtuous woman.

God labels Satan as a father of lies.

John 8:44 Ye are of your father the devil, and the lusts of your father ye will do. He was a murderer from the beginning, and abode not in the truth, because there is no truth in him. When he speaketh a lie, he speaketh of his own: for he is a liar and the father of it.

God, Label Job was perfect and upright.

Job 1:1 There was a man in the land of Uz, whose name was Job; and that man was perfect and upright, and one that feared God, and eschewed evil.

With utmost obedience, he fulfills God's requests, embodying humility. Humble will not add nor subtract in God's command. Archangel Lucifer failed God.

But Moses brought the heavenly law, precepts, and commandments down on earth as it is. Moses, with a heart filled with humility, allowed God to establish His laws, the Torah, on earth. Moses brought the key to success. Do we have this kind of humble people or like Satan, add and subtract in the word of God?

Numbers 12:3 (Now the man Moses was very meek, above all the men which were upon the face of the earth.)

Do you remember the Pharaoh of Egypt? Lord labels him as a hard-hearted man. He brought judgment, not listening and submitting to the highest authority of God. Be careful. Do not let the Lord label you as jealous, liar, killer, adulterer, witch, thief, etc.

Have you seen people label themselves as, I am Trinity, Methodist, alliance, baptist, Catholic, Mormon, Jehovah's Witnesses, or Pentecostal? Lord said, 'I do not know this label. I know only who is righteous, living holy, born again, baptized in Jesus's name, and received the Holy Spirit by speaking in tongues.' Jesus labels them as Disciples or believers seeing their actions.

Mark 16:17 And these signs shall follow them that believe; In my name shall they cast out devils; they shall speak with new tongues; 18 They shall take up serpents; and if they drink any deadly thing, it shall not hurt them; they shall lay hands on the sick, and they shall recover.

You and I need to live right and do right by keeping Jesus as our example. Caring cross and follow Him. How simple it is if we have the truth, but oh no, we know better than God. A different type of product is what we want. We do not believe Jesus is the way and truth. We prefer a religious label and love to follow a false teacher and prophet. Is it worth it? Be careful. Action alert, open Bible read, and follow Jesus. Take heed in Jesus's name. Amen!

LET US PRAY

Lord, we come before your altar knowing you are real and watch us all the time. We ask forgiveness for all our sins and give us a clean heart. Give us wisdom for all situations and guide us through all trials, troubles, and problems. We know the Lord has given us His Spirit. Oh Lord, grant me the ability to listen intently to the voice of God. We ask that all your children bless and walk in harmony and unity. You are the teacher. Teach us so we do not make any mistakes. Lord, be the instructor, so we follow your command. Thank you for the Word, blood, and Spirit of God. There is a mighty war over our soul, so the Lord, keep us in your palm. Let our action be pleasing in the sight of the Lord in Jesus's name. Amen! God bless you!

NOVEMBER 18

SEE-THROUGH THE EYES OF THE PROPHET!

Hosea 12:13 And by a prophet the Lord brought Israel out of Egypt, and by a prophet was he preserved.

The Lord has given us a prophet to lead us throughout and to keep us safe and secure. Humanity broke its relationship with its Creator by disobedience. The Lord always tries to direct, help, and provide for His people. He wants to stay connected for their welfare. But humans always reject God. The prophet is a special office chosen by God. Through prophets, God speaks to us.

We must have prophets to speak to our lives. I know many true prophets have prophesied over me. I listen, tape, or take a note so I do not forget the plan of God spoken by the prophet. To believe, obey, and submit to the prophet makes God's plan successful. We need God, but we think the other way around. God does not need us. God knows that the crooked devil has a plan to destroy God's creation. Our problem is we think differently. Just like many have failed and failed and failed. If we listen to God, then life will become much easier for us.

Another day I was praying for the lady in India; she has some property and wants to build a church. But God is not allowing it. Because all who come to that place know that she is a woman and a widow. They want to take away her land. I prayed and told her that God will send one who is real and true. He will help you release the property to the right person. Nowadays, many thieves come at the angle of light. Pray for the sincere and righteous laborer.

God does not speak to all but one whom He has picked.

Judges 6:8 That the Lord sent a prophet unto the children of Israel, which said unto them, Thus saith the Lord God of Israel, I brought you up from Egypt and brought you forth out of the house of bondage; 9 And I delivered you out of the hand of the Egyptians, and out of the hand of all that oppressed you, and drive them out from before you, and gave you their land; 10 And I said unto you, I am the Lord your God; fear not the gods of the Amorites, in whose land ye dwell: but ye have not obeyed my voice.

Every time God has sent a prophet to warn, correct, guide, and keep us on the right path and plan.

Jeremiah was the prophet not for Israel only, but over the nations. He was born when spirituality almost died in Israel. Everyone did what was right in their sight. It is dangerous when you are taught by a religious leader not to hear God but to them alone. You become deaf and blind to God. So look for spiritual people. In the throne room, they spend time on their knees, praying and fasting. With their connection to the Lord, they fearlessly speak the truth. Taking a risk with their lives, they are willing to do so.

Jeremiah 1:9 Then the LORD put forth his hand, and touched my mouth. And the LORD said unto me, Behold, I have put my words in thy mouth.10 See, I have this day set thee over the nations and over the kingdoms, to root out, and to pull down, and to destroy, and to throw down, to build, and to plant.

They tortured Jeremiah for speaking the truth. It is the same situation today. I go to some places or countries where religious leaders will blow dirty air in the ear. People see the miracle and anointing and still listen to the false teachers, pastors, and so-called prophets. It is the spiritual twilight time where the maximum accident takes place. Isn't this dangerous?

I have had the privilege of meeting numerous exceptional prophets. Each has said the same and they even do not know each other. Many have said, I know you are an author; you have written a book. But I see you write more articles on the internet. I have this prophet who kept telling me that my writing would change. You will have different God-given tools. When I hear the prophet, I become extra watchful and hear God.

The prophets sometimes do not know what they are saying, since God is using their lips and tongue. That is why I always tape and keep hearing until I get it. Always ask God to direct us in His plan. Release His thoughts to us to think as He does.

Micaiah was the most hated prophet since the king of Israel was carnal and ungodly. King was using false prophets who were speaking ear-pleasing words. But Micaiah was not afraid of them, but of the Lord.

1 King 22:14 And Micaiah said, As the LORD liveth, what the LORD saith unto me, that will I speak.17 And he said, I saw all Israel scattered upon the hills, as sheep that have not a shepherd: and the LORD said, These have no master: let them return every man to his house in peace.18 And the king of Israel said unto Jehoshaphat, Did I not tell thee that he would prophesy no good concerning me, but evil?

See, God warned the man but still went into the battle where he was killed. Micaiah was slapped and slanderous for telling the truth. It is not the job of the prophet to believe for you; you believe in yourself and act appropriately. You believe in God, who is looking after your protection and success. I work for God, where false teachers and prophets are the most harmful. They are always ready to take credit. Somehow I never want to help them, but when they ask, I have no choice.

God said,

Jeremiah 29:11 For I know the thoughts that I think toward you, saith the Lord, thoughts of peace, and not of evil, to give you an expected end.

When the prophet speaks to your life, write it down and start working in that direction. A woman who was preaching in the Muslim nation said, I kept praying every day and prophesying revival over that nation. You can do the same. Get a map and study the people of the nation. Be a visionary and prophesy. Prophecy is for the future, and you will see the revival.

In the 80s, I saw the slums of Bombay and the burden of the nation came over me instantaneously. One day, 18 years later, I went to the same slum of Bombay and preached the Gospel. I didn't have any idea, since I never had that strong encounter with God before. I have heard Him, and experienced differently, but not as He showed me the slum where years later I went and practically walked. See what I desire and pray it happens. Your word is a prophecy; you can take the map and speak the blessings, revival, and open the door. Get a glorious vision of the nations and see what God does. Have a forward-thinking mindset and embrace limitless possibilities. Let the Lord take you to the places to preach.

Habakkuk 2:3 For the vision is yet for an appointed time, but at the end it shall speak, and not lie: though it tarry, wait for it; because it will surely come, it will not tarry.

I see visions and have dreamed of what God has to inform me. Dreams and visions are the revealing of the truth or the future. I believe our prayer has the power to change the situation and destroy the mouths of the dog's and tiger's spirits. We have the power to come against, take precautions, and overcome the enemy. All that God is doing is to help, protect, and take care of. Find the true prophets over your life. God will spare your life. Your achievements will soar and your growth will be unstoppable. God will bless you in Jesus's name. Amen!

LET US PRAY

Lord, you are our creator. You have never left us. You have never forsaken us. But we do not listen since we have a hard hearing. God is wonderful and benevolent. Please help us to allow you to be our God. Our God has an interest in protecting and blessing us. How beautifully we are blessed. Our God has true prophets who see and hear for us. God's prophet gives us accurate information, so all those blockers, killers, stealers, and destroyers can be destroyed. Thank you, Lord, for protecting us from destruction. Help us, Lord, to be vigilant, in a season of the season instant. We have you, but the one who goes to witches, warlocks, and false ones are misguided with curses. Lord, teach us to wait for our season and time. All your ways will be established. Your word would not return void, but need our cooperation by believing and obeying. Help us, Lord, to believe in Jesus's Name! Amen! God bless you!

NOVEMBER 19

BE SENSITIVE TO YOUR SURROUNDINGS!

Some people are insensitive to others, needs, emotions, or situations. In today's world, there is a prevailing insensitivity and selfishness, with people expecting to be fed and taken care of. I consider myself to be of greater significance than others. According to God, He understood the needs of His creation on a deep level. Both the father and mother respond to their children's needs. The Holy Spirit is the exceptionally sensitive. While praying, I am able to discern the person's needs. Without fail, they always confirm that the situation I prayed for them about was critical.

When you go to the house where people are sick, do not expect them to feed you and take care of you. Many times, I have seen visitors become burdensome. Worldly people are the most insensitive and selfish. When I and my families were going through trials, some people came to our door to offer help, but some wanted us to feed them and take care of them. How selfish and silly of them! I was unable to take care of myself and my mom because of my sickness during that period. In my driveway, they stood and demanded food. Despite being aware that my mom was in the hospital and I spent the entire day there, thet never bothered to ask how she was or how I was doing. My body trembled due to my deteriorating health and the burden of looking after my hospitalized mother.

While many were blessings, a few caused nothing but pain. Also, when you go to the funeral, do not go there to be a pain to the grieving family. Be sensitive to the people who are hurting. There are times when things become disorganized because certain individuals disregard others. I had compassion for my creation, as Jesus said. God shaded the blood and took the stripes for our sicknesses. He faced trial because humans are incapable of giving or doing what the Lord did for us.

I used to fellowship in Dallas, where the pastor was sensitive to the needs of the congregation. We always had different people come for healing, deliverance, or prophecy. Pastors often refer to it as a good or divine idea. It was never the agenda of man, but the Holy Spirit. Sometimes the Pastor will say I have a message, but the Holy Spirit is telling me to pray for some who are in pain. There are instances when he claims that a lot of people are feeling heartbroken in this location. The process involves him calling out, stating their name, addressing their problem, praying for them, and concluding. In a minute, they will be healed, and they go back to their seats. How nice!

I was amazed. It's surprising how many people are unaware of what goes on within their own community or even their own household.

Colossians 3:12 Put on therefore, as the elect of God, holy and beloved, bowels of mercies, kindness, humbleness of mind, meekness, longsuffering.

1 John 3:17 But whoso hath this world's good, and seeth his brother have need, and shutteth up his bowels of compassion from him, how dwelleth the love of God in him?

My mom had a brother named John. Even in her final moments on earth, my mom held him in her memory. She was calling her brother John even though he died almost 70 years ago. Did she remember all the people? No, she remembered who showed her and her sibling mercy and took care of them when they were little. My mom lost her parent at a young age and this half-brother was more than parents. My mom praised her brother every day. According to her, he was a really nice person who took on the responsibility of caring for his younger siblings when their parents died when they were little. Assisting is one thing, but offering help with love and kindness is a different story. May Lord help us understand that there is a God in heaven who has compassion for our situation. He alone has true love and understanding.

Be mindful of others' needs and feelings. Many are hurting and will make the wrong decision. We need to step in and intercede for the situation, need, or matter. Many add pain over your pain. But some help with love and take care.

I counsel internationally and noticed that people have diverse problems. When you see a need, be helpful and not painful. You will remember on earth and in heaven if you help. No one wants to see you at their door if you show no sympathy. Especially I do not want them at my door. It is true; no one wants people who kindle fire to add pain to life.. Some people are simply born lacking sensitivity.

My days are filled with listening to people complain and cry. By speaking to them, praying over them, and offering words of encouragement, I bring them back to a state of happiness. I learned counseling from the Holy Spirit and I do it wholeheartedly.

While at church yesterday, God instructed me to go visit a specific woman. I called her, and she said she would be home by 1 pm. I said I would like to visit her. So, I purchased something that she could eat, and we spent time together. She has a daughter but is not close. She has no other family. So it was God who sent me and we had a wonderful time. She is recovering from cancer. Little things make people happy. Showing some compassion and giving a little care and love is all that's needed. Don't be someone who only takes and consumes. Give some time as well. People have a dislike for those who take without giving.

When I go to the hospital to pray over the sick, I also ask family members and visitors if they need prayer. Many are hurting out there. A gay colleague once requested his coworker to ask me for prayers. He was in the same hospital where his mother was. I met his mother and prayed over her. I was sorry that she died. But now this young man was dying with aids and was seeing an evil spirit. I went with my prayer partner and prayed. He felt peace. Have some compassion. We know when people come close to death, they may repent. It is our job not to worry about what they were, but definitely what they can be. I visited many people on their deathbeds. At the end of the road, they are so sorrowful and the Lord forgives, just like He forgave the thief.

God heals and saves, so preach them the truth. Our God has shown us great mercy. Do not think someone is evil means you have the right not to believe in God. God is great and always will be there if you call on His name. Keep your faith in the Lord and not in humans. That is the point where people get discouraged. Always remain hopeful and witness the Lord's healing, deliverance, provisions, and blessings. We cannot fathom the greatness of God with our imagination.

I have been in the toughest health trial. I experienced the loss of my job and declining health. Later, the passing of my mother. But I kept my eyes on the Lord and He turned everything around. No one but the Lord has compassion for us. He knows how to take you to shore. He knows how to find the way out. Keep your eyes on the Lord and see how wonderful our God is. Show compassion to those who are around, older, hurting, widows, and orphans. Do not walk away seeing their need, in Jesus' name. Amen!

LET US PRAY

Our heavenly father, your mission was to help the weak, poor, needy, and helpless. You showed great compassion for the lost and hurting! Our job is to reach out to those who are hurting and needy. They never have to look for us, but we must look for them. The Lord makes us sensitive to their needs. The success of your mission depends on our sensitivity to your voice. God, you have done all in the flesh by giving the example to follow you. We must cultivate a deep sense of sensitivity towards the needs of others. If we truly care about the well-being of others, we become neighbors in the truest sense. Take away selfishness and help us be there when someone needs us. Lord, our job is to show compassion and love, so help us. We find many needy people who are hurting. A little help will cheer them up, so help us show them compassion in Jesus' name. Amen! God bless you!

NOVEMBER 20

NOT CONVERTING, BUT PROCLAIMING THE TRUTH!

Give it a try on your own. This has nothing to do with religion, which I can't stand. I never cared about religion. Ever since I started studying the Bible, many questions have been raised. I know I had a question and not curiosity. My quest was to find the God of the Old Testament. The Old Testament is my favorite. The Bible labeled me as a converted gentile and not a Jew, which I didn't like. I wondered why I wasn't a Jew and sought answers from God. I felt the Israelites were blessed and chosen, and I was nothing. My question was, how can I become a Jew? What steps can I take to replace my blood with that of Jews?

My God loves me; He satisfied my desire. Later, as I learned about the New Testament, I got more questions. Where are all these miracles, powers, and healing? All of these tasks needed to be done, but nobody was taking action. In the building known as the church, the religious leaders were seated and standing. I had millions of questions. As a result of spiritual problems affecting a family member, I found myself driven to conduct more extensive research.

I was willing to seek spiritual guidance from anyone. The Holy Spirit is absent in churches that are merely nominal or religious. They claim they do, but they don't. What Jesus did is beyond their capabilities. They cannot be expected to do any better. Religious leaders manipulate their beliefs in order to deceive you.

1 Corinthian 4:20 For the kingdom of God is not in word, but in power.

I had no other option but to pursue the truth due to the seriousness of my need.

After settling in the United States, I started attending churches where they spoke in tongues, danced, jumped, and engaged in some pretty unusual activities, similar to the disciples. When people were sick, they lay a hand, put on Holy Oil, etc. It seems like I slowly but surely started finding the way and the truth. To search for the truth, I started diving deeper into the Word of God. I started having more and more experiences. Being a science student, I will not believe in others' experiences. I need to experiment with proof. As I was baptized in the name of Jesus, once I came out of the water, I had the most powerful, wonderful, and unbelievable experience. Ever since I realized that there was a problem going to religious denominations. I realized it is my job to let others know the truth. I started telling others to study what the Bible says. This is what the former church believed and practiced. This is what I used to believe. I told all whom I met and testified to all about my experience under the water baptism in Jesus' name. Many were convinced and saw early disciples practice baptism only in the name of Jesus. I did not have a religion, so I took them straight to the Bible and pointed out the two or three scriptures to establish the doctrine. As the Bible says, you need two or three scriptures to establish any doctrine.

Ephesians 1:4 According as he hath chosen us in him before the foundation of the world, that we should be holy and without blame before him in love:

All-knowing God knows since there is no past, future, or present in the sight of God. A beautiful life can be given if we follow the truth. Jehovah's Savior, in English Jesus, said I am the truth. Sincerely, search the way out of all trials, problems, sicknesses, and diseases dropped by Eve and Adam. Find the truth of the Bible. The Bible is the truth if you seek to find it. Yes, much lies in the world established by the devil in the Nicea conference by dividing one God into three. Many speak a lie connecting to the spiritual medium.

The Bible is the word of God. Believe and try, you will have the experience to agree. Many reject the truth by following religion. Accepting parents' religion with no evidence or support of the facts. How about inquiring from God about His identity? Who knows the person but the person?

Wherever I go, I preach the truth. These times and days, many religions and voices surround us. The Voice of God is nowhere to be found. I have the truth and I stand on it. The truth will stand for eternity. So do not settle for less. When I say Jesus is a healer, I must prove that. God has my back to protect. He will work and heal. After experiencing the truth, many return to their religion. The roots of the religions are pretty deep, thorny, and stony. You need to take time to find and experiment by believing and obeying it.

Selfish people only seek God when they get stuck, or the situation is beyond. They look for me for prayer or the one who has the Holy Spirit. But as soon as God solved a problem, they say goodbye and goodbye to God. It is ok if they say goodbye to me but do not turn away from God. If God wrote your name in the Book of life from the foundation of the earth, you will be tried and will face problems till your heart softens up.

We hear many testimonies out there, but you need your own. I have many testimonies of my own. You will reach the place where you wouldn't believe anyone but the Lord. How can you trust Jesus? You develop relations by knowing, talking, and spending time with Him.

Read the Bible. Talk to God. search and obey the word. See, life will take a different mode. Only God has the power to help, save, change, and do supernatural things.

I believe in testimony and teaching. I believe in laying hands on sick people and casting out the demons. But we cannot change anyone's heart, only God can. Many places and countries are trying to pass a law against conversion. It is impossible to convert anyone. Passing laws will not stop the convictions.

The Government is trying to stop the hand of almighty God; it sounds foolish. The ruler of a nation and religion needs some sense and wisdom. They will not win a battle against the Lord.

Acts 4:18 And they called them, and commanded them not to speak at all nor teach in the name of Jesus.

Nowadays, ignorant people are coming against Christian leaders, destroying their homes and property. Have you tried God, and read the Word of God, which is in the Bible? It took 1600 years to finish the Bible. Written by God, using many people in a different era. How does anyone dare to come against God?

Acts 5:27 And when they had brought them, they set them before the council: and the high priest asked them, 28 Saying, Did not we straitly command you that ye should not teach in this name? and, behold, ye have filled Jerusalem with your doctrine, and intend to bring this man's blood upon us. 29 Then Peter and the other apostles answered and said, We ought to obey God rather than men.

Let me tell you the truth: there is one God, not millions. God, as a Spirit, resides in heaven and desires to dwell within us. Creating countless gods and goddesses will not bring you wealth, but rather perplexity. The purpose is to provide you with the truth, without any intention to convert. The God of heaven has commanded us to tell the entire world the truth. It is God's command for Christians to let others know the truth. We do not change or convert them, but the Lord transforms them. If you love the truth, then your wondering and toiling will be over, in Jesus' name. Amen!

LET US PRAY

Heavenly Father, we thank you for being our God. The Lord has given the great commission to broadcast in the world. Lord anoints us with the Holy Spirit and fire, so wherever we go, your spirit of truth works through us. The Lord has done this before, and we follow in His footsteps. Lord, we are incapable of changing their heart, but you can do so when we bear witness to the truth. Back us up by proving the facts of the Word. Lord, we give our heart, mind, soul, and spirit to you. By speaking the truth and obeying God's will, we can witness the growth of the Word of God, even on cement ground. The Lord does all and not us. If you put faith in the word, it will happen and there won't be a problem. Lord, you are in full control. Lord, please give us the boldness and courage to preach the good news. Our God is amazing, genuine, and mighty. He said He would do it if we spoke the truth in love. May the Lord have mercy on those lost souls in Jesus's name. Amen! God bless you!

NOVEMBER 21

PREPARE YOUR HEART!

People tend to get caught up in busyness during this time, causing them to forget the significance of Thanksgiving. Good food is something we all crave. We forget Jesus, who has loaded us with all benefits. People from other nations said, we have food, but the quantity is less than in America. They said our country is rich, but we do not have a variety of things and food like the US. Please hear, fear, and serve God wholeheartedly who gives all in abundance. He is real. There will always be leftovers to fill up baskets.

The Lord gives us all. He wants heartfelt gratitude as acknowledgment in return. Always remember to examine our hearts, and never believe that everything is achieved solely by our own power. On the contrary, say, I recognize that it is a gift from the Lord. It is the blessings given by the Lord. Once we learn to be thankful, we will never lose our salvation, which is healing, deliverance, and salvation.

Once a person reaches the height of their blessing, they either see the world through their eyes or God's. Don't allow the devil to deceive you into thinking he provided everything. God is watching you from above. Check your heart. Will you choose to go higher or lower?

It is the loyal ones who bravely soar to witness the beauty of the world. How you see the world depends on your thinking. Depending on God for daily bread, will keep us humble. But those who have much must watch out. Once they reach the top, they might think, oh I can do all this since I have arrived. The focus is not on having everything, but on preserving the soul. Remember to express gratitude at all times.

Psalm 9:1 I will praise thee, O LORD, with my whole heart; I will shew forth all thy marvellous works.

It's unfortunate that we sometimes lose sight of our humble beginnings and become arrogant in our hearts. Always exercise caution when it comes to matters of the heart. The heart is deceitful and wicked. The heart is the source of life's origin.

Another day, I watched a video of homeless people in San Francisco and Los Angeles. I heard a report that San Francisco is depressing. San Francisco is one of the most expensive cities. I was there and had experienced the most wicked spirit in the city. I am very sensitive to the spirit since I fast. Fasting kills flesh and Spirit comes alive. Spiritual senses work powerfully if you fast. I remember this city has many homosexuals and many sexual and gender changes. Once you pass the point of no return, there's no going back, only sliding down.

NOVEMBER 21

Luke 21:34 And take heed to yourselves, lest at any time your hearts be overcharged with surfeiting, and drunkenness, and cares of this life, and so that day come upon you unawares.

Ezekiel 16:49 Behold, this was the iniquity of thy sister Sodom, pride, fulness of bread, and abundance of idleness was in her and in her daughters. Neither did she strengthen the hand of the poor and needy.

We get money and forget our duties toward poor orphans and the needy. Even some forget their parents and siblings. When you get blessings, it is just for your test. Money has wings and will fly away if you forget God. Make sure the one who has given you money, mind, and provision of the job only wants in return is thankfulness. Recognize Jesus and take good care of your heart so it doesn't become insensitive to the surroundings. Giving the heart proper care is crucial, beyond your expectations. Let us remind those lost that listen to God and change. Take the right highway of victory by remembering the Lord. Ensure your relationship with the Lord remains strong to receive ongoing blessings. No one reaches the place without their cooperation with the Lord. It's necessary for you to confirm your identification with the Lord. You can identify as a sinner or saint, homeless, or settled. Going to a church building is not what the Lord is emphasizing, but rather your personal relationship with Him. Your body is a church or His residence. Rid yourself of sin and demons to make way for the Lord's care.

Check yourself and find out whether you are living in God's given territory or not. God has granted us a designated area and region, with the expectation that we behave, act, and think in alignment with His mindset. God didn't make exceptions for anyone. A person who keeps losing and falling further is known as a loser. I always have one thing in mind; continue practicing all you receive. Never assume that you are exempt from the laws set by God. Money has wings and will fly away. God-given wealth has blessing and cursing attached, depending on your heart condition.

Many were rich and became poor. The heart never thinks and recognizes the God of heaven. The people who once walked in the beautiful Garden of Eden became homeless. Rebelliousness is not the right way. When people have it all, then they spend money after drinking, eating, in-store, hair, nails, and shoes. What are you thinking? Investment is good, but where you are investing in the matter of bringing blessings and curses.

Some have given themselves the title of pastor, saints, or wonderful people. But behind the door, they are the most deceitful people. I fear God for them. It is called being deceived by their deceitful heart.

Some have earned more than enough and forgot to help the needy. Help someone who is sick, hurting, and needy. Our job is to make the best out of our life. We can help others if we have a good heart. Have love, long-suffering, gentleness, kindness, goodness, meekness, and peace in your heart. All this virtue attaches to your actions. Righteousness brings peace.

The state of California, particularly its Golden State, has been on my thoughts. Los Angeles was among the cities that many people found desirable. Now there are homeless everywhere. During the year 1980, my mode of transportation to LA was the bus. I said wow, what a beautiful city! I find pleasure in watching beautiful people, clothes, houses, and so on. In the present moment, it is experiencing fire, homelessness, and extreme poverty. What happened? Forgot to prepare the heart to preserve the blessings of God. The glamour of Hollywood is the most deceptive ever. Night clubs, drugs, pride, cigarettes, love for self, and many things worked against them. The contamination starts as you become careless in preparing the heart.

Let me advise you, think about the poor, needy, widow, sick, hurting, and orphan. Through makeup and makeovers, we strive to imitate someone's appearance. Are you contemplating vanishing and transforming into Cinderella? The condition is known as a heart problem. Take care of the heart. You need a double dose of joy in the heart. Many were running from home with a big dream of Hollywood in Los Angeles. But now, how many individuals are interested in fleeing from LA and California?

The country got rich and forgot to teach the oracles of God to their children. First removed prayer, the Bible, and now God. It's not education, people, or country that matter, but rather God, who makes all the difference. Love God with all hearts. Never remembered how they reached up to the mountains. How and when they started sliding back. I thought you should know, the forefather possessed the wisdom to live in a way that pleases God. They sent out many missionaries to teach the truth of God, so they do not have to come to the USA seeking riches. In the present time, rather than educating them with the truth, people followed a heathenish method and observed the result. Can you search and Google what the leaders of the city think? I am praying for God to send someone who can lead this lost generation in the ways of God. This is the key to success. Amen!

LET US PRAY

Lord we thank you, Lord, for your eternal mercy towards those who respect and acknowledge your presence in all aspects of life.

We are born naked and leave this earth naked, without a doubt. In between times, the Lord gives us our necessities and much more. Lord gives all who serve Him with His conditions. He does not withhold any good thing from us. So help us, Lord, that we stay totally in submission to you. Our God is exceptional and always acts in a benevolent manner. One who loves you, Lord, will never suffer hunger, thirst, or scarcity. We do not want to repeat the mistakes of the loser. We want to keep the commandments, precepts, and statutes of the Lord in our hearts. Our heart is called deceitful, but you can create cleanness by teaching your word. We invite you to our hearts. May the Holy Spirit empower us to follow Jesus. In the name of Jesus! Amen! God bless you!

NOVEMBER 22

THANKSGIVING!

"Thank you" is an excellent word. Expressing gratitude to God can lead to unimaginable outcomes. We know the thankful people receive extra. If you desire additional benefits, show appreciation to those who have assisted you.

2 Corinthians 9:11 Being enriched in everything to all bountifulness, which causeth through us thanksgiving to God.

Witness the outcome when you show gratitude for the Lord's blessings.

Matthew 15:36 And he took the seven loaves and the fishes, and gave thanks, and brake them, and gave to his disciples, and the disciples to the multitude. 37 And they did all eat, and were filled: and they took up of the broken meat that was left seven baskets full.

Jesus proved that by learning to thank God, you will find true contentment and abundance.

John 6:11 And Jesus took the loaves; and when he had given thanks, he distributed to the disciples, and the disciples to them that were set down; and likewise of the fishes as much as they would. 13 Therefore they gathered them together, and filled twelve baskets with the fragments of the five barley loaves, which remained over and above unto them that had eaten.

It was demonstrated by the Lord that there is power in expressing gratitude. Give thanks to the Lord for what you have, regardless of the number you need to feed. His blessings will result in multiplication and abundance. Our heavenly father desires us to express gratitude for His blessings. He is a good God and does the wonderful things.

While heading to the Priest, ten lepers were healed, but only one of them came back to show appreciation to Jesus.

Luke 17:17 And Jesus answering said, Were there not ten cleansed? but where are the nine? 18 There are not found that returned to give glory to God, save this stranger.19 And he said unto him, Arise, go thy way: thy faith hath made thee whole.

The Lord Jesus completely healed him, restoring his body, soul, and spirit.

The result of your Thanksgiving heart will bring you great joy and gratitude. We know everybody loves thankful people. Whiners and complainers are universally disliked. Just like humans, God has feelings. Murmurers and complainers are the people Lord can't stand.
An unthankful heart angers the Lord.

Deuteronomy 9:14 Let me alone, that I may destroy them, and blot out their name from under heaven

There is a specific title that God bestows upon unappreciative individuals.

Numbers 14:11 And the LORD said unto Moses, How long will this people provoke me? and how long will it be ere they believe me, for all the signs which I have shewed among them? 12 I will smite them with the pestilence, and disinherit them, and will make of thee a greater nation and mightier than they.

1 Corinthian 10:10 Neither murmur ye, as some of them also murmured, and were destroyed of the destroyer.

Never forget to thank the one who has done well for you. First, thank God and also the people who helped you. You will be blessed. The Bible says thank God for all things good and bad. You might ask yourself why to be thankful for the bad things that occur. Keep in mind, Job lost everything.

Job 2:10 But he said unto her, Thou speakest as one of the foolish women speaketh. What? shall we receive good at the hand of God, and shall we not receive evil? In all this did not Job sin with his lips.

We are unable to share since we have only two fishes, a little flour, and a little oil, and God knows this. All you can manage is to appreciate what you have. By doing this, we will witness the divine intervention of the almighty God. Our God is compassionate and ensures our well-being.

I faced numerous health challenges and lost my job, among other things. I made sure to thank God every day during my early morning prayers. Early morning is when I connect with Jesus in a special way. I approached His gate with a heart full of thanksgiving.

I was overwhelmed with gratitude on the day I started walking. Yet, even in the midst of that trial, I give thanks to God every day. A sense of deep appreciation washed over me as I reflected on the achievement during my trying experience. More than healing, I wanted a thankful heart. I knew God would take care of me, anyway. We gained knowledge of the Lord and refrained from grumbling because He allowed the situation. With knowledge of the Lord, we can stand tall and remain steadfast. The learning process is what it's all about. Expressing gratitude to God ensures that we will never lose our healing, deliverance, and miracles.

Life is full of unexpected twists and turns, making tomorrow uncertain. Only things we must teach ourselves to be thankful for. Our God is a miracle-working God and not a magician. Magic is too little. The miracle is supernatural. To learn and teach your children to be thankful. Entering a miracle is possible through thankfulness.

I visit people in the hospital, at home, or on the phone. Many are so thankful. I talk to one lady; her husband does not know the Lord yet. He gets so evil and violent toward her. But when I talk to her, she always speaks beautiful words to God. Despite her husband causing severe harm last time, she expressed gratitude for being chosen by God. She has no complaints. I trust that God will soon bring about a positive change in her situation.

Job lost all. However, his grateful heart brought double blessings.

If you learn to express gratitude, you will receive abundant blessings and multiplied rewards.

Our God is mighty and all-knowing, and all things are possible for Him. Would you love to know Him at His highest level? We need to know Him and not the other way around. He already knows who He is. The heart aches with sadness as people fail to remember the source of their blessings once they are in abundance.

Today is Thanksgiving; The United States of America celebrates and remembers God's provision, who provided food to pilgrims who came to the United States from Europe.. It was the time many died, and the Lord poured His blessings. The United States of America is one of the most blessed nations in the world. We will survive in the desert, in famine, in scarcity, in poverty, or in any situation if we say thank you to the Lord who said I am your Jehovah Jairah. Our Provider!

I live in the United States of America. My job was taken from me by the Lord in 2000, who then called me to serve Him. He promised me about my provisions. For all these years, He has kept His Word. Many come and eat at my home, and sometimes stay with me. I do my ministry under the Lord, and He has blessed me and blessed me. I have never asked for help from anyone, but He has supplied all my needs out of His riches. Count your blessings and appreciate what you have. Happy Thanksgiving! God Bless you,

LET US PRAY

Heavenly Father, this earth is yours and the fullness of it. We know you love your people, and we are thankful for it. A thankful heart is what we need.

You are amazing, that's exactly what we want to express. You have given us many wonderful blessings. We never got it on our own, but you have provided it. Lord bless people with a thankful heart. Many couldn't reach the promised land for not being thankful to you. As you have shown us, the example of thanksgiving and miracle hidden behind that thank you word. We return to you today to say thank you, Lord. You have done nothing but good. We thank you for another day and year. Every day is a gift from heaven, so we thank you for each day, for our family, friends, loved ones, and freedom to worship you. Our God is good and has taken care of us. You have provided us in abundance, so we say thank you truly, in Jesus' name. Amen! God bless you!

NOVEMBER 23

MAY THE PROPHECY COME TRUE!

If you believe and have patience, the prophecies spoken over you will be fulfilled. Prophecy is constantly centered around strategies and guarantees. To comply with the Lord's instructions, the participant must carry on. Every prophecy spoken in the participant's life will be fulfilled when the time is right. To fulfill God's plan for you as prophesied, you must wholeheartedly follow His instructions. Be mindful of situations and events with all diligence. May God aid you in realizing that His word functions as a two-way agreement, only fulfilled when the condition is active in His divine plan. Allow us to observe a few instances of exceptions.

Isaiah 38:1 In those days was Hezekiah sick unto death. And Isaiah the prophet the son of Amoz came unto him, and said unto him, Thus saith the LORD, Set thine house in order: for thou shalt die, and not live. 2 Then Hezekiah turned his face toward the wall, and prayed unto the LORD,

The prophet was tasked by the Lord, who reigns as the CEO of the entire universe, to reveal the Plan. Later it was changed. Isaiah's prophecy was not false, however, King Hezekiah desperately sought mercy. Avoid stating that the prophet was deceitful or untrue, for he truly was a prophet. The prophet has nothing to do with the situation; he is only the carrier of God's message..

Isaiah 38:5 Go, and say to Hezekiah, Thus saith the LORD, the God of David thy father, I have heard thy prayer, I have seen thy tears: behold, I will add unto thy days fifteen years.

God has the best plan for your life. When you make a plan over God's plan, it will only bring ruin to your life. When the Word is from the living God, have patience until it is fulfilled. The Word of God will be fulfilled at the appointed time in the right season. We may rush God but will not happen, but will happen if we wait. The prophecy within God's word becomes clear when interpreted accurately with the help of prophets and apostles. Understand their interpretation of the word, receive the promised word, and act accordingly. It is the job of a prophet to deliver the message without adding and subtracting. The safety of the Prophet is threatened as unrighteous individuals govern Jesus' kingdom. Remember, prophets serve as messengers, nothing else.

Luke 7:28 For I say unto you, Among those that are born of women there is not a greater prophet than John the Baptist: but he that is least in the kingdom of God is greater than he.

John the Baptist's purpose was to prepare for God's manifestation in the flesh. Let us pray for the Lord to bless us with truthful prophets.

NOVEMBER 23

John 1:23 He said, I am the voice of one crying in the wilderness, Make straight the way of the Lord, as said the prophet Esaias.

The prophet plays a crucial role in God's kingdom. Nowadays, counterfeit denominations and organizations refuse to acknowledge or make use of prophets. This is the end of time, where chaos reigns supreme. Nevertheless, there exist remarkable prophets within this region. We should ask the Lord to send us the true one in our prayers.

Sometimes people become very impatient with the prophecy. According to them, prophecy should be fulfilled without delay. Be patient and trust in God's timing. He will complete the task, as the prophet declared. The concept of prophecy is associated with an uncertain future. David was around ten to fifteen years old when he received the prophecy. He held on to God's prophecy while he was running from his enemy. King Saul was his only enemy. The country turned against David. David relocated his parents to a different country. When God examined David's heart, He found what He was seeking.

May the Lord help His people. Life often takes unexpected twists before finding the right path.

Who is responsible for aborting the prophecy? Do not end the prophecy, but be on guard. You are in charge of your future, take good care of the plan of God. God said I will prepare a place for you. He has mansions, but it doesn't mean you own one until you do the prerequisite to receive one.

Many are not seeking the kingdom of God. Not sincere enough to find the way through Jesus. All registered churches, organizations, the denomination is not the way, but Jesus is. The truth only reveals itself through the path of Jesus. Seek, ask, knock, and find your way to the Promised Land. Numerous individuals are occupied with the hope that there is no hell and that all individuals will be granted entry into heaven. They believe God is good. Good God wouldn't send anyone to hell. Do not buy into these deceitful claims. When blind teachers lead, expect to fall into the ditch together. Be careful.

Think with the right mind, a man came to a prophet searching for healing. The prophet asked the simple things, and he got upset and wanted to go back as he came.

2 King 5:13 And his servants came near, and spake unto him, and said, My father, if the prophet had bid thee do some great thing, wouldest thou not have done it? how much rather then, when he saith to thee, Wash and be clean? 14 Then went he down, and dipped himself seven times in Jordan, according to the saying of the man of God: and his flesh came again like unto the flesh of a little child, and he was clean.

God said to go in the water in Jesus' name and my blood will wash away your sins. Death is the consequence of sin, leading to eternal hellfire. All have sinned. So I give my blood; you just have to go underwater once and you will be cleansed, healed, and delivered as your sins will be wiped away.

All humble went into the water in Jesus' name to wash away their sins. False teachers and prophets affiliated with denominations and organizations will oppose it. False teachers neglect the significance of having faith in the one to whom Jesus entrusted the key, which is Peter and Paul. They will say, we do not have to follow the book of Acts, which is the past church history. Our body, once a church, was bought with blood. Did you know that Jesus wrote every word of God?

So blind leaders are leading blind followers.

2 Corinthians 4:3 But if our gospel be hid, it is hid to them that are lost:4 In whom the god of this world hath blinded the minds of them which believe not, lest the light of the glorious gospel of Christ, who is the image of God, should shine unto them.

There are many who have fallen asleep and many who are like lost coins and sheep, foolish and astray. Wake up. Make sure this prophecy doesn't become a part of your life history. May the Lord grant you a heart that thirsts for knowledge and a wise advisor to guide you in discerning between prophecy and your own words.

Many of my prophecies came true. I cannot imagine my life without a prophet, as I follow God's teachings. Many remarkable prophecies I've encountered have actually materialized. Not everyone has, but it will happen in the name of Jesus. Amen!

LET US PRAY

Lord, we know you cannot lie. You speak to us through your word or true prophet. Please give us a believing heart. Our job is to believe and hold on. Even in the valley of death, or have to standalone or to see the raging water coming against us. May our Lord have mercy on us! Let us see the outcome of all prophecies as we hold on. The ability to foresee the future requires the wings of an eagle for a higher vantage point. We know the prophecy will come true if we trust God almighty. Our Lord has never failed yet and never will. Help us not to fail you. We want to build your kingdom and not destroy it. Our job is to build on one church established 2000 years ago. We will reach our heavenly home by keeping your word and following your commandments. Our future will be bright and great knowing you will do what you said in your Word and through your true prophets in Jesus' name. Amen! God bless you!

NOVEMBER 24

SPIRITUAL ILLITERACY!

The real world is actually the spiritual world. It's important to acknowledge the existence of the spiritual realm. Those who are unaware of spiritual activity are simply ignorant. Poverty results from illiteracy. The lack of basic knowledge among the People of God leads to a crisis and weakens the kingdom of God. The lack of knowledge in God's Word results in damage to His creation. Why? Walking in darkness is the result of not knowing the Word of God. Without the Word of God as a lamp, you're more likely to step on snakes. If you lack the nourishing spiritual food of the Word of God, it signifies feebleness, weakness, and illness. The Word of God acts as a sword to sever the influence of the devil, fallen angels, and demons. If you do not have an experience of the Word as a sword against your opponent, then you will be destroyed. It signifies that it will shatter your life and cannot be restored. Remember, Satan comes to steal, kill, and destroy. How much you should be into the word of God knowing it is your life and death matter? Is it not important to constantly engage with the word of God?

Do not die like a fool. Being in possession of a sword without the understanding of its usage. I received a message from the Lord yesterday, granting me authority and power through the Holy Spirit. Take back what has been stolen by the devil, fallen angels, and demons with force.

Later I talked to the lady, and she said, I am sick. This illness needs to be expelled from my body. I reminded you that you possess the authority in Jesus's name and the Holy Spirit, so make use of it. Tell the devil to get out. Why do you want the devil to use your body since you have the power and authority? She said, true, I have to use authority and destroy Satan's plan to keep me sick. I said that is correct. Biblical illiteracy is a plus for the devil. The devil introduced various denominations, non-denominations, and organizations to discourage preaching, teaching, casting out demons, and healing the sick. They receive training and education to pursue what they truly want, despite the confusion.

What was America's downfall? They took the Bible and prayer out of the School. In modern times, the terms building also used to refer to church. Many families do not read the Bible. It is there, but no time. I carry many Bibles and give them to people when I minister to them. Being aware of your privileges, benefits, authority, and power eliminates headaches. When you become aware and begin using it, it has the power to change not only you, but also the people in your life. Many years ago, when I was living in India, I had the same conditions. We went through a lot for my brother's spiritual situation. My focus is on studying the Word nonstop. While growing up; I did not want to believe in the existence of a demon. I had limited knowledge on the subject and had no intention of increasing my understanding. I made it clear that demons do not exist. I preferred not knowing about the demonic world due to my fear. I wanted to assure myself, as a Christian, that it wouldn't be able to harm me. What a sorrowful situation! But as I started getting knowledge of Ephesians 6 chapter to put on the armor of God, take your only offensive weapon, the Sword, which is the Word of God and above all, the shield of faith. I realized, wow it is a battle. I desire to be spiritually strong, and I believe that consuming the word of God will help me achieve that. I'll provide you with a few cases to demonstrate the difference between spiritual illiteracy and literacy. It will contribute to our understanding.

Genesis 2:17 But of the tree of the knowledge of good and evil, thou shalt not eat of it: for in the day that thou eatest thereof thou shalt surely die.

Is it true that you shall not eat? Now, observe Eve's response to Satan.

Genesis 3:3 But of the fruit of the tree which is in the midst of the garden, God hath said, Ye shall not eat of it, neither shall ye touch it, lest ye die.

God never said thou shalt not touch it but said not to eat. But she added in the word of God. Do not add or subtract to the word of God. It was clear to the devil that this woman had no understanding of spirituality. The devil destroyer, had heard the conversation. The only thing he needs to do is manipulate the Word. Oh, I tell you; the devil is a crook and twister. He tells you it is fun to do it, but never informs the hidden agenda of destruction. Everything appears to be in order. The Devil remarks on its beauty and includes false information. Trying it is a delightful experience, and you'll be just as satisfied as the Joneses. You will be like God and be like the world. It's something that everyone does. Of course, I have to look like, act like, and burn like them in hell too.

The devil never says if you walk naked, I can use your body to rape and molest. By teaching your young daughter makeup, I can operate in the human trafficking industry without fear of divine consequences. I have a method to defeat you in a minute if you lack knowledge of God's terminology. I have the ability to forcibly bring you to my realm of darkness. You'll be trapped forever, no escape route. The devil delights in people's lack of spiritual understanding, encouraging them to focus on worldly matters rather than seeking enlightenment. Satan loves when people attend buildings they call churches, denominations, and false teaching. Hear my false teachers, brag about simple faith, and so on. Ignorant people are beloved by Satan as they love religious education. They do not open the Bible to study, meditate, and practice the Word for warfare. They are so weak that Satan can blow one air and blow out of this world. Satan can give one attack, cancer, or stroke, and take them out of here.

Look at how Jesus handles the devil. It seems that he has a deep understanding of spiritual matters.

Matthew 4:1 Then was Jesus led up of the Spirit into the wilderness to be tempted of the devil.

The devil said to eat when Jesus was fasting. As someone who is literate in the Word of God, I live by its teachings. As per the devil, if you acknowledged yourself as the Son of God, who is God incarnate, he was convinced that you possessed a multitude of angels who would ensure your safety. Jesus, being literate in the Word, used a sword and said, no I know what I have and I know I am God, but I will not tem" The Devil showed and offered a beautiful world, wealth and power, and positions if He worships the Devil. Jesus knew the Devil owned nothing, all that he had was temporary. Illiterate Eve and Adam turn it over to the Devil. Yet, it will be removed. Jesus, knowing all, said, it is written, thou shalt worship the Lord thy God, and him only shalt thou serve.

Is it clear to you now why we have been defeated? We are illiterate, and that's the only reason. Moving through the darkness, as a prisoner, unwell, burdened, controlled, and disoriented.

I read the Bible; because I need it for myself and those to whom I minister to. By not teaching the truth, I become part of the group labeled as blind leaders and false teachers. I want to know the Word. The devil cannot use me. Why do individuals seek to be tricked by themselves or the devil? Only the ignorant fall into the trap of the devil. If you see the religious leaders, so-called saints, holding any positions, or walking contrary to the Bible, then these people are ignorant and illiterate. Just wait and see what happens to them. Judgment will prove what they are. Satan pulls them by the nose; they have no power to cast out demons. Matter of fact, some of them are demon-possessed. It is a sad report. Spiritual illiteracy has done much damage to us, our children, and our families' lives. They destroyed our nation since we do not know ABC and 123 of the Bible, which is for our education. Please open the Bible, study, and get spiritual graduation in Jesus' name. Amen!

LET US PRAY

Lord, we need you. As you said, you will never leave and forsake us. It's possible if we stay focused and don'tlose sight. Lord, guide us in obeying your commandments and walking with you for our safety. Though Adam, Eve, and many who were rebellious and ignorant lost out, we can still study the written word of God. Assist us in utilizing Word as a lamp, light, nourishment, and weapon. Lord, we should walk in victory if we allow ourselves to know and use the word. Teach us to be skilled in utilizing your Word. There are devil-inspired organizations, denominations, teachers, and pastors in this world because the devil has deceived many uneducated authorities. Lord, let the Holy Spirit teach us. We pray for your Spirit to saturate us, as it did on the day of Pentecost, in the name of Jesus. Amen! God bless you!

NOVEMBER 25

GOD GIVES INABUNDANCE NO NEED TO TOIL!

Under God's direction, you do not sweat and toil but receive in abundance! Do you know the way of man is harder than the ways of God? God's way has a simple supernatural computation. Get a heavenly calculator. You need a rhythm of God in your breathing system. When toiling all night for the fish and not catching, Jesus said,

Luke 5:5 And Simon answering said unto him, Master, we have toiled all the night, and have taken nothing: nevertheless at thy word I will let down the net. 6 And when they had this done, they inclosed a great multitude of fishes: and their net brake.

We toil because of not asking God, not knowing the ways of God, and not leaning on God. Our life has a meaning, but we make it meaningless. The Lord has a purpose, but we do not care for a higher calling. Our problem is we are more like swine. It would never benefit you and your children after you.

What a waste of time if we do not care to listen and obey the way of God!

Lord said, Deuteronomy 6:10 And it shall be, when the LORD thy God shall have brought thee into the land which he sware unto thy fathers, to Abraham, to Isaac, and to Jacob, to give thee great and goodly cities, which thou buildedst not,11 And houses full of all good things, which thou filledst not, and wells digged, which thou diggedst not, vineyards and olive trees, which thou plantedst not; when thou shalt have eaten and be full; 12 Then beware lest thou forget the LORD, which brought thee forth out of the land of Egypt, from the house of bondage. 13 Thou shalt fear the LORD thy God, and serve him, and shalt swear by his name. 14 Ye shall not go after other gods, of the gods of the people which are round about you; 15 (For the LORD thy God is a jealous God among you) lest the anger of the LORD thy God be kindled against thee, and destroy thee from off the face of the earth.

Now anyone who wants to sustain this kind of blessing will look nowhere but seek the instruction of God. Our trouble is we do not focus on priorities. We focus on all that is not important. The law says if you have a baby out of wedlock; you get all these free plus money. All jump into the program for free. What about God said I am Jehovah Jireh, I will provide. Having these children, no one wants to raise them. They are on the street hurting, on a drug, misused, and name it. So what do you think? How can you afford this? Many people have to work two or three jobs. Still have nothing but problems. Our problem is not hearing and not submitting to God's ways. Who would not like the free stuff given by God attached to blessings? Satan's free stuff has an attachment called curses. Curses because all that he gives is to break the commandments of God. He gave 30 silver coins to Judas. His reward was suicide, money was worthless since he could not enjoy it.

The Lord gave King Solomon what he asked for as he followed the ways of God. God can give since all belong to the Lord.

2 Chronicles 1:11 And God said to Solomon, Because this was in thine heart, and thou hast not asked riches, wealth, or honour, nor the life of thine enemies, neither yet hast asked long life; but hast asked wisdom and knowledge for thyself, that thou mayest judge my people, over whom I have made thee king: 12 Wisdom and knowledge is granted unto thee; and I will give thee riches, and wealth, and honour, such as none of the kings have had that have been before thee, neither shall there any after thee have the like.

Do not toil for this world. Worldly goods are not satisfactory. The Lord gives without toiling, sweating, and selling selves as a slave. He picks the poor from the dust and setteth him on high. The Lord can crown a shepherd boy as king. Daniel became next to the king by God's given knowledge of dreams, visions, and interpretation of it.

Proverb 10:22 The blessing of the Lord, it maketh rich, and he addeth no sorrow with it.

The reason for our sorrow is not listening to God. Our God is good and gives wonderful riches with peace.

The Bible says to keep the first things first as Muslim people do. We now brought Santa from the North Pole. Look at the spelling of Santa. It is Satan and his seat is on the North side. Our God is good, do not put any idols. It is a manmade character that replaced our God who gave His life. Many foolish people do not recognize and follow the flow.

Our God has given all, learn to continue in His blessings. Blessings of God are amazing, but learning how to continue in it is extremely important. It is the key we should never lose. Many lived in the most gorgeous home. Where are they now? They lost all and are now on the street, behind the bar, living a hopeless life! Many take God's blessings for granted. Some keep God in their tongue but not in their heart. I know many are sincere and know the value of the Word to keep it in the heart so they sin not against the Lord.

Our value of morals is going down, and we put our children in jeopardy. Some parents and grandparents don't have a good night's sleep since they forgot to teach God as their priorities. Many wonder what happened.

Let us see some reasons for our toiling. First, pray, do you? Pray without ceasing, do you? Seek the kingdom of God first and His righteousness, do you? What are you seeking, job, degree, the world, and things of the world? Are you a wise steward of your life? Do you love the Lord with all heart, mind, soul, and strength? Do you see someone in need and turn your face away from them? The Lord sees our toiling. He wants to tell you, wait, why are you up this late? Why are you so tired, depressed, discouraged, and dying like a fool? Do you go cast out demons? Do you give Bibles or words to others? Have you visited the widow? Are you someone who assists the orphan? Do you see hungry and give?

If not, then your toiling will be all night and day. If you care for the vineyard of God, then the Lord will take care of you. Many times I have said, How good God is, many depend on me. And I cannot do all, but the Lord can. He tells me to do this or that. It is no more toiling. Do not go shopping without Jesus. Do not walk without His guidance. God said, I give you all, but do you have the key to open the treasure? It needs the correct key to open your God-given treasure, so help us, Lord. We must not toil all night. If you have two fish, then do not hold back. Give to see the multiplication of fishes to feed all. Seems like we would not have baggers, poor and needy, if we take the instruction of God. Amen!

LET US PRAY

Holy Jesus, the human, is made in God's image and you have been given power and authority. Help us continue in God's given heritage, so we do not have to toil day and night. Nowadays, many are on the street, have rejected their heritage giver, and many turn their back and choose the wrong, hard, and hurtful way. Help us, Lord, to know you correctly, and experience you by learning and learning the ways of God. God has all and owns all. On His command, raging water ceased. Help us, God, to follow faithfully in your instructed plan. Give us diligence and make us sincere. Not to go astray, not to turn left or right without your direction. Help us amend our way. Help us keep continuing in blessing by keeping the ways of God and getting rid of our wicked ways. Make us humble by delivering from our ways, which are wicked in Jesus' name. Amen! God bless you!

NOVEMBER 26

CARELESS LEADERS CAUSE CHAOS IN THE NATION!

God-given direction should be a priority for the leader appointed by God. Once you do, it will become clear to you.

Genesis 1:2 And the earth was without form, and void; and darkness was upon the face of the deep. And the Spirit of God moved upon the face of the waters. 3 And God said, Let there be light: and there was light.

There will be order, laws, serenity, protection, and provision if we follow God's guidance. Nation crisis reflects evil religious leaders. Spiritual leaders are the ones who keep God's order and religious leaders keep Satan's order. In any nation, if its spiritual leaders do not keep God's order in place, the nation will be divided and Satan will rule. Empty promises are Satan's agenda.

God-fearing leaders bring blessings to the nation.

Isaiah 26:1 In that day shall this song be sung in the land of Judah; We have a strong city; salvation will God appoint for walls and bulwarks.

The Lord offers great things if our leaders carry God's instruction.

Is 32:18 And my people shall dwell in a peaceable habitation, and in sure dwellings, and in quiet resting places;

God has angels, a fiery wall of the Holy Spirit to protect, and His presence to take care of His creation. Isn't it nice if we have spiritual leaders who wake up before the sun rises to seek the will of God? God, who lives in heaven, wants His people to look up, stay connected, and cry out to receive what they desire. Connection is the key for the Lord to choose leaders who have an ear to hear and obey.

The Nation has fallen and risen; the cause is its spiritual leaders. My and your job is to cry out to God for the leaders so they hear God.

Deut 31:29 For I know that after my death ye will utterly corrupt yourselves, and turn aside from the way which I have commanded you; and evil will befall you in the latter days; because ye will do evil in the sight of the LORD, to provoke him to anger through the work of your hands.

We need MapQuest of the Lord for every leader to succeed. That is His word for this dispensation. Leaders should know the job given by the Lord. Do not walk blind and deaf to your instruction given by God. Knowing the success and defeat of nations depends on your reaction to the command of God.

Joshua 1:8 This book of the law shall not depart out of thy mouth; but thou shalt meditate therein day and night, that thou mayest observe to do according to all that is written therein: for then thou shalt make thy way prosperous, and then thou shalt have good success.

In 721 B.C. Assyria swept out of the north, captured the Northern Kingdom of Israel, and took the ten tribes into captivity.

What led to the downfall of the Northern Kingdom?

1 Kings 12:26 And Jeroboam said in his heart, Now shall the kingdom return to the house of David: 27 If this people go up to do sacrifice in the house of the Lord at Jerusalem, then shall the heart of this people turn again unto their lord, even unto Rehoboam king of Judah, and they shall kill me, and go again to Rehoboam king of Judah. 28 Whereupon the king took counsel, and made two calves of gold, and said unto them, It is too much for you to go up to Jerusalem: behold thy gods, O Israel, which brought thee up out of the land of Egypt. 29 And he set the one in Bethel, and the other put he in Dan. 30 And this thing became a sin: for the people went to worship before the one, even unto Dan.

The king's selfish motives caused them to turn away from the God who had delivered them from captivity with the help of Moses, instead of working towards the people's prosperity.

Leadership can be compared to the head. Without protection, the brain can suffer damage if the head is not safeguarded. The brain does all the thinking. Some families messed up because of the evil leadership. We had Adam whose leadership was bad and ruined humankind by the flood. Pray for corrupt leaders. The Lord is over all and will send help from heaven if you ask for it.

1 Timothy 2:1 I exhort therefore, that, first of all, supplications, prayers, intercessions, and giving of thanks, be made for all men; 2 For kings, and for all that are in authority; that we may lead a quiet and peaceable life in all godliness and honesty.

So the conclusion is we have to pray for the authorities to stay on the right track. We can let them ruin us if we are sleeping and not taking the matter to God. Esther knew that she and her people had a short time to live. She went on prayer and asked others to pray and fast for three days and nights. She overthrew the plan of Satan.

An evil leader acts carelessly in their role. A responsible leader will stay on the right path by following and obeying God's instructions. David replaced King Saul by playing wise. King David kept God first and nothing else. He was more interested in maintaining his relationship with God than in power and position. God ruled in David's kingdom. Success was not in his strength but through the Lord.

Psalm 75:6 For promotion cometh neither from the east, nor from the west, nor from the south. 7 But God is the judge: he putteth down one, and setteth up another.

Lord removed Eli from Priest's office since he wasn't paying attention to the instruction of the Lord.

1 Samuel 2:29 Wherefore kick ye at my sacrifice and at mine offering, which I have commanded in my habitation; and honourest thy sons above me, to make yourselves fat with the chiefest of all the offerings of Israel my people? 30 Wherefore the Lord God of Israel saith, I said indeed that thy house, and the house of thy father, should walk before me for ever: but now the Lord saith, Be it far from me; for them that honour me I will honour, and they that despise me shall be lightly esteemed. 31 Behold, the days come, that I will cut off thine arm, and the arm of thy father's house, that there shall not be an old man in thine house.

Knowing God is the ultimate judge, one should do their business by keeping fear of God. The Lord warned evil kings by the mouth of prophets but they refused to turn. The judgment lingers on their head like an eminent sword. Grateful for the Lord's promotion, he approached his responsibilities with a humble demeanor, ensuring he fulfilled them diligently.

Micah 3:9 Hear this, I pray you, ye heads of the house of Jacob, and princes of the house of Israel, that abhor judgment, and pervert all equity. 10 They build up Zion with blood, and Jerusalem with iniquity. 11 The heads thereof judge for reward, and the priests thereof teach for hire, and the prophets thereof divine for money: yet will they lean upon the Lord, and say, Is not the Lord among us? none evil can come upon us. 12 Therefore shall Zion for your sake be plowed as a field, and Jerusalem shall become heaps, and the mountain of the house as the high places of the forest.

We need genuine leaders as spiritual authorities. Spiritual leaders should never worry about death or persecution, but stay true to the order of God. When David fell into adultery, seer Nathan said thou art the person.

2 Samuel 12:7a And Nathan said to David, Thou art the man.

Very true, these prophets have to deal with very evil authority

Mark 6:18 For John had said unto Herod, It is not lawful for thee to have thy brother's wife.

John Baptist lost his head because of the corrupt king.

The truth brought John Baptist's head to the grave. Remember, the evil rulers will take you back to captivity. Pray for leaders to have wisdom and fear of God.

LET US PRAY

Heavenly Father, we all handle the trouble we are facing on the earth, in the nation, and as an individual. Our Lord is ready to help if we call on Him. We pray, Lord, please give us the true prophets and true teachers to carry on the work of God and raise the army to face reality. Help us, Lord, to raise our voices unto the Lord. Teach us how to pray and file petitions to the Lord. Our Job is to ask for genuine leaders. We ask the Lord to give us honest leaders who can lead the nation on a righteous path in Jesus's name. Amen! God bless you.

NOVEMBER 27

YOUR CHOICES REFLECT YOUR HEART!

We justify making wrong choices. We suffer the consequences of choices. Some repeat the mistakes over and over. Never find their way out of the tragedy, trouble, and permanent damage. They bring hurt and pain to themselves and the family involved with them.

The Bible gives accurate information about the heart. The heart is a secret agent in your life. Many times, people wonder why, what, and how. Good question, but identifying the problem with a solution is the best. Many go around and around. Never find the way out, always falling behind. God said I blessed you. Falling behind is not a blessing, right? The only way the Lord will bless you is if you have a clean heart. If your heart is healthy, then your choices will give a boost to your life. Life begins in your heart.

1 Peter 3:15a But sanctify the Lord God in your hearts:

Sanctify means to purify or clean your heart. It is necessary to clean and purify the heart. Learn first the condition of your heart. Do you know? No, no one but the Lord knows the heart condition!

Jeremiah 17:9 The heart is deceitful above all things, and desperately wicked: who can know it? 10 I the Lord search the heart, I try the reins, even to give every man according to his ways, and according to the fruit of his doings.

Do you have questions about your heart? Go to the one who knows your heart, and that is the creator of the heart.

David says in Psalms 51, create in me a clean heart.

Do you think we should pray for a clean heart every day, too? I pray every day; the Lord creates in me a clean heart. I do not know my heart, but you do.

Psalm 51:7 Purge me with hyssop, and I shall be clean: wash me, and I shall be whiter than snow.

As you know, our heart needs spiritual help and physical care. Once you balance it out, your life will be the most beautiful on earth. God looks inside of our hearts. Your heart attracts God. People see you as a person, but your actions reflect your heart condition. If the heart has the virtue that God requires, then you are the candidate for His choice.

1 Samuel 16:7 But the Lord said unto Samuel, Look not on his countenance, or on the height of his stature; because I have refused him: for the Lord seeth not as man seeth; for man looketh on the outward appearance, but the Lord looketh on the heart.

The heart gets dirty. That is why we need to continue to work with the Lord. What I mean is, just like you need to take your car for a tuneup, you must take your heart for correction and cleansing. Always take your heart to the creator to fix it. Invite God to clean your heart, since He knows what needs to be corrected. Send your heart to the maker. He knows how to rectify, clean, and take all the action to take care.

Psalm 44:21 Shall not God search this out? for he knoweth the secrets of the heart.

Before you judge yourself, make sure you find out what is in your heart. Our good God wants to secure you. He has given us body, soul, and spirit. He knows each organ of the body. We do not know about the organs of our body, but God does.

Some people speak too highly of themselves. But when you learn or know them, you think, oh this man is a cheater, liar, greedy, adulterer, or whatnot. Do not take the word of man, but watch their actions. Their actions will tell what they are. Their heart is the script of their life.

Often, recurring the same problem will tell you that this person has a heart problem and not a mind. God can correct if they become diligent in searching the heart to correct.

Matthew 5:8 Blessed are the pure in heart: for they shall see God.

The heart needs more attention than any other part of the body. It needs sanctification and purification; it requires sincerity, wisdom, and truthfulness. So having the heart in your body needs your continual care. Learn how to take care of it. Many are experts in flipping, lying, cheating, deceiving, not knowing their action reflects their heart.

When your children do wrong, use the rod of correction instead of helping them find the excuse. When children justify or give excuses proves that they have wicked parents. Parents are also the key factor in raising this wicked generation.

Proverbs 22:15 Foolishness is bound in the heart of a child; but the rod of correction shall drive it far from him.

Proverbs 23:14 Thou shalt beat him with the rod, and shalt deliver his soul from hell.

Proverbs 20:30 The blueness of a wound cleanseth away evil: so do stripes the inward parts of the belly.

The Bible says parents must purge evil by using a rod of iron just for the correction. It will cleanse them and you will sleep quietly. Do you see the faulty generation raised by faulty parents? They did not use the rod to clean away evil when they were doing wrong. Many think it is wrong to punish. Punishment for the right reason is biblical.

It is the parent's job to let children know when they are wrong. You would love to see your children grow up as great saints of God.

I pray the Lord gives us many Jecobad who raised Moses, Aaron, and Mariam. No matter what, parents have the biggest role in raising clean-hearted children. Yes, we can blame TV, society, and other factors. Children do not know what is right from wrong. The moral sense of ethical motive has to be classified and taught correctly.

Of course, parents are busy, leave children at the babysitter, or turn on the TV to watch mind and life-destructive programs. Busy sending them to school, games, parties, and name it.

Parents, you are a God-given child's babysitter. Do not give your responsibilities to someone else.

Once you take your time to raise the children by teaching the law, commandments, and precepts of God, they will become mighty men and women of God.

I have seen wicked parents have children and then grandchildren wicked as well. In the end, the Lord wipes out the nation filled with this kind of wicked and deceitful generation. I lived around multicultural people and I know the raising of the people differed from the different casts. There is no doubt in my mind that a few of them are genuine and truthful. Why? Parents take time to raise their children. Now when you see the children, they reflect their hearts, but also the parents. Take care of your heart and keep it with all diligence so you find eternal life. Amen!

LET US PRAY

Lord, I believe our parents can fail us, but you will not. Give us your Holy Spirit to teach us the truth.

We have a chance if we find the true teachers and prophets. They can rescue us out of hell. Save us from any heartaches. May the Lord help us do what is right. Teach us to take good care of our hearts. We come in your presence, show us the evil, wrong, and wicked things in the heart so we can cleanse within. May the Lord make us a reflection of your Word. Let our life be the life like Jesus. God, grant us a true, sincere, clean, pure, and wise heart. The heart is beyond us, even though it is within us. May the Lord give us a great big clean heart to reach many. Many have broken hearts and their life seems such a mess. Lord, today you heal the broken in the heart so they function well. Our God, we ask you to take care of our hearts and teach us how to take good care of our hearts in Jesus' name. Amen! God bless you!

NOVEMBER 28

SPIRITUAL EXERCISE!

We always want to make sure that we are in good shape. Early morning people are jogging, exercising, or running. In many places, there is a track where people go running, walking, and exercising. Many gyms are there to keep us in shape and healthy. People take membership and pay money for their bodies, so they stay in shape. The body is the biggest matter of people in the US. I met a friend who was much after her fitness. She was always in the Gym, exercising. I mean, she did not care for her husband and children, but for exercise and perfect shape. The body has become an idol for people. They will take every chance to take care of themselves rather than their soul and spirit.

Flesh and spirit are contrary to each other. God made the body of flesh where you camp. Where the Spirit is permanent and God rides on it. Body or flesh is the entry for Satan. Society has taken little or near-to-nothing importance for their Spirit. If the spirit exercises through the Holy word of God, you can enter heaven for eternal rest.

The Holy Word of God is not to read, but to put in action for exercise.

Many people in the world have put the Word of God into action and have seen success. We all do not become Christian since we are born in a Christian family. People who exercise the Word of God get a ride on the Spirit of God. That is associating with the Lord. Remember, your spiritual exercise is a means to enter the spiritual realm. There are many exercises in demonic religions. Which I do not want to talk about, but find out how they become a victim of the evil spirit. You invite Satan and His evil spirit into your body by doing the wrong exercise to shape up.

But when you are exercising the word of God, you are inviting God's Spirit. You can rest easy knowing that you are protected in that place.

1 Timothy 4:8 For bodily exercise profiteth little: but godliness is profitable unto all things, having promise of the life that now is, and of that which is to come.

It is godliness to have reverence for God, His character, and laws. We believe in the Bible, but we know the devil also believes and knows every word. He has convinced our society to break every Word, commandment, and law of God. Look around. The product of Satan is miserable, depressed, homeless, druggy, possessed, oppressed, and sick within and without.

Read scriptures, laws, commandments, and precepts to follow what it says. That is called spiritual exercise. Our problem is we do not find an instructor or teacher who helps us to practice the word of God. Indeed, they care for tithes and offerings, not your spiritual well-being. That is not exercising. If Jesus is around, then He will tell you went to the den. But there are many to make you strong and beautiful shapes. We must know all the scriptures to exercise for better spiritual health.

Today's media is trying to either help or harm. They show a fleshly and spiritual exercise in the media. Sometimes I pause and put my hand on Christians who are bombarded by the opponent. If you are not strong, healthy, and shaped-up Christians, then you will lose your cool. The devil rides on flesh and knows how to push your button. Not only that, but they also are full of demons. Prayer, fasting with the word, is the spiritual exercise for powerful muscles. Before going to the cross-Jesus prayed and was strengthened. He did prayer exercises until the blood sweat came out.

Luke 22:43 And there appeared an angel unto him from heaven, strengthening him. 44 And being in an agony he prayed more earnestly: and his sweat was as it were great drops of blood falling down to the ground.

Where other disciples were tired, couldn't exercise, got weary, weak, and failed.

Many Israelis worked under the instruction of Moses, and Joshua was the strongest one. Once you find an excellent trainer for spiritual exercise,e who will take you to the promised land. You will see your enemy defeated, and no one can stand before you.

Good parents and teachers are excellent instructors. Find a magnificent faith that enforces the laws, commandments, and word of God. Believe me, they are not conservative but will prepare you for the battle. A good instructor will make sure that you are practicing your daily routine. Once you start not stopping, the matter of facts becomes your daily routine.

Your life must have different exercises to follow; it is our job to take care of the Spirit. Do not worry about your face, shape, and other things that Satan has magnified by the Hollywood and Bollywood glamor. The heavenly residence needs different muscles. Different strengths to defeat the devil and his demons. Once you gain strength and boldness, pray up, and fast, you will stand against all forces of the enemy.

Good Christians exercise their faith.

2 Timothy 4:7 I have fought a good fight, I have finished [my] course, I have kept the faith:

Faith is a muscle. You exercise in your daily life by believing in the scriptures and standing on it. You will finish well when the enemy shoots at you.

Ephesians 6:16b wherewith ye shall be able to quench all the fiery darts of the wicked.

Our faith is a muscle. God throws some trouble, trial, and problem here and there. Faith is trying to muscle.

Once you master, you can go forward in battle and defeat the enemy.

Exercise the Word of God, no stealing, lying, adultery, fornication, pride, cheating, or any of the commandments of God forbidding us. Then it will become easy for you to continue your success. Success, championship, and receiving the prize are constant spiritual works. Those who keep forgetting to practice are a failure.

Practice all that in the Word. Joseph did not give in to a woman who was trying him. He defeated her and defeated the power and influence she had to defeat Joseph. Prison was just a means for Joseph to go up the ladder. You cannot go to the top of the mountain if you have not practiced. Our goal should never be the world's acceptance by outer shape but by spiritual shape.

God throws some tests to find out how strong you are spiritual,

1 Corinthians 10:13 There hath no temptation taken you but such as is common to man: but God is faithful, who will not suffer you to be tempted above that ye are able; but will with the temptation also make a way to escape, that ye may be able to bear it.

Do some exercise of love, forgiveness, patience, long-suffering, kindness, faith, and trust. It will give you success. Many times, one who does wrong to you will come for prayer for healing or deliverance. Please help them to the best of your ability. It is necessary; you need spiritual muscles when you are on earth. Remember, you have the great help of angels by the Lord. Fight a good fight of faith. Get stronger by doing spiritual exercise. Amen!

LET US PRAY

Lord, as we are passing by on earth, we have much trouble and trials. We need the best exercise to keep going. Your word gives us spiritual strength and muscles if we practice in our daily life battle. It is our job to pay attention to pray, fast, read the word, and follow in our daily routine. May the Lord give us the best of the best instructors to teach us for the best result. Thank you for the Holy Spirit; it is best if we hear and do as it teaches. Our God did it in the flesh, and we can if we pray, fast, and practice. Help us exercise your Word in our everyday life, so the world may know that we are powerful people of the most high God in Jesus' name. Amen! God bless you!

NOVEMBER 29

HAPPY ARE YE!

Are you happy? Are you content or are you all still sad?

Let us see how to be happy.

John 13:14 If I then, your Lord and Master, have washed your feet; ye also ought to wash one another's feet.15 For I have given you an example, that ye should do as I have done to you.17 If ye know these things, happy are ye if ye do them.

Jesus, the master and creator, walked among us in humble form. Do likewise. Support and care for the orphans, providing them with the least and blessing those in need. You can attain happiness through working for God. Experiment with it. It's not just about you, remember those who are without and need your help. We must lend a hand to those in need. Our feet will walk for someone, but one of these days, it will be all over. There will be a time when you won't be able to walk or work, but then you will realize what God meant. You will face a situation where things will be completely different. You will think why people are insensitive, why they can't help me, and why they are not understanding. So look around and become someone's hand and leg. It will change the chapter of your life.

Have you seen when children get older that they come around to see elderly parents or family? Jesus is the only true family of His creation. Jesus is the father of His creation. As a father, He has to give us the perfect example. But His example was not selfish, limited to His immediate family, friends, or relatives. He was going everywhere to heal, deliver, and help His creation.

He said, Love others as you love yourself. If you love others as you love yourself, then no one will be sick, miserable, without, or depressed. You will see none will walk crazy, hungry, depressed, and naked on the street. All happiness makes the world happy, right?

1 Peter 3:11 Let him eschew evil and do good; let him seek peace, and ensue it. 12 For the eyes of the Lord are over the righteous, and his ears are open unto their prayers: but the face of the Lord is against them that do evil.14 But and if ye suffer for righteousness' sake, happy are ye: and be not afraid of their terror, neither be troubled;

The path to happiness has been revealed to us by our God.

NOVEMBER 29

Now, what is the meaning of the word happy? Happy means merry, joyful, favorable, blessed, and receiving God's favor. Do you want this? You receive this when you follow the ways of Jesus. When you are doing or reaching out to the one who cannot help themselves, is giving favor and provision to the Lord.

My parents were helping and reaching out to the poor, needy, and those who were without. They have always met many needy people since they were in the medical field. Our door was open to the needy. When you do this, your blessing will be beyond and overflowing. They welcomed people from diverse backgrounds, religions, and cultures with open hearts. No wonder why we are so blessed.

In my mission field, I meet many needy people, and I think it has become a lifestyle. You do what your parents are doing. During my younger years, I would often complain about not having a lot. My college friends had way more than me. I told my parents as soon as I got a job, I would do buy all for myself. I will get this and that. Everything will revolve around me. But oh no, you become just like your parents. I am so glad; that I have God, who is the great giver. He provided me with parents who were always givers and never takers. The heart of my brother was filled with kindness and generosity. He will generously give you his last dollar. It is the God-given spirit. Giving heart brings happiness, unmerited favor, and provisions. My brother always found favor.

You know God's provision differs from toiling all night. In the desert, he multiplied fishes and gave water and manna to eat. Your life journey will hit the desert or poverty may take over you, or you may experience want. Remember, the Lord will provide you with that situation. The goodness of God surpasses all limits, leaving us in awe. God hides happiness under your giving.

Proverbs 11:24 There is that scattereth, and yet increaseth; and there is that withholdeth more than is meet, but it tendeth to poverty. 25 The liberal soul shall be made fat: and he that watereth shall be watered also himself.

Proverbs 3:13 Happy is the man that findeth wisdom, and the man that getteth understanding.

Psalm 146:5 Happy is he that hath the God of Jacob for his help, whose hope is in the Lord his God:

I've had the pleasure of meeting someone who makes me happy. Additionally, there are times when you feel terrible and have the urge to escape from certain individuals. Happy individuals bring joy to everyone around them. I'm certain that the happy person is the one who gives. They are not hiding or keeping and have a hoarding spirit. Get rid of this spirit; it will not do good to you and your family.

2 Corinthians 9:8 And God is able to make all grace abound toward you; that ye, always having all sufficiency in all things, may abound to every good work:

Limited giving leads to limited mercy. I am determined not to fall short, and that's my motivation. If you don't give enough, you won't receive enough when you need it. Those who exhibit qualities such as going above and beyond, selflessly giving, and showing compassion will also receive substantial rewards. You will have blessings, provisions, and favors where there is no room to keep them. When you see the needy, sick, poor, or helpless, do not give a lecture. No one wants to hear your criticism. Do something for them.

All happiness is just around us, believe me. God hid it under the needs of your family, friends, parents, or acquaintances who are helpless. Extend your help to others and witness the miracle unfold.

I was visiting an Arab country and met a man who had to leave the nation since he was on a work permit. The people who brought him to that nation took away his passport and started playing the game. As I was there, he asked me to pray, and I did. I have a great connection up in heaven, where things move when I pray. I asked a friend in 2018 about the same man. She said he is still working for her. Back in 2015, I offered a prayer for him. Hallelujah!

My friends always request that I pray because they believe I have a strong connection up there. Yes, I do. He hears my prayer. According to one woman, my sales improved greatly after you prayed three times. Elijah prayed, and the rain stopped and he prayed it rained. We are being a worker; laborers for God, and have a special connection. He honors our prayer. We find favor from Him. It's no wonder that my phone, texts, videos, and emails are constantly buzzing with prayer requests. I'm glad I have the opportunity to make a difference to others. That's the reason I'm here, to carry on His mission. Amen!

LET US PRAY

Lord, it is a privilege to serve you. It brings joy in others' lives but joy and favor to ourselves. Our God is a rewarder of them who diligently seek His face.

We are blessed to have you. Our God wants to establish His kingdom on earth and needs a worker. His kingdom worker has the best salary, benefits, and provision of grace and mercy. We are grateful to be called and chosen. In the example provided by our God, it is clear that our happiness is found in selflessly serving Him. Our children and grandchildren will be blessed. Our God is amazing, beyond, and more than enough for His people. He gives all with the attachment of blessings and brings no sorrow with it. So we say thank you Lord for giving us a great example by coming in flesh. Thank you for giving yourself; we also want to give. We know that is the key to happiness in Jesus' name. Amen! God bless you!

NOVEMBER 30

GOD'S MANAGEMENT IS THE BEST!

Do you seek God's involvement before making plans or decisions? What are your thoughts? Are you smarter than God? Do you blame God for all the chaos? Did you consult God before causing chaos, or did you simply blame Him like the devil does? All the devil does is constantly complain. While the devil remains unchanged, you have the power to transform. You are a creation of God, redeemed by the blood.

Genesis 1:2 And the earth was without form, and void; and darkness was upon the face of the deep. And the Spirit of God moved upon the face of the waters. 3 And God said, Let there be light: and there was light. 4 And God saw the light, that it was good: and God divided the light from the darkness.

The Spirit of God brought about a change in the disorderly earth. Lord is a transformer. Allowing His presence and involvement, He possesses the ability to create anything. Let God take charge before casting blame on Him. You want blessings and want what Abel has; you want what King David has? You covet what Daniel has, yet you reject the inclusion of God in your lifestyle. God can manage your mess and kick the devil out if you welcome the Holy Spirit. I need thee. Every morning I surrender to Jesus. Every day I give my all and ask God to make it new, as your word says.

2 Corinthians 5:17 Therefore if any man be in Christ, he is a new creature: old things are passed away; behold, all things are become new.

Isaiah 43:18 Remember ye not the former things, neither consider the things of old.

God's management is wonderful. Open the Bible to study and find every word to create new. He can create you a new heart if you send Him your deceitful and wicked heart and see what He does. He can give you a good, clean, holy, healthy, and whole body. Worship Him and see what happens.

A little while ago, I had a call. Someone drank and did things that he is not supposed to do. I prayed and told Him to turn around. I asked him to command the devil to get out, which he did. Then I said to turn on the blood of Jesus' songs to worship Him, which he did. In no time, He said anxiety was gone. He couldn't stop crying as the Spirit of God entered. See what he welcomed. The Lord took over and managed the mess of his life and made him new.

Now as we know, the Spirit of the devil does chaos,

John 10:10a The thief cometh not, but for to steal, to kill, and to destroy:

Jesus will come if you invite Him. By the same token, the devil will prompt you to take drugs, fornication, pornography, lies, and cheating to destroy you.

Turn on blood and worship songs to worship the Lord Jesus. His presence will fill you. Command the devil to get out in Jesus' name, wash self and sins in blood. Repent, ask forgiveness, and the Holy Spirit will come. Make sure you surrender every day to Jesus and ask Him to help you and keep you.

If someone offers cigarettes, alcohol, and drugs and you accept, then you are opening the door for Satan. You are volunteering to damage yourself by purchasing from the devil. You are making evil merchants rich with God's given money and strength.

Have mercy on us. Why are we so stubborn and do not understand God's ways of managing our lives? To live for the devil is expensive. You give all that God gives to the stealer, killer, and destroyer. You are giving to the cigarette company, alcohol and drug dealers, and doctors and making them rich. Ask God to give you His wisdom to manage life. Invite Jesus to run your life. Open the door. Jesus is a gentle God.

Revelation 3:20 Behold, I stand at the door, and knock: if any man hear my voice, and open the door, I will come in to him, and will sup with him, and he with me.

Lord Jesus wants to manage your, your children's and your grandchildren's lives. His Spirit wants to move on with your finances, chaos, debt, and addiction, and bring order. Your life needs a leader like the Lord, but you have to invite Him and let Him do it.

We are too busy finding the fault and not seeing ourselves is a mess. God does not buy cigarettes, drugs, alcohol, or dirty movies for you. Despite that, you blame God. You are not a good keeper of His house, which is your body. Invite Jesus and let Him be a manager; He has angels, His blood to wash away all sins, and much more. Try it out.

A creator is only one, no one but the Lord can create,

Isaiah 65:17 For, behold, I create new heavens and a new earth: and the former shall not be remembered, nor come into mind.

Isaiah 43:19 Behold, I will do a new thing; now it shall spring forth; shall ye not know it? I will even make a way in the wilderness, and rivers in the desert.

I receive many calls from other nations for counseling. A few days ago, I received a phone call from a lady. She had pain in the back and leg. I prayed, and she was better. Again, a few days later, she couldn't walk. It was a greater attack from the enemy. I said let me send out a prayer request. Call me when you wake up. Let the Lord send His angels to give her healing. I ask her to call me in the morning to let me know. It will be my nighttime to go to sleep. She called in the night. She said my mom was walking and had no pain. Mother experienced the first time healing from Jesus in her life. She did not know Jesus, but some of her children and grandchildren did.

Some of the family members have experienced the miracle, healing, and deliverance from all kinds of addictions. They invited the Lord to be the manager of their life. Lord did it with no money. They went to many temples, and witch doctors, but Jesus did it with none of their pocket expenses. Hallelujah.

It is God who managed the body, healed, and made new, so when she woke up she said I am fine. She knew where to go and asked for a prayer. The Devil planned to destroy, but Lord Jesus stepped into life.

Invite Jesus in your life, car, work, family matters, in your nation, and see what He does.

His management is award-winning. Lord created his supply from two fishes to a multiple of a thousand. He raises the dead. His shadow even can cure, heal, and deliver.

Why don't you try?

He has managed my life since I invited Him. My life has been beautiful since I served Him wholeheartedly. I am not a fun seeker, but a God seeker. I know I can have it all if I let Jesus be the boss. No worry about the provisions, it will be abundant. No worries about clothes, roofs, food, or water. He got it all.

David had invited the Lord into His life and God kept his life from raging water, sword, bear, and lions. The enemy might have come around you, but the Lord knows how to blind them and keep you under His wings. He is the good shepherd and will hide you under the blood. Abide in Jesus and let Him abide in you.

The Lord is the brilliant manager of your children, your family, your nation, and this world. Introduce Lord Jesus as a skilled manager and CEO overall, in Jesus' name. Amen!

LET US PRAY

Heavenly Father, in the name of Jesus, we welcome you into our life. Please take over our lives and do what is best for us. Lord, we have all and not you, then it will become chaos. You know how to give peace, healing, and deliverance. Lord, take us to the beautiful garden made by you. You know how to bless, provide, and take care of the problem. You know how to make all things new and give us freedom. Only the Lord Jesus, our God, is real and true. We would not have to wonder, worry, and trouble about any situation, since nothing is impossible for Lord Jesus. Lord, give us your spirit, let it freely move on all unorganized chaos. Lord, come into our darkness and bring the light. You have the power to make all new and beautiful. We invite you to please provide, beatify for ashes, heal the brokenness, and heal where it needs healing, in Jesus' name. Amen! God bless you!

DECEMBER

DECEMBER 1

FORBIDDEN BY GOD!

Has someone ever told you that God told them not to do something or not to eat a certain thing? Did you ever wonder why God would say such things to a person? It is because God is a personal God. He has made us, and He knows us personally and wants to talk to us on these matters.

Remember, God told Adam and Eve in

Genesis 2:17, "But of the tree of the knowledge of good and evil, thou shalt not eat of it: for in the day that thou eatest thereof thou shalt surely die.

" Our hearing needs to be tuned up by practicing obedience. God's wisdom ensures that He discerns what is beneficial for us and what may cause us harm. We need to be obedient to what the Lord tells us. It may sound funny or strange, but the Lord did not want me to sit a specific way. Once I was sitting in that position and my little niece was sitting next to me, and she said "can you please remove your hand?" I said okay. God can even use the children to correct us. Many years ago, God told me not to go to Mexico. Now every time someone tries to force me to go, God always lets me know: "Don't go." And the Lord knows how to rescue the righteous.

1 Corinthians 10:13, tells us, "There hath no temptation taken you but such as is common to man: but God is faithful, who will not suffer you to be tempted above that ye are able; but will with the temptation also make a way to escape, that ye may be able to bear it".

I remember times when people were trying to force me to go. I was struck by severe sickness at one point, and on another occasion, someone with a heightened sensitivity to the Holy Ghost had see a negative occurrence befalling me. One friend said I felt like we had to cancel the plans to go to Mexico. The Lord knows how to deliver the righteous.

One time a lady said, my family is Hindu and were going to dedicate to the new house with Hindu customs, and she said, I do not want to take part in that. She said please pray that I can get out of this. Many prayed. God answered the prayers. He did something that she did not have to sit in that ceremony.

Once God told me, I do not want you to eat bacon and Jello. From that day on, I make sure that I do not eat them. God has given me so much food that I don't even miss these two items in my diet.

Genesis 3:1 tells us, "Now the serpent was more subtil than any beast of the field which the LORD God had made. And he said unto the woman, Yea, hath God said, Ye, shall not eat of every tree of the garden?"

Like Satan tempting Eve, people will try to convince you that both this and that are made of pork. I do not care what is what. The Lord's message applies not only to bacon and jello. I only discuss my forbidden things if someone asks. Certain principles are universally accepted, such as not killing or stealing. It is impossible to convince you that it is alright to lie, cheat, steal, or take a life. Once God has forbidden something, make sure to write it down and avoid it. What is personal between you and God doesn't involve millions. Ensure you stay away from the forbidden things that God warned you about. They inquired about God's statement, and I wondered if you had questioned the reason. I said it never crossed my mind. He said it and that's the final word. No further questions. I enjoy life within His boundaries, and I don't mind standing alone or being alone. Where would we be today? If Eve, Adam, King Saul, and many others would have stood in the forbidden territories. Many like to please the flesh, people, and self. I like to please God and Him alone. If I do not fit in the world and its style, I am happy about it. I do not enjoy the World, but I enjoy the Word of God. I live in the Word of God and have no desire for the World. Many things are forbidden to us through the Bible, and also by individual instruction. A preacher claimed that the Lord told him to stop drinking coffee, and he obeyed. It was something personal to him from God. Our God's instructions must be closely seen. Sometimes He checks us out.

Jeremiah 16:2, it reads, "Thou shalt not take thee a wife, neither shalt thou have sons or daughters in this place."

Is this for everyone? No, it was for a particular person only.

In First Kings 13: 8 we read, "And the man of God said unto the king, If thou wilt give me half thine house, I will not go in with thee, neither will I eat bread nor drink water in this place: 9 For so was it charged me by the word of the LORD, saying, Eat no bread, nor drink water, nor turn again by the same way that thou camest. 10 So he went another way, and returned not by the way that he came to Bethel."

But the Prophet disobeyed and listened to the lie of the other prophet. A lion killed the prophet for his disobedience.

LET US PRAY

Heavenly Father, we come before Your altar to worship and praise You. Lord, Your word is final and we say Amen. We cannot override, rewrite, add, or subtract. Lord, open our ears so we can hear and obey You. We must think, talk and act like You. Make us hearers and obedient to Your voice. Your kingdom can be established if you find obedient children. You obeyed to the death of the cross, which is the hardest trial, and never took a shortcut. Lord, we want to follow your will, plan, and instruction. Put it all in our hearts so we sin not against you. May the Lord open the ear and eyes and heart to do His perfect will in Jesus's name. Amen, God Bless You.

DECEMBER 2

PRAYER GIVES BIRTH!

Prayer can give a dead man a life. Prayer makes a man's senses functioning for the Creator. If a man's thoughts, actions, and life are not guided by the Spirit of God, prayers can revive him spiritually. Many people prayed for Saul to bring forth the real Paul, who was called by God, to preach to the Gentiles. Jesus Christ, in the flesh, prayed and brought to life many things. Your ministry and calling need someone's prayer to give life to it. Prayer gives life. Travailing gives birth; learn to travail in prayer and see what happens. Israel was born when the Hebrew slave travail was in agony.

Galatians 4:19 tells us, "My little children, of whom I travail in birth again until Christ be formed in you."

Once you learn to travail, then something will give birth. Prayer with travailing gives birth, strength, and much more. Jesus travail to receive power and strength to go on the hardest trial before His crucifixion, to birth the New Testament Church. The New Testament Church did not show up by making tabernacles for people. It was many years waiting for the Messiah to come and give birth to this beautiful, blood-bought church. It was God who shaded the blood. Messiah means savior. Only one savior brought the sinless blood offering for His creation. No doubt it took travailing in prayer to give birth to this new dispensation. He bought me and you back by His blood, which is available if we repent and be baptized in His name, Jesus. Our Lord knows how and what to do to give birth to a miracle, healing, or deliverance. Prayer gave birth to the apostles to take the gospel to the entire world.

Luke 6:12 tells us, "And it came to pass in those days, that he went out into a mountain to pray, and continued all night in prayer to God. 13 And when it was day, he called unto him his disciples: and of them he chose twelve, whom also he named apostles;..."

The Devil targeted Peter, who had a revelation of Jehovah God walking in flesh. Peter knew Jesus was the one God we were waiting for. God to come in the flesh. He is the Jehovah God in the role of the Savior, Messiah, as the Son of God to save the world. The Devil targeted Peter, who had the key to demonstrate how to be born again. Receiving remission of sins needed the sinless blood of the Great God, whose other title is Lamb of God. Jesus prayed to keep Peter alive. Jesus told Peter in

Luke 22:32, "But I have prayed for thee, that thy faith fail not: and when thou art converted, strengthen thy brethren."

Peter had to stay alive to open the Kingdom by using the key to the new birth by baptism only in Jesus's name and receiving the Holy Spirit. Heaven will rescue us no matter what the devil desires to do if we pray against Satan's target.

Acts 12:5 says, "Peter therefore was kept in prison: but prayer was made without ceasing of the church unto God for him."

An angel opened the door of the prison to rescue Peter. The birth of life, miracle, transformation, healing, and deliverance only happens when someone connects with heaven. Heaven is operating on your request. God hears your prayer and gives a charge to His angels to do the supernatural work. The man who goes into battle without connecting with the Lord will fail himself, his people, and ruin the name of God. Remember, the Devil is free on earth and ready to steal, kill and destroy. If you have an awareness of how to save, deliver and keep, then you will win.

Acts 9:1a reads, "And Saul, yet breathing out threatenings and slaughter against the disciples of the Lord,"

Ananias was afraid of this man Saul (later called Paul). reads,

"13 Then Ananias answered, Lord, I have heard by many of this man, how much evil he hath done to thy saints at Jerusalem:15 But the Lord said unto him, Go thy way: for he is a chosen vessel unto me, to bear my name before the Gentiles, and kings, and the children of Israel:...

Someone prayed for Saul to be Paul. The calling he had was birth when saints prayed without ceasing. Supernatural takes place when the father, the mother, the saints, or someone prays to bring the ministry to life. The killer and destroyer Satan will use its hand to destroy God's work, but when the church is praying, no devil can touch the family. The church is not a building, the body of the saints is the church. Do not think of building when you read of the church in my book, please. Something does not happen without God. It only happens when someone realizes that this needs the power of God to bring it to life. Only God gives birth! Only God can make the dead alive and only God gives life to the dormant. Once you know that your prayer pushes the dead things to life, gives life to the dormant, and removes chains, then you will love to pray. I have seen a difference in many lives. The other day a friend said to me, "Did you remember when I came to your house, and we called a man who had a stage four cancer?" I didn't remember, but she said he is still alive, cancer free and preaching the Gospel. My friend said she met him yesterday at a meeting, completely fine. The Man said, after you guys prayed, I went again to check for cancer, and the doctor said there was no cancer. For the last two years, the result showed that he was cancer-free.

Prayer changes things! A few years ago, someone gave my book 'I did it His Way' to a young man who had cancer. The doctor amputated his leg, but still, the cancer was recurring. After reading the book 'I Did It His Way', he got connected with me. I met him in a meeting and prayed over him. The last time I went to see him was in a children's hospital. That was the last time the doctor ever touched his body. Prayer changes things! Now, he works as a nurse in the same hospital. We have to make the Gospel alive by the power of prayer. The powerless gospel is in the dormant stage, but dead things can come alive through our prayer. Prayer moves God into action. Your prayer results in the birth of the evangelist, apostles, prophets, and teachers of God in your country. Your prayer brings life to a lifeless and hopeless situation. May the Lord wake us up to pray. We will see His angels on earth, delivering the solution, deliverance, healing, and life to the dead and hopeless. May the Lord give us a desire to pray. More than anything, we need praying parents, grandparents, and family. Please pray that the Lord will remove the thieves from the authority. Lord, give us praying women and men on their knees.

DECEMBER 2

Jesus said in Luke 19:46, "Saying unto them, It is written, My house is the house of prayer: but ye have made it a den of thieves.

" Saints, you are His house. Your body is the temple of Jehovah God. Prayer is the heavenly connection to move mountains and to do the supernatural. A mere man, made of the flesh, is limited, but the connection with God gives your matter a mind-blowing result. Always remember, only God gives life and no one else. If we connect with God, then He will work through us. Life-changing, mind-blowing, life-transforming, new birth, heaven operation is only happening if some men and women know how to pray. Prayer brings the power of the Holy Spirit into operation. Amen!

LET US PRAY

Lord, give us a praying heart. Heavenly Father, many are going to hell since we do not pray and receive help from heaven. Many lose their lives since many attend a building that has no interest in getting connected with God. If we get connected with you, then the devil who has bound people with drugs, alcohol, sicknesses, demons, oppression, and the possession of many evil spirits will be destroyed. We know the only powerful weapon is prayer. Much prayer, much power. The Lord sent us many mighty prayer warriors, like King David, Daniel, and the Apostles who prayed. We need people who follow you and not this dead, dormant Christianity we have created in our prayerless life. Help us, Lord, in Jesus's name! Amen! God bless you!

DECEMBER 3

DON'T COME SHORT!

How would you like to wear a smaller dress or shirt that doesn't fit y't fit you? What if you suddenly discover that you have slightly less money than your payment? How would you like to lose a gold prize bit by bit? How would you like to lose (miss) heaven just by a bit?

Be careful and do not play games for eternity. Adam and Eve lost the garden for a slight; by eating one forbidden fruit. King Solomon lost the 10 tribes for a little pleasure of an outlandish woman. Judas lost out with God for 30 pieces of silver. Esau lost the double portion blessing for one meal.

Be careful! Our problem arises when we are looking for a shortcut. Would you like to have a tiny blessing or even lose the blessing? The one who goes all the way will never lose the blessing. The Bible talks about overflowing. Let us do extra, and above, and go beyond even that which is required, so we also receive generous blessings.

A good man, while on his way from Jerusalem to Jericho, met a wounded man. He stopped, picked him up bandaged his wounds, and put him in a motel. A Levi and a priest saw the same man before the good man saw him, but they crossed over to another side of the road and left the wounded man there in the ditch.

Luke 10:33 says, "But a certain Samaritan, as he journeyed, came where he was: and when he saw him, he had compassion on him, 34 And went to him, and bound up his wounds, pouring in oil and wine, and set him on his own beast, and brought him to an inn, and took care of him. 35 And on the morrow when he departed, he took out two pence, and gave them to the host, and said unto him, Take care of him; and whatsoever thou spendest more, when I come again, I will repay thee. 36 Which now of these three, thinkest thou, was neighbour unto him that fell among the thieves?

The good Samaritan had compassion, gave up his donkey ride, paid money, took care of the man's wounds, and paid money to the hotelkeeper. See how much he did! The Lord said in verse.

37, "And he said, He that shewed mercy on him. Then said Jesus unto him, Go, and do thou likewise."

What God is showing and teaching us is that your post, position, the title of your denomination or religion, has no value without mercy in action.

Our God sees the heart. He had compassion for all, and we need to have compassion for people, no matter what they look like. They may not look like us, dress like us, fit in with us, or smell like us, but God expects

DECEMBER 3

us to show mercy, compassion, and love. May the Lord help us! We attend any organization and go through all the religious rituals and customs, but if we forget to be like Jesus, we have failed in our Christianity.

I Corinthians 13:1-3 tells us, "Though I speak with the tongues of men and of angles, and have not charity, I am become as sounding brass or a tinkling cymbal. And though I have the gift of prophecy, and understand all mysteries, and all knowledge; and though I have all faith, so that I could remove mountains, and have not charity, I am nothing. And though I bestow all my goods to feed the poor, and though I give my body to be burned, and have not charity, it profiteth me nothing."

The different organizations try to fit us into their style, custom, and belief. Many times they emphasize the matter which concerns them and not God. So be careful not to come short of His kingdom. Be counted among the five wise virgins and not the foolish. It is the Lord who has set His standard. Jesus did not fit in the religious program of His day. He broke the Sabbath Day many times, letting the Jews, the Pharisees, and Sadducees know it is healing, compassion, loving-kindness, mercy, and doing what is good for the broken and sick is what I want.

Jesus identified them as greedy, jealous, envious, hypocrites, thieves, and much more. They came short of the standard of God. A woman gave two mites in the offering plate, and the rich gave much more, yet the Lord said in.

Mark 12:43 "And he called unto him his disciples, and saith unto them, Verily I say unto you, That this poor widow hath cast more in, than all they which have cast into the treasury: 44 For all they did cast in of their abundance; but she of her want did cast in all that she had, even all her living."

This is the way we should think as we give to God. Are you giving out of your abundance or living? If it is out of your living, that means it is going to be a sacrifice.

I will never forget how the Lord blessed my friend. She was supporting my mission work with her earnings. She was considering my work as a mission work. Once I was going to India for mission work. She gave me some money, and it was a blessing. I prayed a fourfold blessing on her. God said no, so I prayed a hundredfold blessing. Still, the Lord said no. I said now you speak Lord; I do not know how to pray further. Lord said bless her unlimited. How nice! She is now blessed unlimitedly!

In God's dispensation, we have to give to laborers, the poor, naked, hungry, orphan, and the needy. I used to give to the building called church not anymore. After having a revelation on giving, I give to the laborer. Buy Bibles and give, look around and see who is struggling, and help them. Give homeless on the streets, widows, visiting shut-ins, visiting the sick in hospitals and nursing homes, or those in jails and prisons. The Word of God is our test. Do it, then we are a winner. The Lord said when I was hungry, thirsty, a stranger, naked, in prison, you came to me. These are the ones we must consider and have compassion for.

Matthew 25:40 tells us, "And the King shall answer and say unto them, Verily I say unto you, Inasmuch as ye have done it unto one of the least of these my brethren, ye have done it unto me."

Once you learn to do the basics, then you will never lose mercy and grace. If someone asks you to go a mile, go the extra. If someone wants to borrow a coat, give them a cloak as well. The Lord in His Word teaches us how to be received overflowing and abounding. It is not the government, social services, or charity, but we have to take responsibility.

May the Lord help us see the needy, and if we can, we should not hold back. Our job is to help. This month of December is very special. Remember, we must learn to live as Jesus did. He gave all and emptied Himself.

If you live in the US or India, a poor nation or a rich one, we know that there are many things we can do for others. The Lord has given not one but many ways to reach out to others.

Philippians 2:6-11 says, "Who, being in the form of God, thought it not robbery to be equal with God:7 But made himself of no reputation, and took upon him the form of a servant, and was made in the likeness of men:8 And being found in fashion as a man, he humbled himself, and became obedient unto death, even the death of the cross.9 Wherefore God also hath highly exalted him, and given him a name which is above every name:10 That at the name of Jesus every knee should bow, of things in heaven, and things in earth, and things under the earth; 11 And that every tongue should confess that Jesus Christ is Lord, to the glory of God the Father."

Lord Jesus is our example. If we follow Him, then we also will receive our medal and crown, and hear Him say,

"Well done, thou good and faithful servant. You have been faithful over a few things, now I will make you ruler over many. Enter the kingdom prepared for you.

LET US PRAY

Heavenly Father, we come before you to learn your example. We want to avoid any shortcomings. It would be great to hear you say a job well done. We want to make sure that we are on your right hand and that we are called sheep. Lord, your Spirit teaches us and makes us sensitive to hear your voice. Lord, we know the words we would like to hear are good, faithful, and righteous. May You give us that desire to do what it takes and not to take shortcuts. Help us follow You all the way. Please take us to the truth, and our final destination will be eternal life. Life is only in heaven, but hell is where death is. So the Lord helps, strengthens, empowers, and guides us to our destiny. Thank you for you, your angels, and your Holy Spirit. In Jesus's name! Amen! God bless you!

DECEMBER 4

PRAYER REDESIGNS!

Prayer redesigns everything! Prayer to Jesus has a meaningful, overwhelming outcome. Not very many know that there is a power of redesigning in you. Our source is God. Jesus said nothing was impossible. If a barren will have a son, then there is no reason to go anywhere but to the Lord Jesus, isn't it.

Jeremiah 32:17 Ah Lord God! behold, thou hast made the heaven and the earth by thy great power and stretched out arm, and there is nothing too hard for thee:

The powerful secret weapon is prayer. Get what you want on your knee. Parents who have prayed for their children have a power of redesigning their lives. No one can say, I am good unless someone went to the prayer that had stopped the devil from stealing, killing, and destroying their life.

The End of the Nineveh was days apart but citizens repented by praying and fasting. They changed the plan of God. Prayer is the response to avoid judgment. Ones who think they are smarter, more intelligent, greater, and know all things will have a hard time bending their knees before the Lord in prayer. Do you see any prayer in the Church? No, it is the hardest for Christians to go to God.

I give you a few examples of prayer and the outcome. Long back, this lady quit going to church and went back to the world. I came early to pray and started praying as God showed me her face. I interceded for her. I prayed without knowing her decision. The church started, during testimony, she testified about the plan of leaving the church and God. She said the song changed her mind. Now I will not tell her I prayed for her as the Lord showed me her face. Her plan was changed by God as I prayed. Her life was redesigned.

Another example: I was praying for the service before the church. God gave me a burden for a preacher. I prayed for him. On that day, he sang a special song. I was amazed by the anointing of him. The whole church was unglued, dancing, running, and jumping. It was deliverance, healing, and refilling of Spirit took place. I saw the power of prayer. Next time he sang the same song but not much effect.

The third example: I was giving a Bible Study to a couple. I prayed for greater hunger and thirst in their hearts. Later that evening, she called me and said; I am so hungry for the Lord. I want to eat pages of the Bible. See prayer redesign the person's desire.

The Bible speaks of the prayer moving the mountain. When we pray with faith, it has a powerful effect. Many prayers are boring, routine, stagnate, and repetitive. Prayer can get contaminated if you do not use the word of God. Use the word of God and get out of your routine repetition. Pray for those who are dying, depressed, and hurting. The prayerless country is going down, children are losing their minds and confused. When people do not know their gender identity, it shows our religious leaders are sound asleep. Religious leaders are vacationing and forgot their calling and duty. When this happens, then, we are murdering dispensation. Many have started different denominations, ideas, religions since they forgot to connect with God. Do not redesign, let God design.

How sad, life is designed by school authorities, friends, or families. Do not forget your life has the best and brilliant designer. Now, if you say I have no time, then better be cautious. Life will be over suddenly, with many surprises. It is unpredictable and unbearable in the end. If you are born poor, it doesn't mean you have to stay poor.

I speak internationally. Lady said I didn't believe it since you prayed our situation is turning around. We used to be poor, nothing in the house. She said that through your teaching of the Bible and prayers, our finances, life, and family have turned around. Our life is beautiful. We built the house, have a phone, a refrigerator, food, a salary increase, and name it. Poor can become rich; a prostitute can become a prophetess, liar, murderer, wicked and evil can change if you pray. Prayer to Jesus sends help on earth and redesigns life. Provisions will come, manna will come, your vegetables will multiply, lame will walk, and all that you want can be redesigned. Hit the knee, no excuse for prayer. Prayer does great and mighty things. Prayer overthrows the decree of the king. Mordecai, Queen Esther, and the Israelites prayed and the death decree went against the enemy.

Judges 2:18 And when the LORD raised them up judges, then the LORD was with the judge, and delivered them out of the hand of their enemies all the days of the judge: for it repented the LORD because of their groanings by reason of them that oppressed them and vexed them.

Wow! The power of the Prayer!

Mark 8:36 For what shall it profit a man, if he shall gain the whole world, and lose his own soul?

1 Timothy 2 I exhort therefore, that, first of all, supplications, prayers, intercessions, and giving of thanks, be made for all men;2 For kings, and for all that are in authority; that we may lead a quiet and peaceable life in all godliness and honesty.3 For this is good and acceptable in the sight of God our Saviour;

Do you know our job is to stay connected with the Lord all the time? The devil is a destructive designer living around us in invisible form. No one knows what and how he is designing our lives for destruction.
It is your reasonable service to come to God and get intervention and help from the Lord. That is why God instructs us to.

1 Thessalonians 5:17 Pray without ceasing.

We are not raised or taught to pray. The Lord came to set an example and said to follow me. The Lord in flesh prayed and taught the disciple to pray.

Luke 11:1 And it came to pass, that, as he was praying in a certain place, when he ceased, one of his disciples said unto him, Lord, teach us to pray, as John also taught his disciples.

Jesus prayed.

Luke 22:41 And he was withdrawn from them about a stone's cast, and kneeled down, and prayed, 42 Saying, Father, if thou be willing, remove this cup from me: nevertheless not my will, but thine, be done. 43 And there appeared an angel unto him from heaven, strengthening him. 44 And being in an agony he prayed more earnestly: and his sweat was as it were great drops of blood falling down to the ground.

John Baptist and Jesus both taught their disciples how to pray. Please teach others how to pray. This is the first thing we should do. If you pray, it will redesign many lives. If All churches start praying, I believe in 24 hours the world can change. I said the world, not the country. What is our problem? We go to church and do not believe in prayer, but money. Many churches do not pray and will stop if others pray. If you want to destroy the nation, take the prayer out and the devil will redesign their life for hell. Hell is enlarging for God's people. Hell is made for the devil and his fallen angels. Our prayerlessness causes chaos and gives success to Satan. Is there anyone who can say let us pray and fast for three days and night? We will see designer Jesus take over to restore your life. May Lord give us the leader who has a revelation of prayer in Jesus's name. Amen!

LET US PRAY

Lord, mighty God, who has created heaven and earth, we come before you. Lord, you make the lame walk, deaf to hear, blind to see, and heal the brokenhearted. Please redesign as we pray and fast for our situation. Lord, you have made the paralyzed walk. Our job is to call on your name for all matters so you can redesign it. Please renovate our nation. Remove drugs, alcohol, divorces, and sicknesses from the land. It is our job to pray and seek your face. You were not a carpenter but a creator who created all by your mighty power. We need to redesign to be more fruitful and joyful. Let poverty disappear and give us abundance. You can give us in abundance so not enough places to receive. Our Lord has power and provisions. Supernatural God needs someone who prays for the supernatural. Lord, we bring our life to you, redesign it in Jesus' name. Amen! God Bless you!

DECEMBER 5

IF YOU ENFORCE GOD'S LAW!

What can happen if the Laws of God are enforced? The world can be a livable, safe, and happy place. Once laws, percepts, and commandments of God are taken out of our home, society, and country, then the world becomes chaos. Our life story changes, and the story of the country, and the rest change as well.

Every judicial, civil and criminal system is run by the man who has the knowledge of it. So God's given authority must enforce the Laws given by God. And if practiced by God's given authorities. It will make this world better. Ignoring God by ignoring to teach His laws, commandments, and precepts. Do not fail God by stepping on the Laws of God; otherwise, you are coming against the Maker God. As a result, our home, city, and country will face much trouble. Let us see how and what happens when the appointed man of God does not show interest in God or does not regard His laws. God brings the end of the dispensation.

Sovereign God has all the power to do.

1 Samuel 2:6 The Lord killeth, and maketh alive: he bringeth down to the grave, and bringeth up. 7 The Lord maketh poor, and maketh rich: he bringeth low, and lifteth up.

When you read and practice the Word of God given by Him, your mind, life, and heart will change. Especially now He is not working through the priest, levies, and High Priest, but through us by the Holy Spirit. Our God intends to see us rise, be blessed, and prosper in His plan. May I ask what is our problem? No one but our flesh, our poor choices, is our trouble. We are all collectively responsible for the chaos we are in.

1 Samuel 2:25 If one man sin against another, the judge shall judge him: but if a man sin against the Lord, who shall intreat for him? Notwithstanding they hearkened not unto the voice of their father, because the Lord would slay them.

If you ignore the laws of God and neglect to teach your children and grandchildren, then wait for judgment. When you fall in the hand of God where the Lord will pronounce judgment over you with your bloodline.

1 Samuel 2:30 Wherefore the Lord God of Israel saith, I said indeed that thy house, and the house of thy father, should walk before me for ever: but now the Lord saith, Be it far from me; for them that honour me I will honour, and they that despise me shall be lightly esteemed. 31 Behold, the days come, that I will cut off thine arm, and the arm of thy father's house, that there shall not be an old man in thine house.

Lord pronounced the judgment over the lawbreaker. We can stay in jail or prison for years or a lifetime by breaking the laws of the land, but by breaking God's laws we stay in the lake of fire for eternity?

Matthew 10:28 And fear not them which kill the body, but are not able to kill the soul: but rather fear him which is able to destroy both soul and body in hell.

Hebrew 10:31 It is a fearful thing to fall into the hands of the living God.

No one wants to preach a genuine message since no one practices. If no one wants to hear, that is fine, but the chosen and called by God should not be a transgressor or violator. If you have a God-fearing and hearing teacher, prophets, and pastors, then no need for a security system, criminal, judicial, or civil system. The world does not need to have police or guns. God has given many laws, so we enjoy the freedom and blessings of God. Who would like to be behind the bar? No one, right? Then why are you not opening the word of God and practicing the Laws, and commandments of God?

Once, twice, and thrice, a warning from God should be enough to wake up. When the judgment falls on your children and grandchildren, beware. You are stepping into a restricted zone.

Matthew 7:23 And then will I profess unto them, I never knew you: depart from me, ye that work iniquity.

Matthew 13:41 The Son of man shall send forth his angels, and they shall gather out of his kingdom all things that offend, and them which do iniquity;

May the Lord give us the healthy fear of God, who has the last word to say. I have seen the judgment of families and individuals. Certainly, some of them have not changed. Why? They rather live to satisfy the flesh and eyes with all pride than surrender to God. Many cries like Esau and others with pain and sorrow, but turning to God is not. If you choose pleasure on earth rather than heaven, there is no place for you in heaven. Get serious about following Jesus and forget the fear of religious leaders. If we obey God, then where can we be today?

I was never afraid of people, but of God. When I changed my dress code, my coworker criticized me and so did some of my friends. Now, remember the first lesson ever given by God was the dress code. If we have a dress code of God, then many men wouldn't be behind bars. If not, and want to look like Hollywood, remember, you seduced them to rape, adultery, and lusting. So who caused chaos? Go look in the mirror. Clothes are for covering and never to allure or seduce.

Where do we learn to dress? Hollywood or the evil- minded designer? Parents and religious leaders should enforce the laws of God. Their job is to teach what thus saith the Lord. If you don't appreciate the truth, please avoid my door. The dress standard of religious people is some centimeters better than in Hollywood and the world.

Our eternal life begins after physical death. All that you do will bring eternal judgment over you and your loved one.

Being a Christian is not the brief prayer, or going to church, and no one bothers to correct you. We have started many cults or denominations since we want our ways. Jesus said follow me but when the cross gets heavy, we cut and establish Methodist, cut more and establish Baptist and then cut all and established Catholic. Why don't you dare to know the Word of God since you are going to be judged by it?

John 12:48 He that rejecteth me, and receiveth, not my words, hath one that judgeth him: the word that I have spoken, the same shall judge him in the last day.

That is why we have to keep cool when we meet hypocrites who act unthinkable behind closed doors. Remember, when the Lord plays your action video, you have no time but to face the end of your story. We have time. Let us rededicate our lives, repent and baptize in Jesus's name to wash away our sins and receive the Holy Spirit for power to live right. The Holy Spirit will guide and teach the truth. Amen!

LET US PRAY

Heavenly Father, we come to ask for the healthy fear of God to live right. We are a pilgrim and a stranger, passing by. Our action-reaction will bring us judgment for eternity. Please, Lord, give us knowledge, wisdom, and understanding to live right. We want the true prophets and teachers whom you have called and not they have called themselves. We come before you. Give us boldness and courage. Please open our ears and eyes to hear and see. Lord have mercy on us. We know no one can escape from your judgment. Help us, Lord, that we live right in a crowd or behind the door when no one is watching us. Lord, give us a clean heart where the origin of life begins in Jesus' name. Amen! God bless you!

DECEMBER 6

BREACH OF CONTRACT!

What is a breach of contract? In the involvement of the two parties' contract, the terms of conditions are not honored. One party has overridden the contract conditions and set terms. Now when the one-party steps on or outbreak conditions, then it is called a breach of contract. God can rule on earth with His set term and conditions which were between created man and the creator. Now God will not break any term or condition since He is a righteous God, but the problem lies in the human-made flesh.

Once God's given oral condition was broken by a man named Adam and his wife Eve, God had to apply the law. Judgment fell on them by breaking it. After that, He found Abraham, then His descendant, who was later called Israelite. He gave the written commandments to the Israelites by His finger. Later, Torah was given to their leader, Moses. God chose Moses to take charge the God's army to lead them out of the slavery of Egypt, to follow and serve the Holy God by obeying His Laws, precepts, and commandments.

This Holy God needed someone to teach and practice His Torah without personal interpretation. God kept the contract since He found Abraham, who believed in God. He promises his descendants a land to live in. What is the meaning of belief? Accept something as true and trust it. God used the Humble man Moses for His plan to carry on. Lord entrusted him to bring His people to the promised land. God needs someone to follow His condition and not to break or step over His conditions. Jehovah God created us for Himself with His condition. If you do not care to keep commandments, you are following Eve-Adam, King Saul, and Priest Eli. God said Moses was a humble man. Why was he called humble? Moses did exactly what God asked him to do. Do you follow God or Adam and Eve? If you don't follow God, then your relationship with the Lord is already broken, only you do not know.

Our God Gave the Torah to follow and practice by the authorities. When He came, jealous, greedy, prideful, and arrogant people took the office. Does it remind you of this current time? Sure it does. When Jesus came on earth, they kept the laws to fill the pocket. They did not know God of the testament or contract. They got rid of the God of the contract. Hypocrite authorities took over the charge and ruled with harsh conditions and laws.

Our job is to keep the contract.

Jeremiah 5:31 The prophets prophesy falsely, and the priests bear rule by their means; and my people love to have it so: and what will ye do in the end thereof?

Ezekiel 22:26 Her priests have violated my law, and have profaned mine holy things: they have put no difference between the holy and profane, neither have they shewed difference between the unclean and the clean, and have hid their eyes from my sabbaths, and I am profaned among them.

If the authority does not keep the terms and conditions, then it brings the end of the testament. That is why we have two Testaments, Old and New.

His Blood purchased a new covenant. God shed His blood. The Blood seals every contract. It is a blood covenant.

Hebrews 9:22 And almost all things are by the law purged with blood; and without shedding of blood is no remission.

Acts 20:28 Take heed therefore unto yourselves, and to all the flock, over the which the Holy Ghost hath made you overseers, to feed the church of God, which he hath purchased with his own blood.

God shed the blood for this new contract.

Oh, how much I am indebted to His blood. I remembered the day I went under the water in the Name of Jesus. I came out clean, washed, and lighter as a feather. Blood is hidden under the name of Jesus to remit our sins. I have no word to say but thank you, Lord Jesus, for forgiving my sins. I cannot explain the experience of going into the water in the Name of Jesus. Now we have a new contract with the New Testament Faith. His term and condition are to be born of water and Spirit. Water baptism in the name of Jesus, where His blood applies to our sins, and receiving of the Holy Spirit by speaking in tongue gives the power to overcome the enemy. Our God is good.

Matthew 26:28 For this is my blood of the New Testament, which is shed for many for the remission of sins.

1 John 5:6 This is he that came by water and blood, even Jesus Christ; not by water only, but by water and blood. And it is the Spirit that beareth witness, because the Spirit is truth.

Our problem is we do not care for the blood. He shed the blood to purchase the New Testament bride. Let us see the blood-bought Congregation.

Matthew 16:18 And I say also unto thee, That thou art Peter, and upon this rock, I will build my church; and the gates of hell shall not prevail against it.

Let us examine the scriptures and how Peter put the foundation of a blood-bought church. We are the church and not the building. Peter is the one I am going to ask. I want my church built as Peter did. I need a victory over the devil and its tactic, so I rather follow the teachings of the first church. It has the key to opening the kingdom of heaven.

Acts 2:38 Then Peter said unto them, Repent, and be baptized every one of you in the name of Jesus Christ for the remission of sins, and ye shall receive the gift of the Holy Ghost.

Jesus said verily verily three times in John chapter 3. Now, who can stop you from baptizing in Jesus's name for the remission of sins? False teachers and prophets, denomination and churches? The contract breaker!

The one who does not follow the instruction. If you disregard the teachings of the Bible, you are going down the wrong path.

Acts 20:29 For I know this, that after my departing shall grievous wolves enter among you, not sparing the flock. 30 Also of your own selves shall men arise, speaking perverse things, to draw away disciples after them. 31 Therefore watch, and remember, that by the space of three years I ceased not to warn every one night and day with tears.

1 John 2:18 Little children, it is the last time: and as ye have heard that antichrist shall come, even now are there many antichrists; whereby we know it is the last time.

The antichrist will not baptize in Jesus' name since God hid the blood under the name of Jesus to wash away, to remit the sins. My friend, we are at the last hour. No one wants to know the one God, prayer, and fasting. We care about prosperity and the world. We also have broken the terms and conditions of the Bible. So help us, Lord. Amen!

LET US PRAY

Heavenly Father, our Lord, and Master, we asked you to help us keep your laws and commandments. Lord, thank you for giving us the Holy Spirit to teach and guide. Fill those who do not have the Holy Spirit to empower them. Do not let them be deceived by the law, term, and condition breaker false teachers and prophets. Thank you for the wonderful truth and for protecting us from false teaching. The Lord put the drop of blood of Jesus mixed with the Holy Spirit in every eye and ear. Let the misguided people hear and understand the truth of the Bible. Let your Spirit come on them even though they do not know or seek. Our father in your name, we asked you to make us a keeper of your terms and conditions. Help us keep your laws and commandments in Jesus' name. Amen! God bless you!

DECEMBER 7

I KNOW MY GOD!

People behave differently when they have knowledge of their God. Once you develop your relationship by standing on His word, obeying and submitting to God, then you will be on a different level. It is the responsibility of parents to educate their children about God's word. Teach by setting a positive example of obedience to God's Word, rather than teaching when it's convenient. Teaching God's word to our children, grandchildren, and others is part of our duty. There are friends in my life who normally pay close attention to what I say and how I live. Whenever my pastor friend introduces me to someone new, she always mentions that I am her mentor. I am often introduced as a spiritual mother by many individuals whom I have taught and mentored. As we know, knowingly or unknowingly, we are an example.

Follow Jesus' teachings in the Word and select a company.

Psalms 1:1 Blessed is the man that walketh not in the counsel of the ungodly, nor standeth in the way of sinners, nor sitteth in the seat of the scornful. 2 But his delight is in the law of the Lord; and in his law doth he meditate day and night.

Don't allow a troublesome family member to impact you. Please pray to God for help in closing all doors on them. I started going to church in the US in order to learn what is right. I asked God; I want my house so I can serve God the way I want to. God bought me a house where I started living exactly as I was taught through the Word.

I have no interest in spending time with the wrong crowd, especially those who are a mess. The mess will result in a more substantial mess. No matter who they are in your family, find the courage to not let them bother you. You have the option to stay with them, but there's no need to conform or be under their control. Following God's laws ensures that people remain unaffected by their country of residence.

Daniel had a strong connection with his God and didn't concern himself with the opposition. Once you've made up your mind, you will triumph over the opposition. Learn the character of God and live according to His standard. You will not enjoy their get-together party. There's no need for it at all. My mother's character was one of pure goodness, holiness, and righteousness, and she consistently distanced herself from the wrong crowd. She showed great dedication to her children and responsibilities. Our mother was always monitoring us. We have no concerns because she acts with righteousness. If we make a mistake, she immediately sets us straight. I am thankful for that. Having parents and grandparents who are pure, holy, and righteous brings immense joy.

DECEMBER 7

The root cause of many of the children's problems lies with their parents and grandparents, not the environment. Parents experience heartache because of incorrect teaching. You can rest once you've taught them. Abraham was right. He knew God, and He taught Isaac. Isaac taught His sons, Jacob and Esau. They understood the value of God and held on to it. Esau never understood God, left God and God also left him.

Daniel 11:32 And such as do wickedly against the covenant shall he corrupt by flatteries: but the people that do know their God shall be strong and do exploits.

It means one who does wrong does not understand or know of God, even though they teach, preach, or are a missionary, pastor, or church attendees. But one who knows God will be strong and will succeed. Success comes by keeping the laws, precepts, and commandments. You're just like a donkey, always working tirelessly. You are carrying the burden and have made no progress.

Our purpose is to understand God and explore the Bible to deepen our knowledge of Him. If you know God, then there will be no worry. Some gather much, not knowing for whom? My heart aches at the sight of it. Some come together for the benefit of others and perish alone.

Knowing God leads to a rich life and a rich death. When we die, go straight to heaven and be with our Lord. All dogs and tigers fought against us will have no place there. Isn't that great? I am excited about going there. It is not the place where you have to toil and sweat. A place so beautiful it's beyond imagination.

When I mentioned going to heaven early to a friend, she accused me of being abnormal. I said nothing wrong with me, but I knew my eternal home was my destiny. That's what I long for. She said, no, stay until we get old. We will fight with our cane, I said, to find someone. I am ready to go as soon as I finish my work on earth.

The Bible says people lived a long life who walked with Him. The parents and grandparents blessed their children and grandchildren, indicating that the time for deportation had come. How nice! My mom witnessed how her family members spoke of their departure from the earth. They knew when the time came closer. I knew my brother's time. God asked me, "If I take him now, it will save him, but not then there is no hope for him." Make sure God takes you when you are ready.

When it's time to meet Lord Jesus, I would like to leave willingly. Once you miss the time, you will never find the way out. That is what I want to discuss. When Daniel had to go to the lion's den, he was ready since He knew His God. Without knowing God, you wouldn't sacrifice your life for Him.

2 Corinthians 5:8 We are confident, I say, and willing rather to be absent from the body, and to be present with the Lord.

Philippians 1:23 I am torn between the two. I desire to depart and be with Christ, which is far better indeed.

People of God are not afraid of departing the earth. How great is it?

Many experiences struggle to leave since they do not know God. Living in the flesh makes it harder for the soul to depart. We see them sick, struggling, and afraid. They know they lived an evil, unholy life. They were going to chapel but cheating, compromising, and lying to themselves and God. A seeker of little pleasure like Judas, Priest Eli, King soul, and King Solomon left. Even departing time brings sorrow to the soul.

May the Lord give you the wisdom to live a holy and righteous life. Remember, you are not here forever. When life ends, your pleasure-seeking ideas won't come with you to your destination. It is necessary to know God while departing this earth. An angel will escort you to the pearly gates. The entrance to the pearly gate is reserved for God-loving and God-dependent individuals. You are your own biggest challenge. The lust for flesh, eyes, and pride will cost you eternal damnation. I prioritize God over everything else in this world. God said I would never leave or forsake you. God has never left or forsaken me. Matter of fact, I love to be with Jesus. My life has more joy not having worldly people around me. Jesus is a matchless God. Jesus is there all the time and will take care of you. He has angels to help us. His Spirit is amazing. It is given to lead, guides and protect you. I know my God. I do not regret serving and following Him. Life is wonderful and fulfilling with Lord Amen!

LET US PRAY

Lord, we thank you for the people who know and love you. The one who died in Christ left beautiful testimony for us. Lord, help us be faithful to the end.

Join us in shouldering the burdens of our brothers and sisters in Christ. We ask that those who are part of the body of Christ dedicate their lives to you. You will never leave, forsake or forget us. We are thankful for that. Lord, thank you for giving us uncountable blessings, provisions, and privileges. Even their children wouldn't have to beg bread. So thank you, Lord, for your many promises. We ask for your guidance until we depart from the earth. When our time comes, escort us from the earth by your angels in Jesus' name. Amen! God bless you!

DECEMBER 8

WHAT DOES CHRISTIAN THINK?

Christian thinks like their daddy. Spiritual Christians approach matters with love, compassion, and a search for solutions.

John and Peter came to pray at the temple.

Acts 3:2 And a certain man lame from his mother's womb was carried, whom they laid daily at the gate of the temple which is called Beautiful, to ask alms of them that entered into the temple;

John and Peter had no money, but something better than that.

Acts 3:6 Then Peter said, Silver and gold have I none; but such as I have give I thee: In the name of Jesus Christ of Nazareth rise up and walk. 7 And he took him by the right hand, and lifted him up: and immediately his feet and ankle bones received strength. 8 And he leaping up stood, and walked, and entered with them into the temple, walking, and leaping, and praising God. A real Christian has a mind like Christ.

1 Corinthians 2:16 For who hath known the mind of the Lord, that he may instruct him? but we have the mind of Christ.

Once we have a mind of Christ, we think like Him and act like Him. We have exceptional minds, personalities, and thinking other than the people of the world. The world has a worldly mind and Christians have a godly mind. Christian thinks of the solution to each problem. Our mission is to go preach the Gospel with signs and wonders. We do not want people to hear the Word, but to see the healing, miracles, and resurrection of the Gospel. Gospel must spread throughout the nations with signs and wonder. We want people not to just hear but to experience His power in the Word. Every Word has to come alive when we speak.

Just like Jesus, we need to approach the matter with compassion.

Mark 1:41 And Jesus, moved with compassion, put forth his hand, and touched him, and saith unto him, I will; be thou clean. 42 And as soon as he had spoken, immediately the leprosy departed from him, and he was cleansed.

God is compassionate, so ask God to have compassion for the situation.

In the 80s, while I was traveling, I came across a slum in Bombay. My heart became heavy when I saw the slum for the first time. I said to the Lord, who will go to this slum? Not knowing one day, I would come to that slum. At that time, I knew little about the Spirit of God, but felt the heavy burden come over me. I felt like shouting and bursting into tears. It is our responsibility to bear the burden for the nation. Our outreach should include every nation, religion, and racial background. We should seek God's burden to be placed on our hearts. Have compassion for others and cry out to God for help. The destiny of their future rests in our prayers. Our prayer can rescue many people from hell. We cannot walk like a zombie or be insensitive.

Matthew 9:36 But when he saw the multitudes, he was moved with compassion on them, because they fainted, and were scattered abroad, as sheep having no shepherd. 37 Then saith he unto his disciples, The harvest truly is plenteous, but the labourers are few; 38 Pray ye therefore the Lord of the harvest, that he will send forth labourers into his harvest.

As the Lord gave me a burden for the slum, He also made a way to minister to them. Because of all prayers and fasting, much work started in the state of Maharashtra and South India. We must see and think with a heavenly mind. Our God walked on earth with a mission. He had a remedy for His creation. When creation cries, and if we know the answer, then we should not walk away. We see the bagger bagging, widow, orphan, sick, depressed, and bound then we must think about how to help. We are the hand of the Lord. Our blessings hide in your giving to the needy and not supporting the building and business of the word of God. Jesus overthrew the table since He knew they would steal from the poor, hungry, orphan, and beggars.

Many who are bound with fear, depressed, sick, oppressed, and possessed call me for prayer. I get into prayer and things change. Our mind has to go to work to help the needy. Our job assignment is to do.

Without putting in the work, talking about faith is just empty words. Talk is like air.

Matthew 14:14 And Jesus went forth, and saw a great multitude, and was moved with compassion toward them, and he healed their sick.

What and how do you feel when you see sick people? I have a list of people who call me for healing. Sickness brings hopelessness. Haven't you felt that way when you were sick? Sometimes the devil brings black clouds of depression and discouragement. We have to have a mind of Christ to feel what they are feeling. Pray for them. Last night was an all-night prayer. I heard all were praying for a different matter. I said how beautiful it was. All were carrying some kind of burden. We were praying and agreed to all situations and requests. People who have the mind of Christ will wake up and pray. It's something worth losing sleep over. Someone needs restoration in marriages, children, and family needs peace and healing. I admire prayer warriors because they fast and pray. Christian's prayer life is what sets them apart. True Christian goes to God in the middle of the night to intercede on the matter. I love prayer warriors. I believe only prayer warriors bring peace, salvation, and protection to earth.

Some prayed continuously until the matter was taken care of. Peter escaped from the death penalty since someone thought like their father. God is a life-giver. Peter was free from the death penalty.

I see some cases on the computer and feel for them. Come to court with a hand and leg chained. Waiting for life to be over in prison or stuck without parole. I pray for them. My heart goes out to them. Life is a precious gift. Plan correctly to stay away from heartache. I pray against Satan, who has taken over the mind. Crafty Satan succeeds, stealing, and destructive job. He leaves people behind the bar rot and goes about doing business. When I see the case and get into the prayer. Prayer warriors channel them with the mercy seat of the Heavenly Father to rescue them from hellfire. God can save and deliver them if we pray. Probably not from prison, but sure from hell. May the Lord give them the spirit of repentance to escape from eternal death. Christians think differently than carnal and worldly people. We do not look for the party as a good time but to pray and to intercede for the matter of others. We are His ambassador, priest, and high priest. Our mind goes to work to rescue who needs to be rescued. Grateful to God that we have the Mind of Christ, Amen!

LET US PRAY

Heavenly Father, we thank you for the compassion and love you have for your people. Your creation cries around us. Please open our eyes and ears to pray and take care of them. You said when I was hungry, naked, thirsty, and sick in prison, it reminded us it was our job to take care of the situation. We and I say thank you to one who loves and understands others. Our job is to heal, deliver, and set the captive free by your given authorities and power in Jesus's name. Lord, let our minds be filled with the word so we think like you. You are the Word manifested in the flesh. Thank you, Lord, for doing the business of healing and delivering. Let us show the same love and compassion to all. Help us share with the poor. Especially at this time of Christmas, we must think of someone who needs help. In Jesus' name. Amen! God bless you!

DECEMBER 9

RELIGIOUS PEOPLE ARE PRESUMPTUOUS.

What is presumptuous? Presumptuous are arrogant, bold, or overconfident. Since God has asked me to attend service on the Internet, I share with two religious people. One said, Oh, people got hurt, and they stopped going to church. Really? Another person said oh remember what happened to me? Yea, I remembered, he lost his mind when he was a new convert and was led by the lost sheep. Also, I know them personally. They thought they knew it all. They thought they were most spiritual. It only happens when you are a baby and don't let the Holy Spirit lead and guide you.

Now, wise and spiritual people will ask a question and not presume or assume. Presumptuous people are religious or religious people are presumptuous. Some people have the Holy Spirit but wouldn't allow it to lead or guide. Many have fear of doing strange things that God asked them to do or say. I know when I go to other nations; I do not know where I will travel, my meetings, or my schedule. I have nothing to worry about because the Spirit knows all and will take me to all the places where I am supposed to be. I have no problem with it. Religious leaders used to manipulate me too. Once I was also religious, I did not know God. I hated religion. It suffocated me in that box. I was looking for a way out. Once you are in the box of religion, you feel you have no wings, courage, power, and understanding of what to do. The Bible says you shall know the truth and the truth shall set you free. I found the truth of baptism in Jesus' name and believed in receiving the Holy Spirit. Still, there was much flesh involved. One stage of religion is over and enters another box of religions.

The first time when I was baptized in Jesus' name, I experienced the incredible power of water baptism. My experience made me a believer. I believed in Jesus since my family raised me as a Christian. Reading the Bible was the only religious book we had. Very first time I experienced the power of obeying the truth. I went in the water to baptize in the name of Jesus to wash away my sins. When I came up from the water, the weight was as heavy as the mountain was lifted. I did not know that I was carrying this. I felt as light as a feather. This was my first experience of power in Christianity.

It was just the beginning. The Bible says the heart is deceitful. I said no, not mine. See, I have to believe one step further that I know nothing about myself. Well, religious people are blind and deaf, and I was one of them, but still never stop seeking, asking, and knocking.

Let me share a true story of my life to prove how the heart is. One day, the church asked to donate dresses for a lady who was attending my church. Lady was my height and size. I was preparing a bag of clothes for her. That was my day off, and I was working at home and was exhausted. I heard God say to give those two blouses you got from China. Oh my God, I loved those blouses, desiring them for years. It shocked me when God pointed out my favorite blouses. Right away I lay down in bed and said, I am tired and will put it in the bag tomorrow. But in my heart I was thinking, "Lord will forget it tomorrow. And I do not have to give away my favorite blouses." Well, Lord, took away my tiredness in a second. He said you are not tired anymore and put two blouses in the bag. My experience with God was mind-blowing. Wow! He is powerful! Tiredness was gone in a second. That is crazy.

First, God proved to me you do not know your heart. He proved to me I was thinking wrong in my heart. My heart was deceitful and wicked.

Jeremiah 17:9 The heart is deceitful above all things, and desperately wicked: who can know it?

I learn the lesson of my heart. Second, I was thankful to God for taking me the route to know and believe His Word over my word.

Psalm 51:10 Create in me a clean heart, O God; and renew a right spirit within me.

I want a clean heart; I do not want to be a presumptuous religious person. Christian life revolves around the Spirit of God. Christian light shines within the living God. Religious people's life revolves around their church, man- made agenda, routine, and program. I hated that. I wanted what Jesus said and did in the Bible.

I wouldn't let them control me since I had a hunger and thirst for God and not religion. May the Lord lose you from the power of religion to be free to follow Jesus. Look around. How many are sick, hurting, depressed, oppressed, suicidal, druggy, divorced, and in chaos? Do you feel for them or have you also become blind, deaf, and insensitive by following denominations, non-denominations, and organizations? Lord Jesus said, follow me. Let us become God's residents and allow Him to take care of the need of His creation.

Now, when God took away my tiredness, I put my favorite two blouses in the bag to give to that lady.

These beautiful lessons helped me to learn to give my best. There are things that don't pertain to me. Sometimes God gives me so I can share with others. Share your blessing by obeying the Lord. Christianity is based on unconditional love and cheerful giving.

In one brief lesson, I learn different things. God has blessed us with much where there is no room to keep. This lesson delivered me and now I can give without a grudge. I am delivered from the spirit of hoarding.

I slashed the religious chapter of my life out by allowing the Holy Spirit to lead, guide, and teach me. It has given me much boldness and courage to do things I couldn't do before. Jesus gave an example to show us He also faced a religious power.

I am from now on, boundaryless, beyond, and above. The sky is the limit, and so are you! Come out of religion and be free from boundaries. You can be anything that you desire. There is no religious presumptuousness that can tear, misguide, block, or knock you down.

Never worry about your future when you walk with God. Need no approval from people, since the highest authority is Jesus Christ. The Holy Spirit is One God Spirit. He never put your life in jeopardy. Remember that David always went to God and asked for direction. With the same token, King Saul went to a familiar.

Spirit can give you information but cannot guide you to the truth. King Saul, being religious, was unsuccessful. Leaving the legacy of the curse, sorrow, and destruction. Our job is to leave a legacy of truth and blessings.

People claim to have many experiences with God, which I wouldn't doubt. But when it comes to total surrender, coming out of their comfort zone becomes challenging. I am called to follow Jesus. I am called to allow the Holy Spirit to lead and guide. I am instructed to make the Word of God the last word. I want the followers of Jesus to be my true teachers and true prophets. Followers of Jesus spent their time in the throne room, so we hear the same instruction, conversation, and direction. I am glad I never was religious. I love the Lord. I am not lazy to go to the throne room, fast, and pray till I find my answer. Remember, Jesus has called you. Do not let anyone fool you, misguide you, or tell you anything otherwise. Open Bible study to know Jesus. What are you called for? To sit in a pew or to go around the world to preach the Gospel, cast out the demons, and heal the sick. Think for yourself and follow the Lord Jesus. Amen!

LET US PRAY

Lord, we kneel at the altar of God; we are grateful for giving us the spirit of God to guide, teach and lead us. Remove any religious blocker stopper to suffocate the Holy Spirit. Help us not to become religious by having the Holy Spirit. We remember that leading life by the Holy Spirit is not comfortable but unknown and unpredictable. We can only learn and experience the Word by obeying it. Lord, deliver your people from religious demons to have a fresh new experience every day. Help us increase glory to glory. We need your help. We hold our hands since the road is unknown. Help us not to be judgmental, but prayer warriors to let God. Lord, we trust in your direction. Our limited minds cannot predict our God, so we surrender to you. Have your way, but bring us out of religion so we are free in Jesus' name. Amen! God bless you!

DECEMBER 10

CHRIST GAVE!

This morning, the Lord revealed to me that Christianity is about giving. Giving is a central aspect of Christianity's doctrine regarding God. God appeared in order to give Himself. God becomes a human in order to offer Himself.

Philippians 2:7 But made himself of no reputation, and took upon him the form of a servant, and was made in the likeness of men:

During His time here, Jesus went around healing those in need.

Matthew 4:23 And Jesus went about all Galilee, teaching in their synagogues, and preaching the gospel of the kingdom, and healing all manner of sickness and all manner of disease among the people.

Luke 4:43 And he said unto them, I must preach the kingdom of God to other cities also: for therefore am I sent.

God offered Himself as a gift for His own creation. One God, who is Spirit, made our body, so He knew how to repair it. He said I gave you the power and authority through my highest name, 'Jesus,' to go do the same. It is necessary for us to offer ourselves in service to God. Healing should be our priority, not just relying on doctors, nurses, and pharmacists. Their fees are unreasonably high. The Spirit given to us by the Lord empowers us to fulfill His appointed work. The seniors have become homeless as a result of their hard-earned money being spent on medicine and medical bills. If we do our work, they won't end up on the street.

Luke 9:1 Then he called his twelve disciples together, and gave them power and authority over all devils, and to cure diseases. 2 And he sent them to preach the kingdom of God, and to heal the sick.

Luke 10:17 And the seventy returned again with joy, saying, Lord, even the devils are subject unto us through thy name.

We have been granted the authority to work as the Lord did. We are given the power of the Holy Spirit and the authority to act in the name of Jesus. We must now command sickness and the demon to get off. People are being trapped in name-brand cages called denominations, non-denominations, and organizations by a Christianity introduced by the Devil, focused solely on prosperity. In certain churches, engaging in prayer, casting out demons, and visiting the sick in hospitals and homes is frowned upon. How would you address these dishonest teachers and prophets? It's best to leave that place. Their efforts are directed against the Lord.

Despite the Lord's command to go, the church authority wants us to invite people to sit, join us, and be fond of us. No need to be concerned about sickness, fasting, or prayer. Follow Jesus if you want to do what He did. Pay attention to the Lord, not to false teachings, prophets, or church authorities. There is a significant amount of work that needs your attention. Keep working on the assignment that Lord Jesus gave you. The one you see and hear in a church is not the true highest authority.

Jesus drove out evil spirits. Once more, he refrained from seeking amusement, planning the presentation, shopping, hunting, or playing golf.

Matthew 8:29 And, behold, they cried out, saying, What have we to do with thee, Jesus, thou Son of God? art thou come hither to torment us before the time? 32b And he said unto them, Go. And when they were come out, they went into the herd of swine:

This is what Jesus expects from you and me. If you come across someone feeling unwell, possessed, or in distress, offer them assistance. It's the responsibility of both you and me. There are those who have departed from the Lord's teachings and the Bible, embracing false teachings. I assure you, there are those who live in constant fear of losing the people and persist in giving them misleading guidance. Have mercy on you if you do not work for Jesus. Do you pay money to be deceived or what? Jesus overthrew the money and merchant's tables; someone needs to do the same. It is not me but Jesus, whom you believe is asking you to give yourself for His work. Jesus said I am the way, do not follow the lost authorities, check them out and follow Jesus.

Do not take druggy, demon-possessed, sick, oppressed, and possessed people to the hospital, but you teach them the Word, lay hands on them, and heal them. That is the teaching of the Word of God. Pay attention to what you are learning.

What happens if we work? What happens if you decide to give yourself to these needy people? People will be healed and delivered, no bad news, which is the only news we hear these days. No evil existence, all this pharmacy will disappear. All your money-eating demons will be cast out into hell. The prison will be closed down, no rapists or crazy on the street. There will be peace at home and on the street. Our job is to work day and night like Jesus. Once you work as what the Lord did, you will have joy beyond your major.

He gave His blood. He took stripes, so we are healed. So the Lord gave you health and blood to be free from sickness and hellfire. Now you go around and use the blood to wash sins in Jesus' name under the water. Give yourself just like you give yourself for work, school, and the world. Most of the people are busy, I mean very busy. Their preference is mixed up. When I received the Holy Spirit, I wanted to tell the entire world about the powerful experience. I started telling everyone I met. I hired a translator to release Bible courses that uncover the truth. I started praying over individuals and driving out evil spirits. I shared my testimony in the book 'I did it His way. I said, how and what happened here? How was the truth stolen by the devil? Yet, I am filled with joy that I received it and began my service for Lord Jesus. It's not necessary for me to worry about who will give their approval. I have this urge to preach to everyone I come across, without exception.

I explored a wide range of media, including books, videos, and audio, as well as visiting prisons, hospitals, and convalescent places. I worked with people from different faiths and conducted teachings, healings, and deliverances in the name of Jesus. I cannot sit quietly and allow the devil to rob them. I am blessed to have a prayer channel and a phone line to reach many people throughout the world. I realize the load of work is much and understand why Jesus asked to pray for the laborers. Yes, we need laborers who can give themselves. That is why I train new converts for Lord 'Jesus'. I ask them to have faith in Him alone and follow Him. I do not want them to sit in the pew to get bored and sick. Thief collect their money to have a good life. I train new converts to follow Jesus to do greater than what Jesus did. I want them to be limitless. I want them to remove all the idols which cannot help. They should never sit in the box of religious denominations. Following Jesus is to work in the vineyard. Labour to keep it clean, drug-free, kidnapper-free, divorce-free, alcohol-free, and all devil activity of killing, stealing and destroying free. Your vineyard needs you. Give yourself to work for Jesus. We all have to work, but some work, and some follow the lost religions and justify. Open the Bible and see how much work is available. Put this technology to shame. You can put doctors in God's mission field. Drugs can be eradicated from the country.

I am acquainted with people who attend church but are unsure of why they do so or what their calling is. Your body is referred to as a church, temple, and dwelling place of the Holy Spirit. It's evident they're giving their ear to someone else, not Jesus. I encounter many places that try to hinder my work for the Lord, but I always walk away from them. I have no doubt that I am hated by the devil.

I talked to a lady in India whom I mentor. She said, I was praying early morning 4am; I was commanding the demons to get out. I heard the spirit screaming and saying, save me and was running away. I said, good job and told them to stay away permanently. She said my daughter also wakes up and prays with me now. Yes, that is what I want. My Jesus asked us to go, give ourselves, and bring the worldwide revival. I tell you I have no time even though I work almost 18 hours a day. Give yourself for the Work of God. Amen!

LET US PRAY

Heavenly Father, we thank you for giving us work. Help us take care of the assignment. This world needs to see the signs and wonder. Our shadow, our handkerchief, will heal people because of anointing. Anoint us to break the back of the devil. Thank you, God, for taking power and authority back. As you have given us an example of how to work, let us follow you and do as you said. You gave yourself and asked to give ourselves as well. We do not want to give any excuse but to give ourselves. Help us work to see the soul be free from sin, sickness, and demons. Hell will be empty, and your creation will fill heaven up. Lord, we rededicate ourselves for work in Jesus' name. Amen! God bless you!

DECEMBER 11

YIELD TO THE SPIRIT OF GOD!

The Bible says the Spirit of God will lead you to all truth.

John 16:13 Howbeit when he, the Spirit of truth, is come, he will guide you into all truth: for he shall not speak of himself; but whatsoever he shall hear, that shall he speak: and he will shew you things to come.

The Bible speaks about the Spirit of God. Now God is Spirit and there is one Spirit. So one true Spirit is the one God's spirit, and that is what we have to yield. It will not misguide you. What is the reason behind all this chaos? Since no one cares about yielding the Holy Spirit. People have connected themselves to the one they observe and listen to on the pulpit, instead of connecting with God. Please hear the voice of God and not the other voices. When God speaks, it is the final word.

God instructed me once to depart from a specific church. I spoke to the pastor about leaving, but he insisted, "No, I want to remain your pastor." Not listening to God's voice made the last 20 years the worst of my life. On a separate occasion, I was told by God not to go to Canada, and later found out about tour buses mistreating single women. The Lord intervened and halted me. Back in the 80s, I went through all of this right after being filled with the Holy Spirit. I was so deeply manipulated that I had no choice but to obey the pastor as if he were God or the highest figure of authority. Does Jesus' arrival on earth bring to mind the Priest, the high priest, and the Pharisees? Anyway, I learned my lesson, and it was a tough one. From that onward, I decided when I hear God, I am going to obey Him alone. I will run from the misguiding voice of church authorities, and I am sure some of you agree with me. Why do we become people-pleasers? Because some of them have strong words to control and they have followers to attack us. If you don't hear them or comply with their commands, they will consider you rebellious. The church authority will charge you with saying, 'You are your pastor, not me,' and more. There are those who have knowledge about God, yet intentionally reject a relationship with Him. Many have the Holy Spirit but grieves the Spirit. Some people do not open themselves up to the Holy Spirit's communication.

2 Samuel 5:19 And David inquired of the LORD, saying, Shall I go up to the Philistines? wilt thou deliver them into mine hand? And the LORD said unto David, Go up: for I will doubtless deliver the Philistines into thine hand. 23 And when David inquired of the LORD, he said, Thou shalt not go up; but fetch a compass behind them, and come upon them over against the mulberry trees.

May the Lord help us so we inquire of God. If you do, then there will be no mistakes. The presence of God and the Holy Spirit is effective only when individuals let God take control. The Holy Spirit is the all-knowing God's Spirit. Remember, God knows all and not the man. Do not get advice from the flesh. It is good to have a true prophet and teacher in our life. First, we know they are called and assigned by God. Please find the prophet whose motive is clean.

May the Lord give you true prophets and teachers.

The root of our problems lies in negligence, as we hesitate to confront the falsehoods of influential non-denominational organizations and authorities. Fear gripped us, fearing their ability to block us from society and networking. Anxiety grips us as we contemplate the possibility of our reputation being ruined. Why do you care so much about them, anyway? Once you learn to hear the Spirit, then yield to it. All other things will fall off, like withered leaves. Fear and cowardice are not qualities associated with God.

The spiritual situation of the Priest, the high priest, Pharisees, and Sadducees was bad. They spoke evil against their God who walked in the Flesh among them.

John 10:19 There was a division therefore again among the Jews for these sayings. 20 And many of them said, He hath a devil, and is mad; why hear ye him?

Even today, we have divisions between one who yields to the Spirit, and another who yields to the lost authorities. Now, as we know, the Lord has called us, given us the Spirit with five-fold ministers. Look for the one who is staying in the throne room, see what the Bible says.

John 14:12 Verily, verily, I say unto you, He that believeth on me, the works that I do shall he do also; and greater works than these shall he do; because I go unto my Father.

Luke 22:40 And when he was at the place, he said unto them, Pray that ye enter not into temptation.

It is obvious if you do not see this in operation, run from them. Even though they speak in a tongue or operate in spiritual gifts. Many times you are there for the time being and then time to go on. Many times we get comfortable and so we stay. Your progress will be blocked and stopped. Remember, if you yield to the Holy Spirit, then you will Go City to city, village to village, and everywhere.

You can't escape being seen. Christians who are filled with the Holy Ghost cannot go unnoticed.

Is Hebrews 2:4 God also bearing them witness, both with signs and wonders, and with divers miracles, and gifts of the Holy Ghost, according to his own will?

Peter did many miracles. Let us see some of them. Peter went to them, You need to yield to the Holy Spirit and you will go to people just like all disciples did. It is a working ministry and not sitting. At the last church I went to, they gave us a card and asked us to write our names, which allowed us to go out and work. Which was nice! But I go anywhere and find the sick, and needy, and do my work.

Acts 3:7 And he took him by the right hand, and lifted him up: and immediately his feet and ancle bones received strength.

Acts 9:34 And Peter said unto him, Aeneas, Jesus Christ maketh thee whole: arise, and make thy bed. And he arose immediately.

Now Spirit yielding ministry will take you to places, different countries. The job will be easy, I mean it.

Acts 8:39 And when they were come up out of the water, the Spirit of the Lord caught away Philip, that the eunuch saw him no more: and he went on his way rejoicing.

Remember, the Holy Spirit will lead us to the truth. Know what to say, when to say, and not to say. Prepare yourself to yield to the Spirit.

Acts 16:6 Now when they had gone throughout Phrygia and the region of Galatia, and were forbidden of the Holy Ghost to preach the word in Asia,

It is good to know that our God is alive. Do not shut the Holy Spirit down. That is why it doesn't talk to you.

When I heard I was going to move, I became extra alert to hear. I blocked Texas; I never wanted to move there. Almost a year later, I found out it was time and moved a few months later to Texas. Yielding the Spirit of God becomes God's story and not ours.

It was God who took me on a missionary trip to California, Chicago, Dubai, Bombay, Badlapur, the state of Maharashtra, South India, Bangalore, Kodai Kanal, Rajasthan, Vyara, Ahmedabad, and other surrounding cities, and some I forgot already. This happens when you are called and you yield the Holy Spirit. Listen to God.

Allow the Holy Spirit to take you to work. Most of the places where I went where many house of prayer have been built, Bible colleges, orphanages, and much more work has been spread. May Lord give you perception with understanding to yield to Spirit and not religious authority. May you be all that He has called you, Amen! God Bless you!

LET US PRAY

Heavenly father, we have the living God not made of any wood, clay, or metal. It is God who has created us from the dust and put life in it. God takes care of us as we allow you to do so. Lord, we asked you to give us courage and boldness to yield in all your plans. Help us yield to the Spirit of God. Help us go places where we never thought and sometimes even do not want to go. Lord, let your will be done. It is the most beautiful thing that we have the Spirit of God abiding in us. Help us yield the spirit, so we see the mighty work of God. Our God is real and mighty to save, heal, and deliver, so help us trust without question and do as you asked us in Jesus's name! Amen! God Bless You!

DECEMBER 12

GOD GOT ALL!

Yes, you heard me right, God Got all. He is the source of all your needs - food, healing, salvation, deliverance, land, money, knowledge, wisdom, clothes, and more. But that is not what I am looking for. I am looking for God, period. He made me, and I am interested in Him. Nothing I see has ever attracted me but God. I am amazed by the way He thinks of me, even though I am so little in His sight. He saw the giving of the widow lady and said; she gave it all. The God who owns all said that the widow lady gave all.

Luke 21:21 And he looked up, and saw the rich men casting their gifts into the treasury. 2 And he saw also a certain poor widow casting in thither two mites. 3 And he said, Of a truth I say unto you, that this poor widow hath cast in more than they all: 4 For all these have of their abundance cast in unto the offerings of God: but she of her penury hath cast in all the living that she had.

God, who owns all, looked at a little poor widow and was impressed by her giving. The Lord who created the universe told me what He desired of me. I am the one and only God, only to do one thing:

Deuteronomy 6:5 You shall love the Lord your God with all your heart, with all your soul, and with all your strength.

So as long as you have all lined up, mapped out in your mind, and cleared up the channel with God, then you inherit all that God has.

David's heart was on the Lord. Being a shepherd boy, he got kingship, and the Messiah came out of his bloodline. A harlot channeled up with God, cleared up all her past and got salvation of self with family. Once you know how to channel up with one true God who has and knows all, your life will not be the same. He can remove anyone and put us in their place. The Lord gave Esther a position and her beauty. After establishing a spiritual connection with God, she disregarded laws and regulations and successfully abolished the death penalty for her people, which had been enforced by their enemies for a long time. May the Lord clear up your mind and give you total security of all you need on earth. A widow dared to give all that she had. A boy dared to give all his fish. Widow dared to give the first cake from her little flower and oil. What do you know about this God who got all? You may say I know the story of David, Moses, Paul, Daniel, and Jesus. Do not read the story, act on the story. Take a deep breath, and do exactly as it says. Do not doubt you may think it wouldn't. You may have many trials and opposition, and cannot see the way out. Wait, God is creating a way out where you see no way. He has a genius mind. If He puts blessings on a little money, it will start multiplying and never-ceasing finance will channel up to God's bank. He has stored the perfect gifts for you and me.

God got all earth and heaven. The creator has the power to multiply if you learn to help the poor, sick, widow, orphan, etc. No one goes hungry is His policy, but all who finance with Him have to pay attention to those whom you do not value. Help people in prison, sick, homeless, hurting, and of no reputation. How to deliver them from the hand of an abuser, how to pay off their debt, supply their needs and do what it takes. It is little for you compared to them.

When I was in India, we saw many poor, orphans, sick, homeless, and needy. But let me tell you, we have many around us in the US as well. So if you partnered with the Lord, then a simple act of kindness, the act of good Samaritans, will hire you in Lord's company. He is the King of all kings and Lord of all lords.

When the Lord came on earth, He said, I came to do the will of my father who is Spirit God, and not Joseph. He showed humanity to stop focusing on the church agenda and start working on God's agenda, and He will give you all. We lost all focus on God's agenda, committing sins of disobedience, and later regained all new and beautiful things. God said I defeated the enemy who tricked you in the past. I bought it back with my blood. My blood has the power to pay off all penalties of sins. What do you want? Focus on me, I gave you an example. Follow in my footsteps, and you will have no want.

Matthew 6:33 But seek ye first the kingdom of God, and his righteousness; and all these things shall be added unto you.

Revelation 1:18 I am he that liveth, and was dead; and, behold, I am alive for evermore, Amen; and have the keys of hell and of death.

Now Jesus got the key, which was in Satan's hand.

May the Lord give us divine direction by the Holy Spirit, to know the truth. Do not look around. Let me give you information; Jesus is all you need and nothing else.

Philippians 2:10 That at the name of Jesus every knee should bow, of things in heaven, and things in earth, and things under the earth;11 And that every tongue should confess that Jesus Christ is Lord, to the glory of God the Father.

Matthew 28:18 And Jesus came and spake unto them, saying, All power is given unto me in heaven and in earth.

What is our problem? We are looking at places where there is no power and help. We are looking at the place where they give you false promises. Look to God; He got all.

A Lady in India said that she and her husband both are lame. Her husband walks on his bottom. She said, as I left idol worship and turned to Jesus, we built a house of 10 Lakhs. She witnessed that when I was an idol worshiper; we had no food. But now we have plenty. She is an example of her village. She used to always borrow money to buy veggies for her family. Now I have money to buy my necessities. The Lord gave her all. May the Lord open our eyes. I talked to God when I lost my health and job. Lord, please keep my house. Never thought to have another house and forget about the new one. I thought the car was ok to drive. The Lord miraculously healed me from cancer. I was confined to a wheelchair later on due to a back injury. Afterwards, my back was healed and I was able to walk again after being in a wheelchair. The Lord gave me a bigger, brand-new, and better house and a new car. God got all.

Here we have two fish, not enough for a thousand. Lord said, give them to me. I know how to stretch them to feed thousands. Lord said to His people, you are going on a long journey to the promised land. Do not worry, I will make you rich, healthy, and wealthy. May the Lord help us understand it is not our finances but our investment in the hand of God. God wants you to invest your life in His kingdom. Use your strength to work for Him. God knows how to provide for you. Ask God to take you places and live beautifully as working for the kingdom. Cast out the demon, heal the sick, teach the word. It is the most beautiful work I have ever known. Put a word in action and see the outcome. May the Lord give you Mountain-moving, heart-changing, and life-transforming faith in Jesus' name. Amen!

LET US PRAY

Heavenly Father, we come to you; you are the rewarder of those who diligently seek you. Make us a kingdom seeker. We seek the country in which you have promised us. We need your power to overcome every obstacle and hindrance. You are the way of wealth, health, deliverance, healing, and salvation. We come to you for all our great and small needs. Nothing is hard and impossible for you. You got the gold, silver, ruby, diamond, and name it. All the wealth of the world is yours and not devils. May the Lord help us realize you are the creator and you are the owner of all. Our heavenly father, we stand praying for those who are wondering. We pray they look up and find their way through you. It is a great God who has wonderful amazement for those who trust in Him. Please let our direction be in that narrow way through the restricted door. Our God will take us to the street of gold where our mansion is in Jesus' name. Amen! God bless you!

DECEMBER 13

WHO ALLOWED TARE?

Now, what is a tare? In Arabic, it is called Zawan and in Greek called Zizanion. Tare resembles wheat, but not wheat! Tare is worthless. According to Matthew 13, a man planted wheat, and the devil planted tare, which looks like wheat. Tare is not a good but worthless plant that grows in Palestine.

When you see people who look like Christian, talk about the Bible, it is fruitless, and living without faith causes much trouble in God's kingdom. They follow the doctrine of the devil. After planting a good seed, the man went to sleep. That is the time the devil came and planted tare. We need prayer after planting the word of God, otherwise, chaos takes place. On every corner, there is a cross on the building. Your body is the church, and the devil says the building with a cross is. God said I am one, the devil says no three gods. God says to baptize in Jesus's name, the devil says no baptize in the name of the Father, Son, and Holy Spirit.

This tare started growing, and since it is a weed, weed grows fast and harms the Christians. These are the religious groups, organizations, denominations, and non-denominational without knowledge of Jesus as the Son of God or God in the flesh.

Matthew 13:24 Another parable put he forth unto them, saying, The kingdom of heaven is likened unto a man which sowed good seed in his field: 25 But while men slept, his enemy came and sowed tares among the wheat, and went his way.

A man sowed good seed, but when he slept, the enemy who is the devil came and sowed tares. When we are sleeping, it means not working. We can work when we are awake. No one works in their sleep.

We are called to go work and preach the gospel with sign wonder. Well, Jesus worked all the time. His disciple did the same. After His death, the followers of Jesus worked day and night.

Luke 4:43 And he said unto them, I must preach the kingdom of God to other cities also: for therefore am I sent.

Lord Jesus worked everywhere all the time. He preached, cast out demons, healed the sick, and taught. Now we have to do the same. If we do not work, that means we are in spiritual sleep.

Mark 16:15 And he said unto them, Go ye into all the world, and preach the gospel to every creature.

DECEMBER 13

The Lord asked His disciples to baptize those who believe in Jesus. Yes, after seeing signs, wonders, and miracles, they need to wash away the sins. Gospel without sign and wonder is not Gospel. When the Lord Jesus sent His disciples, they did their assignment. They were spiritually awake to work.

Acts 8:4 Therefore they that were scattered abroad went everywhere preaching the word.

Acts 6:2 Then the twelve called the multitude of the disciples unto them, and said, It is not reason that we should leave the word of God, and serve tables.

Disciples kept preaching the baptism in the name of Jesus, miracle, healing, and Holy Spirit baptism.

The leader of the synagog said.

Acts 4:18 And they called them, and commanded them not to speak at all nor teach in the name of Jesus.

Being spiritually awake, disciples continue planting wheat. What is the true doctrine or good seed of the Word of God? If you would have kept working in the field, then false doctrine and teaching wouldn't have come into existence. What did you do after receiving the truth? You may say, I attend the church. The devil has many false teachers to teach false doctrine. Sitting in the pew, attending building on Sunday and midweek is not working. It is the devil's idea to take you astray from the assignment of Jesus Christ. Remember the Lord overthrew the table and said the thief has a den?

False doctrine started in 325 is a tare. Devil's plantation of tare is one God became three. Do you tell others that Jesus is Jehovah's God? Jesus meant Jehovah's savior, that is God walking in the flesh. God manifested in the flesh to shed the blood. When you attend or become a member of the organization, you are helping someone's pocket, but not the Kingdom of God. Wake up and work. A spiritual awakening is needed. What happens once you wake up? You will go to your family, neighbors, hospitals, orphanages, prisons, jails, and everywhere to preach and teach.

There was a time when I was ministering in the Episcopal chapel in Dallas for a couple of months. I don't argue for any doctrine, but teach them the doctrine of a prophet and apostle of God. I saw many got healed and delivered when I laid a hand on them. Even a few times, priests came down for prayer. I gave them different books, and DVDs to learn about the truth of Jesus's name baptism, and Speaking in the tongue by receiving the Holy Spirit. A bunch of ladies always kept the door closed when we prayed in the tongue. Now they do not have to be afraid of religious authorities, I wouldn't. I was there temporarily since God sent me to minister. During that time, many healed and delivered from mental attacks, cancer, and sicknesses and were happy. But they always hid me in the storeroom to pray over people. I prayed over a man, and he said, Oh, I already felt great. He complained about a priest, saying nothing happens when they pray over me.

I refuse to fall asleep; I am awake spiritually all the time. So wake up, go out and do the work of God. I know many churches wouldn't allow it. But God asked you to work. When we fall asleep, that brings the doctrine of the devil, which is a tare. Always work to please God and not some false authorities.

Do you do what Jesus and His disciples did? Do you see a shepherd on a street, city to city, preaching the Gospel? Are they sending out two and two to prison, jail, town to town? It is not a missionary's job, but yours and mine. You are the one who should do it since Jesus asked you to work exactly how He did. He assured us we can do greater than what He did. Now, if you are not working on the work of God, it means you are sleeping. People who sleep cannot work. When you do not want to work, then the devil goes around and plants are tare which look similar to wheat. If you do not work, it causes the tare to spring up. May the Lord give us a spiritual awakening. Tare looks, acts, and speaks about Jesus without sign and wonder. If Jesus removes them from the wheat, it can cause a problem for Christians. But in the end, they will be removed. That is why the Lord said to look for the fruits.

So go around and work. Working people would not allow Satan to plant tare. If you are not working, you are spiritually asleep.

Matthew 13:28 He said unto them, An enemy hath done this. The servants said unto him, Wilt thou then that we go and gather them up? 29 But he said, Nay; lest while ye gather up the tares, ye root up also the wheat with them.

Peter and Paul had a revelation of Jesus's identity. Then it was revealed to other disciples. They continue in this doctrine of truth called apostolic doctrine. But the devil came in when a converted Christian fell asleep. They did not go around and did what Jesus commanded them to do. I tell you this tare is so strong, that many of you and I have experienced it.

Acts 20:29 For I know this, that after my departing shall grievous wolves enter in among you, not sparing the flock. 30 Also of your own selves shall men arise, speaking perverse things, to draw away disciples after them. 31 Therefore watch, and remember, that by the space of three years I ceased not to warn every one night and day with tears.

Paul warned us of a grievous wolf. It will come to plant the tare. They change the true Bible into many false versions. The word of God has been removed, and added, to introduce false doctrine. Our work on the field is to fight against Satan and its tactic. Some are going everywhere to plant tares. Wake up, work, go out, and teach the truth. Change your priorities. When I went around teaching the Word, I found all kinds of false versions of the Bible. I wonder what happened here. No one knows Jesus is Jehovah God Himself in the flesh. Jesus is the highest name of Jehovah. God kept the highest name secret for ages, which is Jesus. Angel revealed it. It is above all Jehovah's previous name. Blood is under this name. One and only God of the Old Testament walking in flesh in the New Testament as Jesus the savior. If you have this truth, then go out and work. Tell the truth to the world. From day one, I found the truth of Jesus and started working faithfully. I will not sleep but work and work. Amen!

LET US PRAY

Heavenly Father, we thank you; you worked on earth and did not go to sleep. You went beyond the temple's boundaries by breaking through the curtain and stepping out of the box to reach your creation. Lord, you gave your blood to all creations. We need a worker who has the revelation of you, so we continue the book of Acts. We are called to work. The apostles and prophets gave and established our doctrine. Help us not to plant tare which is already harming your kingdom. Your people are already being rejected since this grievous wolf in the religious world is destroying the truth. Heavenly Father sends us laborers to work. We cannot sit in the pew and have a good time since you have asked us to go to work. Lord, we ask for spiritual awakening. Open the door, anoint us. Lord, we work to destroy the lie of the devil in Jesus' name. Amen! God bless you!

DECEMBER 14

DON'T LET ANYONE CONTROL YOU!

We are called to fulfill our mission with all those who have repented, been baptized in the name of Jesus, and are filled with the Holy Spirit. When you learn the truth, it becomes your responsibility to spread it to others. Your task is to preach the Gospel in every place. Are you doing it? Are you unable to move from the pulpit, pew, or any other location in the city? You have been summoned to work as a laborer. First, we must pray, teach the word of God, cast out demons, and heal the sick. If you are not doing it, that means someone controls you, or you are just careless.

Luke 4:42 And when it was day, he departed and went into a desert place: and the people sought him, and came unto him, and stayed him, that he should not depart from them.

Can you believe people wanted to cling to Jesus? Do you have this experience? When I was called to go to Texas, many said, no you cannot go to Texas. An individual tried to remove the sale sign for my house. Some try to counsel me saying your ministry is in California. Even some of my family members tried to discourage me. After receiving a message from God, I quickly departed California. Was it easy? The answer is No. It was the plan of God.

Luke 4:43 And he said unto them, I must preach the kingdom of God to other cities also: for therefore am I sent.

You are not called to make a friend, settle down, and rot to contaminate. It gets so horrible that no one likes to go to some buildings they call churches. Unproductivity and power struggles often result from too many clicks.

Luke 2:49 And he said unto them, How is it that ye sought me? wist ye not that I must be about my Father's business?

John 9:4 I must work the works of him that sent me, while it is day: the night cometh, when no man can work.

You received the power of the Holy Spirit to work, cast out demons, teach, and heal the brokenhearted and sick. Avoid sitting on a pew, raising your hand, giving money, and then leaving. You will be loved by the thief in the building/church. With no work, he still makes time to meet you once or twice a week for less than three hours. Easy money! What your heavenly father said, GO and do what He did, isn't it? You may not go since it will harm Satan's kingdom. They have stopped me from working outside their organization's beliefs. I still did what the Lord asked me to do. I'm still unable to comprehend the why behind it. They missed out on what Jesus said to His disciples and us. Many laborers, including myself, were stopped by various denominations, organizations, and pastors. It's often the internal issues, not external factors, that cause many problems. Please pray for them. They need compassion for sick, possessed, lost, and hurting people. I mean what I said. In this dispensation, our priority should be street preaching, not going to the building. If you want to learn the New Testament, then practice laying hands using the authority in Jesus's name.

Matthew 21:23 And when he was come into the temple, the chief priests and the elders of the people came unto him as he was teaching, and said, By what authority doest thou these things? and who gave thee this authority?

They dared to ask questions to the God incarnate. Jesus encountered individuals who were deaf, blind and lacked religious authority. I faced opposition from religious authorities as well. They demanded that I no longer engage in preaching, teaching, laying hands, and casting out demons. You have been summoned by the Lord. Carry out His request. According to someone, it is not advisable to host a prayer meeting, healing, and deliverance in my home. Some religious authorities act in opposition to the Lord's teachings. Do not stop God's work, continue working for Jesus as he asked. Somehow, someway, the devil wants to stop you and me from spreading the good news. I am not here to sit on the pew and go home. Keep your distance from barriers.

We must do what Jesus did.

John 6:15 When Jesus therefore perceived that they would come and take him by force, to make him a king, he departed again into a mountain himself alone.

Luke 13:22 And he went through the cities and villages, teaching, and journeying toward Jerusalem.

Matthew 9:35 And Jesus went about all the cities and villages, teaching in their synagogues, and preaching the gospel of the kingdom, and healing every sickness and every disease among the people.

I am privileged to find the truth. It has freed me from the burdens of religious beliefs. The day I received the Holy Spirit; I kept working and laboring for the Kingdom. This is the powerful, precious, life-giving gospel. You can take any promises in the word of God and practice to see its reliability and trustworthiness. Much time through our lifestyle, people get converted. Their relationship with the Lord strengthens as they live out the principles of the Bible.

A woman converted to Christianity from Hinduism and experienced a life-changing transformation. It positively affected her supervisor; He was an angry man, but by her prayer, he became the kindest and nicest man. Another day, her supervisor said, I want to change my religion. Lady said, it's not about changing" Lady said, it's not about changing religion, it is about changing the heart and turning away from sin. Joy overwhelmed me as I listened to the testimony of a new believer. They encourage their colleagues to try Jesus for a better outcome. This is our ongoing responsibility, no matter the time or location. That is what you are called for. Signs and wonders will be confirmed by God.

Mark 16:15 And he said unto them, Go ye into all the world, and preach the gospel to every creature Friends, please go out and preach, do not sit on the pew and get contaminated. Disregard any advice or comments from others.

Mark 8:35 For whosoever will save his life shall lose it but whosoever shall lose his life for my sake and the gospel's, the same shall save it.

Traveling to different nations may be risky, but we can trust in the Lord's guidance and protection. If a disciple had stayed in one place then, Roman, Italy, Asia, Corinth, Ephesians, Collisions, and all cultures and colors would have never found salvation. I continue to encourage you to serve Jesus through your work. God's kingdom and mission depend on you and me. Don't please people. Please the Lord. Do not deprive yourself of a little favor, handshake, visitation, or a phone call. The Lord will take care of you if you work for Him. See the apostles.

Acts 5:19 But the angel of the Lord by night opened the prison doors, and brought them forth, and said, 20 Go, stand and speak in the temple to the people all the words of this life.

We have to continue the work by surrendering to God. Don't stay in the same place, but go everywhere and preach the Gospel. May the Lord give you an understanding of the seriousness of His business. Once you go out to work, He will lead you to people with provisions.

2 Corinthians 10:16 To preach the gospel in the regions beyond you, and not to boast in another man's line of things made ready to our hand.

Our job is to meet new people, new cultures, and new souls with the Gospel of God. We are blessed to meet people from all over the world. Call a random phone number and witness. When the weather gets bad, I pick up the phone and call randomly and ask if I can pray for them. So gird up your loin and prepare with shoes of Gospel of truth to preach to all nations of the world. This is what you and I have to do. From today, open your mouth to preach the gospel, and give Bible study. Go out to cast the demon of the drugs, lies, cigarettes, cancer, and alcohol out. Amen! Lord, anoint you to destroy the yoke of Satan in Jesus's name! Amen!

LET US PRAY

Heavenly Father, we thank you for being faithful. You said if you seek me, you will find me. Let us seek, ask, and knock to reach you. Lord, our job is not to get comfortable on the pew, in the same city, and same place. Lord, help us do what you have asked and called. Open many doors to preach and teach. Lord, please give us a burden for the soul so we can reach them with prayer and fasting. May the Lord give us many souls to win. We want to work for the kingdom and not for anybody. Lord, you will provide every need. Send us true prophets and teachers. Send us laborers to work in the field of the Lord. Redeem the Soul from the bondages, yoke, and chains in Jesus's name. Amen! God bless you!

DECEMBER 15

POSITION YOURSELF TO SAVE!

We all hold some kind of position in the family, at work, and in the kingdom of God. God positioned Adam and Eve on the earth at an address called the Garden of Eden to dress the Garden.

The position of mom and dad has a major role in raising the children. Children born to a couple are called daughters or sons. Parents will see the outcome according to the time they spent training children correctly. Their product is the future parent of their grandchildren. So the cycle is going on and on. God gives each person a position to take responsibility.

Psalm 75:6 For promotion cometh neither from the east, nor from the west, nor from the south. 7 But God is the judge: he putteth down one, and setteth up another.

Abraham positioned Isaac on the altar to sacrifice. Lord rescued since He had an ultimate plan to rescue His chosen. The choice Abraham carried out shows that he never had to worry, since the Lord would rescue them. Father positioned Isaac to die, but the Lord had a position to rescue him. Isaac represents us, the chosen, and the lamb represents Jesus Christ.

Joseph positioned himself as a rescuer of God's chosen people. He focused on God and His works. Once you focus on God, then God will position you to save the people. He will rescue you from all trouble and not leave you and take time off. May the Lord help us position ourselves by focusing on God. Focus on His word, focus on calling. To surrender to God is scary. Feels helpless, without remedy. As you do, act and be faithful to your calling, you will be fine. God will save you from the death penalty, jail, prison, famine, starvation, and problems, in Jesus' name. May the Lord use us to warn the hurting, helpless, discouraged, lost, confused, and misguided world. You understand what I mean, right? The world is lost. They do not know where they are heading. Their minds have been stolen by the devil through identity. To save lost and hurting generations, the Lord wants you to position yourself in Him.

A one-world government is being orchestrated by the devil through strategic networking. My major role is to help and show the people that Jesus is the way of truth for eternal life. Life can be more abundant on earth and after that, as well.

Only if I position myself to reach out to the lost. Pray and cry out for the situation that the world is facing.

Why do I and my group fast every week, and longer fast once a month? We want to be ready in season and out of the season. We know there are many demons in the war for general, fallen angels, and the chief in command, Satan. I also know that I am here to come against Satan for myself and others. The Lord God gave me this mission.

You must do the work of warfare against the enemy. Position yourself to save the lost. You cannot fast and pray after you are defeated. I must fast, pray, and exercise my faith ahead of time. Do you get it? You do not know where you are heading, and you do not know the plan of the enemy against you. Once you have fortified yourself through early morning prayers, diligent study of the Word, deep meditation on its teachings, and unwavering fasting, you will feel invincible and ready to face any battle that comes your way.

As you know, the five fools did not position themselves to meet their groom. May the Lord make us five wives. Now, do you understand why we pray and fast and read words? You do not know when the trial, problem, and situation will happen again. It comes without alarm. May I suggest it to you? Pray as you have never prayed, fast as you have never fasted, and get into the world of God as you have never done before. Matter of fact, please pray without ceasing. May the Lord help us be ready all the time. Understand the time and season. I remember one little girl who always went to sleep with socks on and her hair tied up nicely. She said if Jesus comes in the night, then I do not want to meet Him with messy hair and barefoot. Wow!

Esther positioned herself as a rescuer to her people. She was not like the religious queen Jezebel, but a vigilant, sharp by putting on the armor of God. Queen Jezebel had her make-up on and provocative attire. See what the difference is. May the Lord do the greater work for us, so we do exactly what it takes to save this dying, druggy, alcoholic, depressed, suicidal, and hopeless generation? Our Lord is a rescuer, but He needs an employee to work for Him. Please enroll in His kingdom.

We all have a position; some are like Adam and Eve and some are wise and righteous like King David. Joseph was focusing on his calling. He reached next to the Pharaoh to save the people of God from the famine. Esther did not worry about the king's rule, death, or self-righteousness. It was against the king's reign to fast. Esther fasted and rescued the bloodline of the Messiah. May the Lord position you to rescue many nations everywhere. You may be in a communist country, in a nation of idolatry, in a Muslim nation, and maybe in some Christian religious nations that have lost the way of God. Position yourself to rescue people.

When I was working in the Post Office, I met many people who did not know Jesus. I had a great opportunity to witness other nationalities. By my preaching, many received healing, were baptized in Jesus' name, and believed in the Lord.

I acknowledge you have a role that requires concentration. Focus so your shadow can cast out demons, heal the sick, and many receive salvation. We messed up our position. That is why our city has great crime, shootings, drugs, divorces, and poverty. We are vacationing, hunting, and studying to impress, but not focusing and going out and doing some work of teaching and preaching. We all have a call from God to heal, deliver, and preach the gospel.

How have we positioned ourselves? It is so off that some congregations have many demons. They only care about wealth. Den of Thieves has positioned itself on the pulpit.

I want to position myself to take the Gospel everywhere. If there is an open door, then I would like to preach the Gospel. No matter who they could be, as long as they let me. I pray for everyone who allows me. It is all up to me how I position myself. I need to wake up and pray to prevent stress and unpreparedness.

Why couldn't the Disciple cast out the demon? They didn't prepare themselves. A deaf and dumb spirit was in the young man, but the disciples were not prepared. Jesus commanded the demons to get out, and the demons left.

Mark 9:28 And when he was come into the house, his disciples asked him privately, Why could not we cast him out? 29 And he said unto them, This kind can come forth by nothing, but by prayer and fasting.

Position yourself to the calling or we will see sick, depressed, confused, possessed, lost, and helpless people around us. May the Lord prepare our hearts in Jesus' name. Amen!

LET US PRAY

Heavenly Father, we thank you for positioning yourself on earth to save us. Lord, help us keep our eyes on you. Order our feet in your footsteps through the word of God to take care of the work you left for us. Lord, help us know you through following to do your word and will. Heavenly Father makes us light, since we see much darkness around us. We pray for all who need help. We need to be light for all. So help us, strengthen us, give us wisdom, love, and burden for the lost soul. We bring our children to you and guide them with godly parents, teachers, and authorities. We thank you for the words of God. It is good all the time, so help us to a position in the word of God in Jesus' name. Amen! God bless you!

DECEMBER 16

PRESS THROUGH!

Learn to overcome all obstacles in the way. Don't expect a rosy road, the road without obstacles, no hindrances, stopping, and blocking. Our road will encounter both fierce water and fire. May we learn from the Lord how to face obstacles and reach the savior's throne.

Press thought to touch the garment. Reach to the throne of God. Find His shadow, His healing touch, or His Spirit for the purpose of healing. It takes an effort to reach the Savior Jesus. Savior refers to someone who brings healing, delivers, and saves. All that you need is in Him.

Mark 2:3 And they come unto him, bringing one sick of the palsy, which was borne of four. 4 And when they could not come nigh unto him for the press, they uncovered the roof where he was: and when they had broken it up, they let down the bed wherein the sick of the palsy lay. 5 When Jesus saw their faith, he said unto the sick of the palsy, Son, thy sins be forgiven thee. 11 I say unto thee, Arise, and take up thy bed, and go thy way into thine house. 12a And immediately he arose, took up the bed, and went forth before them all;

The man encountered challenges but ultimately caught the attention of the Savior. You must press through to receive the help. You can do it. Seeing the result makes it all worth the time and effort. People were pursuing Jesus across mountains, oceans, and rivers to locate Him. He helped, gave, healed, and delivered those who reached Him. Why don't we do the same?

We are granted authority in His name. It's common to witness people traveling around the world to meet a real prophet for problem-solving. Hungry and thirsty people of God will fly anywhere to find one true prophet. I solved a similar situation by doing the same thing.

Mark 5:21a And when Jesus was passed over again by ship unto the other side, much people gathered unto him: 23 And besought him greatly, saying, My little daughter lieth at the point of death: I pray thee, come and lay thy hands on her, that she may be healed; and she shall live.

Jesus went to the little girl's house to heal her. Even though she had passed away, he managed to resurrect her. Jesus was surrounded by a multitude of people. A lady was suffering from blood issues for twelve years. With resolve, she fought her way through to touch the garment and receive healing. To reach His throne, we need to learn how to pray, fast, and persevere.

He is the same yesterday, today, and forever.

Mark 5:29 And straightway the fountain of her blood was dried up; and she felt in her body that she was healed of that plague.

Scream to get Jesus's attention and find a solution to your problem. When Blind Bartimaeus heard that Jesus was nearby, he shouted to catch his attention. Many tried to stop him. Jesus heard and called him. The man without sight requested to have his vision restored.

Mark 10:52 And Jesus said unto him, Go thy way; thy faith hath made thee whole. And immediately he received his sight, and followed Jesus in the way.

Don't stay blind, deaf, lame, or limbless, but cry out to get help. The Lord will hear and help you. He will give full attention to your needs if you cry out. It's all up to you to get His attention. Worship is also one way of pressing through. Just worship Him; you will get His attention. Ask the Lord to cleanse you of all diseases.

Matthew 8:2 And, behold, there came a leper and worshipped him, saying, Lord, if thou wilt, thou canst make me clean. 3 And Jesus put forth his hand, and touched him, saying, I will; be thou clean. And immediately his leprosy was cleansed. Turn on some music to worship, pray in the tongue and when His presence comes, say, Lord, heal, help, touch, and make me whole. He will do it. David also asked for the minstrel who sang and played music to help David enter serious worship to bring His presence.

Learn to pray with a musical instrument. Speak and claim His promises given in His word, even give an extra offering to get what you want to get from God.

With the last bit of oil and flour, the Lady baked a cake for the Prophet of God. God provided a survival miracle for her and her son during the famine. May God guide and teach us the way to reach His divine throne. God can solve the problem as soon as you press through to touch the throne of God. We are our problem. We do not want to wait, seek, ask, and knock. May the Lord have mercy on us. Our remedy is on our knees. May the Lord make us sensitive in the spirit realm. We can be healed if we find someone who has the gift of healing. I get many calls in a day to receive healing and deliverance since I use the authority given to His saints by the Lord Jesus. The power of the Holy Spirit guides me as I follow Jesus and His instructions. As soon as we touch heaven, all healing comes down. It should be everyone's desire to touch the garment of Jesus.

Mark 3:7 But Jesus withdrew himself with his disciples to the sea: and a great multitude from Galilee followed him, and from Judaea, 8 And from Jerusalem, and from Idumaea, and from beyond Jordan; and they about Tyre and Sidon, a great multitude, when they had heard what great things he did, came unto him. 10 For he had healed many; insomuch that they pressed upon him for to touch him, as many as had plagues.

The key to finding Him lies in our approach and actions. Learn how to reach, press through to touch Him. We live in a time and age; where no one knows how to cry out. Pray till all mountains of problems move. Find the true prophets of God where you find help from God.

Lord Jesus has been replaced by pharmaceutical drugs, witchcraft, homeopathy, and other means. He took 39 stripes to cure all illnesses. We had the power to destroy demon attacks. He said in our language that you can do greater. Yes, I believe it. I pray over the phone and healing, deliverance and miracles happen in Jesus's name. The power of God is received when one perseveres, cries out, and seeks the Lord God. Many people reject God's ways, but I encourage you to read the Bible. May your faith be restored by the Lord. Our relationship has been hindered by following false denominations and organizations. Find the true believers of Jesus Christ who demonstrate spiritual gifts. Seek places where they know how to travail in Spirit and cry out. May the Lord God help His people by sending the true fivefold ministers. Many will not even believe the prophet's prophecies.

People may experience temporary healing, but without understanding how to maintain it, sickness can return. People have never been taught how to get violent against Satan. Take what belongs to you by force. Command the devil to release all he is hiding, stealing, and has already destroyed. Truth belongs to God, however, He depends on someone to enforce His way, remedy, and provisions. How much you're willing to sacrifice will determine everything. God will notice your sacrifice of fasting, seeking, and crying out. He will remember you. Once, I had severe shoulder pain and prayed and prayed, but one day, it ended. In the middle of the night, I cried out because accidentally I slept on that shoulder. Sure enough, my prayer was different, since the pain was great. Whatever it was, it was consumed by the Holy Spirit's fiery descent. I was healed completely. Your effort, action, desire, and continued seeking will draw His attention to heal, provide, bless, and deliver you from everything and anything. Today, people are too occupied to spare a moment. The way of God is forgotten. And replaced by all man-made ways. Have mercy on us, Lord, help us in Jesus's name. Amen!

LET US PRAY

Please, Lord, teach us to press through. Lord, you spent many nights praying. You were praying on the mountain. The house is warm and we don't want to cry out. We are numb and ignore our needs and others. We go to doctors and pay for expensive insurance and expensive medicine. Lord, some medicine has the warning to kill us, despite that, we do not depend on you. False teachers and prophets taught us not to believe in the accurate word of God since they do not care. But Lord, today you teach and bless us with a true teacher and prophet. We desire to see God in operation again. Lord, give us a desire to reach you. We desire to have you close to our hearts. Please help us in Jesus' name. Amen! God bless you!

DECEMBER 17

USE YOUR TALENT!

Each one of us has been blessed with a unique talent from God. God asked Moses what you have in your hand. He said just a stick. He used that stick to make people wonder. May the Lord use whatever you have in your possession to give God glory. I pray to the Lord to use all that I have. Use my talent. If I do not have, then please give me some to give you glory. Rather than criticize, people should think about how they could be of help to others. All day long, I counsel, pray, and teach. I have seen the fallen, broken people's lives turn around. Praying has the ability to raise up those who are impoverished. I look at my hand and pray to the Lord to use it for His glory. I do not have a stick but a hand.

Luke 13:13 And he laid his hands on her: and immediately she was made straight, and glorified God.

Paul heard and did as the Lord has asked us in His word.

Acts 28:8 And it came to pass, that the father of Publius lay sick of a fever and a bloody flux: to whom Paul entered in, and prayed, and laid his hands on him, and healed him.

Our hand holds more power than the stick possessed by Moses. When we utilize that hand, everything transforms. Utilize any talent given by God to advance the kingdom. I look around and see many talented people, but they use their talent for Satan. Some use their talent for fame, money, and power on earth. I wonder sometimes what and how their story will end. God grants us everything, so why not use it for His purpose? I had a wonderful experience of baptism in the name of Jesus. I dedicated myself to studying it thoroughly in order to fully comprehend its revelations. I am so happy that many who have accepted the name of Jesus and are baptized, their sins are forgiven, and they walk in the newness of life. Remembering my experience is a constant reminder of my struggle against the truth. I wanted to baptize in the title of Father, Son, and Holy Spirit. The roots of false teaching were so deep that I needed a powerful Lord to deliver me from my disbelief of jesus's name Baptism. The Bible says Jesus of Nazareth learns by obeying the scripture. I learned by obeying Acts 2:38 as well. Experience is only attainable through obedience, not explanation. Today, my talent has blessed the kingdom of God. Many have entered the Kingdom of God by washing away their sins in the blood. The people who have good and perfect gifts from God guide many. I want to use my talent for the King of Kings and the Lord of Lords. May the Lord help us distinguish the blessings and curses.

Matthew 25:15 And unto one he gave five talents, to another two, and to another one; to every man according to his several ability; and straightway took his journey.16 Then he that had received the five talents went and traded with the same, and made them other five talents. 17 And likewise he that had received two, he also gained other two. 18 But he that had received one went and digged in the earth, and hid his lord's money. Our God-given talent should earn 5 more. We must work for the one who has given us these talents. A man worked hard for God, and God blessed Him with double blessings. My question is, what are you doing for the talent given to you by the Lord? Once I discovered the truth, I spread it worldwide. The Lord guided me to other countries, cities, and states to enlighten people with the truth. How can you stay in one place, not letting others know about your experience? How long does it take to transition from crawling to walking and running? It's common to witness people dedicating ample time to work, household chores, and other matters, while neglecting Jesus due to exhaustion or lack of time. The one who does not labor for Jesus has time to find the fault of God's work. May the Lord assist you in utilizing your limited abilities for the kingdom. Paul spoke different languages; he traveled around the world to preach in every language.

If we use our talent, knowledge, wisdom, wealth, and all that God has given, then this world will have no sorrow, failure, crazy people running around, depressed, and unhealthy people. May the Lord help us so we can take over the world by using our talent.

We get stingy when we have to give God's laborer. We think laborers live and eat air. Many times people spend all their money on themselves, but for God and His people, they have nothing.

If we take care of God's word and His people, we will have many blessings on our way. The woman's husband possessed exceptional building skills. She constructed a room specifically for the prophet. Because of that, she received blessings.

Our job is to give instead we have become takers. Everyone has some kind of gift. The Lord said He gave some gifts to each person. Some refuse to use their talent because of twisted thinking. If you utilize your skill to give glory to God, the Lord's presence will be acknowledged in the town, state, and country. What are you doing to the gifts given by God? Hiding it? Use it. I always knew that I could multiply the talent that God gave to me if I used it for the kingdom. I had no knowledge of computers, but dedicated myself to learning. I learned how to record, write, and make a movie. My passion is to reach the world with the truth of God. Jesus never sends anyone without talent. We all are unique. I can't be you and you cannot be me. We all use our talent and make the world new and beautiful to live in. The 12 children of Israel were blessed with extraordinary gifts from God. Some people were given the gift of singing by God.

James 1:17 Every good gift and every perfect gift is from above, and cometh down from the Father of lights, with whom is no variableness, neither shadow of turning.

God gave Bezaleel the wisdom.

Exodus 31:3 And I have filled him with the spirit of God, in wisdom, and in understanding, and in knowledge, and in all manner of workmanship, 4 To devise cunning works, to work in gold, and in silver, and in brass, 5 And in cutting of stones, to set them, and in carving of timber, to work in all manner of workmanship

God gives the wise heart detailed wisdom to do the unique work.

6 And I, behold, I have given with him Aholiab, the son of Ahisamach, of the tribe of Dan: and in the hearts of all that are wise hearted I have put wisdom, that they may make all that I have commanded thee; 7 The tabernacle of the congregation, and the ark of the testimony, and the mercy seat that is thereupon, and all the furniture of the tabernacle,

Daniel had a God given understanding to interpret of the dreams. So Joseph has the same talent in different times and eras. Use your talent to give God glory. Do not say, I do not have time. Some are good at serving people and working with their hands. I heard the man was working in the hospital; his wife was a housewife. She always cooked for any Christian admitted to the hospital. See, do something for others. Little things will always be remembered and admired. Amen!

LET US PRAY

Heavenly Father, we come to you; we thank you for your example. You use all your talent to heal, deliver, and set the captive free. Now it's our turn to go do the same. We thank you for blessing us with talents. Help us not to bury them, but use them. The Lord, our heavenly father, all is yours. Make us faithful to you and your kingdom. Do not let us get too busy. Do not let it be wasted away by the devil. We know all perfect gifts come from you. Your love is the biggest gift. So help us do as you have asked. We are here on earth to do the job given by you. We want to be sincere in all our activities for God. May the Lord send us His Angels and take us wherever we go. Help us find the place to work and give your name a shout, clap, and hallelujah. We want to be faithful laborers for your kingdom, in Jesus' name. Amen! God bless you!

DECEMBER 18

BE A MEDIATOR!

The Lord is looking for the mediator to stand before the throne to plead a cause. Wages of sin are death, sin has a consequence. Sinners face divine judgment from God. However, if God finds a mediator, He can alter His judgment to show mercy. To enforce a judgment on Nineveh, the Lord chose Jonah as the messenger to inform them of the consequences of their sins and the exact date and time of their judgment. Nineveh was not among the chosen people of God. How great is our Lord! His mercy endureth forever! We, as humans, can work together and put an end to this chaos. It is our privilege to show mercy to others. If we can offer aid, we are obligated to take action. Our mission is to save everyone, even if it's just one person. All it takes is our time and attention to take the necessary steps on our part.

1 Timothy 2:5 For there is one God, and one mediator between God and men, the man Christ Jesus;

The Jehovah God put on the flesh, shed blood, and did all to save you and me. He becomes a mediator to the same me and you. My job is to follow the example of Jesus and do what it takes. Every judgment came with a warning from God. Our job is to take extra precautions and necessary steps to escape from pronounced judgment. Remember, the judgment could be on one or many or an individual, city, state, country, or the world. The judgment of the flood of Noah was over the entire world. Brimstone and fire rained because of the sinful lifestyle of Sodom and Gomorrah. There was an individual judgment pronounced over King Hezekiah.

2 King 20:2 Then he turned his face to the wall, and prayed unto the Lord, saying, 3 I beseech thee, O Lord, remember now how I have walked before thee in truth and with a perfect heart, and have done that which is good in thy sight. And Hezekiah wept sore.

He interceded for himself and the Lord heard and gave an increase of 15 years. Now, do you understand it is a life and death matter? Believe it or not, you are called to be a mediator. So stand for your children's family or situation. But the best is you stand for your Nation. You will be a blessing to this world. You have the power to change any judgment for anyone or all.

Ezekiel 22:30 And I sought for a man among them, that should make up the hedge, and stand in the gap before me for the land, that I should not destroy it: but I found none.

The Lord is looking down, seeking one who can carry His burden. Stop God's hand to pour out His wrath. He is asking you to go to Nineveh. Instead of going there, we ran away to Tarshis. People run to the party, golfing, fishing, hunting, and movies and are extra busy to avoid God's assignment. Why? Nowadays people do not care about others. Sad, isn't it? We see many burning in hell, in crazy houses, prisons, jails, and hospitals, since someone does not want to go. They look for another way to avoid taking any responsibilities. Our carelessness and irresponsibility to the situation, matter, and problem will bring an earthquake, lava, storm, and disaster to the world. Wake up to intercede. Interceding to God for the situation, children, elderly, depressed, possessed, and homeless are facing. God cared for you and me. God put on flesh to save us. He gave life, which is in his blood. He did it all, even today He is standing in the gap. You and I find all excuses to get away from our responsibilities. Please stand and cry out for this dying world. How to pray as a mediator? We know sin brings separation between God and His creation.

Daniel 9:20 And whiles I was speaking, and praying, and confessing my sin and the sin of my people Israel, and presenting my supplication before the Lord my God for the holy mountain of my God;

The story of how Moses became the intermediary between God and His people. Can you stand and pray for the sick and dying world? Pray not only for yourself. If you fail to intercede, they will be subjected to the judgment of hellfire. I understand my responsibilities, which include standing in the gap, praying, counseling, and teaching. I've seen countless individuals being rescued.

Exodus 32:30 And it came to pass on the morrow, that Moses said unto the people, Ye have sinned a great sin: and now I will go up unto the Lord; peradventure I shall make an atonement for your sin. 31 And Moses returned unto the Lord, and said, Oh, this people have sinned a great sin, and have made them gods of gold. 32 Yet now, if thou wilt forgive their sin--; and if not, blot me, I pray thee, out of thy book which thou hast written.

Many individuals who said "yes Lord" have been used by the Lord. Embrace and accept God's will and ways. He is looking, His eyes go to and fro to see who can hear and stop His hand to pour the judgment. Inform them of the truth, so they can renounce their evil ways and be saved from God's judgment.

Amos 3:7 Surely the Lord God will do nothing, but he revealeth his secret unto his servants the prophets.

The greatest mediator is Jesus. Daniel, Moses, Abraham, Noah, Esther, and now us, if we do what it takes to stop the chaos. How are you fulfilling your mission? Is it just your burden and the burden of your children that you are carrying? Are you compassionate towards individuals battling drug addiction, alcoholism, depression, cancer, and other health challenges? Are you taking a stand in support of missing children? Do you have compassion for those who are misled by false religious leaders? Extend mercy to those imprisoned in our country and abroad. Do you care for the homeless? Nowadays, many live hopeless lives. Could you visit them and provide food, clothing, or some assistance? May God's guidance enable us to stand for His creation. I see everything is little, a little prayer, little Bible reading, and nothing of fasting. Not fasting according to the word of God. We don't hear life-changing messages because the person teaching doesn't care about changing your life. If the change comes into their life, then it will be in yours as well. People, it's time to wake up. Stop following the lost heads, follow Jesus.

We started fasting and praying all night. It's my responsibility to ensure that we are standing up for the people of this world. Please pray for the nations. Nations are in a big crisis. By carrying their burdens and praying earnestly, our families will experience automatic transformation. Changing the drug situation, the behavior of unholy individuals, eliminating alcohol, and uncovering the truth will result in a change for our problem and family. The Lord will find joy in you taking on His burden and not just focusing on your own. Nowadays, people are short-sighted and have no interest in caring for others. Please give yourself to the service of the kingdom. Don't forget, your influence in heaven is significant. Jesus prayed all night. Did He pray for His family only? No.

John 17:20 Neither pray I for these alone, but for them also which shall believe on me through their word;

In the present moment, Christians are being attacked by devil worshipers who are praying to Lucifer. We must attack back, praying to the Lord Jesus. Our mission is to stand up for all people. Defeating Satan's plan and idea is our ultimate goal. Amen! May the Lord send us many mediators, in Jesus's name. Amen!

LET US PRAY

Heavenly Father, we are in your courtroom, kneeling and asking for the forgiveness of our and others' sins. Lord, let your precious blood wash away all our sins. May the Lord show us his grace. We know we sin and it is in our flesh. Your blood has the power to wash our sins if we repent and baptize in Jesus' name by submerging in the water. You will forgive all ours and others if we call on your name. Lord, help us wake up early to pray. Pray at midday and at night. It is our job to intercede on all the problems since you said nothing is impossible. You will raise the people from ruin. Let us pray for others as we pray for ours. As you died for all, then we should pray for all too. Lord lay a burden for those who have no one to intercede for. We desire to be a mediator in Jesus' name. Amen! God bless you!

DECEMBER 19

IMPORTANCE OF THE ROOT!

What is the definition of Root? The bottom or lower part of anything, the first ancestor. The root is very important for the plant. It sucks water and nutrients and provides them to the plant. It's similar to a vein or artery. Firmly rooted plants ensure a secure supply. Jesus traced his ancestry to David, but in reality, he was the incarnation of Jehovah God in human form. The person involved was Jehovah, not Joseph. If you have a strong foundation, you're guaranteed success. Where you come from says a lot about who you are. If you declare your identity, expect people to dig deep into your lineage.

David and King Saul had distinct family lineages. One came out of Judah and another from Benjamin. Finding out someone's bloodline is now done through DNA testing. Currently, it's the most advanced test available.

In the Bible, the Lord mentions the roots of righteousness, bitterness, and David. The evil root is the root of bitterness. This will bring about the downfall of the person. The root of righteousness will bring blessings. Why does it hold such significance? Our righteous God remains connected to a righteous root.

Frequently, a cursed root results in a contaminated seed that harbors a plague, sickness, or disease. Some of our problems continue with our ancestors. It needs the savior's blood to clean and wash your roots. You need to find when and where it started. Let it out. Let the Lord denounce and send His angel to remove and cleanse in the blood of Jesus.

Certain people have a root in genius. The Lord has granted them with a sound intellect and intelligence. Aaron possessed an honorable ancestry. The reason God picked him as a priest and high priest was because their mother Jochebed taught them the truth of the Lord. They had a righteous root.

Exodus 20:6 And shewing mercy unto thousands of them that love me, and keep my commandments.

Psalm 103:17 But the mercy of the LORD is from everlasting to everlasting upon them that fear him, and his righteousness unto children's children;

Make sure you do it right. You believe your deeds towards your spouse, in-laws, families, or anyone have gone unnoticed. Lord saw and you are reaping good or bad, blessing or cursing, eternal life or death. You've been tagged by God. You have marked your bloodline with either diseases or eternal blessings. You're asking if I should show mercy towards you, isn't that right?

DECEMBER 19

The descendants of Aron were given a wise heart by God to maintain the laws. Additionally, we must enforce, teach, and adhere to the instructions found in the Holy Book known as the Torah. Once you have a good heritage, your children automatically inherit blessings.

Have you wondered why some are so cursed? Because someone in that bloodline had done evil and unjust to someone, and that is why they have been tagged with certain curses and illnesses. Baptizing in Jesus' name can remove the tags of curses and diseases. Cleansing from the evil root is possible for anyone through the blood of Jesus. The blood of Jesus has the power to wash away sicknesses, curses, and trouble if you repent and are baptized in His name.

Is it clear to you know why certain individuals pass away at a young age? Certain families experience issues like alcohol, heart attacks, diabetes, and high blood pressure. The bloodline's roots are associated with various illnesses.

I observed that my friend has a particular fondness for her. She was favored by the root, who is favored by the Lord. Her ancestors likely had a close relationship with God. Our parents' good roots have brought us blessings from God, and I understand that. Our origin is a source of blessings for others.

It's important to pray for your children to marry someone with a blessed lineage. Curses or blessings will be passed down to future generations. A married couple is a combination of blessings and curses, blessings and blessings, or curses and curses. Can you perceive?

Righteousness was a defining characteristic of David. The bloodline was blessed with the arrival of the Messiah, thanks to a righteous ancestor. Jesse's lineage traced back to its origin.

Proverbs 12:3 A man shall not be established by wickedness: but the root of the righteous shall not be moved.

Those pursuing God are different from those pursuing fame, money, power, and position. How would you make the most of a short lifespan of 70 or 80 years? The decision is up to you.

1 Timothy 6:10 For the love of money is the root of all evil: which while some coveted after, they have erred from the faith, and pierced themselves through with many sorrows.11 But thou, O man of God, flee these things; and follow after righteousness, godliness, faith, love, patience, meekness.

Sword, famine, poverty, and plague will haunt every generation of this wicked root. There is no escape from God's grasp. You are constantly being observed by the Lord. God will erase you from His world on the Day of Judgment.

Hebrews 4:13 Neither is there any creature that is not manifest in his sight: but all things are naked and opened unto the eyes of him with whom we have to do.

Job 26:6 Hell is naked before him, and destruction hath no covering.

Ecclesiastes 12:14 For God shall bring every work into judgment, with every secret thing, whether it be good, or whether it be evil.

Yesterday, I was blessed with a prayer from a prophetess. She wanted to know if anyone had sought to cleanse my bloodline through prayer. I said, "no". She said, cleaning the bloodline takes 30 minutes. And I said, 'Go for it. She blessed me, praying for the spiritual protection and guidance of my entire lineage, tracing back to the very first humans, Adam and Eve. I said, wow, amazing! I was glad I allowed her to do so. There is so much available to us, but by joining churches, denominations, and non-denominational organizations, we get theological blinders only. I don't want to be caught off guard by anything. I seek forgiveness and cleansing of all wrongdoing by both sides of my family. She referred to Deuteronomy 28 and urged me to repent. She said we were in the courtroom of God; angels dispatched to arrest demons, cleanse and take care of every hidden sin, unpronounced and unknown sins, and the sin of ignorance removed from my bloodline. Isn't that nice? We all must do cleansing of our and our ancestor's sins. Many can't see because of spiritual blinder, deafness, and ignorance. May the Lord provide us with truthful mentors and prophets who are guided by the Spirit. I have been watching Prophet Alph Lukau on YouTube. I love the operation of gifts of the Spirit. He contacted the young woman and informed her that all of her family members had experienced failed marriages, which she acknowledged as accurate. It was revealed by the prophet that your great-grandfather took the lives of innocent foreigners on his property. The chaos of broken marriages in your bloodline is a result of innocent bloodshed.

If parents, their children, and their grandchildren all have a history of alcoholism, divorce, or the same illnesses, investigate the underlying causes. Repent of sins, get baptized in Jesus' name, and witness the outcome. Your life story will change. Transformed from evil to good, sickness to health, liar to purified, killer to sanctified, murderer to washed clean - all by the name of Jesus. Jesus is your root now. You have a good heritage. Amen!

LET US PRAY

Heavenly Father, we come before your altar asking you to forgive all our maternal, paternal, and spouse's bloodlines to Adam and Eve's sins in the blood of Jesus. Let the Lord keep our roots in the blood of Jesus. We want your righteousness. Our righteousness is a filthy rag. Help us experience you by keeping your commandments. God will bless our descendants after us. They will continue to reap as we live the legacy of righteousness. It is a privilege to forgive those who have done wrong to us. Lord, we forgive and you forgive their sins against us. We know it will free them from sickness attached to sins. Lord, as we repent, let your righteous blood speak today that we are not guilty. Our roots begin with righteousness and the holiness of God. So we inherit the legacy and blessing of Abraham, Isaac, and Israel in Jesus' name. Amen! God bless you!

DECEMBER 20

TIME INVESTMENT.

It's important to monitor and manage your time. Once time is gone, it can never be retrieved. Just like a waterfall on the ground cannot gather again. Everything has time and season. Make sure to utilize your time wisely.

It came to my attention, through a friend, that you are always reading the Bible. She advised me to wait until I'm older to read the Bible, rather than doing it now. She advised to prioritize enjoying life at the moment, with the assurance that there will be time to read later. No, I read the Bible now when I am young. The Word of God is my light, lamp, food, sword, director, and everything for my life. I invested my time in studying the Bible. Achieving success requires a perpetual investment in learning the Word. I complete reading the Bible within a year consistently. I complete reading the New Testament over summer vacation. Wise time investment is a passion of mine. Investing time in God is never a waste, regardless of what you say. Investing time in good soil is how you gain a fulfilling life.

My hobby is to learn. I'm constantly expanding my knowledge. There's no better way to invest your time.

People often acquire false knowledge and misapply it. How do we become our enemy? No playing right from the start. Have you ever seen a demon, which is the devil, or fallen angels? Do they come with a horn? He employs the living human, a precious creation of God. To fulfill his mission of killing, stealing, and destroying, the devil exploits God's creations of time, life, and money. The path of Satan involves tempting you with what you are willing to permit. Jesus says I am on the way. Investing time, money, and God-given knowledge in His kingdom brings immeasurable value to life and world production.

Your ability to manage time greatly impacts your ability to manage your mind. Progress is the result of effectively managing and directing the mind. Life goes through different stages, and I understand that. Different stages bring about different mindsets. Healthy thoughts require the development of the mind. Your abilities decline as you age. Be mindful and productive while you still have the chance. Do not say, 'later'. Later is a notion that never materializes. Don't hesitate to dive into any opportunity that presents itself. You'll be surprised by how effortless it is to create. Support the divine mission on earth by investing in God's work.

In the early morning, Jesus went to pray and continued praying all night. His investment provided us with an excellent illustration. It is fulfilling time management. No one will disturb you in the middle of the night and early morning. You can talk to your heavenly father peacefully. I love early morning timing since my connection is without interruption. I am sure you understand that very well.

Luke 6:12 And it came to pass in those days, that he went out into a mountain to pray, and continued all night in prayer to God.

Mark 1:35 And in the morning, rising up a great while before day, he went out, and departed into a solitary place, and there prayed.

Upon connecting with the Spirit God, He received His divine schedule and immediately started working. Many times, we don't know the plan of God and we waste our time. Many big fights, accidents, troubles, and sorrows come because of that. If you aspire to live a successful life, investing significant time is essential.

Time management was a challenge for me when I was younger. I had a Muslim friend; she was good at managing her time. I learn to manage my time through her example. She always kept her god first. Her study methods made her the class leader until I mastered her time management techniques and overtook her. Notice the influence your company has on you. Time investment in a valuable friend brought change to my life. If you invest in the wrong people, your life will be a big mess. Choose a wise, smart, truthful, and honest friend, spouse, prophet, and teacher. It will change the direction of life. It's truly a blessing to have great friends.

Among my friends, you'll find people of all ages, from young children to the elderly. Currently, my friend who has known me the longest is 93 years old. I was trained in the old-fashioned manner by her until she passed away in July 2021. Her sole focus was on teaching and preaching. Her presence in my life is a valuable asset. She still calls me and tells me; I am glad you came into my life. And I say the same for coming into my life. I am thankful to God for her.

My goal is to find opportunities to invest my money in the poor, widows, and orphans. To invest my money, I need a trustworthy prophet and diligent laborers. My money will grow abundantly in their hands, like two fish. Locate the soil that is enriched by prayers and fasting. Observe their work, then consider investing in their ministry. They have the power to pronounce a blessing on you. Put your resources into a ministry that reinvests in God's kingdom. Do you get it? Please do not give to the thief and robbers. They will blow your money away.

I invest my time in making connections with countless individuals. Teaching, praying, counseling, and encouraging are my business. It's important to connect with the right individuals to succeed. The name of the game is teamwork. There must be no divisions within the body. It's important for us as the body of Christ to stand together, avoiding divisions and groups that tear us apart. To expand the kingdom, it is essential to connect with like-minded people.

The incarnate Jesus, who is Lord and Jehovah, traveled and brought healing miracles. Jesus was engaged in carrying out His father's work.

Luke 2:49 And he said unto them, How is it that ye sought me? wist ye not that I must be about my Father's business?

Acts 10:38 How God anointed Jesus of Nazareth with the Holy Ghost and with power: who went about doing good and healing all that were oppressed of the devil; for God was with him.

I have invested much time, money, and strength in the kingdom of God. When we dedicate time to the kingdom of God, life becomes meaningful. Time is the greatest weapon against the devil. What occurs when

DECEMBER 20

we go out and do as Jesus did? Sight will be restored to the blind, hearing will be restored to the deaf, and someone will be saved from suicide or making a wrong choice.

Putting scripture into action is how we come to know God, plain and simple. Treat the given directions as a recipe.

While employed at the Post Office, I planned and saved for a trip to India where I ministered in various locations during my vacation. The truth has been revealed to many through my ministry. I am involved exclusively in the real world. The pulpit, position, or religion do not appeal to me. I find satisfaction in God alone. As He opens the door, he travels to another part of the world and accomplishes something amazing. I'm noticing more and more people are embracing Jesus. The Kingdom is the only place where we focus our efforts on guiding the lost towards Jesus. God's work is truly amazing. I have no requirement to be involved in mainline churches or mega-churches. I am solely guided by the Holy Ghost. I served the Lord by visiting hospitals, convalescent homes, jails, and homes in various cities and nations. Time investment is crucial, but the choice of where to invest is paramount. Amen!

LET US PRAY

Lord, we thank you for giving us the mind, health, and direction for how and what to do with our time, money, and life. It is our choice to manage time. May the Lord help us do it promptly and in the right season. Let us match our programs with yours. Make us sensitive to your voice. We know that our time is short on earth. If we lose then, we will never come back. Give us the wisdom to invest all in the plan of God. You are the greatest example we must follow and no one else. We know your creation needs us. We have to carry on with your mission. Help us not to make it a secondary but primary investment of time, strength, and life. It is the best investment not for us only but for the thousand generations after us. Blessing who has invested their time for us, who brought the truth and delivered us from this dark and evil world. We thank you for investing your blood, life, and time by delivering a Torah and the Bible to us. How great are you, Lord! We give you all. We surrender to you and love you with all our minds, hearts, souls, and strength. Let our mission on earth be pleasing to you in Jesus' name. Amen! God bless you!

DECEMBER 21

OBEDIENCE IS THE FOUNDATION!

That means Disobedient has no foundation, Right?

Luke 6:49 But he that heareth, and doeth not, is like a man that without a foundation built a house upon the earth; against which the stream did beat vehemently, and immediately it fell, and the ruin of that house was great.

Now you know why people stumble and fail? Not having a foundation is a sign of never getting established. Now, what is the foundation?

The foundation is the establishment and settlement. We have Jesus as our foundation. If you have the revelation or knowledge of the identity of Jesus Christ, then you have built on the foundation of truth. Built the church with the revelation of Jesus, that church will not fall. Any storm can come and it will not destroy. And who is Church? You are a Church, residence, and house of God.

Luke 6:47 Whosoever cometh to me, and heareth my sayings, and doeth them, I will shew you to whom he is like: 48 He is like a man which built a house, and dug deep, and laid the foundation on a rock: and when the flood arose, the stream beat vehemently upon that house, and could not shake it: for it was founded upon a rock.

Listen to the word of God carefully, prayerfully, and with a sincere and obedient heart, and see what happens. May the Lord help you today to hear and obey. Let the Lord do some ear surgery to keep us on the right way and path. The bottom line is you do what thus saith the Lord without adding and subtracting. Why Christianity is failing and falling? Why people are not at the place where the disciples were? Because they laid other foundations and built Baptist, Methodist, Mormon, Seventh Day Adventist, Catholic, Pentecost, and name it. It is our job to keep our foundation, which was laid by the Apostle and Prophets who had a revelation of Jesus Christ.

Isaiah 28:16 Therefore thus saith the Lord GOD, Behold, I lay in Zion for a foundation a stone, a tried stone, a precious cornerstone, a sure foundation: he that believeth shall not make haste.

Ephesians 2:20 And are built upon the foundation of the apostles and prophets, Jesus Christ himself being the chief corner stone;

DECEMBER 21

Built your church on the revelation of Him. Jesus is the foundation for the New Testament covenant. Baptize in Jesus' name, cast out the demon in Jesus' name, and heal in the name of Jesus. Do all in Jesus' name.

Jesus is the manifestation of One Jehovah God in the flesh.

Colossians 1:17 And whatsoever ye do in word or deed, do all in the name of the Lord Jesus, giving thanks to God and the Father by him.

If you do not use the name of Jesus in baptism, then don't expect remission of sins, healing, deliverance, etc. The devil would talk you out of the first step of getting baptized in Jesus's name. Once your sins are not forgiven give the devil easy access to your flesh. Why because of Disobeying the truth? Obey and have a foundation.

Go back to the basics. Go to the church founded on the foundation laid by the Apostles Peter and Paul. It cannot be destroyed.

Matthew 7:25 And the rain descended, and the floods came, and the winds blew, and beat upon that house; and it fell not: for it was founded upon a rock.

Why is God warning constantly of false teachers and prophets? They are laying another foundation. That is why they are failing. One denomination after another is being established by those who do not have the revelation of Jesus Christ. Jesus never builds or establishes a denomination. So who did? The devil.

Galatians 1:6 I marvel that ye are so soon removed from him that called you into the grace of Christ unto another gospel: 8 But though we, or an angel from heaven, preach any other gospel unto you than that which we have preached unto you, let him be accursed. 9 As we said before, so say I now again, if any man preach any other gospel unto you than that ye have received, let him be accursed.

Do you see? Even when Paul was alive, the devil was removing the foundation of Jesus Christ. No one does but the devil. Now, these people did not have the revelation of Jesus, since many of us came from practicing polytheism. Many God worshipers will have no problem believing in the Trinity. There is no trinity or Holy Trinity word in the Bible. It is Satan's idea to divide one God and rule. One God put on flesh to shed the blood and now His spirit, which we say is the Holy Spirit, is abiding in us forever. We have one God throughout the Old Testament. He is working as a creator, as Jehovah-Jireh, El Shaddai, Jehovah Shammah, Jehovah Sabaoth, Nissi, and Shalom. At present, in the plan of redemption, He came with the name Jesus, which meant Jehovah Savior. All the above names dissipated in the name of Jesus. How nice! Every knee shall bow, in heaven and on earth and under the earth, to the name of Jesus.

Once you have a revelation by obeying the Word, all confusion about religion, denomination, and organization will disappear.

Our problem is not going to God, who has the answer, but we go to the man standing in front of us. They are not God; they are flesh and blood. Only Spirit gives revelation because Our God is Spirit. Spirit, God can tell you who He is.

Titus 1:16 They profess that they know God; but in works they deny him, being abominable, and disobedient, and unto every good work reprobate.

Matthew 11:27 All things are delivered unto me of my Father: and no man knoweth the Son, but the Father; neither knoweth any man the Father, save the Son, and he to whomsoever the Son will reveal him.

No matter where you live, or what you listen to, we cannot change the foundation since apostles and prophets lay already. That is in the book of Acts. Some revels that do not know the identity of Jesus discontinued it. Once they twist and turn, then words become ineffective. You know it is the Lord who works through us if we yield to the Spirit. We are to listen and obey. So, my friend, hear and obey what God has written in the Bible.

God is in business to help those who have ears to hear and eyes to see. May the Lord help us understand One God stays one till eternity. Even though you preach three or many.

Another day someone called me. He said sister Das is God, a man or woman. I said, think He is coming for His bride. Our heavenly Father, so what do you think? He said I knew God is a man. We have this confused generation. They do not know if they are men or women, then what they know about God. They have no foundation of truth.

Why are nations falling? Get rid of the truth, get rid of the Bible, prayer, and connection with God, but build the building and label it as a church. What good does it do?

Psalm 11:33 If the foundations be destroyed, what can the righteous do?

Do not read the Bible, do not practice His word. You will fall and fail. Is there anyone there who can call on God and repent, believe, and obey? Let me warn you, the devil is ready to show up since you allowed it.

Satan has done the job since someone did not do the job right. The foundation needs obedient people. Once you hear, then obey and see what happens. Amen!

LET US PRAY

Heavenly Father, we come to you for the truth. We know only your word is true. Help us obey, so our work and life have a solid foundation. Everything needs a foundation. If not, it will fail and fall. We are his Church. The Word of God says that obeying the Word of God is the foundation. If we obey, we will not fall, be removed, or be destroyed in any circumstance. It is true since we know, Lord; that you thrust many disobedient people out of position. Judas, King Saul, and many others unrighteous are gone in the storm of life. We want to obey and follow you. Your word is going to stand eternally and if we stand on it, we will too. Lord, there is no other foundation we want, but the one laid in the book of Acts. We repent, and baptize in Jesus's name to wash away our sins, for a clean conscience, and receive the Spirit of God to continue to stand against all storms, trials, and trouble in Jesus's name. Amen! God bless you!

DECEMBER 22

CRITICISM!

What is criticism? It is a disapproval attack, fault finding, or appraisal. Some are very strong in criticizing others to make them feel the low.

Low esteem is the part of someone who already murders their value. I know some people; nothing is good enough in their eyes. They are experts in focusing on others. All is well till they murder a billion-dollar idea by not having a wider vision.

I deal with many personality cultures and nationalities of people. In reality, some parents, friends, and spouses are low and will play a destructive role in others' lives. Inferior personality people will bring others down. It will damage your thinking and relationship with other people. Be careful of those people. No one needs their opinion, still, they criticize anyway.

In reality, if you stand and say I am good because God said so.

Psalm 139:14 I will praise thee; for I am fearfully and wonderfully made: marvellous are thy works; and that my soul knoweth right well.

1 Peter 3:3 Whose adorning let it not be that outward adorning of plaiting the hair, and of wearing of gold, or of putting on of apparel;4 But let it be the hidden man of the heart, in that which is not corruptible, even the ornament of a meek and quiet spirit, which is in the sight of God of great price.

Have an immovable foundation if we live by the word of God. No one will dare to govern your life. May the Lord help us in a dark age where people do not know how to wear clothing and other things. If you live in a conservative country or if you have a conservative view or a biblical view, then you will be criticized.

They criticized me for my style, especially the dress style. Friends always said people talk against your dresses. You know; I dislike the way they dress, but I wouldn't criticize. I changed since it taught me how to dress according to the word of God. The word of God speaks concerning life, dress code, and our behavior. Eve was wearing a robe and not an apron since God taught her. I am not hot and cold. The cloth is to cover my body. Every 16 minutes, one girl is raped. Who causes this chaos? Don't blame the devil. Confess that I am not living by the instruction of God. Confession that I am just like my parents, Eve and Adam. Extra expenses for personal beauty. Now, who is watching you in so many details? Critics, right? If you do not believe me, read the Bible about how they tried to mess up Jesus.

Matthew 11:19 The Son of man came eating and drinking, and they say, Behold a man gluttonous, and a winebibber, a friend of publicans and sinners. But wisdom is justified for her children.

The Bible says, Woe unto these people since they are too busy tearing and misleading others. Critics need help. Some are good critics who can make you a better person. But when it is against the Word of God, then ignore it.

Have you seen some people wear long clothes covering their heads? No matter where they go, they will not change. Teaching with conviction is so powerful that they do not care what you say or think. They are careless of critics. If you like it or not, that is the way they will dress up. Now, what is this called? Powerful teaching. Nothing is bothering them. May the Lord transform us through His teaching of His Word. Once you know the truth from the word of God, you will never have to change as the prince of the air; the devil is trying to change you. Devil's designer is trying to conform us to trap us into looking trashy. Why does everything keep changing? The devil comes up with ideas and plans by criticizing God's creation. How can you so easily deceive? Why are you letting the devil beguile you? I do not care what the devil likes. I want to live the way God has designed me with His dress code.

Many girls in Asian countries want to look Western. Not having a word of God in them, they get easily discouraged and spend money to change their nose and eyes. Many want to fix wrinkles and go for everything to look younger and prettier. Why can't they use the money for the ministry?

We see people putting on so much makeup since no one told them they are good-looking. No need to waste money to ruin God's given beauty. All the word of God is to put a hedge of protection around us. It will protect us against the storm that vehemently blows against our lives. Nowadays, a little girl is facing the peer pressure of the world system. Who poisons their innocence and teaches makeup. Parents and grandparents need to change the word of God instead they help them conform to the world. The devil has crept into many spiritually illiterate parents' and grandparents' minds. They are teaching them to put on worldly attire, makeup, and styles. Little girls are not free anymore. The prince of the air is doing its little tactic.

Now, why are we surprised when their little body is being attacked or kidnapped?

2 Corinthians 2:11 Lest Satan should get an advantage of us: for we are not ignorant of his devices.

Why does Satan go to others' noses, wrinkles, eyes, and eyebrows? I mean, everything is not good anymore. It is Satan's world, and he wants to make money by fooling you if you are not letting the Word of God protect you. Obeying the Word digs the deep foundation, your house will not fall or be destroyed. Keep Word in the heart. I live in the same world and see how seductive it has become. May the Lord help you think the way the Lord thinks and sees. He used mud and created you. You can be beautiful by having the Holy Spirit shine through you.

Ecclesiastes 3:11 He hath made everything beautiful in his time: also he hath set the world in their heart, so that no man can find out the work that God maketh from the beginning to the end.

Psalm 149:4 For the LORD taketh pleasure in his people: he will beautify the meek with salvation.

When parents live a righteous life, nobody dared to touch little children, but now, with the cooperation of parents and grandparents, their lives is in jeopardy. Little children are innocent, they are under their parent's protection and guidance. If the foundation of parents is not right, and the teacher is TV then what God can do? All this plastic surgery costs no less than 4,000 dollars. In today's world, people want to look like someone but not themselves. Learn to see your inner beauty. The devil only plays with the minds of people who are pulled by their lust and finally throw them away. Why are you your enemy? I live in the same world, but having the word of God written within, I do not sin against God. We handle good or bad. If you have obeyed the word, then you are above Satan's tricks and tactics. Satan's power and plan will not work. Lust of eyes is the biggest problem. Lust is the biggest problem, period. Look up, see through the eyes of God. We all have Eve and Adam in our house. We are watching Forbidden! Lord help us. May the Lord make us the light of this evil and dark world. Help us raise the Godly strong little girls and boys for the kingdom. Do not raise children for Satan and his kingdom to destroy little life. Attack critics by the word of God, with a made-up mind and steadfastness. Remember who you are. You are head, first, above, and beautiful King's daughters and sons. Amen!

LET US PRAY

Lord, we are grateful to be your children. You made us and clothed us in the garden of Eden. You knew the crafty devil was coming to destroy it. The devil misguides those who are ignorant of the word of God. But we will not get trapped in its old dirty trick by your given instruction on the Word. It is not fun but a trap to trap us with ruining the plan of God. We know our inner beauty is more important than the outer. The aging process is just as beautiful. It is the way of God to deliver us from this earth. Thank you for the eternal home. Teach us the wisdom of God through your word, knowing we are the light and example. Our Lord has placed us on this earth to represent Him. We are His bride and an ideal model if we keep the commandments. No criticism is good, but we know the word of God is the weapon against all the fiery darts of the devil. We quench them all in Jesus' name. Amen! God bless you!

DECEMBER 23

DO YOU SEE THE STING OF DEATH IN SIN?

Avoid regarding sin as fun, a party, a momentary pleasure, necessary sustenance, beauty, authority, wisdom, or enjoyment. I hope and pray that the sin appears to you as a hell, filled with burning and screaming.

What is sin?

Sin refers to actions such as crime, transgression, offense, or trespass. According to the Bible, sin is an act of transgression against God's divine law. Sin is an idea or action endangering a relationship between God and a person.

See as permanent separation of your soul from God. Whenever you picture yourself in hell, it's a realm of never-ending agony and torment. Just a reminder, it's not done yet. When justice is served, it will be over. Lord Jesus has the final say on when it's all over. Guard against allowing your flesh to become comfortable with sin. Repent with utmost urgency. Repent and abandon your sinful actions. Your flesh will be pleased by sin, presented in an attractive package. Sin is already a part of our being. The blood became corrupted due to Adam and Eve's sin. The presence of sin runs deep in our blood. By obeying the laws and precepts, you will remain on the heavenly path.

The devil is knowledgeable and skillfully influences each individual. Satan keeps a close eye on those who are living in righteousness, hoping to lead them astray. The Devil prepares all plans to trap you and me in hell. He has an understanding of both the process and the actions required. His plan and strategy are worthless if you disregard them.

The devil will plan a different tactic. Destroying all plans of Satan requires a made-up mind, unconditional love for God, total obedience, and submission. It is all over when we step into heaven.

It can't be changed, that's the reality. Beware of the deceptive illusion caused by sin. It's not about satisfying your senses or seeking pride, but rather about embracing pure deception and death. The devil has a new idea from hell sending a new package to destroy your soul. God is there to handle the usual responsibilities of caring for your soul. Very simple, but powerful. The Lord utilizes the uncomplicated word of God for His work. Because God is eternal and unchanging, the commandments, laws, and precepts will always remain the same. There's just one way to heaven and one way to save the soul. Embrace the word of God so tightly that it becomes inseparable from your heart and mind. There's no need to be afraid, the furnace is burning seven times hotter and the lions are hungry for an extended period. The Lord has the power to save, while the devil does not. The purpose of his packages is to trick the fool and allure the innocent.

God is not a dictator, but rather a creator, sustainer, and protector, conditional upon your alignment with His loves and hates. No other way! God, who is all-knowing, has a purpose for your creation and constantly thinks of you. The way of Satan is deceptive, while God plans to lead you to truth and guide you on the correct path.

I only trust and believe in the Word of God. God's Spirit is a trustworthy guide and instructor. It will empower you to do the supernatural.

Many do not fear God but continue living in sin.

1 Timothy 4:1 Now the Spirit speaketh expressly, that in the latter times, some shall depart from the faith, giving heed to seducing spirits, and doctrines of devils; 2 Speaking lies in hypocrisy; having their conscience seared with a hot iron;

We all know the *Roman 6:23a For the wages of sin is death;*

Take some time to think about what the Lord is saying directly to you. He is communicating the precise message He shared with Adam and Eve.

Genesis 2:17 But of the tree of the knowledge of good and evil, thou shalt not eat of it: for in the day that thou eatest thereof thou shalt surely die.

Everyone experiences physical death, but the soul's eternal separation from God happens in the lake of fire. This is the subject the Lord is addressing in this statement.

Genesis 5:5 And all the days that Adam lived were nine hundred and thirty years: and he died.

Upon sinning, Adam sought to hide from God. Sin is incompatible with the presence of God. You avoid being in the presence of God.

Proverb 28:1a The wicked flee when no man pursueth:

Genesis 3:8 And they heard the voice of the LORD God walking in the garden in the day's cool: and Adam and his wife hid from the presence of the LORD God amongst the trees of the garden.

A common belief is that hell is a place of misery. Let me clarify that people's suffering on earth is a result of their sins. The pleasure sin offers is short-lived, while the misery it causes is long-lasting.

I've witnessed individuals being apprehended for a crime and standing before a judge in handcuffs. They are at the mercy of the judge. In the presence of witnesses, the judge will administer punishment by the seriousness of their transgression. Pay attention to their faces while they work for an extended period behind the bar. All have different reactions. It's too much to handle for them and their families. It's especially cruel to sentence children to life in prison without any sympathy. How sad and sick it is! Imagine being under a curfew for a few days, unable to leave your house. It's understandable if you feel disconnected from the world. Lately, numerous storms have served as a reminder for us to disconnect from the world, lacking light, food, water, and daily essentials. We cannot stand that. Picture it being permanent. What follows? You have disappeared for good. How sad!

Isaiah 59:2 But your iniquities have separated between you and your God, and your sins have hid his face from you, that he will not hear.

This is why the Lord found the remedy for you and me. He has created a life filled with mercy and grace. Animal blood cannot remove our sins. The effect of animal blood is temporary and lacks deliverance and forgiveness.

Isaiah 59:16 And he saw that there was no man, and wondered that there was no intercessor: therefore his arm brought salvation unto him; and his righteousness, it sustained him. 17 For he put on righteousness as a breastplate, and an helmet of salvation upon his head; and he put on the garments of vengeance for clothing, and was clad with zeal as a cloke.

You and I, my friend, should spread the message of hell. The focus of preaching has shifted from Hell to prosperity. It is you who observes someone prospering every Sunday, not yourself. The Lord has hidden hell from the eyes of His creation's creation. We have a clear view of the opportunity, the right timing, and happy hour. Can you provide information on Satan, unholy fallen angels, and demons? To succeed, we must have a complete understanding of our opponent. We are being encircled by Satan and his team. We must be a source of light for demons to cry out and escape from judgment. Demon will beg you, don't subject me to torture. The demon must identify and verbally acknowledge that they are aware of who you are. Your dedication to the Holy One of Israel must be acknowledged by the demon. Our response should be to expose the devil's new tactics, rather than accepting them as mere amusement. Everything is not okay. There's a snake undercover in Santa, involved in sins like games, drugs, alcohol, and adultery. Wake up and prepare yourself with armor to resist the Devil, and he will flee from you and me. Amen!

LET US PRAY

Lord, we come before your altar, asking you to please forgive all our sins. You are the same yesterday, today, and forever. We repent of all our sins that we know or do not know. We asked you to take us to the right route of righteousness. Give us the true prophets and teachers of God. We desire you and love you. We want more revelation, wisdom, and understanding to know you and walk with you. Give us a daily prayer life. Help us know all your laws, commandments, and precepts to keep us away from falling into sin in Jesus' name. Amen! God bless you!

DECEMBER 24

DO YOU HAVE ROOM FOR ME?

On that day when it was time for the Lord to be born, His parents went from inn to inn to find a place for Him, but there was none... He came as a baby of a humble carpenter's home.. Nobody can view this baby as the one who made heaven and earth.

Luke 2:7 And she brought forth her firstborn son, and wrapped him in swaddling clothes, and laid him in a manger; because there was no room for them in the inn.

Joseph, the father, searched for a room to keep the baby safe and rest. There was no space available for Jesus. Today is no different from before, the situation persists. There's no space in our busy lives to make room for Jesus. The manger is where Baby Jesus was born, surrounded by animals.

We celebrate Christmas to honor Christ's arrival in this world. We understand that people can become extremely busy. The devil possesses greater intelligence and wisdom compared to Daniel. Satan issued a challenge to replace Jesus. Satan has successfully filled people's lives with busyness, leaving no space for the Lord.

Christmas is a busy time for us, filled with food, parties, shopping, gifts, flying, and driving. There is no place for Jesus among Christians. According to Satan, Jesus's birth can be nullified by his numerous ideas. Have you observed the high level of activity we experienced during this period? Sometimes, our busyness causes us to forget the incredible acts of Jesus during His time on earth. Jesus came to give himself to the vulnerable, impoverished, suffering, sick, oppressed, possessed, and heal those with broken hearts.

I came across information about someone who sadly committed suicide recently. The holiday season prompts people to recall the good old days. The loss of loved ones and divorce cause feelings of sadness and depression. It only gets worse after the Holidays. Ensure that Christmas does not revolve around me, myself, and I. Christmas marks the birth of Christ. His birth is a reminder to make a place for the needy, widow, poor, hurting, and all who need Christ's attention. It is about the Lord Jesus. It's not about what we can get, but rather about fulfilling His mission. It's sad to witness the selfishness of certain individuals who prioritize personal gain over their own families.

I have always advocated for giving to the impoverished and homeless instead of keeping it for personal use.

Today, I had a great time visiting elderly residents in convalescent homes, rehabilitation centers and assisted living facilities. They require the healing touch of Jesus.

ELIZABETH DAS

My friend's sister Tammy, her husband brother Shield, and I went to some convalescent or rehabilitation homes today. It was a time of giving and sharing. We selected some items, offered prayers, and distributed them to numerous elderly individuals. We were filled with joy, and so were they.

Make space for Jesus to carry out His mission on His Birthday, despite being busy.

This is the time to demonstrate the true purpose of Christ's coming to Earth. Show them sympathy, love, and care. It's not solely about spending money on food, gifts, shopping, and various other things.

There was no space available for his birth. Today, he is looking for a room despite our busy schedule.

While we are consumed with our pleasures, do we see those who are hungry, cold, and in need? I'm aware that Santa has taken the place of Jesus, according to the devil. Santa originates from the North Pole, which is believed to be Satan's dwelling. The devil wants to undermine the purpose of Jesus Christ and focus on worldly distractions. May we be guided by the Lord to realize that it is not about us. Avoid purchasing excess, instead seek out those who are in need. When Jesus was born, there was no place for Him. Today, He lives in us as a Holy Spirit and we say, Lord, I do not have time for you. " I am busy entertaining myself, my family, and my party, so I do not have time for your mission.

Matthew 25:35 for I was hungry and you gave Me food; I was thirsty and you gave Me drink; I was a stranger and you took Me in; 36 I was naked and you clothed Me; I was sick and you visited Me; I was in prison and you came to Me. 37 "Then the righteous will answer Him, saying, 'Lord, when did we see You hungry and feed You, or thirsty and give You drink? 38 When did we see You a stranger and take You in, or naked and clothe You? 39 Or when did we see You sick, or in prison, and come to You? 40 And the King will answer and say to them, 'Assuredly, I say to you, since you did it to one of the least of these My brethren, you did it to Me.'

Our plans involved organizing Christmas festivities for the newly converted individuals in a foreign country. As they transition away from their religious faith, we need to educate them on the importance of embracing others and practicing kindness. Taking a moment to ponder Jesus' deeds on earth is timely. I was approached by a lady who wanted a calendar with scripture readings for each day. The idea was absolutely fantastic. A large number of people are unfamiliar with the Bible.

I was told by another brother to give the brand-new blanket to the homeless. I said, "Well, if we give, then give the best." I provided free lunches and nice stainless-steel boxes as a gift, teaching them the importance of giving during Christmas. I distribute a range of items to the new convert every year during Christmas. They are my brother and sisters. They should never feel that they are alone. It's important to learn how to give and not just constantly take.

We paid visits to homes for the elderly. They asked for prayers for their families. Some people prayed for me.

They expressed their happiness and devotion to Christ with us. We applied oil and prayed for those who were waiting for healing and deliverance, having faith that the Lord would grant them healing.

It was Christmas for Christ and not for me. It wasn't about receiving, but about the act of giving.

In India, we are hosting a meeting. We buy them lunch and the New Testament.

DECEMBER 24

Their knowledge and understanding of Jesus will come through reading the word of God and His promises. It's important for the broken, hurting, needy, sick, and oppressed to understand that Jesus, not Santa, is the one who came to save us. He came to unveil His creation. He came specifically for you and me.

We should not forget about those in prison, jail, orphans, widows, and the homeless who eagerly await visitors. I am searching for these individuals.

May the Lord help us look beyond the superficiality of this world. Our eyes should be fixed on those for whom Jesus took on human form. It's my responsibility to remind both of us to teach our kids about sharing the Love of Christ. Let's remember that Jesus came to save the world, and we should follow His example. When making our Christmas list, we must exclude Santa and focus solely on Jesus. Keep the devil where it belongs, in the north. Angels declared it, and now we join in celebrating Jesus's coming. He arrived for both of us, granting us a life of abundance. I have the duty to bring the message of salvation to those who are in need and helpless. Amen! God Bless you!

LET US PRAY

Lord, we know you are the reason for the season. It is not mine or any other birthday. It is the Birthday of Jesus. We know your mission does not change. Never let us remove Jesus but keep the Lord as a center in the Christmas season. Help us keep Jesus in everything. Jesus is the only way to the truth and life. Never get into Satan's shopping system. Do not lose your mission in the trap of buying, eating, and forgetting Jesus and His mission. We must remember what is the reason for Christmas. We must remember it is all about Jesus. It is our job to let the world know who cannot return. It is the part of our blessing we share with needy, helpless, and hopeless people. Our Savior is born to set the captive free and heal the broken-hearted. We must go around and let others know Christ must be the center of Christmas. In Jesus 'Name Amen,! God Bless You!

DECEMBER 25

JESUS MADE ME ROYAL!

Royalty is in my blood. The King above all kings arrived to conquer the prince of darkness and purchased back all that was lost and stolen through His blood. An earthquake, sign, and wonder are the outcome of a significant shift in the spiritual realm. The star reader understands the celestial sphere's signs and transformations. The birth of Jesus was accompanied by an angel delivering the news of peace on earth. The mother of the Lord was visited by Arc Angel to disclose the arrival of Lord Jesus.

Luke 1:34 Then said Mary unto the angel, How shall this be, seeing I know not a man? 35 And the angel answered and said unto her, The Holy Ghost shall come upon thee, and the power of the Highest shall overshadow thee: therefore also that holy thing which shall be born of thee shall be called the Son of God.

A great King arrived on Earth, who was not only a ruler but also a creator. The name's disclosure came as a surprise to Joseph. A divine direction was unveiled by the heavenly Father. Revelation is not derived from physical beings, but from the Spirit of God.

Matthew 1:20 But while he thought on these things, behold, the angel of the Lord appeared unto him in a dream, saying, Joseph, thou son of David, fear not to take unto thee Mary thy wife: for that which is conceived in her is of the Holy Ghost. 21 And she shall bring forth a son, and thou shalt call his name Jesus: for he shall save his people from their sins.

What makes the name of this king so significant? It was kept secret for ages.

Judges 13:18 "And the angel of the LORD said unto him, Why askest thou thus after my name, seeing it is secret?"

With their understanding of celestial object shifts, astrologers provide divine information. The Bible talks about the Star. Angels are called stars.

Revelation 1:20 The mystery of the seven stars which thou sawest in my right hand, and the seven golden candlesticks. The seven stars are the angels of the seven churches: and the seven candlesticks which thou sawest are the seven churches.

Acting as intermediaries, angels are celestial beings that connect heaven and earth. Heaven is the dwelling place of Jesus, while earth is where His creation exists.

DECEMBER 25

God's throne is located in heaven, where He governs.

Matthew 2:1 Now when Jesus was born in Bethlehem of Judaea in the days of Herod the king, behold, there came wise men from the east to Jerusalem, 2 Saying, Where is he that is born King of the Jews? For we have seen his star in the east, and are come to worship him.

God-authorized individuals with knowledge of the celestial realm share divine information with us. Angels, dreams, visions, God's word, and true prophets are all ways in which God reveals His messages to us.

I proclaimed that Jesus has made me a person of royalty. Yes, I have experienced a new birth, through water and spirit. My new birth is from above. The meaning of Again is "from on high."Have you experienced the New Birth?" Birthing in the Kingdom is necessary. You feel like a royal. The children of the Most High are known to the devil as well.

Psalms 82:6 I have said, Ye are gods; and all of you are children of the most High.

The exact date and time of Lord Jesus' birth are unknown, but his purpose was to defeat the kingdom of darkness on earth. Adam and Eve's sin held us captive for a long time. He redeemed me with His valuable blood. Now do not repeat the same sins. Keep His commandments and you will do great.

1 Timothy 6:14 That thou keep this commandment without spot, unrebukable, until the appearing of our Lord Jesus Christ:15 Which in his times he shall shew, who is the blessed and only Potentate, the King of kings, and Lord of lords;

The Lord had a different plan than watching our defeat - He intended to come as a little child. Now is the moment to worship and exalt Him as the conquering King. He has restored you and me. If you find the way to Jesus, you will find Him. Everyone is invited to repent and cleanse their sins by getting baptized in the blood of Jesus. Receive the Holy Spirit.

Our desire should be to serve the King of kings. My heart yearns to understand Him in His strength and supremacy.

Revelation 17:14 These shall make war with the Lamb, and the Lamb shall overcome them: for he is Lord of lords, and King of kings: and they that are with him are called, and chosen, and faithful.

To celebrate His birth, people engage in various activities such as enjoying good food, visiting different places, dancing, drinking, going to church, and preparing for days in advance. The true significance of his birth is often overlooked by many. Those who are lost, possessed, and held by their enemies are the ones for whom He is born. Throughout generations, the Devil has kept many under his possession. Jesus came to his world, offering them complete deliverance from sins. Jesus protected us by covering us in His blood and hiding us from the enemy. The bloodline serves as a barrier that the devil cannot cross. The ones purchased by His blood rejoice the most at this time.

A lot of individuals were eager for the arrival of Jesus but failed to witness it because they had knowledge about God but lacked a personal relationship with Him. Due to their lack of revelation of Jehovah God's highest name, they remain unaware of the significance of baptism in Jesus' name. Those who did not keep His commandments were unaware of the hidden name of Jehovah God for salvation.

The Lord's instruction is clear: loving him means keeping His commandment. Instead of following Jesus, we often end up following churches, organizations, and denominations. It's not going to work, ever. Jesus is the only way, there is no alternative.

Today, you may be focused on consuming, unwrapping gifts, and neglecting those who are less fortunate. Don't forget about those who are needy, sick, hurting, poor, orphaned, widowed, oppressed, and possessed. You make a visit to them during this time. Instead of waiting for them, remember they are unable to come to you. Jesus came to us from heaven. The Holy Spirit descends upon us and resides within us for eternity.

Our responsibility is to make sure the world knows the name of King Jesus. We need to spread the good news worldwide, letting everyone know that they can experience freedom. The name of Jesus conceals the blood that washes away our sins. He will arrive as Spirit to guide, empower, and educate us. How wonderful it is, isn't it? Spread the good news to everyone else. Merry Christmas! God Bless You!

LET US PRAY

Heavenly Father, we come to say thank you from our hearts for Jesus coming into this world. It is the King of the universe who thought of me. We want to keep you in our hearts and do what you did for us. We must go and do the same for others who are still sitting in darkness, bound by chains of drugs, alcohol, and lustful sins. Lord, free all sinners, wash them in the blood of Jesus. Keep them clean, pure, and Holy to meet you. It is the wonder-working power of the Holy Spirit working through and in us to do marvelous deliverance and healing. Lord, we ask for fresh anointing with your Spirit and Power to do what you did. It is for that very mission we remember you today. We remember your birth and celebrate it as a healer; savior, deliverer, and merciful King of King and Lord of Lord. Thank you for coming to pay the price of our sins and for bringing us out of eternal death in hell in Jesus 'name. Amen! God Bless You!

DECEMBER 26

IT WOULDN'T WORK!

When changing the Word of God by adding, removing, or subtracting from the Bible, it wouldn't work. What do I mean? The Bible Says, who has an ear, let them hear. Do you have an ear to hear? Moses had an ear to hear. When a person hears, they put it in an application. This is called true hearing. A young girl listened to the message about tithing. In that particular week, she got a ten-dollar gift. In the following week, she placed one dollar as a tithe inside the envelope. The pastor questioned how she could pay tithes without a job. She mentioned receiving ten dollars, which she used to pay her tithes.

Her heart was convicted by the truth. To obey, preaching must be heard by a spiritual ear. Be honest and don't sugarcoat messages when talking about hell. A little leaven leaveneth the whole lump. A little fox devours the crops. What you're saying can be somewhat risky.

Acts 2:37 Now when they heard this, they were pricked in their heart, and said unto Peter and to the rest of the apostles, Men, and brethren, what shall we do?

Our responsibility is to preach the message, word, seed, and truth as it truly is. Addition and subtraction won't yield the desired outcome. You didn't do it correctly, so there was no result.

On Earth, Jehovah God took the form of Jesus and offered Himself as a sacrifice. He fulfilled the long-standing prophecies spoken by countless prophets. It has been completed, as per his statement. Finishing, he did a great job! It is not how you start, but how you finish that will count. Finish well!

Many efforts to modify the word led to the formation of numerous denominations, churches, organizations, and even non-denominational churches. It won't work if you've made even a small change, whether it's an addition or subtraction. How sad? Do as it says!

My question is, why do you have to add and subtract? Have you seen the outcomes experienced by Adam, Eve, Cain, King Saul, High Priest Eli, Ruben, Esau, and others who attempted it?

Living in a country that worships idols does not give you the right to modify the Word of God. By doing that, you are giving the devil an opportunity. Making His word non-effect. The Word of God is God.

Read the Book of Kings, Chronicles, Samuel, judges, and Ruth and find out what happened to those hard-hearing people. It is a lesson to learn, remember, and not repeat.

Jeroboam, who was called and anointed by God as king, showed little regard for hearing His voice. If you are blessed with power, position, wealth, and blessings, make sure to carefully abide by His commandments and statutes. Look up to God, who gave you all. Stay connected to God, who blessed you with a promotion.

Daniel, Shadrach Meshach Abednego, Esther, John, and the Baptist were all attentive and obedient to the Lord's words. Many Did not care for the consequences but kept the Word. The Lord can both grant and remove blessings. Always uphold the integrity of the Word. The Lord converted their grief into joy, the battle into success, and promoted them to positions of prominence. There are those who departed from this world without yielding or abandoning their resolve.

Anyone who added or subtracted faced a curse, demotion, or expulsion. They brought judgment over the nation. They were removed from the land of flowing milk and honey. God gave you a car, money, wealth, and blessings. So, you're under the impression that it's fine to have a small affair with the Word of God? Do you believe it's fine to make slight alterations in His Word through adding, subtracting, or removing? If you remove the word, you are removing God by losing all that you received from Him. You are inviting the curse.

Many people only seek God for elevation, but ignore the Word after they are elevated. They believe that power and position are in their hands, therefore God should be eliminated. The flesh seeks to fulfill its desires.

Humans have a natural tendency to be their own worst enemy. Once we grasp the correct and perfect way of God, the flesh will never hinder our relationship with Him. Remove disobedience and rebellion from the equation.

Jesus demonstrated the process of obedience to us, step by step.

Luke 9:23 And he said to them all, If any man will come after me, let him deny himself, and take up his cross daily, and follow me.

Jesus did not give a lecture or a good message, which you hear today. He practically lived what He preached.

1Peter 2:21 "For even hereunto were ye called: because Christ also suffered for us, leaving us an example, that ye should follow his steps:

John 13:15 For I have given you an example, that ye should do as I have done to you.

Don't forget that your actions speak louder than words.

Acts 18:24 And a certain Jew named Apollos, born at Alexandria, an eloquent man, and mighty in the scriptures, came to Ephesus.

In order to serve Jesus's Kingdom, the man's eloquence had to be combined with truth. In the Kingdom of God, there are only truths and no lies, and everything will function perfectly.

Acts 18:25 This man was instructed in the way of the Lord; and being fervent in the spirit, he spake and taught diligently the things of the Lord, knowing only the baptism of John. 26 And he began to speak boldly in the synagogue: whom when Aquila and Priscilla had heard, they took him unto them, and expounded unto him the way of God more perfectly.

DECEMBER 26

He learned the valid baptism for the forgiveness of sin was in Jesus' name. Only truth has the power to set us free. Word is only effective when it is used without adding and subtracting. If you add or subtract then, it is the devil's work and not God's. The devil has added and subtracted to attack the truth. He divided one God into three; He removed the Name of Jesus from the Baptism, to remove blood. By twisting the practice of fasting, he jeopardizes the kingdom of God. So on and so forth! The devil has the mastery to deceive and lie. The point where you will stumble is precisely what Satan's wisdom aims for. May the Lord give us wisdom and understanding before we answer the question coming out of the mouths of religious or unbelievers. Be careful!

The words of the Lord hold the highest authority. Zechariah received news about the arrival of John the Baptist, the son. He couldn't believe it since his wife was old.

Luke 1:20 And, behold, thou shalt be dumb, and not able to speak, until the day that these things shall be performed, because thou believest not my words, which shall be fulfilled in their season.

Remember, power is in believing and in doing. Do not fear death, but believe and obey.

Luke 1:38 And Mary said, Behold the handmaid of the Lord; be it unto me according to thy word. And the angel departed from her.

The keys are belief and obedience. Do as it is instructed in the Word of God. God asked me to be baptized while I was searching for truth, and I agreed. The power of the Word became evident to me when I fully embraced the name of Jesus. Believe what it says. By obeying, you can achieve the same result I had in the water. Amen! God Bless you!

LET US PRAY

Heavenly Father, we come to you knowing we are called to obey, submit, and surrender. No matter what, it is our responsibility to carry on the truth and to experience the power in it. Lord, there is no lie in the word of God. God said and it will happen if we obey. Lord, send us true teachers and prophets. Your Spirit helps us to understand the Word of God. It is a zone of truth and light. Life-saving, delivering, healing, and saving power is in truth. Help us stand on the true word of God. Help us follow you. Help us believe the true prophet and teacher who established the doctrine of having a revelation of who Jesus is. Give us the revelation of you, Jesus, as you did to Peter and Paul. Help us love the light, the truth, and obey and believe in it. We can show the word it works only if we believe as it is in Jesus' name. Amen! God Bless You!

DECEMBER 27

THE MIND IS THE GREATEST ASSET!

Guard your mind by sharing accurate information. The mind can download what you allow. The mind is a computer you must watch for bugs and viruses that can contaminate your future and family and will mess you up. A rational mind is necessary for us to become the men and women God intends us to be.

God's book, the Bible, has the power to transform minds. Some claim I switched churches due to their acceptance of certain things. Due to my disagreement with their beliefs and my dislike for conservatives, I am looking for an alternative worship place. People are leaving men made church because they value worldly desires over God's Word. The devil has permitted certain things in churches that people are accepting of.

Jesus remains constant, but His Word can transform you if you're open to it. When you find the truth, then obey and practice. The simple act of obedience will help you to continue in the truth.

John 8:31 Then said Jesus to those Jews which believed on him, If ye continue in my word, then are ye my disciples indeed; 32 And ye shall know the truth, and the truth shall make you free.

Change can occur through church transitions, marriage, or embracing the lifestyle of this world. If you are constantly changing, it means you are as steady as water. Water is never stable. You cannot stand on the water. Water is the most unstable ground. Refrain from conforming to the world by feeding incorrect information to precious minds.

Be careful, only the Word of God is everlasting. Why don't you stabilize your life by putting the Word of God in your mind, computer, and heart? I love to obey the word of God. It is very special to me. Why? First, it is the word of God. Second, it is written for me. Third, it will never change. Fourth, it is going to change me. Fifth, It will deliver me since the truth has the power to deliver. Sixth, if I obey, then it is a shield and buckler to me. I can count it as a number in the hundreds. It's important to protect the mind. It is the roof of our house. We are the House of God. If we disobey Word then, we are putting holes in the roof which will leak and damage the house. Obeying the word of God protects the mind from leaking, while disobeying it can cause leakage.

Philippians 2:5 Let this mind be in you, which was also in Christ Jesus:

Resist the constant changes imposed by the world systems.

Romans 12:2 And be not conformed to this world: but be ye transformed by the renewing of your mind, that ye may prove what is that good, and acceptable, and perfect, will of God.

In recent times, we observe a lot of people losing their sanity. From birth, even children have an underdeveloped mind. Disobeying the word of God leads to nothing but curses.

Isaiah 26:3 Thou wilt keep him in perfect peace, whose mind is stayed on thee: because he trusteth in thee.

The mind is very important, if you do not have a mind then your life will be tossing and turning. There is no use in living.

Philippians 4:7 And the peace of God, which passeth all understanding, shall keep your hearts and minds through Christ Jesus.

Normal functionality depends on the health of the mind. When your mind is sound, you can think right. The simplicity, fruitfulness, and promises of the Bible are unlocked through simple obedience. The Word of God reveals life's simplicity, but those with complicated minds struggle to see it. Our lives are secure when we permit the mind to operate through the Word of God.

I counsel people from many nationalities, ages, and countries. People always say that you have great wisdom. I always seek guidance from God on how to assist, teach, and respond when others are in need.

2 Corinthians 11:3 - But I fear, lest by any means, as the serpent beguiled Eve through his subtilty, so your minds should be corrupted from the simplicity that is in Christ.

Do not open the door to Satan. He is an expert in taking away your peace with freedom. With Jesus, we have peace, tranquility, and freedom. Having a sound mind is the most significant factor in our lives. The mind is a door for Satan. Many invite Satan by downloading the evil material of false religion even though Jesus said, I am the Way of Truth. It's not simply curiosity, but rather a lack of caution on the part of humans. We understand poison is bad for the body and will kill you. So is pornography, a TV program that comes as a virus. It does hijack your good data from the mind. It is our responsibility to read and memorize the Bible. Learn the Bible and meditate. In the Bible, the Lord provides the healthiest material.

Avoid reading materials that obstruct your ability to hear God's voice. While I was growing up, my father made it a rule for us not to engage with any type of reading material or movies, and we didn't have a TV at home. I perceive the experience of a person who did not follow the rule. The input and output information we encounter shapes our thinking. May the Lord guide us in obeying both the Lord and our good parents. Bad information contaminates good information.

I never read a magazine, novels, or bad materials, and avoided the movies. I never liked it, but had no time for nonsense. It's important to protect our homes from harmful information by being discerning about the books, TV shows, and other materials we allow inside. Our home should never be contaminated with the poisonous air of Satan.

Ephesians 4:27 Neither give place to the devil

1 Thessalonians 5:22 Abstain from all appearance of evil.

All harmful and toxic information is present in the world. Be careful what you read, watch and hear. No need to allow it in your family's life. Satan is not coming without your permission. Do not volunteer for the killer, stealer, and destroyer. The devil is doing a mighty destructive job by altering many minds and continues inventing evil to trap our minds. Although the Bible is widely regarded as the best-selling book, is it truly the most useful for practical application? The Bible is our life manual to meditate day and night. Word is for light, lamp, food, sword, and help. The mind, created by God, is the most powerful computer; it should not be destroyed.

The confusion you witness today is due to the incorrect information inserted into the mind computer. Life presents us with viruses, violence, suicide, and confusion about gender, among other things. Stay protected from harmful influences by saturating your mind with the word of God, the ultimate virus protection. Hallelujah Amen! God Bless you!

LET US PRAY

Heavenly Father, we come to you. We know that no one can make the mind as you do. But also it is our job to protect this beautiful computer-like mind. We ask for wisdom from God on how to fix the holes and damage. We have great responsibilities to keep it from all types of viruses. Teach us how to clean our minds with the word of God. We know how to block our computers from all kinds of viruses. Teach us how to use anti-virus for our mind computer. We allow all bad information without any filter. Your word says For as he thinketh in his heart, so is he: We want to think like you by reading your word. We do not want to be one of those who are called mind-damaged people. The mind is the most important for the good life. Let our mind download everyday good data by reading, hearing, and practicing what thus saith the Lord. Our world can become healthy, safest, and good if we all allow the Bible in our minds. Thank you, that the Bible is the healthiest data, tonic, and virus-killing book given by the one who has created the incredible mind.Thank you, Lord, in Jesus's name Amen! God Bless You!

DECEMBER 28

IMPORTUNITY!

What is the meaning of importunity? Strongs concordance definition from the Greek word anaideia, an-ah'-ee-die-ah' meant shameless. Persistence in carrying out God's plan. Unembarrassed baldness in the dignity of faith!

I am working in the field of God; I meet different religions, nationalities, and cultured people. It is a great privilege to serve and work for Lord Jesus alone. I am gifted with many spiritual gifts. So I receive many calls for healing, deliverance, counseling, prophecy, and other reasons. I learned people who are working for themselves, denominations, and o't interested in healing, situation, deliverance, or salvation.

I was surprised to find out that a lot of truth-preaching churches have experienced changes. My commitment has always been to the Lord Jesus alone. So I am not worried about misleading messages. It did not surprise me, but was sad. What is the difference between working for Jesus in His field and working for churches, denominations, or organizations?

It is two different scenarios. When it comes to authority, you obey and act accordingly. When led and connected with God, they will be in harmony with God's plans. If not, it's better to stay away since they are brimming with self-interest. Please pray to hear the Holy Spirit lead, guide, and teach all truth. You are not called to fill up the pew of a building so-called church to let someone milk you. Spend your life investing in the advancement of the Kingdom of heaven on earth and refrain from assisting the devil in establishing religion.

I am more concerned about the lost, sick, hurting, and depressed sinners. I do not worry about who says what. Churches nowadays have abandoned their mission by substituting God.

I always teach and disciple new converts to go lay hands on sick people, cast out demons, and then preach the Word. When there is evidence, people will listen to the Gospel. Today, a lady said, I want to see the lame walk. I want to lay my hand on lame, blind, and deaf and see the miracle. I said go for it. It needs a hand and the name of Jesus with the power of the Holy Spirit. His capability to do anything and everything is dependent on your importance. God never changes, but you have to have faith to work. Of course, God will not heal through sinners and nominal or so-called Christians. God has a standard for choosing His workers. The Lord did many miracles through Paul.

Acts 19:11 And God wrought special miracles by the hands of Paul:12 So that from his body were brought unto the sick handkerchiefs or aprons, and the diseases departed from them, and the evil spirits went out of them.

Why don't we see these today? I have seen mighty miracles, healing, and deliverance. I always keep company with righteous people. Not all can come to my door.

Pray continuously. It is also the work of God. Keep praying and don't give up, even if it didn't happen the first time. You pray again and again. The key is to keep going. Do not stop, do it again, and again until it happens. People who believe in God are seeking healers to find healing. I just seek, ask, and knock till I find the answer.

When I am sick, I send out a prayer request to many prayer warriors. Most time I get better right away. If not, the next day I send prayer requests again. I won't stop sending prayer requests until everything gets better. Many times, healing comes in one-time prayer. When nothing occurs, individuals without belief turn to medicine, surgery, and alternative resources. Many Christians get help from a witch doctor or psychic. Churches have misguided people asking them not to look for a spiritual healer but going to a medical doctor is ok. Go for doctors and surgery since they have raised the faithless generation. I do not believe God's healing power working through everyone. Paul or Peter is laying hands,, but it is the Lord Healing through His Spirit. He uses humans. I go to the one who has the healing power to help me. You must get deliverance from Jesus alone.

I've labored countless times, yet when someone identifies themselves, my prayers heal them. I stated that it was okay. God has a notebook, and He is a writer. If He is not then, he does not have to blot out something from his writing.

The Bible says I have given gifts to people so God can get the glory. If you are one of the 12 disciples, like Paul or Peter,r then your name will have the record of your work in heaven. David's name is recorded. Disciples of Jesus were importunate, persistent, and one hundred percent using the unadulterated word of God. They didn't add or subtract. God will use you too if you are not deviating from the truth. He seeks those who captivate his complete focus, never allowing God to rest No matter the hour, I'll persistently knock until you open. God can be moved by persistent solicitation or banging on heaven's door.

Luke 18:2-8 is the example of the judge even did not believe God, since the woman pressed him, and being persistent Judge took care of her problem.

Luke 11:5 And he said unto them, Which of you shall have a friend, and shall go unto him at midnight, and say unto him, Friend, lend me three loaves;6 For a friend of mine in his journey has come to me, and I have nothing to set before him?7 And he from within shall answer and say, Trouble me not: the door is now shut, and my children are with me in bed; I cannot rise and give thee.8 I say unto you, Though he will not rise and give him because he is his friend, yet because of his importunity he will rise and give him as many as he needeth. 9 And I say unto you, Ask, and it shall be given you; seek, and ye shall find; knock, and it shall be opened unto you.10 For everyone that asketh receiveth; and he that seeketh findeth, and to him that knocketh it shall be opened.

When you ask for it just once, it holds no meaning. I visited this elderly lady, she said I had this knee pain, every day. I said command the mountain you have to move. She did it every day. The pain was gone. Another lady said I prayed for my unsaved husband every day. Now he preaches the Gospel.

DECEMBER 28

When I was working, I gave the Bible to all non-Christian coworkers. One lady refused to receive the Bible. She said I didn't believe in the Bible. I tried to witness it for ten years. At one point, she was afflicted with cancer. After requesting a prayer, she experienced a complete healing. She was baptized in the name of Lord Jesus. Just to clarify, my understanding is confined to God and the Word. I know nothing about medicine. My parents were in the medical field. According to the Bible, Jesus endured 39 stripes for my illness. It was because of my sickness too. That is why I always look to pray for people. I need them to pray when I need prayer. It is persistence and nothing else. If you're sick, the family is in a difficult situation, or you need help with any problem, go knocking on heaven's door in the middle of the night. Cry out, fast, repent, and do what it takes for His attention. His ear will be inclined towards you, ready to fulfill your desires.

I was blessed with a brother who possessed great wisdom and faith. I was once told by him that I am a go-getter who perseveres until I reach my goals. According to God, we should continuously seek His presence by knocking, asking, and seeking at different times of the day. His tiredness will cause him to give in because of the persistent banging on His door. Can you do this? It is your importunity; persistence will bring change, in Jesus' name. Amen!

LET US PRAY

Heavenly Father, we come before you knowing you will never reject us. It is a lesson to learn from the devil; he is persistent and never gives up or gives in. Let us do the same, pray without ceasing. Knock, ask, and seek till we find and receive what we desire. Lord, encourage people, give them boldness, courage, and persistence to move the mountain, to establish the mission on earth and in their life. There is a part on our site that gets lazy, tired and discouraged. Lord, today, give desire, courage, and persistence for the mission. We know your word is true, but we get too busy and lazy to ignore you. We commit ourselves fresh to the mission given by God. Our Importance will make a major change on the earth in Jesus' name. Amen! God Bless you!

DECEMBER 29

I AM OPEN TO THAT!

We are all open-minded when it comes to allowing something. Your house is not open to strangers, correct? Our body is a house of God.

Hebrew 3:6a But Christ as a Son over his own house; whose house are we.

If you open your ears for Jesus, He will communicate with you. Jesus is not a product of human craftsmanship; rather, as God, He is our creator. Whenever you ask a question, He will respond to you. Ask who the true God is and see what the answer reveals. Keep your mind open to the truth.

When you are open to sins,

Romans 5:12 Wherefore, as by one-man sin entered into the world, and death by sin; and so death passed upon all men, for that all have sinned:

Now choices are yours. We are given the power to make decisions. Making both good and bad choices has visible outcomes. For guidance in every situation, turning to the word of God is the best approach. Making the correct decision often necessitates seeking assistance, counseling, advice, and information. King Solomon, who was once wise, lost his way when he married women who worshiped foreign idols. He had no one to turn to for advice or guidance, be it advisers or prophets. What a sad story!

Ezra 13:26 Did not Solomon king of Israel sin by these things? yet among many nations was there no king like him, who was beloved of his God, and God made him king over all Israel: nevertheless, even him did outlandish women cause to sin.

Don't let Satan and hell have access to your children by opening the door. If you decide to do it, be accountable for the resulting consequences. Who has the authority to make decisions for the children and grandchildren? The time we are living in is dangerous. Parents and grandparents are sending their children to hell, or a kidnapper. They are training their children to look like Hollywood or Bollywood. What a lost generation! Get wisdom. I observed multiple instances of judgments within families, however, their pride in worldly possessions and physical desires blinds them. Fear God and make changes for the sake of your little children. Instead of introducing them to the world, introduce them to the Word of God. The devil gained entry because of your poor choices, just like Eve, Adam, and other foolish individuals. Shut the door using the Word of God.

DECEMBER 29

By opening yourself to God's plan, similar to David, Joshua, Daniel, and many more, your story will be preserved in the book of Life. The Book of the Chronicle intentionally excludes any mention of the sinful northern kingdom of Israel. God blotted out all the wrong people and their names. I find reading history and chronicles fascinating. A comment was made by my friend stating that you only talk about the Old Testament. I said, yes, it is written for me.

1 Corinthians 10:11 Now all these things happened unto them for examples: and they are written for our admonition, upon whom the ends of the world have come.

Our job is to walk, think, act, live, and do right. We have the power to choose and discover the truth for ourselves.

Jeremiah was constantly warning the king of Judah. They were closed off from the teachings of the Lord. Finally went into captivity in Babylon for seventy years. In Babylon, God sent sword, plague, and famine to eradicate evil from the land. Open self for the right Spirit. Be receptive to God's communication through the word, genuine prophets, and educators. Amazingly, we repeat the same mistakes. When God turns your slavery, poverty, and trouble into triumph and freedom, be especially careful.

We refuse to accept the word of the Lord, which is why we removed the Bible. See the consequences. The answer is in the Bible; it is within your hand's reach. Open and live right to make the right decisions.

When individuals call upon me for prayer, I receive responses from God and deliver them. However, not everyone is receptive to God's guidance. Modern-day figures like Adam, Eve, King Saul, and King Solomon face repeated consequences for their wrong choices. Blessing to those who open for God and curse those who do not. I have devoted my life to Jesus. I am open-minded about His intentions. I have my own plans, but I prioritize Jesus above all else. In season and out the season is ready. I cannot be devoted to both money and God.

My openness is limited, but the Holy Spirit has my full attention. Obeying and following God's will helps me gain a lot of knowledge. I can tell when someone tries to sneak in, like Satan in the form of a snake. I rebuked it right away. Open to the right people and spirit; it will do good. Opening oneself to Satan invites sickness, trouble, and disaster into life. Religious, friend, or family connections can be used by Satan to infiltrate. You will never understand unless you are aware of the word of God. Every four generations, power and truth fade away. Why? Your family will welcome many through marriage, some of whom may be vulnerable to Satan's influence. They are more supportive of Satan than they are of God. Not a fan of God's ways, but definitely enjoy movies, the world, and everything around them. Keep an open mind and heart towards God, His Spirit, and His word. The world offers more than what life requires, as life is short. In India and even in America, I was occasionally offered modeling opportunities, but both God and a close friend always said no immediately. You won't be accepting this offer. Do not settle for something you see in your surroundings. Be open to One who is beyond the limits of your vision. Keep your eyes, ears, heart, and mind fixed on Jesus. Don't let anything negative affect your ears, eyes, and mind.

Both women and men often hold strong religious beliefs or customs from their upbringing. I've gained knowledge, but my learning journey isn't over since I demand evidence before believing anything. Prove me. Being open to all and guided by the Holy Spirit is wise when searching for the truth.

When you open yourself to God, He will purify you. There will be many who argue that they are not ready. Let me tell you; you will never be ready, just open for God, and He will do the rest. It is not by might and power of yours but by the Holy Spirit. The Holy Spirit gives the power to fight against the devil, lies, Satan, and religious demons.

Always ensure that the voice you hear, even from your loved ones, belongs to God. Some in your family could be like Cain, Eve, Adam, Priest Eli, Absalom, and Joseph's jealous brother. Also, be careful of yourself. If you permit the wrong things, you can find yourself in trouble. You have the power to open or close.

God has constantly directed through His word. I tell you; it is marvelous to know the Word. I am in love with the book called The Bible. It is God's book. When you open the book, make sure your ears, heart, mind, and eyes are receptive to the Lord's teachings.

No harm or wrong will be allowed to come to you by the Lord. Avoid being excessively intelligent, stay mindful of your surroundings. Those who open doors to the wrong create their own mess. Always remember, the burden of responsibility is on you. Drama and hopeless messes? No thanks. Amen! God Bless you!

LET US PRAY

Lord, it is a great thing that you have given us the right to choose, open, and shut. Lord, we are open to your guidance and the Holy Spirit. How wonderful it is that we have true prophets and teachers, the Holy Spirit, and the Word of God available in our languages. Lord, help us to open our eyes, minds, and hearts to such healthy tonic, wealth, and power of God. Help us, Lord, to shut the door for poisonous things available out there. We are blessed to have the word with the Spirit of God. Many are lost, homeless, sick, and dead since they have been exposed to the wrong information. Once the devil comes into the house, life, or our body then we are done. We see AIDS, HIV, cancer, stroke, heart attack, and name it. We make choices and our choices are sometimes very poor. It is our choice to smoke, drink alcohol, and keep ourselves busy in this world. We open ourselves to these destructive poisonous things. Lord Deliver us and give us power so we close the door to the mind, heart, life, family, and country-harming things. We know all are available easily, but we shut today for Satan, who is killing, stealing, and destroying in Jesus's name. Amen! God Bless You!

DECEMBER 30

GOD HAS NOT CALLED LAZY OR COWARDLY!

A person who is afraid cannot participate in war. Many battles are there in the real-life field. If you are not bold and courageous, then ask for boldness and courage to stay on the field. Many battle sights will be scary, but God has your back if you trust Him. Ask Daniel, Moses, Joshua, and others.

God has no use for people who are cowardly, fearful, or lazy. It's possible that they'll say I'll go later. According to the word of God, we should always be prepared, regardless of the timing. You cannot use the word NO, only Yes sir and Amen!

I once flew from India to the US with a fractured leg. In India, I faced a spiritual battle. I encountered resistance because I was spreading the truth. Truth can only be revealed through the Spirit of God. Religious leaders and their followers struggle with truth and light. I was faced with opposition from all directions. Religion claims godliness, but rejects the power of God within. Followers are too scared to stand against these false teachers and authorities.

When heading into battle, courage and boldness are essential.

Judges 7:3 Now therefore go to, proclaim in the ears of the people, saying, whosoever is fearful and afraid, let him return and depart early from Mount Gilead. And there returned of the people twenty and two thousand; and there remained ten thousand.

Those who followed the Lord experienced a similar situation when Jesus was captured by the Romans.

John 20:19 Then the same day at evening, being the first day of the week, when the doors were shut where the disciples were assembled for fear of the Jews, came to Jesus and stood in the midst, and saith unto them, Peace be unto you.

Jesus' disciples abandoned Him out of fear when He was taken during the night.

Mark 14:46 And they laid their hands on him, and took him. 50 And they all forsook him, and fled.

In the end time, fear will consume many, as Lord predicted. The environment will become frightening and everything will occur unexpectedly. Numerous locations are disappearing right in front of us. Natural disasters such as lava, floods, tornadoes, and earthquakes are currently happening. In the presence of this, God has advised us to stay alert and pray. This battle necessitates divine intervention.

Luke 21:26 Men's hearts failing them for fear, and for looking after those things which are coming on the earth: for the powers of heaven shall be shaken.

We are witnessing an incredibly frightening and unbelievable scene unfolding before our eyes. We see bad news every day. Our job is not to be lazy around but to hit the knee and cry out. Travail in prayer, so the Lord sends help by the heavenly host. Pray as you have never prayed. It's time for us to pray and do whatever is necessary.

Matthew 26:41 Watch and pray, that ye enter not into temptation: the spirit indeed is willing, but the flesh is weak.

God said,

Joshua 1:9 Have not I commanded thee? Be strong and of good courage; be not afraid, neither be thou dismayed: for the Lord thy God is with thee whithersoever thou goest.

There is a need for laborers in God's kingdom. I'm talking about someone who can work in the service of God. Go out and preach, teach, baptize in Jesus' name, cast out demons, heal the sick, in season out the season willing and ready to work.

The Garden of Eden was created prior to the man who would care for it. The Garden required someone to look after it. Lazy will destroy the Garden. You have been given the responsibility and you are handling it like a professional. If you don't feel like working for God, request His help in cultivating a strong desire to do so. You have made money to eat out; vacation, and have a good time. Are you rich in this world but poor in heaven? Be rich toward God.

Genesis 2:15 And the LORD God took the man, and put him into the garden of Eden to dress it and to keep it.

Matthew 9:37 Then saith he unto his disciples, The harvest truly is plenteous, but the labourers are few; 38 Pray ye therefore the Lord of the harvest, that he will send forth laborers into his harvest.

This demonstrates our investment in unimportant matters. It's impossible to find time for God anywhere. Attending church and contemplating our religious routine offered us a means of self-justification. Be fruitful to the kingdom of God. In all our activities, there is time to work on God's vineyard. People claim that I pray, read the Word, and attend church. Do you go out and work for Jesus? Do you go to prisons, jails, convalescent homes, or the next city to visit the sick? If not, make this your top priority. I want nothing to do with these misguided followers and leaders who are blind and deaf.

Every morning, I dedicate a few hours to prayer, seeking His will and purpose. Afterwards, I managed to establish contact with several villages in India and ministers over the phone. There are a large number of individuals who are sick, searching, and in need of God's assistance. Providing telephone Bible study sessions and praying for the sick is what I do. I used Holy Spirit power and authority to drive out a demon with the help of Lord Jesus. In this day and age, technology allows us to spread the teachings of Jesus Christ to every corner of the world.

I prayed for God to inspire you to help those who are lost. If not, they will be lost forever. It's not just about secular work and financial gain. The general belief is that having a job is necessary to meet societal standards of living. On a magnificent mission, God came to heal the sick, mend broken hearts, liberate captives, and restore what was lost. The Lord wants to know if you are maintaining my vineyard today. Are you answering your calling? Are you continuing the mission of God?

Attending a church under a different organizational name is simple. It is the time to wake up, shape up, and shake yourself off from the world and its contamination. Our spirits have been infected and our souls have been destroyed. Why do we go to church and Bible colleges? It's not making sense to me. Numerous individuals go about collecting money and enjoying a lavish lifestyle. But what about getting dirty? When you work in the field, visiting hospitals and praying for the needy, you end up getting dirty. Getting dirty is part of the job when working in the Field of Jesus. Jesus was constantly engaged in labor without rest.

Mark 6:31 And he said unto them, Come ye yourselves apart into a desert place, and rest a while: for there were many coming and going, and they had no leisure so much as to eat.

My sleep duration on the mission field is limited to 4 hours or less. I am always engaged in teaching, preaching, casting out demons, and healing the sick through laying my hands on them. Traveling long distances is normal. It's always on the move. You are completely exhausted when you return home. On one occasion, I arrived back from India and slept in my bedroom despite having a broken foot. As I looked around, I hoped and wished this could be my bedroom. I was exhausted after traveling for nearly two months. Lack of sleep, unfamiliar food, and everything else you can think of. I came to the realization that I had been in my bedroom for nearly 10 days. The room was unrecognizable to me due to extreme tiredness. This type of work is challenging, you know.

It's the same scenario whenever I return from California. Meetings after the meeting, hospitals, and constant visits constantly leave you feeling tired. It's a lot of hard work. We are not meant to stay in one place and donate, but rather to go out and preach to those who are lost. By overcoming laziness and reaching out to Hindus, Muslims, Buddhists, addicts, alcoholics, prisons, and jails, we can change the world. May the Lord awaken us and grant us the bravery to spread Jesus' message to those who are lost. Amen! God Bless you!

LET US PRAY

Lord, we are so glad that You have given us the Holy Spirit; You have empowered us with your Spirit. You have given us the Spirit of Love power and a sound mind. We do not have a spirit of fear or laziness. The Lord helps us to discipline our lifestyle to work regularly in the vineyard of God. We want to be like you. All knew that you were the big prophet; they never have seen anything like it. Lord, you said we can do greater than what you did, yes we believe you. Just help us to be a worker in the field. We must be laborers. Give us a good working habit. Help us find a way to our vineyard and make us sincere and diligent to work for you. You have been such a great example. Help us pick up our cross and follow you in Jesus's name. Amen! God Bless you!

DECEMBER 31

HEAR, OBEY AND SUBMIT!

God is searching for someone who will carry out His requested commands without deviation. The plan is God's, not yours. He'll do exactly as he stated. It's God's way of presenting His creation to the world. Maintain the formula without making any changes. Master the art of following instructions. Once you learn to follow His instructions, you'll experience incredible fulfillment. God is good. He said prove me. And He meant it.

I managed to contribute almost 25 percent of my paycheck to tithes, offerings, and missions without ever having to borrow. I never took on the role of a borrower. God has fulfilled His promises. Abraham was a rich man. He gave God tithes. By whom was it given? Tithing only requires giving ten percent to God. Always remember to give in accordance with our dispensation's requirements. Our dispensation requires us to provide workers with land options of 30, 60, 100, and unlimited. Do not go inside the den where the thief steals money. Help those who are poor, naked, hungry, orphaned, and widowed.

What is the amount you receive instead?

Malachi 3:10 Bring ye all the tithes into the storehouse, that there may be meat in mine house, and prove me now herewith, saith the Lord of hosts, if I will not open you the windows of heaven, and pour you out a blessing, that there shall not be room enough to receive it.11 And I will rebuke the devourer for your sakes, and he shall not destroy the fruits of your ground; neither shall your vine cast her fruit before the time in the field, saith the Lord of hosts.

Proverb 3:9 Honour the Lord with thy substance, and with the first fruits of all thine increase.

Follow the instructions in the Bible to witness God's supernatural intervention in the situation. In order to prove its authenticity, the Bible requires someone to follow it. The reader's digest is not comparable to the Bible. Begin to practice and follow His instructions. It's part of my routine to talk to Lena, a woman from India, on a daily basis. Everything I teach Sister Lena from the Bible, she will do without fail. According to her, the coworker's wife is in the advanced stage of cancer. Sister Lena sent the prayer cloth and Bible that were anointed. The hospitalized woman was released after coming into contact with the prayer garments. Initially, the ill woman was furious. Her face transformed like the devil. However, she decided to follow the advice of some wise individuals and accepted it. Now she is healed and reads the Bible. Lady Lena's husband was causing trouble, but now he's decided to go to a prayer meeting. He described the Bible as a divine and excellent book. He claimed that when you enter God's door crying; you leave with happiness.

I appreciate your obedience and submission. Listen and follow what the Lord says!

DECEMBER 31

On January 1st, 2018, while I was sitting, the Lord instructed me to write. I prayed to the Lord every day for a whole year. He said yes, so I got up and started writing. Initially, it took between 8 and 9 hours. I need to receive God's guidance first and then complete the steps of writing, editing, recording, and publishing. There are times when a company shows up, but I can't sleep until I've posted it on YouTube. At times, I find myself needing to respond to a large volume of phone calls for counseling and prayer. Nevertheless, I follow God's commands. It's the final day of the year.

Praise God! Despite Google suspending my channel, I continued writing. I was prepared by God in advance. Before I got suspended, I had to create an additional YouTube channel. By the mercy of the Lord, I was guided to carry on with my work. Behold, He is a provider of solutions. Before my first YouTube video got suspended, he had already prepared me to create another channel. The devil is always one step behind the Lord. Be attentive to His voice, for He is a way-maker.

I was asked by a prophetess about what I had done on another day. I mentioned I published a book, and she pointed out that I already have the second, third, and fourth ones ready, as God is downloading them. The Lord has already informed me that the Daily Spiritual Diet will greatly benefit the Kingdom of God.

People who prioritize material possessions and wealth do not feel a need for God. People like me, who have complete faith in God, require his guidance. Jesus is the path to follow. Furthermore, I had no intention of writing the first book "I Did It His Way." I thought it would bring me honor. The devil is skilled at twisting and messing with our minds. The Prophetess was sent by the Lord to my door to prophesy about the book. According to the prophetess, God will be glorified by the book you've been working on. God gave the name for the book "I Did It His Way" to another lady. I made a note of it in my notebook because I know I'll forget while being sick.

My book 'I did it His Way' received an A grade in Religious World and is being considered for a movie adaptation. Publishers are constantly calling me to request permission to republish my book.

While you may appear as a single individual like Abraham, if God is within you, he can transform you into a nation like Israel. From the lifeless womb of 90-year-old Sarah, God can bring forth a new life.

Jeremiah 32:27 Behold, I am the Lord, the God of all flesh: is there anything too hard for me?

Genesis 18:14 Is anything too hard for the Lord? At the time appointed I will return unto thee, according to the time of life, and Sarah shall have a son.

Seek God's help in having a heart that is obedient. Do not jump at every opportunity to come by. Seek God's plan by asking Him. Consider the divine advice for the offers you're getting. I feel sorry for the people who sell God's plan for fame, money, and power. I do not want that. Golden Street is where I'll be walking one day. I will have a mansion, but the most beautiful thing is that I will be with Jesus forever. He has chosen to call those who are faithful, obedient, and submissive.

I need to distance myself from the counsel of the religious leader. I have an immediate understanding of where their attention lies. It is dangerous. Love yourself. Consider yourself here with a purpose and for a specific time. Look for it.

As a woman, I travel to different countries for missionary work. My brother, who was wise, always guided me about what to be cautious about. I can relate to his concern because I also have to go in person. It's a different story because God is the one behind it, so no worries.

Mary declared her lack of fear, and that settles it. She showed no concern in revealing God's plan to her soon-to-be husband, Joseph. Despite the consequences of being stoned to death, she was still careless. The Savior was brought forth by her. Through a ministry, a plan of salvation, and following the example of biblical prophets, we can bring forth God's will.

Many great prophets from different nations have foretold numerous remarkable prophecies in my life. Certain promises are made directly by God. I'm patiently waiting for it to be fulfilled. It's been over 34 years since they were spoken, but I've never felt the need to question it. Once God has spoken, consider it final. Time and seasons are under His control.

Jesus' prophecy of coming to this world has been fulfilled, and the second coming is approaching rapidly. All we need to do is whatever is necessary. Let our lamp contain an abundance of oil. Let us pray and get ready to meet the groom. Direct your attention towards God. We need to ready ourselves mentally and emotionally for what we couldn't achieve in previous years. As we enter the New Year, let's prioritize prayer, Bible reading, reaching the lost, fasting, and preaching of the gospel. Can we wear the armor of God as we battle for God's kingdom? Make sure everyone is aware that Jesus is Jehovah. The highest name was attained by walking in the flesh. The name Jesus signifies Jehovah's Savior, sent to save us. Our mission in the upcoming years is to spread the Word of God to those living in darkness. May the Lord bless you and yours as you enter the New Year. Please pray for me. I finished this year writing a Daily Spiritual Diet and waiting for the next assignment from God. God Bless you! Happy New Year!

LET US PRAY

We thank you for showing us new days. Let Our day become new as the Lord said, I make all things new. Show us your grace and mercy every day. Do not let your grace and mercy depart from us. We come with a made-up mind to carry on our mission throughout our lives. We know our life is a blessing from God. We ask for forgiveness for our sins. Forgive what we could not do in past years. But we ask for the strength to follow you, as you said, pick up your cross and follow me. Make us more sensitive to the instruction of the Holy Spirit, since it is our guide and teacher. We have been living in the grace of time since the Holy Spirit, which is your Spirit, abides in us. We rededicate the coming years in Jesus's name. Amen! God Bless You!

ABOUT THE AUTHOR

Hello, I am Elizabeth Das Author of the Book Daily Spiritual Diet a devotional for each day and I did it His Way. As I mentioned I am not the author but I obeyed the voice of the Lord to write.

Daily Spiritual Diet is a series of 12 months in English, Hindi, and Gujarati with many languages. My books are published in different languages. The English name is, I did it 'His Way'.

The French name is : Je l'ai fait à "sa manière" The Spanish name is 'Lo hice a " a Su manera "

The Gujarati name is 'me te temni rite karyu'....

Hindi name is 'Maine uske tarike se kiya'…'

And many other languages

It is also narrated in different languages. Praying to see you saved and most important you find hope.

May the Lord Bless you.

ELIZABETH DAS

Contact: nimmidas@gmail.com, nimmidas1952@gmail.com

YouTube Channel:
1. http://youtube.com/@dailyspiritualdietelizabet7777/videos
2. http://youtube.com/@newtestamentkjv9666/videos

Web Addresses: https://waytoheavenministry.org/

www.ingramcontent.com/pod-product-compliance
Lightning Source LLC
Chambersburg PA
CBHW081838230426
43669CB00018B/2744